More Praise For

BROTHERHOOD

"In rugby, we often talk of 'going into battle' with your team. It's just a game, of course, but in *Brotherhood*, sport, war, and friendship leap from the pages as players really do become warriors—and heroes."

—DAN LYLE, US Rugby Hall of Famer
and NBC Sports Analyst

"*Brotherhood* captures men working through shared hardships, the lessons learned, and bonds forged through that journey. Ultimately, the book shares the stories of young men and their families who were willing to give everything for our country—and some who did."

—MATTHEW SHERMAN,
West Point Men's Rugby Coach

BROTHERHOOD

BROTHERHOOD

WHEN WEST POINT RUGBY
WENT TO WAR

Martin Pengelly

INTRODUCTION BY
H. R. McMaster

Godine • Boston • 2023

Published in 2023 by
GODINE
Boston, Massachusetts

Frontispiece: West Point Rugby, Class of 2002.
Photo courtesy of Cpt. Pete Chacon.

LIBRARY OF CONGRESS CATALOGING-IN-PUBLICATION DATA
Names: Pengelly, Martin, author. | McMaster, H. R., 1962- writer of foreword.
Title: Brotherhood : when West Point Rugby went to war / Martin Pengelly ;
introduction by H. R. McMaster.
Other titles: When West Point Rugby went to war
Description: Boston : Godine, 2023.
Identifiers: LCCN 2023002507 (print) | LCCN 2023002508 (ebook) | ISBN
9781567927115 (hardcover) | ISBN 9781567927122 (ebook)
Subjects: LCSH: Iraq War, 2003-2011--Participation, American. | United
States. Army--Officers--Biography. | United States Military
Academy--Biography. | Rugby football players--United States--Biography.
Classification: LCC DS79.766.A1 P46 2023 (print) | LCC DS79.766.A1
(ebook) | DDC 956.7044/34092273--dc23/eng/20230214
LC record available at https://lccn.loc.gov/2023002507
LC ebook record available at https://lccn.loc.gov/2023002508

First Printing, 2023
Printed in the United States of America

To the memory of
Philip Pengelly, my dad, and to Jean Pengelly, my mum.

For the reading and the rugby.

If in describing a rugby match, I write, "I saw adults in short trousers fighting and throwing themselves on the ground in order to send a leather ball between a pair of wooden posts," I have summed up what I have seen, but I have intentionally missed its meaning. I am merely trying to be humorous.

—JEAN-PAUL SARTRE

I'm afraid of Americans.

—DAVID BOWIE

CONTENTS

Lock Bryan Phillips takes the ball up in a May 2002 match of Army versus Saint Mary's.

PREFACE

R UGBY UNION is a fifteen-a-side ball-handling contact sport that arose from the schools of England in the mid-1800s. Its great stadiums are in London, Cardiff, and Edinburgh, in Dublin and Paris, in Johannesburg, Auckland, and Sydney. It is played with passion in Argentina, Samoa, and Japan, in Fiji, Uruguay, and Kenya, in Romania, Russia, and Georgia. It is generally held to have come to North America in 1874, when Harvard played McGill.[1]

Thanks to hooped cotton shirts by Ralph Lauren, or that Clint Eastwood movie about Nelson Mandela and the World Cup, or even the episode of *Friends* where Ross tries to impress a British girlfriend, most Americans know what rugby is. But in the American mind, rugby lost out to football long ago.

Still, American rugby is a flourishing subculture, passionate and resilient. Most Americans who pick up the game pick it up at college. Presidents Bill Clinton, George W. Bush, and Joe Biden did so.[2] So did senators like Ted Kennedy and Chris Murphy, cabinet secretaries like James Baker and Gina Raimondo, and captains of business like Mark Cuban.[3]

Kurt Vonnegut didn't play rugby, but he did write about it. It was May 1941, and he was reporting for the *Cornell Daily Sun*. The college rugby club, he wrote, "Needs more players and more student support to survive. Is there anyone in this school that would like to play a damned good game, faster than football and harder than soccer?"[4]

Any reasonably arch observer of American rugby and its struggles over the next eighty years might be tempted to add, *So it goes.*

This is a book about American rugby.

But if they want to read this book, as Vonnegut wrote, "A person doesn't have to speak with an English accent or know a blessed thing about the game." It is a book about the sporting spirit, the thrill of the chase and the tackle. I do happen to speak with an English accent, and this book could not exist if I had not played rugby through my childhood and youth, then spent large parts of my adult life writing about it for money. I married an American and moved to New York; the game stayed with me.

This is also a book about something Kurt Vonnegut, who wrote *Slaughterhouse-Five*, knew rather more about: the US Army.

This book tells the stories of fifteen young men who went to West Point before 9/11 and were senior cadets that dreadful day and officers in the wars that followed. Because those fifteen young men graduated in 2002 and served from 2003, this is a book largely about the invasion of Iraq and the war there rather than the one in Afghanistan; many of the West Point rugby brothers went to Afghanistan, but in the years covered by this book, those who saw combat did so in Iraq.

While this book touches on many aspects of the Iraq War, it is not about why America chose to take Baghdad, how the case for war unraveled, how sectarian conflict bloomed, how nearly four thousand six hundred US troops were killed, how almost thirty-two thousand were wounded, and how hundreds of thousands of Iraqis were maimed or killed.[5]

This is a book about one group of young American men who found rugby together, became soldiers together, and served their country, right or wrong. It is a book about how I set out to learn what happened to them when they went to war. To reach for Shakespeare, as the cadets did, it is a book about a band of brothers.

—MARTIN PENGELLY

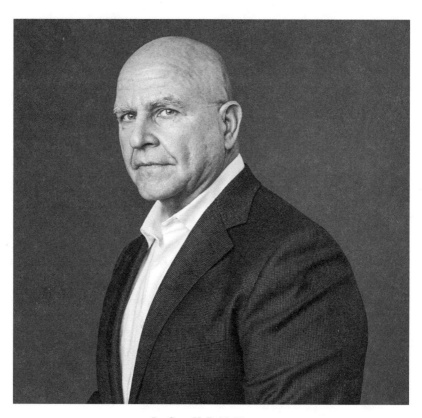
Lt. Gen. H. R. McMaster.

INTRODUCTION

THIS IS a story of a rugby team. Martin Pengelly played lock forward in London in 2002 against those to whom he is about to introduce you. *Brotherhood* is a brilliant group biography of the individual cadets who played against Pengelly's Rosslyn Park Football Club. But it is also much more. Readers will not only learn about the sport for which the author and I share great affinity, they will find in these pages an abundance of what seems scarce in society today: exemplars of comradeship and the willingness to sacrifice for one another and one's fellow citizens.

The "brothers" of West Point's 2002 rugby team came from diverse backgrounds and grew into a team bound together by common purpose, mutual trust, and affection. They cared not from whence their teammates came nor for any identity categories into which they might fit. They earned respect from one another based on their character and athletic prowess. Their stories shed light on something that few Americans understand: an ethos grounded in honor, courage, and loyalty that binds warriors to one another. The brothers internalized this ethos at West Point, exhibited it on the rugby pitch, and carried it with them onto battlefields abroad.

In contrast to popular culture's tendency to cheapen and coarsen the warrior's ethos, Pengelly reveals the sense of honor that motivates young men and women to lead soldiers in our army. Colonel Joshua Lawrence Chamberlain, an erstwhile professor of languages and rhetoric at Bowdoin College who, on July 2, 1863, led the soldiers of the Twentieth Maine Infantry Regiment in a bold bayonet charge that blunted a Confederate attack at the Battle of Gettysburg, observed that in battle, "the instinct to seek safety is overcome by the instinct of honor." Good rugby teams play tough, and good army units fight hard, in part, because teammates expect one another to display virtue and avoid dishonor. A sense of honor is a crucial component of effectiveness. It also underpins the expectation that rugby players behave like gentlemen on the pitch, as well as the moral and ethical standards that make war less inhumane.

The cadet ruggers were commissioned as officers in the United States Army eight months after the most devastating and deadliest terrorist attack in history took the lives of nearly three thousand of their fellow citizens. They selected army combat branches and went to war. They built teams and led them in battle. They and their soldiers fought with distinction in dangerous places. Readers might be tempted to contrast the leadership these young men displayed so soon after graduation with the safetyism that pervades so many academic institutions today. There are no safe spaces to which one might retreat on rugby pitches or on battlefields overseas. Thankfully, our nation still has stoic warriors who are willing to face dangers much greater than those one confronts in even the fiercest rugby maul.

At West Point, the brothers learned from military history and from rugby that the need to develop cohesive, confident teams to withstand the test of battle is timeless. Cohesion is essential for combat effectiveness and resilience. Good combat units take on the quality of a family in which its members have deep affection for their brothers- and sisters-in-arms. As John Keegan observed in *The Face of Battle*, his classic 1976 study of combat in the same geographic area across five centuries, from Agincourt (1415) to Waterloo (1815) to the Somme (1916): "What battles have in common is human: the behaviour of men struggling to reconcile their instinct for self-preservation, their sense of honour and the achievement of some aim over which other men are ready to kill them." He observed that the study of battle is "always a study of solidarity and usually also of disintegration for it is toward the disintegration of human groups that battle is directed." The warrior ethos is foundational to maintaining the cohesion of one's own "human group" and generating the fortitude and combat prowess necessary to disintegrate the enemy's.

Cohesive rugby and army teams have trust and confidence in their leaders. Pengelly tells us how young leaders put mission accomplishment and the survival and well-being of those they led before their own well-being and thereby inspired soldiers to act in ways contrary to the natural drive of self-preservation. Confidence and unit cohesion are necessary ingredients for courage because they form a psychological and emotional bulwark against fear. Fear is debilitating in rugby and in battle because it can lead to hesitation and allow the other side to gain the initiative.

Sacrifice is part of this story. These young men faced hardships and traumas associated with their service—including physical adversity, separation from family, physical wounds, and, most difficult of all, the loss of friends in battle. Readers will get to know men who died far too young and those who gave what President Abraham Lincoln described in the Gettysburg Address as "the last full measure of devotion." Pengelly tells us how the families of the fallen and their teammates grieve their loss and honor their memory.

He also helps us understand how West Point and the United States Army are living historical communities in which younger generations look to earlier generations for inspiration and to understand better their calling as soldiers. Consider the lyrics of "The Corps," a poetic hymn written around 1902 by West Point Chaplain Bishop H. S. Shipman, which every cadet must memorize:

We sons of today, we salute you. You sons of an earlier day;
We follow, close order, behind you, where you have pointed the way;
The long gray line of us stretches, thro' the years of a century told
And the last man feels to his marrow, the grip of your far off hold.

At West Point, monuments and memorials appear at every turn to remind future officers about the legacy of courage and honor that they have inherited from those who went before them. Pengelly tells us how teammates visited the beaches of Normandy and felt a visceral connection to those who summoned the mettle to assault Nazi defensive fortifications on June 6, 1944.

The best army leaders draw strength from the past as they mold future generations through their example and their mentorship. You will read about one of those leaders, Colonel Mike Mahan, who served as assistant and then head coach for West Point Rugby across more than three decades and remained connected to army rugby teams even after he moved to California. Commissioned during the Vietnam War, Mahan witnessed many changes at West Point and in the army. But he was a source of one of the greatest continuities in the profession of arms: the opportunity to develop the next generations of leaders. Mahan epitomized the positive leader whom no one wanted to let down. He and his fellow coaches motivated and inspired my teammates and me in the early 1980s.

Pengelly's focus here in *Brotherhood* is the class of 2002, but the comradeship and commitment to one another he writes about evoked memories of my experience as an Army rugby player. I still count among my closest and most trusted friends the men I met when I first stepped onto a rugby pitch more than four decades ago. It is my hope that young men and women who read this book will be inspired to serve based on the story of these brothers, who bore hardships and made sacrifices but also reaped rewards associated with fulfilling their duty to their country, to their soldiers, and to one another.

—H. R. McMaster
USMA class of 1984
Stanford, California

THE TEAM:
WEST POINT RUGBY 2002

A rugby team consists of fifteen players: eight forwards (wearing jerseys numbered 1 through 8) and seven backs (numbered 9 through 15).

Jerrod Adams
POSITION: Wing
FINAL RANK AND POSTING:
Lieutenant Colonel, 164th Theater
Airfield Operations Group

Matt Blind
POSITION: Fullback (Team
Captain)
FINAL RANK AND POSTING:
Captain, Third Battalion, Twenty-
First Infantry Regiment, First
Stryker Brigade, Twenty-Fifth
Infantry Division

Pete Chacon
POSITION: Wing
FINAL RANK AND POSTING:
Captain, Third Battalion, 187th
Infantry Brigade, 101st Infantry
Division (Air Assault)

Joe Emigh
POSITION: Center
FINAL RANK: Second Lieutenant,
Field Artillery

Mo Greene
POSITION: Fly Half
FINAL RANK AND POSTING:
Colonel, Professor of Military
Science, Western Kentucky
University ROTC

James Gurbisz
POSITION: Hooker
FINAL RANK AND POSTING:
Captain, Twenty-Sixth Forward
Support Battalion, Second Brigade,
Third Infantry Division

Jeremiah Hurley
POSITION: Prop
FINAL RANK AND POSTING:
Lieutenant Colonel (P), Deputy
Chief Technology Officer and
Director of Innovation, Joint
Special Operations Command

Andy Klutman
POSITION: Prop
FINAL RANK AND POSTING:
Captain, 165th Infantry Brigade,
United States Army Training and
Doctrine Command

Dave Little
POSITION: Number 8
FINAL RANK AND POSTING: Major,
Executive Officer, Missile Defense
Agency

Brian McCoy
POSITION: Flanker (Team Vice
Captain)
FINAL RANK AND POSTING:
Captain, Fifth Battalion, 158th
Aviation Regiment and Eighth
Army Aviation Staff

Zac Miller
POSITION: Flanker
FINAL RANK: Second Lieutenant,
Infantry

Clint Olearnick
POSITION: Center
FINAL RANK AND POSTING: Major,
First Battalion, 327th Infantry
Regiment, First Brigade Combat
Team, 101st Airborne Division
(Air Assault)

Brian Phillips
POSITION: Lock
FINAL RANK AND POSTING:
Captain, First Battalion, First
Air Defense Artillery Regiment
(PATRIOT), Sixty-Ninth ADA
Brigade

Scott Radcliffe
POSITION: Back Row
FINAL RANK AND POSTING:
Captain, Speechwriter to the
Multinational Corps Iraq
Commander

Nik Wybaczynsky
POSITION: Lock
FINAL RANK AND POSTING:
Lieutenant, Third Battalion,
Forty-Third Air Defense Artillery
Regiment (PATRIOT), Eleventh
ADA Brigade

Mike Mahan
POSITION: Coach
FINAL RANK AND POSTING: Lieutenant Colonel,
Associate Professor of Chemistry, West Point

BROTHERHOOD

Lt. Matt Blind cradles a mortar in Iraq in 2004.

Shitsucker

IRAQ IS home to nineteen species of scorpion, some among the deadliest in the world. There is *androctonus crassicauda*, the "mankiller." There is *leiurus quinquestriatus*: the "deathstalker."[1]

Scorpions stir primal fear. Before the US invasion of Iraq in March 2003, the CIA trained Iraqis "to foment rebellion, conduct sabotage, and help . . . target buildings and individuals."[2] Such paramilitary groups were involved in abuse and torture. They called themselves the Scorpions.

Hammam al-Alil is a small town in northern Iraq, forty kilometers south of Mosul. In November 2004, American soldiers there took soda bottles and cut off each of the ends. Then they put a scorpion in one end and a mouse in the other and made bets on the fight. Their officers winced a little, but there wasn't much real fighting to do. Apart from the odd burst of mortar fire, Hammam al-Alil was quiet. Three-Twenty-One Infantry, part of the Second Stryker Brigade, had been in-country a month. In their redoubt—a concrete office block, fully wired, four corners, four machine guns—the soldiers marked time. There was an insurgent cell in town, hence the mortars, but there were not enough troops to go find them. There were patrols, but mostly the redoubt held everyone. It was close and dull and hot.

Matt Blind was two years out of West Point, where he had captained the rugby team. Now he was a green lieutenant watching his men bet on the scorpions. His two years since graduation had been filled with training. Driving and flying, too, up from Fort Benning, Georgia, to his home in rural Ohio, in the farm country around

Akron, to Athens to see Erin, his girlfriend who became his wife. Back to Georgia. Assignments. Florida, California, Louisiana. On his first day at Fort Lewis in Washington State, he was given his platoon. The commander, Lieutenant Colonel Kevin Hyneman, was a rugby player, coach of the Tacoma Nomads, a local team of last-chancers. Hyneman gave Blind forty-six soldiers and some Strykers, eight-wheel troop carriers coming in to replace vulnerable Humvees.[3] At West Point, Blind had led fifteen men from fullback, a general behind the lines. Two years later, with his forty-six men in Hammam al-Alil, he was still in the back field, wondering where the action would be.

In the soda bottles, the mice put up a good show. Their paws were coated with glue from improvised traps, but all the scorpions could do was skitter back and forth, arching their tails, making hopeful strikes. Blind didn't encourage his men in the grisly pursuit. But he didn't discourage them either. Bored soldiers must fill time. Thousands of years before, in the nearby city of Hatra, Roman legionaries probably did similar, using earthenware pots. Maybe they scooped up the scorpions their besiegers catapulted into the city.[4] In late 2004, the insurgents of Hammam al-Alil weren't trying that. If they had, the soldiers might have run out of mice. The town stayed quiet.

Later, when all of Iraq was in flames, the US Army established a forward operating base in Hammam al-Alil. They called it FOB Scorpion.

ONE FINE spring day, years later, I went to Hingham, Massachusetts, a couple of towns down the South Shore from Boston, on the way to the Cape. At the Black Rock Country Club, where Bill Belichick, coach of the New England Patriots, has a house on a fairway, the lush greens and white sand bunkers were quiet. Matt Blind strode into the bar—fit, mid-thirties, neatly pressed in golfing gear and West Point polo shirt, aviator shades pushed back over short blond hair, hand out, smiling. He was on vacation from his investments job in Boston and had driven his pickup from Scituate, where he lived then with Erin and their three young boys.

Out on the balcony, after lunch, Blind stretched back in his chair. He straightened his shades and thought back to Hammam al-Alil. The dust, the scorpions, the boredom. The hurry-up-and-wait. As we spoke, Mosul and its surrounds[5] were occupied by Islamic State, the brutal militant group which spawned in the chaos of Iraq and Syria after the American invasion, dislodging al-Qaeda as US enemy number one. Blind had been home eleven years, out of the army for nine. US troops were still in Iraq. They would soon be in Syria. Blind had fought in a vicious, many-sided war. It had not ended. Worse, it had mutated.

He thought back to October 2004, when he led patrols in a town that was nothing next to what came later in Mosul. But there was foreboding. Hammam al-Alil was "a goofy place," he said, "because you could tell that the people didn't want us."[6]

"When you went through a neighborhood that wasn't supportive of Americans, you could tell. You could tell by the way the kids reacted. Kids react the way their parents do. My kids like the same sports teams I like. They like the same restaurants I like. In Iraq, most neighborhoods we'd go through, the kids would be cheering and waving and the parents would wave too and we'd hand out candy and soccer balls and footballs. Down there in Hammam al-Alil, it wasn't like that. You'd drive through and people would turn their heads away; they'd try to get their kids out of the street. It's not that they were afraid of us. It was probably a function of there being a fairly active insurgent cell in town. But we didn't have the firepower or intelligence to go after that, so we basically just stayed put."

After a while, the scorpions and mice began to lose their pull. There was another way to pass the time.

"There was no running water or facilities. So it was three weeks without a shower, a running faucet, a toilet, or anything like that. So we had some porta-potties delivered. And one of the biggest things to do was we'd call the Iraqi guy who came to suck the porta-potties—'the Shitsucker.' That was the activity of the day, when the Shitsucker would come up to the gate, and I'd be out there negotiating with him: 'I'll pay you seventy-five dollars to go suck the shitters.'"

West Point's motto is "Duty, Honor, Country." It was his duty, Blind supposed, to get the Shitsucker to the lowest possible price. His duty to his country. There wasn't much honor in it, but it was one way to serve the American taxpayer. Save some dollars on the Shitsucker as Iraq went to shit. Some of the soldiers started placing bets on how low the Shitsucker would go.

"I actually took that post over from Ryan Southerland, who was a lieutenant in the First Stryker Brigade and a good friend of mine at West Point. He and I did the whole transition together, and he couldn't have called it more accurately: 'The guys are going to be bored. You've got to keep their minds off bad stuff, and you just kinda gotta get through it.' We were down there three weeks, and that was our first three weeks in-country. We thought, 'We gotta do this for a year? Watch scorpions and mice fight each other? Negotiate with the Shitsucker? Really?' But then we got the call that we were going to abandon the Hammam al-Alil outpost, the last few days in October. And then we came up to Mosul, and shit kind of blew up."

FOR EIGHTEEN months or so, after the invasion in March 2003, Mosul was relatively quiet. The 101st Airborne occupied it, and its commander, Major General David Petraeus, kept the peace with Sunni tribes and the Kurds to the north.[7] But in October 2004, serious fighting broke out in Fallujah, and a battalion of the Twenty-Fifth Infantry Division, a successor to the 101st in Mosul, moved south to join in. As it did so, insurgents moved back up to Mosul. On November 8, 2004,[8] US and Iraqi forces were attacked with small arms, machine guns, and mortars. Americans were injured. Strykers hit roadside bombs. Matt Blind and his men went to find the enemy.

At the Hingham golf course, Blind took a sip of his beer. "The battalion commander just said, 'Go out and turn over every stone that you possibly can, uncover everything, knock down as many doors as you possibly can, and let's draw a line in the sand.'"

At first, the Americans worked with caution. Blind was in one Stryker, his platoon sergeant was in another, and they sat at a Y-shaped intersection in a densely populated area. There was some mortar fire, some small-arms fire, ineffective, from rooftops or behind buildings. Blind took a look out of the hatch of his Stryker, then consulted the systems within. This was it. Contact. In training, instructors posited situations and demanded action. There was no live fire. Nobody was trying to kill you. Rugby, if Blind had thought about it, posited immediate, changing circumstances, situations that demanded decisive response. If you didn't go in hard, you could get hurt. But not too badly, most of the time.

"I was on the radio, talking to my platoon sergeant, saying, you know, 'We've got to go in there. We're sitting there in all this fire; we're a sitting duck. We gotta go in there.' And Sergeant Sanchez says, 'Yeah, I think that's the right move,' so I say, 'Okay, well, what do we do now?'" Blind laughed. "I remember telling Sergeant Sanchez, 'Well, I guess I'm the platoon leader. I'll move first.'"

And so he moved. After three hundred yards, he told his driver to stop. Sanchez followed, then stopped fifty yards further on. It was a "bounding overwatch," a move off the training grounds of Yakima, out in the desert in Washington State. On the balcony in Hingham, Blind made chops at the air by his face, describing shorter and shorter bounds. In Mosul, gunners fired MK19s, air-cooled forty-millimeter machine guns that fire armor-piercing grenades. It was mostly to keep the enemy's head down, short bursts of unfocused fire. Blind rode low in his seat, eyes peeking over the top of the hatch.

"We were doing these bounds that were like fifty yards at a time," he said. "Like, *inching* forward."

He laughed. "So we got into where we thought the fire was coming from, and this probably took, y'know, three or four minutes. But we needed to go into this neighborhood, and the streets were very narrow. I took a left-hand turn, and there was a guy sitting in the middle of the street with an RPG. And he fired the RPG."

The man aimed right at Blind's Stryker. He missed. The heat of the rocket scorched Blind's helmet, but the rocket-propelled grenade roared past and exploded behind him. Blind blinked. The man disappeared.

"And then we started firing. It was just kinda chaos after that. I don't remember a whole lot. We ended up going through that neighborhood a little bit and then back to the original position. And then a car pulled up; a guy got out and started to pull something out of the trunk. So we went up and engaged. There were two guys there. We lit up the car with MK19, and the guys were still there. And MK19 will set a car up, set it on fire, lift it up off the ground. And the guys were still there. They had rifles, shooting. We did what we had to do."

The fighting went on all day and into the next. On November 9, the first Americans were killed: Army Major Horst Moore and Air Force Master Sergeant Steven Auchman, by mortar fire at Forward Operating Base Marez.[9] On November 11, Specialist Thomas Doerflinger was shot in the head by a sniper.[10] Insurgents took a bridge on the Tigris River. Insurgents took police stations. Members of the Iraqi security forces were executed in public. Kurdish Peshmerga helped the Americans fight back. US planes made bombing runs. Reinforcements came from Fallujah. By November 16, US forces had reestablished control in the north, south, and east of the city. The west was still full of insurgents. The Battle of Mosul was over. The Americans found the bodies of seventy-six Iraqi security personnel and an al-Qaeda propaganda lab. After the fact, Blind said, the Americans found out that they had come close to capturing Abu Musab al-Zarqawi, the leader of al-Qaeda in Iraq. He had been surrounded, briefly, at the al-Sabreen mosque.[11]

Matt Blind was in Mosul for nearly a year. He patrolled, he took prisoners, he took cover when fire from AK-47s—some shot off by Iraqis on his side—rattled the narrow streets. Nobody in his platoon was killed, but four men in his company were. Blind made executive officer. On December 21, 2004, he was across town when a suicide bomber killed twenty-two in the dining tent at FOB Marez.[12] At FOB Freedom, near Mosul's palace, once home to Saddam Hussein's sons, Uday and Qusay, Blind heard and felt the explosion. He saw the mushroom cloud.

In Hingham, eleven years later, memories of Mosul were a blur of gunfire and confusion, frustration and anger. Blind remembered how two sergeants, David Mitts and Salamo Tuialuuluu, big, popular guys, were shot dead in a convoy ambush.[13] How another sergeant, Ken Ridgley, died in a blast of gunfire from a car at a checkpoint.[14] How a specialist, Jose Ruiz, was shot and killed just before the end of the tour.[15] How others were hurt.

Some images were clear. There was Sergeant Hughes, one of the men in Blind's Stryker. On the first day of battle, his 50-cal machine gun jammed. A Stryker carries as many computers as weapons. But as Blind put it, "When a gun jams, a gun jams. There's nothing technology can do." So Sergeant Hughes did it instead, jumping up out of his hatch to open, clear, and reset his gun while bullets whipped by. In Hingham—as in Mosul—Blind laughed.

"I was on the vehicle intercom, shouting, 'Sergeant Hughes, you gotta get the fire going, get the fire going!' And meanwhile, my eyes are like that far above the sandbags in front of me or whatever. And he shouts back, 'Sir, I can't get it firing, it's not firing, it's misfiring.' Which is not all that uncommon for a 50-cal to do. And that dude jumped out of his hatch, stood up on the top of this vehicle, and cleared that 50-cal, opened it up and got it going again. And meanwhile, I've got about a centimeter of sight between my helmet and my hatch, and this guy, he works for me and he's clearing that weapon. I'm thinking, 'Maybe I should be up there . . .'"

The adrenaline could not last. That night, Blind made it back to his bunk. He took his helmet off, and looked at the scorch marks left by the RPG. He put his rifle down, and took off his gear, and lay on his back on his bed. He had engaged the enemy. Killed some, or helped to. He had not lost any men. He was not hurt. But he did something he never expected to do. He cried.

"I was in a bunk by myself," he said, pondering the last of his beer. "And so, I . . . like . . . cried. I mean, really *cried*." He grinned. "I'm not a crier. But it was just so . . . For the first time in my life, I was legitimately scared. I was a month into this deployment with the next eleven or fifteen or who knew how many months to come. And now I knew what it was going to look like."

*Hooker Jim Gurbisz takes the ball up in a
March 2002 match of Army versus Rosslyn Park.*

Aldershot

O NE COLD day in 2001, I lost the first professional job I'd ever had. The magazine I wrote for closed. It had hired me straight out of college, but it was about and for lawyers, about whom I knew very little. Frightened, twenty-three years old, adrift on the vast gray sea of south London, I wrote to two more magazines about which I knew rather more: *Rugby World* and *Rugby News*. The editor of *Rugby News* replied.

We met for coffee on the Tottenham Court Road and I wore my one blue suit and he asked how much I'd been earning. I told him the real figure and he suppressed a smile. I went out for a beer with my housemates. The editor called. I couldn't start right away but the job was mine if I wanted. I wanted. My brain bat-squeaked a warning— entirely prophetic—about life at a magazine owned by Independent News and Media, a press empire down on its uppers. I ignored the bat squeak and went back to the bar for another.

The next morning I called my parents to tell them the astonishing news. They weren't astonished. They'd spent twenty years shuttling me and my brothers to rugby clubs around the north of England and sometimes further afield. When my older brother played in Russia, Dad went along for the ride. Some boys we'd played with went on to professional clubs. There were three Pengelly boys: Owen, Robin, and me. We were all big forwards, but we hadn't made it—not even Owen, the one who went to Moscow, the only one remotely so mean as required.

This was to be the payout on Mum and Dad's money and time: one son writing about the game for a wage that wouldn't make rent.

Then again, Mum and Dad were never in it for gain. They came to love rugby, thought it good for their boys, if relentlessly brutal. Neither grew up with the game. Mum made it from a Durham mining town to Manchester University, then taught English. Dad was a navy kid from Plymouth who went to Cambridge then taught high school science. They voted Labour, read the *Guardian* and sent us to state schools. By the time I landed at *Rugby News*, one brother, Robin, was teaching and the other, Owen, was in Washington, DC. In time off from embassy life, he played rugby for the Maryland Exiles.

Mum and Dad liked that I wanted to write. I asked if they could pay my rent while I waited for *Rugby News*. They could, so I spent the cold spring of 2001 playing instead of writing, for Rosslyn Park, a grand old club in southwest London. During the week, when teammates worked, I lurked in museums and galleries. I told anyone who asked that I was researching a novel: a dreadful piece of wish fulfillment about a long-lost Titian. When *Rugby News* called, the novel went in a box. It's still there—beneath three other tries.

At the end of my first day at *Rugby News*, the editor sent me to Shepherd's Bush, to a pub where antipodean backpackers brayed questions at three ex-international players. An ex-captain of South Africa said something spectacularly rude about the Welsh town where he was paid to play. My tape recorder wasn't turned on. I asked inane questions, got the tube south and sat into the early hours, hyped, pounding out my very first story. In the morning, the editor cut half of it and told me it wouldn't make print.

I worked hard. After a year, I'd been to Australia for a Lions tour, covered Six Nations games at Twickenham and European finals in Paris and Cardiff, interviewed big names and young hopefuls. The editor kept me on.

"ALWAYS REMEMBER the detail," the old man said. "Always, always the detail."

Wine bar, Rathbone Street, Fitzrovia. Lunchtime, a Thursday, April 2002.

The old man in corduroy and tweed was drinking red and smoking indoors, blue wisps curling to the ceiling, nicotine yellow, speech furred by the wine. I clung to his every dancing word. At night, I would scramble to write it all down.

> Harry Secombe's birthday at the Trocadero, Stanley Baker,
> Richard Burton a "murderous bastard on the flank."
> Richard Harris having tapes of Munster matches sent to
> his agent in Hollywood, opera singers in mufflers watching
> Welsh trial games at Cardiff.

"All great, great men," the old man said. "And so bloody romantic."

For me, life was not so bloody romantic. Home was a shared flat in Balham. But I was trying. Still lurking in galleries. Still telling myself I was writing. That evening, according to my diary—forensic proof that I should've known why I stayed single—I also "read a little Cellini then watched Barbarians vs. All Blacks, 1973."

Art and sport. The old man knew both. He was Cliff Morgan, in the 1950s a little giant of world rugby, fly half for Wales and the British and Irish Lions, later a presenter of sport, music, and praise for the BBC. In rugby, he was the commentator who, in that greatest game of all, Cardiff 1973, spoke a symphony over the greatest try ever scored. The overture: "Phil Bennett, chased by Alistair Scown. Brilliant! Oh that's brilliant!" The theme: "David, Tom David, the halfway line! Brilliant by Quinnell!" The crescendo: "This is Gareth Edwards! A dramatic start! Whatascore!" The encore: "If the greatest writer of the written word would've written that, no one would've believed him."[1]

Cliff was a national treasure. As his obituary would have it, "Like so many Welshmen growing up with chapel sermons in their ears, he reveled in the sonorous phrase."[2] The valleys poured out of him, each tale richer by the glass. As he smoked, he didn't command the room so much as caress it with skeins and tendrils of story. In April 2002, more prosaically, he was honorary chairman of *Rugby News*, his salary a perk from our owner, Sir Tony O'Reilly, an Irish millionaire also once a Lion. Lunch with Cliff was the richest perk of my job.

That Thursday in London, did I tell Cliff about West Point? Testimony to so much wine at midday, my diary doesn't say that I did. But the game against the Americans was only two weeks gone. Its scars—red welts on temples or back, a blackish eye, nicks and cuts to the hands from foraging stupidly in rucks—couldn't have faded entirely. But they could've been added to. Since West Point, I'd played a couple more matches for Park's Emerging Players, effectively the thirds, out on the rough-cut pitches in Richmond Park where once we stopped for a stag in the home twenty-two, the royal beast staring us down before taking a shit and going its way. My diary says Camberley "kicked everything, including our heads." We won 62–0. Esher were captained by a New Zealander who tried to maim his opposing hooker—one of the team's eight forward positions—and was sent off, berating the ref as he went. That finished 36–15.

After the games, a pattern. Clubhouse food, a couple of beers, home, sleep, wake up to spend a stiff Sunday stalking the Charing Cross Road, rifling through bookshops for secondhand gold. Back to work on Monday, back to the club for training. At *Rugby News* the office was three rooms over a travel agent, above a furtive Capper Street door. There were four of us in there on the editorial side, a mile north of Fleet Street but entirely in thrall to its charms. That said, the only staffer who actually looked like he'd stepped out of a novel by Evelyn Waugh—"a man of impossibly fly-blown and lugubrious appearance; his skin sallow and wrinkled, an unfiltered cigarette in his mouth; his eyes like piss-holes in the snow"[3]—actually sold small ads. On the reporting side, we were the editor, from New Zealand, small and sharp; his deputy, a solid south Londoner, trained on the tabloids; the chief reporter, the son of a Fleet Street legend; and me, three years out of college, drawn to the idea of writing as much as to the game we covered.

That Thursday, after lunch with Cliff, I skipped training. It was close to the end of the season. Nobody would mind, much.

Go back, then. Two weeks. Back to West Point.

Midweek games were rare. On Thursday, March 28, 2002, I got up early as usual, filled a kit bag with shorts and socks, boots, gumshield, scrum cap, and towel. Shirts stayed at the club. I carried the bag up the Northern Line to Capper Street and threw it under my desk in the corner. After a day's work on the May issue, I caught a train to where Park played at the Rock, a green field on a small cliff over the South Circular Road.

The team bus was always a fragile place, everyone nervous about the battle to come, each with his own way to hide it. Most players buried their heads in a paper. Rosslyn Park was strictly amateur, conservative in more ways than one. Most of the players had old school ties and jobs in the courts or the city. No one else read the *Guardian*—the backs took the *Telegraph*, the forwards the *Sun*—so my paper with its book reviews and feminism got me marked down as some sort of dangerous Bolshevik, tolerated for a reasonable supply of lineout ball and match reports for the email. For those, in steamy changing rooms filled with the smell of blood and embrocation, I took requests. Did Dave the prop really run twenty yards to score? He said he did. Jacko the fullback fancied the physio too. Did I *want* to give him credit?

Twenty years later, I work for the *Guardian* in Washington. That means I can access the archive, so I know what I would've read that Thursday in March 2002, on the way to play West Point.

Dudley Moore dead at 66; Briton on death row in Florida gets reprieve; earthquake in Afghanistan; suicide bomb in Israel; London Arabic newspaper receives "email from Bin Laden"; U.S. humiliated at Arab summit in Beirut.

Six months earlier, the season had started with 9/11. At the magazine, one of the sales team—a former New Zealand Maori flanker—stuck his head into our office and urged us to watch TV. Six months on, Afghanistan had fallen. Plans for war in Iraq were afoot. And here we were, in the belly of the military beast.

In fading light, the bus pulled into Aldershot, a small Hampshire town keen to announce itself as the "Home of the British Army," something any visitor knows from the low brick buildings, whitewashed fenceposts, windswept barrack yards, and, to employ a technical term whispered as our bus slid up to the Army Stadium, huge great fuck-off tanks. Off the bus, we grabbed our bags and piled into the clubhouse to change.

Why had we come here, on a cold spring night, to spend eighty minutes trading blows with Americans? In one sense, to adapt a British song of the First World War, we were there because we were there. Why and how didn't matter. We just had to get on with it. Every rugby player knows that feeling, before kickoff. We could hear them, the cadets, the bare stone walls and floors magnifying the clacking of their studs, their conversation, their shouts. The accents were strange, but the nearness wasn't. At rugby clubs the world over, rough and intimate places, the opposition is always close by, warming up while you do, running drills, casting looks across the field like Trojans sizing up Greeks by the ships. But on that Thursday night in March 2002, the opposition *was* different. It was foreign. To my mind at least, the Americans even *sounded* big. Soon we would run out and know.

Why were we there? We were there because our faces fit, because West Point had come to Europe to play École Spéciale Militaire de Saint-Cyr and the Royal Military Academy Sandhurst, and Sandhurst had recommended us as jolly good chaps for a game. Three weeks earlier, after the same sort of bus ride out into the heathland where Britain trains its killers, we'd beaten the British cadets. My diary records it.

> 48–20. One try, collecting a loose ball close in. One great tackle.

I remember the try, which chiefly involved falling over, but I *really* remember the tackle. A prop came onto a short ball and ran straight at me. I picked him up, drove him back and dumped him down on his arse, shoulder in his guts all the way. Glory.

> A kick in the head. A dummy and pass for Conrad's try.

Conrad was a center, one of the South Africans who showed up at Park each season, come from their Shepherd's Bush bedsits, casually brilliant and terrifyingly hard and off home after a year.

West Point. Aldershot.

We won 41–25. It was fast, furious, and physical.

Rugby hurts more when it's cold, which that night was, and when the ground is hard, which that pitch was, and when opponents come clattering at you in wave after merciless wave, which West Point inevitably did. They wore yellow shirts with Athena's helmet and sword on the breast, black shorts, and black socks. They had a big pack of what looked like football linemen, and their backs were all running backs, cornerbacks, and safeties, cubes of muscle on jackrabbit legs. They ran hard, supporting players driving over the tackled man tough and low and fast. Rugby snobbery holds that Americans, reared in pads and helmets, don't know how to tackle. These ones did, waist- or chest-high, wrapping their arms and smashing their man to the floor. Nearly twenty years later, Mo Greene, the West Point fly half who watched the game thanks to an injured shoulder, told me the cadets had their assumptions too.

"Brits were supposed to be better rugby players," he said, from Western Kentucky University, a professor of military science, fresh off ten combat tours in Special Forces. "But they were supposed to be, uh, not tough, right? And Americans were not supposed to be very good rugby players but were supposed to hit like all devils because we played American football. And I remember that game being one of the most brutal rugby games I have ever seen, tough play on both sides, punishment dished out and taken. I know you guys won, but I remember it being just one of those blue-collar, punishing games."

Out of the ordinary indeed. No Brit ever called Rosslyn Park blue-collar.

Played moderately well, winning lineout ball and making hits but dropping the ball with the line begging.

I'm surprised I won anything at the lineout, the restart after the ball goes off the field, in which I jumped to contest possession as two mates lifted me high. To reach again for that technical term, my opposite number was as big as a fuck-off great tank. But I clearly remember dropping the pass that I had only to catch for a try, the equivalent of a touchdown in American football. Right-hand corner, American fullback covering, pass coming, line open. I lowered my shoulder to meet the tackle and took my eye off the ball. No try. Scrum, West Point. I remember teammates' howls, being called a useless cunt. The company of men.

Still, so what, we won, even though the two sides didn't agree on the score. I had it 41–25. West Point made it 41–20. Either way, midway through the first half they dropped a goal for three points and celebrated as if Baghdad had fallen. We looked on, hands on knees, chests heaving, ten points clear and nonplussed.

There were other misunderstandings. Jerrod Adams, the cadets' own player-author, thought we were "a semi-professional team." Nope, though most of us had played with pros at some point. Dave Little, West Point's number 8 forward (a position typically held by one of the team's most powerful players, someone capable of carrying the ball hard, breaking tackles and making yards), would reminisce happily about spending the game trading punches with his opposite number. That was Jim Ryan, a terrifying Yorkshireman who told me he couldn't remember a thing. One thing I didn't remember was that West Point put out another team the same night, against some Oxford students. Therefore, Adams wrote, "Substitutions were very limited." We were nowhere near as fit. If the cadets had been reinforced, we might have waved the white flag.

After the game, speeches in the clubhouse bar. The cadets were impeccably friendly. Our captain was given a beautiful West Point shirt, gold and black, folded as reverently as a US flag. My opposite number, the giant, loomed like a grizzly bear. His name was Bryan, and he gave me a shot glass engraved with the West Point crest.

Over the years, from club rugby in Yorkshire to college at Durham and then down in London, I stood through so many such sessions.

Game done, out of the showers, back into everyday clothes. Hair gel and steam. Walk stiff-limbed to the bar. Beer on a split lip. Antiseptic sting. Stand carefully, raked skin raw on trousers and shirt. Vision muddied. Tired weight behind the eyes. A sort of cracked bliss. That evening in Aldershot we got on the bus back to London, climbed into cars, cadged lifts, or limped to late trains home.

It was a night out of the ordinary, a hard game against hard men being groomed to fight hard wars. Men I knew at Sandhurst were also preparing to fight in the mountains of Afghanistan, the heat and dust of Iraq. Before lights out, earnest as ever, I turned back to my diary:

> As we drove away, I couldn't help wondering how many of our opponents might yet die for their country, somewhere out in the Middle East, in the impending future.

The next morning, I picked up a *Guardian* as usual. Headlines, Friday, March 29, 2002:

> U.S. defies France by seeking death penalty for alleged 20th hijacker; 50 Taliban reported killed on new front: border region battle may herald fresh campaign; Discovery of 90m smallpox doses eases U.S. fear of attack; Iraq and Kuwait strike reconciliation deal: settlement could hit U.S. bid for backing.

Statue of Gen. Dwight D. Eisenhower at West Point.

Point

I VISITED WEST Point in May 2015, thirteen years after the Aldershot game.

I lasted one more year on the rugby pitch. My last game for Rosslyn Park was at London Welsh in February 2003. I was twenty-five. My opposite number, a hulking nineteen-year-old, pounded me into the ground. I limped off and sat under a coat in the mud. There was a strange last hurrah that summer, for Rugby Klub Ljubljana. I went to Slovenia to write for the magazine but took my boots just in case. The opponents were a touring team from Wales. I scored a try, busted my nose, dragged myself off, and watched the Welshmen drink themselves dumb. It was a burning day in June. The Julian Alps shimmered. A Slovenian looked on in awe.

"I like these men," he said. "They are like the ancient Romans. They drink till they vomit, and then they drink some more."

I couldn't argue—or keep up.

I left *Rugby News*, tried my luck at freelance. My luck held. I worked as a sub-editor on the sports desks of the *Independent* and the *Guardian*, clocking in for shifts, learning a craft, hitting print deadlines, going home late. Spare days and nights were for writing. A thought lingered, of writing seriously about rugby, this strange sport and its violent delights. The thought refused to take hold, so I swapped the terrible novel about a lost Titian for a masters in the history of art. Two nights a week for two years I lurked in Bloomsbury, haunting the great old squares. I used the degree to get work on arts desks. But if I'd always been a little too *Guardian* for rugby, now I was a little too rugby for the *Guardian*. The books editor didn't understand why I wanted a permanent job. Did rugby players read? Really? I protested that they did, really. Could write and edit too. Nothing going.

I went back to sports. In my spare time, I poured my masters into a new novel about modernist painters in the First World War. It was really a self-serving screed about a girl who left me. I grew a beard and when I turned thirty I packed some Hemingway and got on the train to Paris. I rented an attic under the bells of Saint-Médard, on Rue Mouffetard in the Fifth. The bells woke me at eight, I wrote till one, walked the city till six, had a drink in a café, edited and read in the evenings. I found it true and good to do so. I threw the Hemingway out. The novel grew like bindweed. The girl wasn't impressed. The novel went into the box in the closet.

In an instant, life changed. A friend in Edinburgh, finishing her PhD, invited me up for Thanksgiving. Her partner was American—a rugby player from Dartmouth—and her family was flying in for dinner. There was a sister. Kate. I took the train up, then walked to a flat where the New Town slid down to Leith. Kate opened the door. I fell for her right there. She was blonde and beautiful, wide-eyed, a pale New Englander brought up facing Europe. She made tea and we talked. We walked, climbing Arthur's Seat. We talked. She'd been an actor, had lived in Los Angeles, now worked in TV in New York. Her laugh was sudden and raucous. It hit me like caffeine. I bought the drinks for dinner. We talked. We washed up. We talked. In the dregs of the evening, she wrote her number on the back of a packet of Advil. By March I'd flown to New York to take her out for dinner. By August I wanted to ask her to marry me. By October I'd summoned the guts to do it. We married the next May, in Farringdon, near the old *Guardian* newsroom. We celebrated on the South Bank, lived a year near Waterloo station.

The *Guardian* opened up in New York. We packed and moved. I worked news in a loft in SoHo. Obama versus Romney, Snowden and the NSA, Sandy Hook—a crash course in what Philip Roth called "the indigenous American berserk." We had a daughter, first of three, at

Columbia-Presbyterian, uptown Manhattan, the place where Roth would die. I changed diapers and worked shifts and carried on writing, sometimes in cafés, my daughter asleep on my chest. Still looking around for a subject, I turned back to rugby. Like the mountain to the mountaineer, American rugby was simply there. A small mountain, granted. A foothill to the alps of France or New Zealand. But the man who ran the national union was an Englishman who had coached me back in Leeds. I called him and wrote a story. I wrote more.

By 2015, the war in Iraq was over but Afghanistan dragged on. I wanted to find the West Point players I'd faced in 2002. To report what they had seen and done. The sports editor indulged me. I took the train from Grand Central.

To TRAVEL from New York City to West Point is to travel in time and American lore. From the apartment we had for ten years, at West 183rd, the walk to the subway crosses Bennett Park, the highest point in Manhattan. In November 1776, it was Fort Washington. The British attacked from the east. German mercenaries came from the north, wearing hunting green. George Washington escaped west, over the Hudson to Jersey, where the bridge now named for him stands. Captured Americans were herded south to prison ships in Brooklyn harbor. Thousands died.[1]

From Bennett, down to the A train south. At 125th, back up to the street. Walk east, past the Apollo Theater and Marcus Garvey Park. Climb again, at Park Avenue, to the Hudson Valley line. From there, the train winds through time. Crossing the Harlem River to the Bronx, the track skirts Yankee Stadium. Back over the river is Inwood, where supposedly in 1626 Peter Minuit bought Manhattan for the Dutch.[2] The story may be apocryphal, but the tribes were there. Middens and shell mounds have been found, near beckoning woodland caves.[3] The train runs tight to placid water that belies its name, Spuyten Duyvil.[4] A tale for wide-eyed children: one of the first shark attacks in the New World, an unsuspecting Dutchman grabbed by a monstrous fish. It's Washington Irving, so it isn't remotely trustworthy.[5] But it's a good story, and I tell my girls it was a bull shark, the sort that comes up rivers. They shudder, deliciously, and gaze at the gentle water. Some years, whales reach the George Washington Bridge.[6]

What happens next is thrilling. The train clacks round a curve, the road traffic of the Henry Hudson Bridge passes overhead—the explorer was here in 1609—and suddenly the world opens up, all water and sky, the "vista the Lenapes and the Wiechquaesgecks saw."[7] Silence falls, so close to the yawping city. On a wind-whipped day in the brief New York spring there are whitecaps out on the river. After rain in summer, the water seems to swell. There are ships, upriver for Albany, down to harbor and sea. Even the ships look small on the Hudson, a riverscape splayed to the sky.

The train hugs the eastern bank. To the west, the Palisades, the great cliffs of New Jersey and New York. Two military helicopters fly north, gray-black, rotors droning, insectoid reminders of journey's end. Stations reel past. Glenwood and its dead power plant. Yonkers, selling riverside life. The Tappan Zee Bridge. Tarrytown, for Irving's Sleepy Hollow. Ossining, home to Don and Betty Draper and Sing Sing prison. Croton-Harmon, which gave Gotham its water.[8] Just before Peekskill the engine flushes an osprey up from its nest. The great gray-black back lifts on huge wings and cruises over the river. An eagle watches the water.

Stay on the train to Cold Spring and Beacon, in the Hudson Highlands, and the riverbanks close in. Storm King Mountain is a boulder thrown by a giant. In the stream, on Pollepel Island, Bannerman Castle, a ruined military depot. But when you're as incurably urban as I am, which means you don't drive, and you want to get to West Point, you have to cross the river. You have to get off the train at Peekskill. A cab. The driver is from a Latin American country that has a flag of red, yellow, and blue. Maybe Ecuador, maybe Venezuela, either way bemused to hear you're going to West Point to talk rugby rather than football. He laughs as he drives over the Bear Mountain Bridge, high and elegant where the hills plunge down to the water.

British ships once sailed the Hudson, seeking to split the colonies in two. The Americans threw a great chain across the river. Benedict Arnold tried to sell West Point to the British.[9] In 1802, ten years shy of another war with Britain, the military academy was born.

The main road in goes through Highland Falls. Side streets climb the hill, the river rolls below, there are diners and delis and banks. At Thayer Gate, named for a great superintendent, a miniature castle tower. ID checks. The guard is Samoan. Hard by the gate there's a huge green sports field, named for the Buffalo Soldiers, Black cavalrymen who fought in the West, the field dotted with posts and lines for lacrosse, soccer, football. Behind that, the great gray buildings of the academy itself.

When Charles Dickens saw it, in 1842, it was love at first sight. West Point, he wrote, "Could not stand on more appropriate ground, and any ground more beautiful can hardly be."[10] When I first went there, in May 2015, I felt something similar. Not everyone falls so fast. Much depends on the season. As the *New York Times* put it in 2009, reporting cadet suicides, January to April is "gloom period," when the trees are leafless and the hillsides bare, "when the pewter skies seem to mirror the gray fortresslike buildings on campus, and cadets hustle from class to class to avoid the cold winds whipping off the Hudson River."[11]

Cadets and staff are impeccably polite and call any visitor *Sir*. But West Point isn't built for a friendly welcome. It's half college, half barracks, staffed by soldiers tasked with making soldiers. The novelist James Salter arrived—as Cadet James Horowitz—in summer 1942, a hundred years after Dickens. Fifty years later, he remembered a place like "Joyce's Clongowes Wood College, which had caused such a long shiver of fear. . . . There were the same dark entrances, the Gothic façades, the rounded bastion corners with crenellated tops, the prisonlike windows. In front was the great expanse which was the parade ground, the Plain."[12]

The Plain is a great green lawn fringed with metal bleachers. Outside Washington Hall, the giant central building where cadets eat, an equestrian statue of the first president guards the great front doors. Up the hill is the Protestant chapel, also Gothic, forbidding and huge. Michie Stadium, the cathedral of Army football, is up the hillside too. Down toward the Hudson, there is a new library, Jefferson Hall, fortresslike, a citadel of books in uniform gray. There are offices and gymnasiums, fields for soccer and baseball. There are statues of generals. Kosciuszko, Sedgwick, Grant. Eisenhower, MacArthur, Patton. Behind Washington Hall are the barracks, ranks of windows over yards for formation and punishment drill. Cadets who live three to a room cross and recross those yards, rushing to academic or physical tests.

Eighteen-year-olds arriving at West Point are greeted with the calculated brutality of Beast, a six-week barrage of indignity and hard training to break down civilian habits and instill military order. Dickens thought the "course of education . . . severe, but well devised, and manly."[13] Many who have endured its modern forms beg to disagree. Mike Mahan, a 1970 graduate who became the coach who put West Point rugby on the map, remembers "institutionalized harassment."[14] The culture changes. There are more cadets nowadays, around a thousand in each class, up to ten nominated by each member of Congress, service families, enlistment, and officer training also offering paths to admission.[15] Women have been admitted since 1976, and, perhaps correspondingly, hazing is much reduced. But in any era, memoirs of life as a "plebe," academy argot for freshman, are often scrolls of misery. James Salter became an army flier, then reached the heights of American fiction. His description of plebe life sketches the experience as well, and as concisely, as any: "It was the hard school, the forge. To enter you passed, that first day, into an inferno. Demands, many of them incomprehensible, rained down. . . . We stood or ran like insects from one place to another. . . . Some had the courage to quit immediately, others slowly failed. . . . Life was anxious minutes, running everywhere."[16]

Most make it through. And even Salter found poetry in memory, even of the gray days of winter, when "the river is smooth and ice clings to its banks [and] the trees are bare."

"Through the open window from the far shore," Salter heard "the sound of a train, the faint, distant clicking of wheels on the rail joints, the Albany or Montreal train with its lighted cars and white tablecloths, the blur of luxury from which we are ever barred.

"At night the barracks, seen from the Plain, look like a city."[17]

NOWADAYS, A train runs past the home of West Point rugby. It is not the passenger line to and from New York, on the eastern bank of the river. On the west, commercial trains scroll endlessly south for the big ports, diesel tanks coupled to grain silos, shipping containers two high. The heavy wheels click next to the road, which runs down to Anderson Rugby Complex at the far north of the post.

On a wet day in May, the hills rich green and fringed with ominous cloud, the men's rugby coach stops his car by the rails. Matt Sherman was once a fly half for Cal Berkeley and the Eagles, the US national team. Now he's mustachioed, efficient, the very image of a college coach. He lives in Cold Spring with his wife and children. Sometimes, when the tides are right, he kayaks the river to practice, past Constitution Island, site of a revolutionary fort. He's also an Oxford-educated historian with a well-stocked office library.

We've stopped at the edge of a nondescript field, marked out for football. Matt reads from a plaque in the ground: "Near this site stood the home of American patriot, Revolutionary War soldier, and previous owner of the West Point lands, Colonel Stephen Moore. Moore's home served as General Washington's headquarters from July to November of 1779."[18] This is Target Hill Field, where in 1961 West Point rugby was born.

Long before then, football was West Point's true religion. But rugby has been in America just as long. Rutgers, in New Jersey, claims the first game of college football, a 6–4 win over Princeton in November 1869—and says it was played under "rugby-like rules."[19] Most sources say the first game of actual rugby, the handling and tackling game that arose in England alongside gentler soccer, was played in Cambridge, Massachusetts, in May 1874. Harvard and

McGill, from Canada, fought out a scoreless tie. Again, though, the records give pause. Harvard-McGill is also widely said to have been the first game of college football.[20]

According to historian Stephen Ambrose, there was football of some form at West Point, most resembling modern soccer, as early as 1825. In the 1850s, Philip Sheridan, who would become the little Civil War cavalry general who laid waste to the Shenandoah, received a demerit for kicking a ball near barracks.[21] But organized football grew faster elsewhere, and West Point did not field a team until 1890. Until 2014, when rugby was given varsity status, in part as a way of corralling it in the aftermath of a scandal over inappropriate emails sent between cadets,[22] most came to the club sport having come to West Point to play football. Most had never played rugby before. Such pioneering spirit had precedent. In 1890, Dennis Mahan Michie, the son of a professor, was one of only two cadets who had played football. He arranged a game against the US Naval Academy. Army lost heavily. In 1891, Army beat Navy. The rest is sports history.

In America, ever since, rugby has been to football what the Hudson freight train is to the Amtrak on the far bank. It runs far slower. There was a brief time when it might have seized its chance. In both games, the violence has always been half the point, for players and fans alike. But by the early 1900s, football was outright lethal. Theodore Roosevelt intervened, demanding codification of laws and play in the proper spirit.[23] Some colleges switched to rugby. Stanford led the way, providing most of the US players who won Olympic gold in Antwerp in 1920 and Paris four years later.[24] Alas for rugby, football got its house in order. Soon rugby was rare, kept alive at Ivy League schools, in pockets out west, and in clubs in coastal cities often formed by migrants from the empire. But then, a cadet decided to bring the game to West Point.

John Taylor became a colonel of infantry and after that an entrepreneur. In the summer of 1960, he was an upperclassman, preparing to push the class of '64 through Beast. Up at Michie Stadium, he came across a game staged by the New York Rugby Club. In a history compiled by members of the first West Point team, Taylor recalled being "intrigued by the constant flow of the game, seemingly without rules and [with] players of average build and weight."[25]

It was a telling first impression. If football, ordered to the finest degree, sometimes seems an odd fit for the land of the free, it could have been made for its military academy. Superbly fit foot soldiers perform precise roles, following orders from on high. But West Point is also a college like any other, and even in the cold barracks yards rebellious instincts persist. Most cadets who come to rugby were reared on football. Handed a rugby ball, told they can run and pass, the simple freedom proves intoxicating. It helps that they're all supposed to tackle too, as hard (and legal) as they like. Without pads.

Sixty years ago, up at Michie Stadium, Taylor spoke to the New York coach. Taylor now had a mission: to bring rugby to West Point. First he bought a ball. It was like a football but fatter and rounder, familiar but enticingly different. He put it on display in the library, with a sign-up sheet and a spread from *Life Magazine*. Today, somewhere toward the end of the long, slow death of print journalism, it is hard to imagine the reach *Life* had in the sixties. If you made *Life*, you'd made it. The man who made John Taylor's copy was Peter Miller Dawkins.

He was born on March 8, 1938, in Royal Oak, Michigan, the son of a dentist. At eleven, he was treated for polio. At seventeen, he was accepted by Yale but chose West Point instead. A halfback in football, Dawkins was recognized in 1958 as the best player in the college game, winner of the Heisman Trophy. The next year he graduated as the only cadet ever to be brigade commander, class president, and captain of the football team *and* to finish in the top 5 percent of his class. But that wasn't why John Taylor made Pete Dawkins part of his pitch. Dawkins had won a Rhodes scholarship, which sent him off to Oxford. He studied politics, philosophy, and economics, and he enjoyed the old university town: quiet rooms in a medieval college, an "ancient bicycle bought for 25 shillings,"[26] cups of "instant coffee with powdered milk."[27] He also took up rugby.

In 1959, Art Buchwald met Dawkins in his rooms at Brasenose. The columnist wrote, "Not since Robert Taylor rowed in that memorable

film *A Yank at Oxford* has any American captured the imagination
of this famous university town as Peter Dawkins . . . now the fifth
American in Oxford history to win a rugby blue."[28] Dawkins said he
played rugby because he "had to do something or get fat." Like John
Taylor and others who would follow him to rugby—like Bill Clinton,
who would play in the forwards for University College on his own
Rhodes scholarship ten years later[29]—Dawkins took to the game
straight away. "Rugby is different," he said. The ball must be passed
backward or kicked forward, and "when you tackle you are usually
using the ball carrier's momentum to stop him. Therefore you need
no protective padding—when you've got the ball you're not trying to
burrow through the other team. There's no future in it. The idea is to
keep moving and pass when you see you're being tackled."[30]

Dawkins was six foot one and more than 200 pounds, in those days
huge for a wing. His football-formed aggression and high-stepping
run caused trouble. He later admitted "a penchant for what [the Brit-
ish] called 'crash tackling.' That is, rather than using my opponent's
momentum to bring him to the ground . . . I would attack directly at
my opposite number and tackle him, as violently as possible, by driving my shoulder through his chest."[31] He also remembered games
against the two most formidable teams in rugby, the All Blacks of
New Zealand and the Springboks of South Africa. One thing he did
had an impact even in those mighty countries. Dawkins was charged,
as wings were then, with throwing the ball at the lineout. Rather than
lob a gentle parabola, as rugby players did, the American threw over-
hand, football-style, fast as a naval torpedo. Sometimes he bypassed
the lineout entirely, putting his backs on attack. Reporting the annual
game between Oxford and Cambridge at Twickenham, the home of
English rugby, the Associated Press said Dawkins "found himself a
sensation—all because of his long American football tosses."

"Twice he heaved the ball about 30 yards straight into the hands
of a waiting teammate. Millions saw such a move for the first time
on television. It came naturally to Dawkins. But to Britons it was
something near a revolution."[32]

It was also effective. Oxford won 9–3.

◆   ◆   ◆

DAWKINS HAD two seasons in dark blue. He served in Vietnam. After that, he went into business and Republican politics. Eight West Point rugby players did not come home from Vietnam. At Anderson Rugby Complex, their portraits hang on the wall, along with the year they graduated, and where and when they died:

Clair Hall Thurston Jr., Class of 1964, killed War Zone D, November 1965

George Everett Perry, Class of 1963, near Dak To, 1966

Chuck Hemmingway, Class of 1965, Route 1 near Hue, June 1967

Bob Serio, Class of 1964, Binh Duong, April 1968

Jim Brierly, Class of 1967, Binh Dinh province, December 1968

David Sackett, Class of 1968, Boi Loi Woods, October 1969

Alex Hottell III, Class of 1964, near Bao Luc, July 1970

Bill Pahissa, Class of 1969, Firebase Ripcord, July 1970

Norton Bailey Wilson Jr.—Butch to his teammates in the Class of '63—is on the wall too. He died near Kirchgoens in West Germany in March 1964, pushing another man from the path of a train.[33]

Alex Hottell III wrote his own obituary. A year before his death in a helicopter crash with Major General George Casey, the commander of First Cavalry, he sent it to his wife. It said, "We all have but one death to spend, and insofar as it can have any meaning, it finds it in the service of comrades-in-arms. And yet, I deny that I died FOR anything—not my country, not my Army, not my fellow man, none of these things. I LIVED for these things."[34]

At home, the first West Point rugby teams lived for a fluid schedule of games, mostly against New York clubs, and for the ingestion of certain kinds of fluid in dark bars after the final whistle. They learned their game as they played, first in kit scrounged from the soccer team and coached by one of their own, Ric Cesped, a cadet who had grown up around British expats in Chile.

On May 12, 1962, the first team played the last game of its first season. The same day, Douglas MacArthur came to the academy to accept an award. MacArthur was both a star cadet, first in the class of 1903, and an influential superintendent in the 1920s. In the 1940s he led the conquest of Japan, then ruled it. His last campaign was the Korean War, during which President Truman fired him.[35] At West Point in 1962, aged eighty-two, MacArthur delivered a farewell speech based on the academy motto, "Duty, Honor, Country." Like Alex Hottell's obituary, the speech became part of West Point lore. But something else MacArthur once said holds greater sway: "Upon the fields of friendly strife are sown the seeds that, upon other fields, on other days will bear the fruits of victory."[36]

Any cadet knows the line by heart. At Michie Stadium, it is carved in granite. It is also in Bugle Notes, an exhaustive book of facts, statistics, and willful nonsense each plebe is required to learn.

For half a century,[37] most West Point players came to rugby from football. When they did, there was another holy text to learn:

> *He to-day that sheds his blood with me*
> *Shall be my brother.*

It's Shakespeare, from the Saint Crispin's Day speech delivered by Henry V before Agincourt in October 1415. It's also preceded by a line—"We few, we happy few, we band of brothers"—that was made more famous still by Laurence Olivier, who delivered it to the embattled British in 1944, and by Steven Spielberg and Tom Hanks, who produced the 2001 HBO miniseries *Band of Brothers,* which follows a company of American paratroopers in the Second World War.

Shakespeare's words have long found a home in rugby. Land on any website selling cheap gear and you'll find them printed on T-shirts and hoodies alongside slogans from "Give blood, play rugby" to "Rugby players do it with odd-shaped balls" and tired double entendres about hookers. At a slightly more exalted level, Brian

Moore, a great English hooker of the 1990s, has written powerfully about how he used *Henry V* before games against France, "tears of passion running down my cheeks as the Harfleur speech" played on the bus to the game.[38]

Moore was using Shakespeare to foster team spirit in violent action, a process West Point takes very seriously indeed. At the Aldershot match in 2002, I looked on, as sardonic as anyone can be when truly knackered, as the cadets exhorted each other as brothers. As the great reporter Seymour Hersh once said, the US Army doesn't do irony.[39] When West Point rugby players call each other *brother*, they mean it.

Brian Moore meant it when he talked about Harfleur, the speech Henry gives his men as they besiege a French town. Perhaps he was most taken by the opening:

> *Once more unto the breach, dear friends, once more;*
> *Or close the wall up with our English dead.*
> *In peace there's nothing so becomes a man*
> *As modest stillness and humility:*
> *But when the blast of war blows in our ears,*
> *Then imitate the action of the tiger;*
> *Stiffen the sinews, summon up the blood,*
> *Disguise fair nature with hard-favour'd rage;*
> *Then lend the eye a terrible aspect . . .*

Or perhaps he was thinking of the end:

> *I see you stand like greyhounds in the slips,*
> *Straining upon the start. The game's afoot:*
> *Follow your spirit, and upon this charge*
> *Cry 'God for Harry, England, and Saint George!'*

Either way, *Henry V* is effective stuff when you're psyching yourself up for the first scrum or tackle. At West Point, Henry's words also suffuse a painful rite of passage. Many rugby players sport the word "Brothers" on a tattoo—a Ka-Bar knife through a rugby ball, perhaps wrapped with "He today who sheds his blood with me"— on shoulder, thigh, or breast. Bryan Phillips, my enormous opposite number at Aldershot, told me about his tattoo, the first he ever had: "A sword and shield through a rugby ball that says 'Brothers' on it."

"It's on my right shoulder. It was drawn by Brian McCoy, and a lot of us have versions of the same tattoo. It has an XV on it"—for the number of men in a rugby team—"and a V for my number."[40]

I cherish an old Rosslyn Park shirt, time-honored red-and-white hoops, a black "5" stitched to the back. Same thing. Sort of.

Liz Samet is a West Point English professor and the author of *Soldier's Heart*, a book about teaching cadets the canon.[41] For her, the popularity of *Henry V* among cadets and rugby players is not without its problems. At West Point, all first-year students are required to memorize a text. "Saint Crispin's Day" and "Harfleur," Samet said, are particularly "popular among football teams, perhaps not to the extent that it textured the rugby team, but certainly locker-room favorites." *Henry V* is "also a favorite among military officers. And in some cases, in order for that to be a favorite, you can't have read all of that play very carefully. There are elements of it that don't work at all for this notion of brotherhood, though it's a very powerful one indeed."[42]

Samet was referring to passages in the Harfleur speech in which Henry threatens rape, murder, and "naked infants spitted upon pikes" if the town does not yield.

"I know why the speech is attractive in isolation, and it's attractive for military officers," she said. "I think it's actually more dangerous for military officers not to know it than for rugby players, per se, because rugby players are going to a kind of war but not to the same war, that kind of war that Henry was fighting. So the brotherhood is the romance of course, and I understand the appeal of that. It is also the reason that I see it as a potential problem for army officers. It ignores the other kinds of solidarity that Henry creates."

Do West Point rugby players pause to think such matters through before facing Penn State, Dartmouth, or Cal? Possibly not too deeply.

English is optional after the first year and most of the '02 team majored in science—and rugby. But *Henry V* abides, throughout the US Army. In 2002, American soldiers were fighting in Afghanistan. At home, a charitable effort resurrected the Armed Services Editions, cheap paperback books modeled on those shipped to US forces during the Second World War. Titles in the new run included *The Art of War* by Sun Tzu, the speeches of Teddy Roosevelt, the witticisms of Christopher Buckley . . . and *Henry V*.[43]

Craig Mullaney could have received a copy. A 2000 West Point grad, he was a Rhodes scholar, a wrestler, and briefly a rugby winger, until he injured a shoulder. In his memoir, *The Unforgiving Minute*, he describes taking leave of his platoon in 2003, after a sharp fight near Shkin in Afghanistan:

"As I waited for the Chinook to take me to Orgun, Story assembled the platoon to bid me farewell. I had learned since my first introduction in January not to bore them with a long speech. This time I recited only the few well-worn verses I had memorized years ago as a plebe studying Shakespeare. For the first time the words seemed appropriate to recite outside a classroom. 'We few, we happy few, we band of brothers.' What brothers, I thought, as I looked in their eyes. I was proud of the medals my men had earned. . . . I stood in the company of heroes. I mangled the rest of Henry V's speech and spoke from my heart, 'Thanks for the privilege of letting me fight with you.'"[44]

AMONG WEST Point rugby brothers, Mike Mahan is known as Father. As a cadet in the late 1960s, loathing the hazing by instructors and older students, he came to treat as a talisman "a coffee cup that said 'Out and alive in '75,' being that I would graduate in 1970 and I had a five-year commitment" to the army, as all cadets do.[45] But Mahan's commitment to West Point came to last rather longer. He led an infantry platoon in Germany, an experience that "turned the whole thing around for me as it was so exhilarating and exciting, it was everything I had dreamed about as being a leader. So I pursued that and I did very well." He hadn't known rugby at West Point but he came across a game or two during a posting to California. Then, one day in 1980, during a postgrad course at MIT, he went to watch the cadets play Harvard Business School. A coach spotted him, and when Mahan came back to West Point, he was asked to coach the team.

"Rugby was my vehicle to teach cadets leadership," he said, a retired lieutenant colonel, settled in California. "What I quickly found out was that if you're in the classroom, teaching chemistry, you've got to teach the ideal gas law to a bunch of kids who have other things on their mind. You don't have time to talk about leadership. But after school, when I was with the rugby team, that was the spot where you could really demonstrate and demand good leadership."

Mahan did so for four years, spent three years away, then came back in 1987. He found a club more devoted to partying than propping, to "beer parties after games, naked carrier landings on beer-covered tables." He backed off. A British exchange officer had inherited the team. But as this Brit was not a rugby player, he asked Mahan to change his mind.

"I said yes, I would do it, but only if it was a serious endeavor, that our goal would be to win the national championship. Because I thought we should be using this vehicle to give cadets an advanced experience in leadership before they went out into the army, where they had to be a good leader."

Plenty of people at West Point will tell you that when it comes to training officers, rugby is a useful tool. Perhaps the most direct expression is a recent one, from athletics director Mike Buddie in 2022: "Rugby *is* ground combat. It is the epitome of how we're going to be able to fight and win wars, and that's by being more mentally, physically, and emotionally tough than anybody or anything we come up against. Rugby is like this awesome petri dish of teaching diverse, effective, winning teams. It's a tangible example of all the things we try to teach—we learn about military history, tenacity, grit, toughness, effort, strategy, organization . . . and we get to keep score."[46]

Mike Mahan thought the same way. He told his players, "'We're going to train like a military unit,' because that's what my experience was. And we were going to pursue the national championship, which they had never reached before. The US never had a national championship till 1980. It was 1988 when I was there, and we hadn't even been in the final four during those eight years."

Under Mahan, West Point rugby got serious. The cadets made the final four their first time out, losing narrowly to Air Force. It was, as Mahan says with a laugh, "one of the few years that Cal didn't win," but it started a run of finals appearances.

Like other US colleges, West Point accords some sports varsity status, bringing financial support and recruitment. By the time rugby acquired that status, it had a gleaming new home, Anderson Rugby Complex, opened in 2007.[47] But in the Mahan years, rugby was a club sport, outside the inner sanctum. It didn't have a clubhouse or much in the way of support. Mahan didn't mind. In every relative hardship, he saw a chance to strengthen his players.

"We didn't care about what support we got from the administration. We were in this on our own, we were going to excel, we were going to work as hard as we possibly could. We were going to be good leaders and good teammates, and it worked."

Coach Mahan retired from the army but took a civilian job in fundraising, close to the superintendent. He kept coaching. By the time the Class of '02 found their way to rugby, West Point had repeatedly found its way to the final four. A championship remained elusive. The drive to win one remained.

James Gurbisz, senior photo, West Point Military Academy, Class of 2002.

Eatontown

ROM PENN Station, out of the long black tunnel bored through the Palisades, the New Jersey–bound train crosses swamps and flats. There are reed beds and channels, herons watching for fish. There are freight yards and fulfillment centers, mosques and beaten-down churches. At Newark Airport, jets arrive and depart. This is no grand journey through time like the trip up the Hudson, but the army and its history are here too. At Elizabeth in 1780, the Americans won the Battle of Springfield, beating Wilhelm von Knyphausen, the German victor of Fort Washington.

The train tracks south. Out in Raritan Bay, ships lie at anchor. A different Jersey reveals itself: green, watered, and prosperous. The stations reel past. Aberdeen-Matawan, Hazlet, Middletown. Next stop, Red Bank. Out in the parking lot, Ken and Helen Gurbisz are waiting.

Ken is bearish and genial, seventy or so with gray hair, mustache, and an engaging, barking laugh. Helen is shorter, darker, pleasantly inquisitive about family, life, and work. She was a teacher; he was an engineer. Both had Polish forebears who landed in Jersey. Helen grew up in Jersey City and Nutley; Ken was in Bayonne.[1] In the car, they finish each other's sentences, point out landmarks, squabble good-naturedly over the map.

They had two children, Kathleen in 1977 and James three years later. The kids grew up in Eatontown, in a spacious house on a quiet street with a tree in the yard. Ken and Helen have moved on, but the house still sits amid the swish of the sprinklers. We drive past.

Two-car garage, driveway with space for roller hockey, broad roads for riding bikes.

Thanks to the phenomenon of archived virtual tours on real estate websites, I can see the home's interior, frozen in time before the Gurbiszes moved: In the living room, a table with framed pictures. Kathleen on her wedding day. James on his. James's graduation picture, proud in West Point gray. In the den, another portrait of James, his sports trophies on one side of the television, with a team picture and two medals. Kathleen is on the other side, caught in full flow on the track. Up over the window, there's a model Chinook, the helicopter that moved troops in Vietnam. In the study upstairs, two sketches of the lighter Huey hang over a desk. In the garage, tools and fishing rods over a workbench, a plaid shirt over a chair. Out back, porch, deck, lawn, and whitewashed shed.

The neighborhood is so sylvan, you expect to hear radios by raised windows, broadcasting Ike warning the nation about the military-industrial complex. The house is hard by Fort Monmouth, a huge army base that opened in 1928 and closed in September 2011.[2] We drive through. The officers' housing is neat and desirable, barracks blocks stark and empty. On either side of the main drag, big midcentury buildings sit prey to weeds and vines. Hall, theater, bowling alley. CECOM—Communications-Electronics Command. Later, in the shade at the Little League field where Gurbisz played and his father coached, the mayor of Eatontown, Anthony Talerico, tells me some buildings haven't been touched since the day the base closed down.[3]

Talerico went to school with Gurbisz. Now, on his watch, change is happening, buildings are being reclaimed. Towns round the fort are changing too. Many in Eatontown, Tinton Falls, and Oceanport arrived after the base closed.

To each generation, Fort Monmouth means less.

It meant a lot to James Gurbisz.

There were Memorial Day services and there was the bowling alley and on Armed Forces Day you could visit and sit on a tank. Families showed up from Korea or Germany, the parents posted to Jersey. At Memorial Middle School, the principal, Jay Medlin,[4] walks a corridor lined with pictures of spring visits to Washington sponsored by the American Legion. There Gurbisz is, thirteen, blond and broad in shirt and tie, poker-faced on the Capitol steps in 1994. At Monmouth Memorial High, the superintendent, Andy Teeple, taught math to Gurbisz.[5] He guides us to a hall where Gurbisz's baseball and football uniforms are framed. Number 52 in baseball, number 68 in football, captain of both as a senior. A plaque lists other achievements: Board of Education, student council president, mock trial, National Honor Society. Teeple remembers Gurbisz as one of those kids who could joke *and* work. The fields for baseball and football are decked in black and gold.

Over lunch at the Pour House, a dark bar in Tinton Falls where the Reuben is the size of a baseball mitt and Coke refills come in missile-silo glasses, Toby Stark remembers his friend.[6] They grew up in the shadow of the fort. Once, someone called a bomb threat to the school. Gurbisz took charge of the evacuation, directing traffic, offering to carry friends to safety.

In 2002, not long after the day the Twin Towers burned over the horizon, the reporter Seymour Hersh spoke to the editor of the *New Yorker*. US troops were in Afghanistan. The Iraq War drew near. Hersh discussed his work uncovering My Lai, the massacre at the black heart of Vietnam. Two years later he would report the shame of Abu Ghraib, the prison where US guards abused Iraqis. Despite such disasters, Hersh insisted, the US military was "still one of the most idealistic societies we have. There are more people there who believe in the Norman Rockwell version of America."[7]

At the Little League field in Eatontown, there is another plaque for Captain James Gurbisz.

BY PHONE from Palo Alto, California, where she works in tech investments, Kathleen Gurbisz Forte remembered sports at home—"all the kids would come by, especially when my dad was playing roller hockey with us"—and at high school, where she still holds track records.[8] She remembered a typically annoying little brother, the "chubby, husky, fat kid," standing awkwardly, aged nine, at Grace United Methodist Church, in cub scout uniform and holding the Stars and Stripes.[9]

"He was bigger than other kids," Kathleen said. "My parents wouldn't let him play football, but they let him play baseball. He wasn't a runner. I was the runner. But he liked basketball, was always very athletic. He was three years younger. We fought a lot, probably because we were both very stubborn and very competitive. It wasn't until my senior year in high school, his freshman year"—by which time Jimmy was playing football—"that I really got to see him. I bought this 1977 Volvo, a car my own age, for like twelve hundred bucks, like all my summer money, and my mom gave me gas money to take Jim to school. I didn't want to do it, but honestly it could have been the best thing ever. Because that's when we really forged a good, solid relationship."

Kathleen watched her brother "blossom into someone that was super-disciplined, willing to push to the point of exhaustion, I think more than others on the academic side, and then also on the sports side, almost like in a robotic way, which also probably led to some of the injuries he had," including problems with his knees. She remembered him pulling all-nighters to hit deadlines then sleeping the whole weekend. Ted Jarmusz, Gurbisz's coach for baseball and football, confirmed Gurbisz's will to win.[10] Sitting by his pool on a hot suburban morning, Jarmusz said Gurbisz was the heart of any team, owner of the dirtiest uniform, runner of the most punishment laps for answering back, instigator of parties after victories and extra training after defeats. In football, Gurbisz played on the line as a guard. Off the field, he ran with a group including Anthony Bongi, a wide receiver, an army kid whose dad brought him back from Korea.

"The entire culture and everything about our teams came from Jim," Bongi said, twenty years later, just out of the army himself. "There's no ifs, ands, or buts about that. Jim might not have been the biggest guy, the fastest guy, the strongest guy, or the best player, but he was the leader. It was a close-knit group of guys."[11]

Kathleen laughed. "Whenever I think of Jim at school, I think of 'balls to the wall.' That was kind of their motto. I always think that was in part because of Jimmy. He was a jokester. People loved him. I don't think his jokes necessarily had cruel intent. It was always just funny. He was like a magnet. People gravitated toward him."

When Gurbisz was fifteen, he gravitated toward Tori Richardson. She was a slight, elfin girl from the Philadelphia area, and one day in her sophomore year at Monmouth Memorial High, she found herself with Jim Gurbisz "in some stupid extracurricular session."

"It was like Students Against Driving Drunk," she said, from Charleston, South Carolina.[12] "Everyone signed up just because they went on really good field trips. And it wasn't long after we met that we started dating. We held hands down the hallway. We went to the mall on Friday night. Classic New Jersey."

On the one hand, Tori said, going out with Gurbisz was "annoying, because he never seemed to really have to work hard. He had a natural work ethic. I would be the one the night before the test, like, 'Oh, crap, maybe I should study.' Meanwhile, he's done."

On the other hand, in a very Jersey way, she is keen to push back on any idea that he stood out from the crowd.

"Yeah, sure, he was captain of this and captain of that. But it was high school. Everyone has their own little faction and group. He wasn't this shining beacon above the school and the town. He was just the one guy who could get along with everyone, and did well at what he did."

FORT MONMOUTH was not the only military presence in Gurbisz's life. His father, Ken, flew Huey helicopters in Vietnam.

"My brother was always interested," Kathleen said. "And my dad, every so often, if we asked, would pull out his maps of Vietnam and Cambodia and would tell us where he was, where he flew over. I think he shared some of those stories with Jim."

Nonetheless, Gurbisz's interest in West Point caught his parents off guard. At high school, he did the things ambitious students do, including attending Boys State. Sponsored by the American Legion, in Jersey the program takes kids to Rider University in Lawrenceville, where for a week every June they form a mock government, conduct elections, and hear from prominent speakers. Graduates include the New Jersey Democratic senators Bob Menendez and Cory Booker and the Supreme Court justice Samuel Alito. Gurbisz approached it with slightly ironic detachment. Rather than try to make mayor, congressman, or senator, Ken said, his son ran for dogcatcher. But Gurbisz's irreverent streak didn't prepare him, Helen said,[13] for the day a kid from Paterson, Newark, or some other Gomorrah on the Passaic River, started a dice ring and got himself thrown out. All parts of Jersey are tough, Jim understood, but some parts are more tough than others.

Gurbisz didn't attract recruiters from the big football schools, in part because the Monmouth Falcons "went without a win his junior and senior year."[14] But his grades were good, and he had Ivy League interest. In 2011, Ken Gurbisz sat for an interview with the Rutgers Oral History Archives.[15] He discussed growing up in Bayonne, Vietnam, marriage, and family life. He also remembered the day his son, who had told him the Army football coach was coming to talk, called him at work, confused.

"He said, 'Dad, I don't know if I did the right thing.' He says, 'I gave a verbal commitment to go to West Point.' Now, I know Jim—we lived near Fort Monmouth, and I know he loved it. I know he was raised around military families, so he knew the deal. I said to him, 'Jim, we're just going to talk when I get home, okay,' and we talked, and I said to him, 'You don't do West Point for a free education, you don't do West Point for your parents.' I said, 'You don't do West Point for anybody but yourself, and you've got to really, really want it in order to go there.' And he had that commitment. He wanted to go."[16]

Kathleen saw her brother achieve "something so prestigious pretty much on merit, not having other avenues or other ways that people have gotten into West Point, whether that's pulling strings or whatever."

Tori, however, "was the first person trying to convince him against it. *Viciously.* I mean, look at it from the perspective of an eighteen-year-old girl. We'd been dating all through high school. I knew he always respected his father's military service and all that, and obviously I knew he had applied, because it's a big deal to apply. But I thought, 'He's not gonna be accepted and it's fine. Or even if he does, he's got Princeton in the bag, he's got Columbia in the bag.' Like, why would you go to West Point when you can go to Princeton and play baseball?

"I knew West Point meant we were not going to see each other for months, when I'd literally seen Jim every single day. Back then, we didn't have cell phones. There would be one weekend when we could go up and talk for a little while. And it wasn't just that. I knew it was a big commitment afterwards. You have to go into the military. And at that point we knew Fort Monmouth was shutting down, pretty much. No one was getting stationed there. So I'm like, 'Well, no, he's gonna be away for a long time training.' So, for me it was purely selfish. You know, 'Out of all the career paths you could take, this is going to be the most dangerous, even though you completely want to be a mechanical engineer. So go to Princeton.' His dad's a mechanical engineer, my dad's a mechanical engineer. Get a job, there's plenty of them in Jersey. I'd already been thinking that after we'd been together for so long, we were gonna stay together. I was like, 'This is not the life I pictured for us.'"

It was what Gurbisz pictured for himself. It was also what Anthony Bongi's dad pictured for him, although Anthony wasn't an academic or sporting star, so a prep year beckoned. The US Military Academy Preparatory School still works to whip kids into shape in one intense year. Nowadays, it's on West Point's campus. Twenty years ago, it was on the grounds of Fort Monmouth.

A lot of things were once at Fort Monmouth. It was home to the US Signal Corps, which for forty years included the US Army Pigeon Breeding and Training Center.[17] Julius Rosenberg, executed as a Soviet spy with his wife Ethel in 1953, worked there on radar research.[18] Fort Monmouth engineers and technicians invented the aircraft altimeter and the walkie-talkie. By 2004, when James Gurbisz had graduated West Point and was serving in Iraq, teams at Fort Monmouth were working to counter the key threat to US forces: improvised explosive devices, IEDs. As one reporter put it, the scientists were engaged in a race against time.[19]

West Point's hulking Taylor Hall was designed by Ralph Adams Cram, who would go on to design the Cathedral of Saint John the Divine in New York City.

Beast

A T WEST Point they call the Class of 1915 "the class the stars fell on," because fifty-nine of its 164 graduates made brigadier general or higher. Among them were Omar Bradley, first chair of the Joint Chiefs of Staff, and Dwight D. Eisenhower, supreme commander of the Allied forces in the Second World War and, from 1953 to 1961, the thirty-fourth president.[1]

The Class of 2002, which James Gurbisz joined, might challenge 1915. There were more of them, and, as the bicentennial class, they were marked for attention.[2] They entered West Point in 1998, twenty-five years after the last major war. In 2001, their final year began with 9/11. In an instant, they knew they would be the first cadets to graduate in wartime since Vietnam. They were the bicentennial class. According to Bill Murphy Jr., a former soldier who wrote a book about the Class of '02, they were "quickly named the Golden Children by the envious cadets ahead of them. They were celebrated at every turn, the upperclassmen complained, but the only thing special about them was the year they were born."[3] Writers and reporters kept coming.

Lieutenant General Daniel Christman was superintendent from 1996 to 2001. First in the class of 1965, tall and gregarious, he wanted to show West Point to the world. He hired a New York public relations firm, which led to an invitation to *National Geographic* to film a reality series, *Surviving West Point*, which would screen in 2002. Christman also allowed two authors to observe the cadets closely.

Ed Ruggero, a West Point graduate, infantry officer, and novelist, wrote *Duty First: A Year in the Life of West Point and the Making of*

American Leaders. It was published before 9/11, when most cadets figured they would see Kosovo as peacekeepers if they saw a war zone at all. The book is an insider's account, in some ways a description of a lost world, as innocent as one focused on training killers could be. Even Ruggero's brief description of rugby leans toward the archaic, describing a scene the pioneers in 1961 would have known: "Under the lights of their practice field, the Army rugby team churns the turf into mud. Wearing throwback uniforms of striped jerseys and thick, knee-high socks, they slam into each other at full speed. When they pause, they breathe like horses after a gallop."[4]

Years later, on a hot September day, I visited Christman at the US Chamber of Commerce in Washington, across Lafayette Square from the White House. He marched me to an office decorated with Civil War art—Grant at the Wilderness, weary but resolute—and pictures with Reagan, Clinton, and both the presidents Bush. Back in 1998, Christman said, he went to see Jann Wenner, the great editor of *Rolling Stone.* The magazine had published a piece about life on an aircraft carrier. Wenner was "full of appreciation for what the Navy was doing and what young naval officers were like." To a man who bled Army black and gold, that was a challenge to meet. "So I pitched a ten-thousand-word piece to him: full access for the writer. He introduced David Lipsky to us."[5]

Lipsky was a prizewinner with no need to impress any general. "He was scruffy and had long hair and ripped jeans and a rumpled shirt," Christman laughed. "I told him he could have unfettered access, and he was interested. A few things ended up in the book that some people didn't like"—possibly a reference to the tale of Lieutenant Colonel Hank Kiersey, a revered leader discharged in a scandal over a joke[6]—"but what the heck, you know? That's journalism. And the funny thing was that Lipsky came to live on the campus, and by the end of it he'd smartened up: sports jacket, haircut, and all of it."

Lipsky ended up writing a book, *Absolutely American: Four Years at West Point,*[7] which became a bestseller. He lived with the cadets for four years. Marched with them, ate with them, celebrated their victories, shared their defeats. He was there on 9/11. As David Brooks wrote in the *New York Times*, Lipsky produced "a superb description of modern military culture, and one of the most gripping accounts of university life."[8]

Lipsky realized that "of all the young people I'd met, the West Point cadets—although they were grand, epic complainers—were the happiest." The academy was "a place where everyone tried their hardest. A place where everybody—or at least most people—looked out for each other. A place where people—intelligent, talented people—said honestly that money wasn't what drove them. A place where people spoke openly about their feelings and about trying to make themselves better."[9]

Brooks wrote, "Lipsky obviously came to admire West Point, but [his] book is not a whitewash or a sales brochure. It essentially describes a contest between two competing values systems. There is first the pure *huah* value system of the military, emphasizing discipline, self-sacrifice, duty, honor, courage, and controlled but savage violence. Then there is the value system of society at large (and of *Rolling Stone* in particular), emphasizing freedom, self-expression, pleasure and commerce."

When I began to write about West Point, I didn't read *Absolutely American* so much as ingest it. I read other books too, including *Once an Eagle* by Anton Myrer, a huge novel of twentieth-century war[10] used to teach leadership at West Point,[11] and the other nonfiction classic, *The Long Gray Line: The American Journey of West Point's Class of 1966*,[12] Rick Atkinson's epic on the tragedy of Vietnam. But when I came to write about how the rugby brothers of 2002 lived at West Point and found their game and their brotherhood, Lipsky provided a perfect introduction when he described Jeremy Kasper, a nervous high schooler, a prospective recruit like James Gurbisz:

"He made his candidate visit in the winter. Snow everywhere, bleak and gray. 'I was just having flashbacks to Wisconsin.' He watched a rugby game, four cadets were carried off on stretchers, next morning he watched the medevac helicopters fly in. 'I was like, 'I am not coming here, I don't know what these people are smoking, they are *nuts*." Six months later, Jeremy was marching the same fields on R-Day."[13]

R-DAY, OR Reception Day, happens each year in June, when the wooded highlands bake. In its way, it is even more of a calculated shock than the relentless indignity of Beast, the six weeks of basic training which follow.

Ty Seidule, a retired brigadier general and former West Point history professor, has described how R-Day works. The new cadets arrive in buses. They are hustled to a huge lecture hall. Then, "After a short brief—the army loves briefs—a loud voice announces, 'You have ninety seconds to say goodbye to your families and your time starts—now!' So starts a stressful day. The upper-class cadets yell at the new ones purposefully."[14]

R-Day is there in *Surviving West Point*, the documentary Dan Christman commissioned. The new cadets say goodbye to their parents. They are taken to be turned into soldiers. Men have their heads shaved. All are assigned to companies led by older cadets and ordered this way and that. It is James Salter's "inferno" or "forge." As when Salter arrived, sixty years before, unchanging "demands, many of them incomprehensible, rain down."[15] The new cadets learn four responses: "Yes, sir. No, sir. No excuse, sir. Sir, I do not understand."[16] They learn how to salute, right hand at the brow. They struggle with huge bags of equipment. Seidule again: "R-Day finishes with a parade. Cadets march through the sally ports, past Washington's statue onto the Plain wearing their smart gray uniforms as their families look on from the stands, proud and worried. The parade climaxes with the oath."

It's all there on the screen. The cadets march onto the Plain. They take the oath: "I do solemnly swear that I will support the Constitution of the United States, and bear true allegiance to the national government; that I will maintain and defend the sovereignty of the United States, paramount to any and all allegiance, sovereignty, or fealty I may owe to any state or country whatsoever; and that I will at all times obey the legal orders of my superior officers, and the Uniform Code of Military Justice." They march away, to their meal in Washington Hall, arcane demands hurled in the clamoring din. The new class is in, swallowed by the great granite maw.

Sometimes cadets quit on R-Day. More often, some in the class of a thousand or so wash out during Beast. The "institutionalized harassment"[17] Mike Mahan remembered is less now, but Beast is still terribly hard.

First, cadets learn to march. David Lipsky opened *Absolutely American* with a description of how much cadets hate marching, calling it "a suck or a haze," but how he came to love it.

> "There's something wonderful about being in a column of marching people: the gravel popping under soles, the leather flexing in boots, the kind of saddle-top sounds as the ruck (what the backpack gets called in the Army) frames settle. Occasionally someone, out of sheer misery, sighing *Oooh*, or just blowing out air, which in the general silence is like a whale breaching and then slipping back under the surface. You can watch a leaf float down from a tree or stare at the guy's rifle in front of you. The boiling down of life to its basic questions: Can you do this? What kind of person are you, and what can you make yourself finish? Can you hang with the rest of us? Those questions don't get asked much, in the civilian world."[18]

Cadets are shown military life. They are introduced to tactics and weapons, they are pushed over assault courses and through lake swims, they discover bug-flecked life under canvas and on overnight guard duty, in fierce heat or drenching rain or both. They learn to behave like plebes, lowest of the low, below yuks (sophomores), below cows (juniors), and the furthest below firsties, as West Point seniors are known. It means learning to be told what to do and how to answer those doing the telling. How to get it right next time. Most often, there is "No excuse, sir!"

In one particularly strenuous ritual, the cadets learn what it is like to be gassed. They stumble out of a sinister brick chamber in the woods, vomit, and cry—and run to the next test. They run and run and run. They march and march and march. They shed weight. It is meant to weed out those who fail to conquer thoughts of quitting.

Among West Point rugby players, finding one who will admit to hating R-Day and Beast is a bit like finding a Republican in Washington Heights. They're there, but they're not lining up to say so. R-Day? Beast? West Point life? No problem. Really.

James Gurbisz, the big blond football player from Eatontown, New Jersey, counted himself fit and ready. He had strength, built on gridiron and diamond, and he had determination. He was going to apply all of that to football. Eventually, in rugby, it would make him a fit at hooker, the spearhead of the forward pack, one of the toughest positions. But he'd done his reading too. He knew what to expect. R-Day, said his father, Ken, was more of a shock "for the parents than for the kids."[19]

"You're sitting there, and they say, 'You got thirty seconds to say goodbye to your kid.'"

"No," said Helen, his wife. "A minute."

"Yeah," said Ken. "It was not a long time. Right? Like . . ."

". . . So, picture . . ." said Helen. "You have your son sitting with you. Then all of a sudden, he's got to get up and leave. They're marched across the field."

"And next time you see him," said Ken, "it's five o'clock. And I think if anybody tells you they weren't apprehensive, they're lying. That's my feeling. Because, you know, I've been through the military. Going through basic training, there's a million questions. 'How am I gonna do this? How am I gonna do that? How am I gonna fare through this whole thing?' It's just normal human nature that you're going to be somewhat apprehensive."

"And at five o'clock at night," Helen said, "when we see them again, now they have their uniform on, the white shirt, the gray slacks, the hair is cut."

After eight hours at West Point, Gurbisz looked like a soldier. There's proof, carefully kept. A book published in October 2001: *The Spirit of West Point: Celebrating 200 Years.*[20] On the cover, a phalanx of new cadets, led by older students in crisp white uniforms, marches across the Plain. There, second from the left in the front row, is Gurbisz. He wears glasses, a white shirt with shoulder tabs, gray pants, and black shoes. Arms at his sides. Hair shaved. Eyes front. Full parade order.

One cadet quit. Ken and Helen remember names called, the kid coming out, the parents driving away. Elsewhere on the Plain, Gurbisz's future teammates stood. Among them was Zac Miller, a high achiever from western Pennsylvania. Church leader, big brother, academic whiz. Tall, broad shouldered, and strong but as far from a meathead as could possibly be. I asked his parents, Keith and Rosalyn, how he dealt with R-Day and Beast. Keith laughed.

"You know, it takes a certain type of individual to go to West Point, to be a soldier. You're going to have some that are just really into it. I mean, it's a mentality. It's like football players, wrestlers, and rugby players, right? They're not quite *right* in rugby."[21]

Miller would end up a back row forward, a forager and tackler, one of the light infantry, relentlessly in close-quarter combat.

On R-Day 1998, Joe Emigh also stood to attention. He was a laid-back kid from southern California, but he'd been through a year at the prep. That helped lessen the shock, but he had another weapon all of his own. Faced with shouting upperclassmen, he fell back on a resource he would draw on all four years at West Point: his relentless sense of humor.

"Joey was a funny kid," said his dad, George. "He never really talked about much. I asked him, 'How did you handle the hazing part?' And he said, 'You know, the biggest problem I had was just trying not to sit there and laugh and smile, because that only made it worse.' That stuff never really bothered him. It was tougher for him academically. Joey wasn't the best, but they had all the resources. He couldn't get lost at West Point."[22]

Emigh went up the Hudson with Jeremiah Hurley, his prep roommate at Fort Monmouth, a big wrestler from North Carolina who would become a rugby prop, binding onto Jim Gurbisz when the packs locked together. Brian McCoy, a football safety from Texas, who, like Zac Miller, would end up in the back row of the scrum, had been to the prep school too. On R-Day, those with a year in the system already knew how to keep equipment and uniforms in order, how to make their bunks, how to lessen harassment and punishment or cope when it landed regardless. Those who did not know all of that were more vulnerable—and the upperclassmen knew it. But most found ways to adapt. Among the future rugby players, Bryan Phillips and Nik Wybaczysnky, giant football linemen from California, were simply too big to care. Both would end up in the second row, the engine room of the scrum. Dave Little was a linebacker who became the number 8, at the back of the scrum, linking forwards and backs. He came from San Diego. Like Emigh, Little came east to play football, figuring the academics would be tougher than the physical challenge. And like Emigh, he was "not particularly bothered. But the old reputation it had for how hard it was, with the hazing and so on, didn't seem particularly earned."[23]

Clint Olearnick, eventually Emigh's partner at center, came from Colorado. He didn't have football interest, but he had the grades and the physicality, over six feet and square. Unique among the rugby players, he had played the game in high school. After a flirtation with the Naval Academy, he was able to persuade Senator Ben Nighthorse Campbell to recommend him to West Point.

"I didn't have a problem," Olearnick said, of his first days in Salter's inferno. I actually enjoyed it. You know, when I showed up for R-Day and Beast, I had already started shaving my head in high school. So the whole culture shock, the guys getting their head shaved? I had to grow my hair out before I went to West Point, because they *wanted* to shave it. It was probably only a half inch of anything. And so I showed up, and Beast was easy for me. R-Day was pretty easy. I'd always lived somewhat of a structured existence, playing a lot of sports. My dad was, I wouldn't say *hard*, but he was a disciplinarian, expected a lot. I think a lot of the folks were scared when we showed up, but I knew it would all balance out in the end."[24]

If Olearnick approached life with a sort of brutal Zen, Pete Chacon, who in rugby would be a wing, revved himself up every day.

He was from California, too, from a hardscrabble corner of Oakland. He couldn't afford college, so he planned to join the Marines. His dad suggested he try the service academies because he was smart and a good wrestler, small and wiry, and the government would pay his fees. Like Clint, Chacon looked at the Naval Academy on the Maryland shore. Then he realized "they make you do all the swimming, and screw that."[25] Like Olearnick, he secured support from a senator, Barbara Boxer, and with it a place at West Point. When he flew in for his candidate visit. it was his first time out of California, give or take a visit to Lake Tahoe, Nevada.

"So that was kind of crazy," he said. "It was a little bit of a shell shock for me to leave California for New York, climate-wise. But I was a freak. I loved school. People always tell you not to volunteer for things. Don't volunteer in Ranger School. Don't volunteer for extra duty when you're at the academy. That's bullshit. If I was going to be there, I was gonna make the most of that time. I volunteered and did extra stuff, and I just loved it."

Of R-Day, Chacon remembers "some big speech. It was, 'Hey, look 'round. Everyone here, to your left, to your right, was the team captain at school, was an MVP of their sport. He got straight As. So did she. But here, they're just average.' And I'm thinking, 'Who wants to be average?' You know, that speech impacted me significantly. Like, they were trying to get us to just accept that we were just going to be middle of the pack. Or that we were just there to experience West Point. It just pissed me off. I thought to myself, 'Fuck that. That is bullshit.' I just rejected it."

Chacon was able to channel his frustration into fiercer effort, to forge a path through what Craig Mullaney, the Rhodes scholar from the Class of 2000, would call the "chaos, noise, and dumbstruck terror"[26] of much of academy life. Chacon applied the same ferocity to academics as to physical challenges. Among the rugby players, some were smarter than others—Zac Miller seriously so, specializing in computing and math. Mo Greene, Matt Blind, and Jerrod Adams, three football players who would become backs in rugby, were academic highfliers too. Andy Klutman, a big man who became Jeremiah

Hurley's fellow prop, would end up a doctor. Others found the classwork tougher. But another thing Mullaney noted was that as his squad leader told him, R-Day and Beast were meant to teach a serious lesson: "Your only chance of surviving . . . is to work together. The only way to fail is to fail one another." As George Emigh told me, even those like his son Joe who found classwork tough found support among classmates and teammates.

Rugby reinforced the process. Simply by not being the Great God Football, it fostered an outsiders' bond. It was tribal, irreverent, and fun. That suited those for whom the hardest part of West Point was the adjustment to military discipline.

Particularly for plebes, life is undignified by design. They are required to memorize *Bugle Notes*,[27] the small leather-bound compendium of academy arcana. The honor code: "A cadet will not lie, cheat, or steal, nor tolerate those who do." The Alma Mater—"Hail Alma Mater dear / To us be ever near / Help us thy motto bear / Through all the years"—and other rah-rah songs. How many gallons of water in the reservoir: "78 million gallons when the water is flowing over the spillway." How many lights in Cullum Hall: "340 lights." The right answer to a question about a cow: "She walks, she talks, she's full of chalk, the lacteal fluid extracted from the female of the bovine species is highly prolific to the nth degree." The right answer to a question about "the definition of leather": "If the fresh skin of an animal, cleaned and divested of all hair, fat, and other extraneous matter, be immersed in a dilute solution of tannic acid, a chemical combination ensues; the gelatinous tissue of the skin is converted into a nonputrescible substance, impervious to and insoluble in water; this is leather." More, to be thrown up whole on demand.

In the long run, *Bugle Notes* helps instill understanding of order and discipline and how to pass it on. But some will always have difficulty keeping a straight face, and it wasn't a coincidence that some found a home under Mike Mahan, the rugby coach who once chafed at officialdom himself. There was a good field to play on, up by the Plain in the shadow of Washington Hall and the Chapel, and the superintendent, General Christman, was fond of the sport and said so. But there wasn't much equipment, and there wasn't much money, and the team trained on a rocky field up a steep hill at the far ass-end of the fort. Most of those who slogged up there to train, who traveled economy for games at Dartmouth, Harvard, Ohio State, and Penn State, drank and sang together, thriving on their outsider identity. Some admit to struggling with the orders and rules. Matt Blind, the captain, happily remembers incurring and walking off his fair share of hours—official punishment in the form of marching, weapon shouldered, across the bare barracks yards. And yet he and his players happily say they would die for their own authority figure, Mike Mahan.

If there is one rugby player from the Class of '02 who sums up this outsider-insider model, it is one whose army career shows both why he thrived at West Point and why he might have flunked out altogether. It is the fly half, the quarterback of the team, Mo Greene. Born in 1980 in Binghamton, New York, he grew up in northeastern Pennsylvania on a farm he helped to work. After West Point, he ended up in Special Forces. When I first wrote about the rugby team, he chose not to take part. Years later, a lieutenant colonel, he was heading for civilian life.[28] Asked why he didn't speak to me the first time around, he directed me to a memoir by Stanley McChrystal, the general who led Joint Special Operations Command and in 2005–06 supervised the hunt for Abu Musab al-Zarqawi, leader of al-Qaeda in Iraq.[29] I read this description of men McChrystal commanded, from a unit, as fate would have it, called Green:

> "The operators shared many traits. They tended to be hyperfit, opinionated, iconoclastic, fearless, intelligent, type-A problem solvers who thrived without guidance."[30]

West Point is not designed for iconoclasts, which means that in small numbers it breeds them. In the summer of 2021, when I met the players for a weekend at Matt Blind's place in Massachusetts, Greene's place in the team was clear. Shorter than the big forwards, dark and intense, supremely fit, he spent the whole weekend with his shirt off (or would've, if the stewards at Fenway Park had let him). He sat at the center of every conversation, argument, or song. He didn't bark orders—the other big dogs, Clint Olearnick and Jeremiah Hurley, wouldn't have let him, never mind Matt, the quiet captain, hosting, watching, shaping—but there Greene was, at the hub of the drinking, nostalgia, and laughter, forty-eight hours straight.

"I was an excellent student," he said of how he came to West Point, an eager free safety or fullback.[31] "I was a good athlete. I had a love for football in particular, even though I was just five foot ten, 160 pounds. My junior year of high school, I started getting recruited to play at West Point. My father's cousin was a retired major, a pilot, flew in Vietnam. And so we had a dinner where it was time to talk about the benefits of West Point, of the army. This is like 1996, '97. Still largely a peacetime army. And so we talked about all that good stuff.

"I wanted to play Division I football. And I wasn't getting Division I recruiting letters from anywhere else. So I pursued the West Point deal. I had the grades. I thought, 'Whatever, I can do it.' And then in my senior year at high school, they got a new football coach, and I got a letter that said they were not recruiting me anymore. The process to apply to West Point, it's not a short process. So I was more than kind of committed. And my thinking was, 'Well, I'll just go walk on. They recruited me. Surely I can do this. So full speed ahead.' And I don't come from a wealthy family by any stretch. We're poor. The idea of going to college for free? It resonated. And so football and scholarship, that was what put me at West Point."

In the summer of 1998, for those not recruited for football but still dreaming of pulling on the gold and black, there was a chance to impress the coaches.

"There was a big cattle call for all these scared-to-death cadets. 'Those who want to try out for the football team, go over here.' I didn't know him at the time, but Blinder and I were there."

Matt Blind was the same sort of kid as Greene, if blond and less of an extrovert. He was from rural Ohio ("forty-five minutes south of Cleveland, fifteen minutes west of Akron, out there in the farms"[32]), and like Greene he had strong grades. Also like Greene, he wanted to play Division I football. Also like Greene, at five foot six and 160 pounds, he was undersized. West Point took an interest, but it faded. Luckily for Blind, Sherrod Brown, then a representative from Ohio, nominated him, so off he went. Like Greene, he went straight to Michie Stadium.

Greene said, "We did some dips, and we did some running, and then they took heights and weights and stuff like that. And essentially, for I think almost all of us, it was like, 'No thank you. We have'—and pardon my crass language here—'a lot of five-foot-ten, 175-pound, slow white kids,' you know? We have our pick of the litter of those. So it didn't work out. But like most determined people or people that were overachievers at high school, I was determined to not quit. And so I spent my freshman year as best as I could continuing to train in the weight room, and I played intramural football, doing all the things I thought I could do. I thought I was going to get another shot. And it just never came. And so I was pretty crushed."

The same went for Blind. No Division I football meant no real purpose outside the classroom. In it, they did fine. Greene would finish fourth in the class, Blind in the fifties. But both needed physical release. Both needed the bonds of a team.

To Blind, the hierarchies of West Point weren't much of a problem—"kind of a joke, almost, hard but not unbearable." He got more of a surprise when he met his roommates.

"In Beast I roomed with Andre Wright, a kid from San Bernardino, California. Actually, he was the first Black guy I'd ever known in my life. And I loved him. Then my first roommate for the academic year was another Black kid named Korey Hines, from the Bronx in New York. And my third roommate was a kid named Jonathan Childs, from Trenton, New Jersey. Also Black. To me, then, it was just crazy. Where I came from, in Ohio, there were white people. It was a 100 percent homogenous white farm community. And then my first three roommates at West Point just so happened to be Black kids from kind of rough neighborhoods."

They say college opens your eyes. For Greene, it was a mental challenge too. Without the hierarchies of football, the coaches, plays, and orders, he struggled to contain his natural iconoclasm, his resistance to the accepted ways of getting things done. Luckily for him, like Blind, he found his way to rugby.

Greene said, "An outsider would probably look at the cadets and say we're all kind of cut from the same cloth. But when you're in that world, you know, there's obviously tribes of people. And I'd say the rugby team was definitely, like, my people. And the thing it gave me, for better or worse, was an escape from the academy.

"As an underclassman, you need a place to go. To be with your people. Your brothers. You need something to pour yourself into, emotionally and physically. To just absolutely drain yourself, in practice or a game. That was what kept me going—what made me able to persist through the drudgery of the academy."

West Point is a test. It is meant to make cadets struggle. When Mo Greene found rugby, he found in Mike Mahan a mentor who felt the same way about the harassments and indignities, but loved the place nonetheless. Greene found what he needed. He could make it through four years.

Zac Miller, senior photo, West Point Military Academy, Class of 2002.

Stoneboro

"OUT HERE here, you're closer to God."[1]

Keith Miller steers his Honda through the quiet lanes of Stoneboro. Fields of corn and soy line the road, interspersed with neat single-story houses behind scrupulously maintained lawns. The land is green, the sky blue.

Keith is a retired teacher, a coach of football and wrestling. He moves slow, says little. He has brown eyes, a silver goatee, and, he says with a gruff laugh, a temper quick when roused. Laughing again, he says he could've been good at rugby had he only known it existed. He's broad shouldered, has hands like shovels and legs like pillars of stone. Just in this far western corner of Pennsylvania alone, I suspect, a scout from London or Auckland could find twenty top-quality props just by throwing a ball into the corn and whistling.

Many wonder if America will ever take rugby seriously. Many think that if it does it will dominate, using converts from basketball, football, and track.[2] Most rugby people dispute that. Many rugby people don't know much about wrestling. Keith Miller wrestled at school, then coached for thirty-five years. If he'd played rugby, the ball would've been one thing, the grappling and tackling another. His strong handshake and steady gaze confirm it. You can see him working you out.

Keith's wife, Rosalyn, sits in the back of the Honda. She's also a retired teacher, seventy-ish, short-haired, slight, and neat, and she does most of the talking. She has muscular dystrophy. Coming into Sandy Lake, she points out the place she goes for physical therapy. "If

I stop walking," she says, "I won't walk again." Trips from the Millers' house on Swartz Road avoid steps and slopes. When the car stops, Rosalyn leans on Keith, gets by with a cane and his arm.

The Miller house is low at the front and drops at the back to a basement. There is a tree house for the grandkids in grounds that run twelve acres, back to where the woods begin and deer sidle out to graze. Keith mows and weed-whacks weekly.

The township where the Millers live is made up of two small settlements, Sandy Lake (population 621) and Stoneboro (974),[3] each with a main street and a brick bank. Sandy Lake is dry. Stoneboro isn't. The big thing in the area is the Great Stoneboro Fair, first staged in 1867 and "Always on Labor Day" through two world wars until the COVID-19 pandemic. Keith mentions an ancestor who fought in the revolution and in the War of 1812, when timber was cut around here for ships to fight the British on Lake Erie. In the 1900s, Sandy Lake was a summer draw for the steel cities, Pittsburgh, Sharon, and Youngstown. Now its banks are lined with quiet holiday rentals.

Keith and Rosalyn give a tour: the sole stoplight in Sandy Lake, the sole bar in Stoneboro, the churches, Wesleyan, Methodist, Presbyterian. A new stop: the house in Sandy Lake where Rachel Powell lived.[4] On January 6, 2021, Powell used a bullhorn to direct the mob that attacked the US Capitol. A month later, the mother of eight was arrested.[5] Her house sits silent, toys capsized in the yard. We drive on. Some houses have Trump signs. Most don't. Many fly American flags. Outside the Miller house, in a neat rock garden, stands a small white cross.

ON JUNE 19, 1980, in nearby Franklin, Rosalyn gave birth to a son. They named him Zachariah Robert Miller. Everyone called him Zac. On nights and weekends, Keith built the new house. Back then, Swartz Road was still gravel.

Zac attracted attention. When he was two, Rosalyn says, "We were riding in the car, and he said, 'That sign says thirty-five.' I thought, 'Well, he's probably heard me say to Keith, slow down.' And then we drove a little bit further, and he said, 'That sign says fifty-five.' And then I thought, 'That's weird, for a two-year-old child to know the difference between thirty-five and fifty-five.'"

We are sitting at the Charltons' place. Denny Charlton serves us coffee at the kitchen table. Denny was Zac's dentist. His wife, Lynn, Zac's teacher in first grade. Rosalyn continues.

"And then when we would ride in the car, we would count or add, or I told him, 'You know, multiplying is just a quick way of adding.' And so then we would do multiplication tables. And when he went in for kindergarten testing, we went by Jeff Thompson's room, and we stopped in there, and the kids quizzed Zac on multiplication facts, and he knew them all. He was five. He was already doing third grade."

Lynn Charlton laughs: "I taught that child *nothing*."[6]

Zac's brother, Nate, was born in 1984. The two boys read widely, the Hardy Boys a favorite. Evenings were for schoolwork. Keith is proud to point out, "There was never a Nintendo in this house."[7] All the same, Zac gravitated toward computers.

"He was exceptionally gifted in most areas," Rosalyn says, "but especially in math and computer science. He was in the gifted program at school, and as part of his enrichment we took him to a private computer class in a nearby town when he was in first grade."[8]

Zac went to Lakeview High School. He also took classes at Grove City College, a small Christian school. In homes around Sandy Lake and Stoneboro, at the school gym, at basketball camp, the same story comes up. In a logic class at Grove City, a student asked Zac if he was a freshman.

"Sort of," he said. "I'm thirteen."

The college class meant Miller missed a regular lesson with his high school math teacher. But when he came back, Jeff Engstrom says, "He would come to me and say, 'Hey, what do I need to do today?' He did that at home. He completed my course without having to attend. And he did very well."

The Charltons remember Miller's babysitting shifts, featuring epic Nerf gun battles but all the kids asleep and the house tidy when the adults came home. His mother remembers her son's eager role in Sunday school at the Presbyterian church. Anne McLain, a year ahead at Lakeview but a future West Point classmate, as well as a future rugby international and astronaut—suggesting that there might be something in the water—has recalled his "little kid's curiosity."

"He looked at me as someone he could learn from, not someone he was better than. I think that was why Zac was so well liked . . . He did not try to make people feel important; to Zac, people truly were important."[9]

Zac told everyone that he wanted to be president. Most believed it possible.

"He had an acronym," Keith says. "W-I-N. 'What's Important Now.' If he was at football practice, that's what was important. If he was at the college taking classes, that's what was important."[10]

Such determination could bubble over. Zac played Little League. One day, a line drive hit him flush in the face. Rosalyn rushed onto the field, only to be ordered back to the bleachers by son and husband, each furious and eager to get back to the fray. Where younger brother Nate took after his dad—foursquare, a wrestler, quiet—Zac was more like his mom. But the Miller temper was there. In the summers, Keith ran a roofing crew. Zac worked with him. So did the math teacher, Jeff Engstrom.

"He was much younger and stronger and could carry the shingles up onto the roof easier than I could," Jeff says. "And his mother often told me, 'You protect him from Keith.'"

"I'd fire him a couple times a day," Keith says, laughing.

"I wanna get off this roof!" says Jeff, channeling Zac in high dudgeon.

"He'd fire him, but then he'd have to hire him back," says Rosalyn, dryly.

"He'd quit, and I'd have to take him back because I had to take him home once he'd finished," says Keith.

"It could get ugly," Rosalyn says.

Pat Engstrom, Jeff's wife, cuts in: "He had his mother's smile."

◆　◆　◆

IN MAY 2002, aged twenty-one and just short of graduating from West Point, Zac Miller spoke to Chuck Lueckemeyer, a writer for *USA Rugby* magazine. Asked how he had coped with academy life, Miller harked back to those summers on the roofs of Mercer County.

"I was used to getting up early and working hard all day . . . coming here wasn't that much of a difference. You have to get up early, you have to work hard, and you get yelled at a little bit too. It's all vaguely familiar."[11]

When Miller was in high school, however, West Point wasn't remotely on his mind.

"We had nobody in the military," Rosalyn Miller says. "My husband wasn't. My brother, my father, they weren't. Keith's father was in World War Two, but he never really talked about it."[12] Her son's decision to apply to West Point was, she says, "Kind of out of the blue."

In Eatontown, New Jersey, Jim Gurbisz grew up next to Fort Monmouth. In Stoneboro, Pennsylvania, up in Oak Hill cemetery, there are flags and markers for men who fought in the Civil War, the First and Second World Wars, Korea, Vietnam, Iraq, and Afghanistan. But there is no institutional presence.

"I think he loved the idea of the challenge," Rosalyn says.

West Point has a searching gaze. In 1997, it swept western Pennsylvania. Miller's SAT scores stood out, so Keith and Rosalyn took their son to Indiana, a small city near Pittsburgh, for a first interview.

"There were probably about forty people there," Rosalyn says. "Males and females, mostly males. I can distinctly remember only four had what I would call proper attire for something that important, because we made Zac wear a suit. And two of those four got in."

A cadet spoke to Miller and his parents. "He said, 'Well, you'll be part of the bicentennial class.' And as soon as he said that, I thought, 'This is where it's going to end up.'"

Miller applied. In his essay about why,[13] he quoted Woodrow Wilson: "There is no question what the roll of honor in America is. The roll of honor consists of the names of men who have squared their conduct by ideals of duty."[14]

Miller wrote that he wanted "to be one of the men whose name appears on President Wilson's roll of honor." On his academy visit, he was "impressed with the library holdings and especially the computer facilities." He wanted to attend law school, but he was "willing to endure in order to become better." He also quoted George Bernard Shaw: "Liberty means responsibility. That is why most men dread it."[15] He himself, he wrote, "Was one of those men who does not dread liberty. I do not dread responsibility. I want liberty for all Americans, and I am willing to accept the responsibility for protecting it. By attending the United States Military Academy at West Point, I will be on my way to providing this liberty for my fellow man."

Zac Miller wanted to be president. Senator at least. To no one's great surprise, West Point welcomed him in.

*Number 8 Dave Little carries the ball in an autumn 2002 match
of Army versus Dartmouth.*

Rugby

WEST POINT rugby welcomed Zac Miller too. But unlike many others who found their way to the team, Zac did not come to rugby from football. He played football in high school, sure, but western Pennsylvania is a long way from being a hotbed of gridiron talent. As Zac's mother, Rosalyn, told me, when Zac went east he was planning to try out for track.[1] But as he would tell *USA Rugby* magazine four years later, when he arrived at the academy, his platoon leader "was a rugby player, and saw I was the approximate size and shape of someone who might be good at the sport. He didn't ask me to come out for the team—he kinda told me."[2]

Miller did as he was told. He fell for rugby, hard—and not just for the physical challenge. As his roommate R. J. Johnson put it, Miller may well have been some sort of genius. He may have been destined to win the Robert E. Lee Memorial Award[3] for math and to win a prestigious Rhodes scholarship and a place at Oxford. But he loved the rugby brotherhood—and he had "a little bit of a wild side" too.[4]

Most of the West Point players had that, to one degree or another. But not all of them. There is a rugby player from the Class of '02 who admits to struggling to love life at West Point and finding it hard to fit in.

Scott Radcliffe was a football player from Ohio, a dark, quiet guy who on the rugby field became a back-five forward, a mid-sized big man switching around the second and back rows of the scrum. He came to West Point after a brief spell at Duke, where he met a football player who had dropped out of West Point.

Radcliffe recalls something the footballer said to him. "He said, 'You know, I always thought to myself before I went there, like, you're always gonna wonder, what if you don't? You're gonna wonder what you missed. What the challenge was.' And he was more right than he could have ever conceived of being."[5]

In the end, inspired by a cadet summer in Germany under H. R. McMaster, a famous armor officer and West Point rugby player,[6] Radcliffe went into the cavalry. He did two tours in Iraq and one in New Orleans after Hurricane Katrina. Out of the army, he ran for Congress,[7] then settled in Austin, Texas, with his wife, Mandie, and their three daughters.

From his home in the heart and heat of the Lone Star State, Radcliffe thought back on close to twenty-five years earlier, to when West Point seemed the thing to do. The football team was interested, but he declined its offer of a year at the prep school and plunged straight in.

"I was just kind of a mental wreck from the start. Beast was such a cultural shock. I was not in peak form when I got to the football team. I got cut. I was a mess. I had this really hard transition to military life. You can probably tell from me being the only person on the rugby team that went armor, I kind of do my own thing. And that doesn't fit in super well at a place like West Point, right? Certainly not when you're going through Beast and you're learning how to follow before you learn how to lead. I already knew math was going to be a challenge, because I wasn't gonna have to get a bachelor of science anywhere else. I didn't really care that I had barely taken trig, but here I was at an engineering school. So I was just in a bad place, that first month or so."

West Point doesn't only make engineers, but it does make a lot of them. Being an army officer is often about knowing how to build and mend stuff or to fire things or drive or fly. The academic challenge is steep. After the second year, when cadets are committed to five years in the army and three in reserve, the pace goes up again. Another back-rower, Dave Little, "got kicked right in the teeth with the academic curriculum"[8] and had to adapt to avoid flunking out. He did so by "completely backing away from the hard sciences and engineering" and completing a general management degree. It was a disappointment, softened by committing to rugby. Dave found other players like himself and Radcliffe, cut from football, in need of a challenge to make classroom struggles worthwhile. But he also found some who piled athletic endeavors on top of academic excellence.

"You couldn't ignore them," Dave Little said. "They're a mystery to me still, because they're so smart but they also have this sort of wild streak that counterbalances that smartness. Like Mo Greene, right? You got a brain that works so, so well, he's so intelligent academically, but also he has that fire, that animal side as well."

The same sort of cadet brought Scott Radcliffe to the rugby pitch. After that bad first month, dropping out seemed possible. "And then this guy that was in my company, they called him Swamp Thing—I wish I remembered his actual name—he was on the rugby team, and he was a firstie. And he came to my room, and said, 'Scott, I really think you should come with me to practice.'"

In colleges across America, there is often a rugby club. Often, that club, for men or women or both, is home to somebody everyone else calls Swamp Thing. In America, since the college game sprung up in the sixties and seventies, rugby has been a sport of the outsider, the eccentric, the nonconformist. The hardest of hard drinkers. A home for waifs and strays but also for type-As. Recruitment is informal, often involving likely specimens in danger of going adrift. Phaidra Knight, a US Eagles great and member of the World Rugby Hall of Fame, has spoken of how she found rugby at the University of Wisconsin–Madison and how rugby helped her find herself.[9] Her story is a version of what happened to Scott Radcliffe at West Point.

Very few in the United States arrive at rugby by a straight line. Jay Atkinson, a writer from Massachusetts, fell for rugby at Acadia College in Nova Scotia, discovering that "running full tilt into the opposition was an existential moment that could not be faked."[10] Atkinson's account of the sport and all that comes with it, much of it involving drinking, would be familiar to players from the public schools of England to the company teams of Japan. And to the University of Indiana. Mark Cuban, the billionaire owner of the

Dallas Mavericks NBA team, played rugby there. One hot summer afternoon, as I dozed on a bus to DC, my phone kept waking me. An unidentified Texas number. Finally, irritated, I answered. It was Cuban. Accepting my woozy apologies, he said rugby "taught me that you can beat the hell out of each other and then drink together afterwards. It taught me that a good rugby song and a party makes you lifelong friends no matter what. It taught me the value of fitness. ... The beauty of rugby is that it's so irreverent that you learn not to take anyone else too seriously too. You learn to accept other people for who they are. We had doctors, lawyers, day laborers, jobless, homeless guys even, you know? There was always someone who slept on someone else's couch. They're still my best friends to this day."[11]

Odds are that at some point in Cuban's rugby days, there was someone called Swamp Thing. In Scott Radcliffe's case, Swamp Thing was able to persuade him to give this strange game a go. Scott had seen rugby, knew a few who played, but when he went to his first practice, he "couldn't tell at that point what was Australian rules football, what was this rugby thing." At West Point, that didn't matter. If you were willing, you could try out. Craig Mullaney, the Rhodes scholar in the class of 2000, made a confession to me.[12] His shoulder injury, the dislocation he would re-dislocate boxing at Firebase Shkin,[13] he sustained playing rugby. There was always a place for novices even if, like Mullaney, they were not converted, and in fact came to see rugby players as "crazed ... would-be Vikings."[14] The club was strong enough to run four teams, after all.

"I messed around," Radcliffe said. "I was on the C or D side first [new players, gathering experience for a gradual climb to the A team]. I can't remember." Either way, he was hooked. The club had a close bond, nurtured by a hundred contrasts with football. The training field was a long way from anywhere, next to the old PX, or military store, in a neighborhood called Stony Lonesome. As Mike Mahan described it, "The field was fifty yards wide and one hundred yards long and had berms on both sides, with trees."[15] The field was used for tailgating during football games, which meant that "there were bottle caps and beer bottles and charcoal briquettes and condoms and whatever on it every Monday. It was recovered land, where they dumped all of the soil when they excavated for the PX. So every once in a while a huge sinkhole would appear in the middle of the field. The cadets were fond of putting somebody down there and only their head showing, and then we would fill the hole back in."

There were big characters to learn from. Among them was Duncan Smith, Class of 2000, headed for Special Forces, in rugby an openside flanker, foraging and smashing, the sort of berserker who might easily have been called Swamp Thing.

"I think he had prior service," Radcliffe said, referring to cadets who come from the regular army, enlisted men older than their peers. "He looked like a tough guy. As tough as you possibly can. And he always had headphones on before the game. And somebody asked him, like, 'Duncan, what are you listening to?' And he said, 'Sarah McLachlan.' And the guy said, 'What? Why are you listening to Sarah McLachlan?' And he said: 'The thought of girls crying makes me mad.'"

JIM GURBISZ fired himself up in a more conventional way. The big blond from Jersey, Radcliffe said, listened to "System of a Down and all the heavy stuff, just to get good and ready."

Armenian-American metal is a niche interest, but maybe it gave Gurbisz a way to channel his frustration. He had plenty. Like most of his teammates, he had to deal with a lost football dream. As described by his dad, Ken, it was fairly standard stuff. A big fish in high-school ball, Jim swam up the Hudson and found himself a minnow next to the leviathans of the Army team. Not long after the start of plebe year, the coaches told him to add fifty pounds to make weight as a linebacker. But Beast was brutal: he'd shed weight, the physical punishment continued, and classes were terribly tough. He called his parents.

"It was a surprise," Ken said. "Football's a big deal, and playing Division I is a big deal, so I was a little disappointed. But he thought it out. It was the best thing for him. I was just proud of him to have admitted that to have the best chance of making it through West Point, he was going to have to make a change."[16]

It helped that in Beast and after it, Jim fell in with the one guy who'd played rugby before.

"We were very fast friends," Clint Olearnick said.[17] "We did everything possible together. I would go down to Jimmy's house all the time, Eatontown, a quick drive down to Jersey. As plebes, we would always do all the duties and stuff together. And Jimmy and I kind of ran our freshman class. We were the jokers. The two of us together? We were extreme trouble. And everybody knew it. And we just had a great time. Just loved hanging out with each other. That's not to say we were more like brothers than anyone else. We had our ups and downs. We had our fights. But, man, when we were getting along and doing our stuff, it was amazing. We had so much fun together."

Olearnick went straight to the rugby team. He worked on Gurbisz to follow.

"I dragged him kicking and screaming," he said, with a slightly evil grin. "I would talk it up every day, like, 'Dude, I'm going to rugby practice, you gotta come, you gotta come, you gotta come.' I got him to come up and play rugby with me. And he just loved it so much, and that was our identity, done. We come back from practice just *reeking*, you know, filthy, mud from head to toe. We go shower, we go down and eat. We did everything together. You know, our backs were to each other every time we slept, right across the room, every single night."

Olearnick was a back row forward. Gurbisz proved a perfect fit for the demanding position of hooker, slung between two props in the dark heart of the scrum, hooking for the ball with his foot. He threw the ball into the lineout too, and was a fourth back row forager when play broke loose. In soccer, goalkeepers are different. Even Vladimir Nabokov said so.[18] If the man who wrote *Lolita* had played rugby, he'd have been a hooker.

"Coach Mahan identified Jim as a hooker," Olearnick said. "And that was exactly the perfect spot. We couldn't have asked for a meaner, more intense dude out there. He'd play number two for you.

On the field, he was slightly insane. He would put his head through walls, if he needed to. He would go after anything. He was bright but extremely tough as well."

Jim didn't slow down in training.

"Coach was onto Jimmy and me more than anybody else on the team," Olearnick said, with more than a bit of pride. "We'd be doing a drill at one side of the field. Jimmy and I would be messing around, and Coach would say, 'Go run to the other.' So we go run to the other goalpost, we get back, and we'd be together. And we get back, and he'd say, 'Go do it again.' And we go run to the other goalposts and come back. He'd be like, 'Go do it again.' And he's still putting everybody through the drills. And Jimmy and I are just running around the field. We needed it. I mean, I don't think it ever changed us. We didn't take ourselves too seriously. We enjoyed messing around more than we enjoyed playing the game, I think."

The players made their way to the club. By the start of their final year they were ready to take command. In summer of 2001, they voted Matt Blind captain, Brian McCoy his deputy. Blind said, "It was kind of like a grow-up moment. All of a sudden, we're not eighteen anymore. We're now twenty-one or twenty-two, and this shit is really serious. This is our life. We're bleeding Army rugby at this point. And then all of a sudden your buddies you've been partying with and playing with for two or three years decide that you're supposed to lead the team. You're excited about it, you're honored. But then there's times when you're the captain, you're like, 'Why the fuck do I have to do this?' You know, you're dealing with Jimmy and Clint.

"I would sit down with Coach Mahan and talk to him about the rules for the weekend. He would never micromanage us. We would have our walk-throughs on Friday night, when we got to the hotel or at home at West Point, before the game the next day. But Coach Mahan was very much like, 'Brian, and Blinder, make sure these guys get to bed. You know, you guys will have plenty of time to have fun after the game. We got a tough game tomorrow.' He'd say, 'Make sure that these guys are doing the right thing.' And that is Father Mahan. You listen to Father Mahan.

"But now all of a sudden, you're the person that's in charge of making sure that Clint and Jimmy and Mo are not up until one or two o'clock in the morning when we've got a game at ten the next day. What was crazy about it was that you'd sit and you'd *negotiate* with Jimmy and Clint, because they would tell you, 'Blinder, we actually play better when we're drinking.' And you know what, it was actually true. So you got Coach telling you one thing, and you got Jimmy and Clint telling you another thing. And, you know, both things are factual. And so you end up in this negotiation where you say, 'Okay, well, all right, you guys are allowed to go out, we're all allowed to go out, but we're only allowed to have two beers.' I think we got to that point on a number of occasions, and, of course, once you have two beers, and that turns into three ...

"We would take it a little bit more seriously when we were playing a really good team, like Ohio State, or in the Sweet Sixteen or the Final Four when everything was on the line, or even Dartmouth or UConn. They were good rugby players. You could get caught off guard and end up beaten, and you don't make the Sweet Sixteen. So the stakes, at least for a twenty-one-year-old group of guys, were actually pretty high. And I loved the party and level of drinking just as much as the rest, so ..."[19]

MATT BLIND wasn't the only player grappling with the demands of leadership. Off the field, West Point runs on a company system, older cadets taking charge of younger ones, both sides learning from the arrangement. Even Gurbisz and Olearnick assumed leadership roles. In terms of proper academy order, that might have been a bad idea. But when it came to rugby, they both became Swamp Things to a new generation. Charlie Erwin, a second row forward from the Class of '03, remembered their version of pastoral care.

"As a freshman, you get an upperclassman, a sophomore, as your team leader. They're responsible for your military development that first year. And so that kind of kept Clint in my room, as an excuse to come bother me. Clint and Jim too? They were just merciless."[20]

Charlie Erwin came from Texas, where high school football is huge. Unfortunately, his school was terrible, so though he got an appointment to West Point he was never going to make the football team. As fate would have it, though, "a week or two before I'm supposed to fly out, I see this rugby game on television. I'd never seen it before. I thought it looked awesome. I was going to have this adventure, to go see what kind of man I was going to be. And I thought, 'Nothing looks tougher and cooler than that game on TV right now.'"

Come R-Day, at mealtime in Washington Hall, an upperclassman at Erwin's table asked the plebes what they wanted to do at West Point. Erwin mentioned that he'd seen rugby and it looked pretty cool. "And he goes, 'As a matter of fact, I'm on the rugby team. So if you don't screw it up, we might let you on.'"

That was Dave Birie, a mainstay of the Class of '01. He summoned Erwin for tryouts, which meant throwing the new guys a ball and telling them to "just play and tackle each other." Erwin "went out there, and I broke my nose and kept playing and just had a great time. I ended up on the developmental side. And that was my introduction to rugby."

Gurbisz and Olearnick quickly converted the third in a trio of fast friends, adding Pete Chacon, the wrestler from Oakland. When Erwin showed up, they took him on as a project. They'd all run up to Stony Lonesome for training, except those who nabbed a place in the van that carried the cones, tackle shields, and balls. After practice, Erwin "would walk back with Pete and Clint and Jim. We'd go eat chow. It was really nice as a freshman, because I'd be with these tough guys, these upperclassmen, and no one was going to screw with me in the mess hall. Clint and Jim were like my protectors. And so we would eat dinner and tell stories and jokes, and then we'd go back to barracks, to get cleaned up and study."

West Point companies function like army platoons. Older cadets are sergeants, harrying their charges into order. The proper storing of rifles, the proper way to hang clothes, the proper spacing of books. It's easier to deal out than to deal with, but cadets make it work. Erwin said Gurbisz and Olearnick "never ragged their freshmen. We just wanted to be good dudes and tell jokes and stories. And that's what we did."

Any bunch of "good dudes" can seem not so good to others, of course. Any group will seem exclusionary to some, and if that group is composed of big male rugby players, it may not seem amusing to all. Any amount of horseplay may seem more harmless to those involved than not. Either way, there was plenty of it among the rugby players, and some of it involved one of Olearnick's testicles. The story goes that he'd been playing baseball at high school and had taken a pitch in the groin, and then the thing swelled up huge and never shrank back to normal size. Alternatively, as Olearnick said, it might've been genetic. His brother had one too, and in time normal testicle size returned. But at West Point, Clint Olearnick's testicle acquired a name, Gigantor, and a disciplinary role.

"It was the size of a grapefruit," Charlie Erwin laughed. "It was getting bigger every year. It was really something to behold. I was in a room with a couple other guys, and I'd just be sitting on my computer, working. And Jim and Clint would come in. And I just knew they were coming to jack with me. My first response was to ignore them. But then Clint would lay his testicle on my shoulder. As quickly as I could, I would try to punch back at it. And then it's him and Jim and me, rolling about, wrestling. One of them would usually start biting my ears. Put me in a bear hug. And the only remedy for that was to just punch for the throat or the face. Grab whatever I could and twist and try to inflict as much pain as I could. That was the quickest way to get back to my homework. Then they'd kind of roll off and laugh and giggle and just go back down the hallway."

It was all very male, and it was not unique to Gurbisz and Olearnick. Zac Miller roomed with a couple of soccer players, both from New Jersey, Jay Landgraf and R. J. Johnson. Zac was a hard worker.

"The first summer," Jay Landgraf said, "we had a meeting, and we were given a chance to kind of stand up in front of a platoon, right at the end of Beast, and just say, 'I'm going to such and such company, you know, keep track of me and, you know, we'll stay, we'll stay friends and help each other out as we go through.' And Zac stood up. He goes, 'Yep, I'm Zac Miller. I'm from Stoneboro, Pennsylvania. Listen, guys, I got 1500 on my SATs. I'm pretty good at school. So if you need any help, please come to my room, because I'd love to help you."[21]

At times, Johnson said, Miller seemed to be tutoring half his year, particularly in computing. Their "big corner room, right in front of MacArthur statue, on the third floor, 301 Mac Long"—one of two sections of MacArthur Barracks, the other being Mac Short—got crowded. Sometimes the superintendent, Lieutenant General Christman, would drop by to see Miller, who had become class secretary. Sometimes, though, rugby players would pounce.

"We were right as you came up the stairs," Johnson said. "People would just come and screw around. One day Matt Blind came in and put some body parts on my desk, so I threw my seat at him. And then Matt and I got into a sword fight. We'd worn our sabers to lunch. So I'm defending myself with my saber, and he stabbed me in the leg. I was like, 'He really stabbed me.' We all knew he stabbed me. So we did a field dressing, and I had to limp to class because you can't be late. And the teacher, basically, was like, 'Cadet Johnson, you're bleeding.'

"I'm like, 'Yes sir, I know that.'

"He's like, 'What happened?'

"I'm like, 'I don't want to talk about it.'

"He's like, 'I'm a major in the United States Army. What happened?'

"I'm like, 'Cadet Matt Blind stabbed me in the leg with a saber, sir.'

"The major just sighed.

"He's like, 'Go get fixed up.' There's a million stories like that. And Zac? He would, like, needle around the edges a little bit. He was a little bit of an instigator but like, 'Oh, it wasn't me.' Zac was the perfect child, but he had a little bit of a wild side too."

A kid fit for rugby.

So was Joe Emigh. Unlike Zac Miller, he was recruited for football, and unlike Scott Radcliffe, things went according to plan, at least at first.

"Joey played as a plebe," said his dad, George,[22] "but then they switched him from linebacker to fullback. And then he kind of just blended in with the crowd, kind of lost focus. Eventually they made the decision for him. He was on the team until the spring. At the end of spring practice, he got an email stating he was cut from the team. He called me. And I said, 'Hey, Joe, you can decide whatever you want to do. If you want to leave West Point and go play college football someplace else, we can find you another school. It won't be the same level as West Point. But there's many small colleges like I went to that would welcome somebody with your talent. So you decide what you want to do.'

"You are able to leave West Point up until you start your junior year and not be bound to the army. And so he kind of contemplated that. But between that point in time and before the end of the year, he found rugby, somehow. And then everything changed."

Emigh could deal with West Point life—as his father said, his biggest problem was trying not to laugh—and he could get by in the classroom, like Dave Little switching to management, doing what he needed to do.

"There's only twenty students in a class," George Emigh said. "So, if you're not doing it, those teachers pretty much know who's failing and who's not. Joey got the help, and he made it. Don't ask me how, but he survived. I think I'm surprised, but very proud that he did that."

Rugby helped. Emigh went into the centers, one of two players at the fulcrum of attack and defense, in football terms both running back and safety. He made quick progress, and became close to Jerrod Adams, another former football player who ended up on the wing.

George said, "I saw quite a few of the games, and I still never figured out the rules, why the whistle blew or anything like that. I tried to ask Joey about it, and he said, 'I don't know either.'"

Bryan Phillips didn't know the rules either. He was an offensive lineman who got cut, went to rugby practice, and had a game in the second row for the B side at Towson down in Maryland.

"And then we went on spring tour, spring of 2001, my junior year, and we went to California. My second game of rugby ever, I found myself against Cal Berkeley on their home pitch. I was a backup and one of the locks went down and Coach Mahan put me in. I had to learn pretty quickly."²³ Bryan tried cut-blocking, hurling himself at the ball carrier's ankles. The ref blew his whistle, told Bryan to use his arms, and reached for his yellow card. That would mean ten minutes off the field, as opposed to red for permanent banishment. It was explained that Bryan had played only once before. The ref relented on the yellow, but the penalty stood. Undeterred, Bryan "fell in love, especially being an offensive lineman in football where you don't get to tackle anyone and you don't get to touch the ball. Rugby was absolutely all for me."

Others followed. Nik Wybaczysnky would have formed a monstrous second row with Bryan Phillips had he not struggled with injury. Matt Blind played fullback, the last line of defense. Mo Greene ran the attack from fly half. Brian McCoy was a safety who became a flanker. His first game was "up in Canada, at the Royal Military College in Kingston. I broke every rule there was—I didn't know there were rules. I blocked as much as I could, I did everything you were not supposed to do, I hit with my head, I led with my head, everything that was bad for my body. And I fell in love with the game."²⁴

Andy Klutman was another big football player who became a natural prop, binding up with Jim Gurbisz and Jeremiah Hurley, Joe Emigh's prep-school roommate. Of all the Class of '02 rugby players, Hurley was the last to make the leap, the summer before senior year. Like Pete Chacon, he came from wrestling. Unlike Gurbisz, who turned down football's invitation to gain weight, Hurley grew tired of having to lose it.

"I was wrestling at 197 pounds, so I was cutting about forty pounds every week to compete. It made more sense to eat like a normal person and not potentially kill myself every day. Propping was the fun part—I grew up playing contact sports, so that didn't discourage me."²⁵

Propping is dangerous, whether you know what you're doing or not. In a scrum, each member of the front row binds to the others then engages with the other front row, lacing their heads with their opponents', channeling the drive of their own forwards and resisting the enemy eight, fearsome force on neck, shoulders, and back. The higher the standard, the greater the pressure. Jeremiah didn't have much time to learn, but he had two things in his favor: wrestling holds and throws weren't much different from propping techniques and cheats—and he happened to be built like a warhorse. Hurley, Klutman, and Gurbisz were basically the same size, "three huge fucking lumps of human flesh with gigantic, oblong heads" as someone, probably Mo Greene, put it, amid beers and shouts years later in Massachusetts. It also helped that like the others, Hurley came to relish "the shared hardship" of outsider sport.

"Whether you're doing suicides up at H Lot for practice, or jingle-jangles, or whatever torture that Coach Mahan had for the day, that was the toughening aspect of it," Hurley said on a call from Fort Bragg, South Carolina, Joint Special Operations Command. "That was pretty significant. A suicide is the run from the goal line to the five-meter line and back, then to the twenty-two and back, and so on. The running drill. The run up to H Lot would make you want to commit suicide too. It's a shitty run. You had to do that two or three times a week."

I didn't dare ask what a jingle-jangle was. Hurley sighed.

"Good times," he said. "Good times."

The players all said so. So did some of their parents. George Emigh said, "That group of guys, the rugby team? Truly, it was a band of brothers. And that's pretty much, I think, the only reason Joey stayed at West Point."

Joe Emigh, senior photo, West Point Military Academy, Class of 2002.

Fullerton

"ARE YOU writing the facts or the truth?"[1] Julian Smilowitz—Coach Smilowitz—smiles. He's big and bearish, near seventy, moves slow, wears shades. At Roscoe's Famous Deli-Bar in Fullerton, California, he orders a Coke while the rest of us tackle sandwiches the size of footballs. It's December, but we sit in the shade. Most of the Fullerton fire department is at the next table for lunch.

"Just the facts," I say, resisting the temptation to add "Ma'am." *Dragnet* wasn't filmed too far away, after all.

Until today, California was just a state of mind to me. I was born and schooled in the north of England, went to work in the south, moved to the east coast of the United States. In ten years of work and kids, I made it as far west as Chicago. Now, finally, after a flight from Newark and fitful sleep in a hotel by the John Wayne Airport in Santa Ana, here I am. Where Joe Emigh grew up.

George Emigh conducts a tour with his daughter, Marianne, in the back of the car. Their old house at 425 Sunny Hills Road sits on what George calls a "pie-shaped lot" at the end of a quiet cul-de-sac.

"They've changed my windows," he says. "Kept my wall, though."

George was born in Fullerton in 1954 and grew up in a house his father built. Joanne Stary was born in Cincinnati and came to Fullerton when she was ten.[2] Like George, she went to Fullerton Union High. He played football; she was a cheerleader. They married in 1975. George had played defensive end at Adam State, and they lived in Colorado a while but soon came home. George was a salesman, away a lot. Marianne and Joey went to Union High too.

Fullerton is in Orange County, named for the citrus groves that were there before the suburbs came, covering the hillsides like ivy. In a state turned deep blue, Orange County still runs red.[3] Richard Nixon was born there in 1913. After 1968, in power, Nixon established his "western White House" in San Clemente. After 1974, in disgrace, he planted trees at the high school in Fullerton but put his library in Yorba Linda.

George's dad was a Democrat, a carpenter and a union man, but George liked Ronald Reagan, the president who said Orange County was "where the good Republicans go to die."[4] George's only regret about the family's old house is that it sits on Sunny Hills, a road with the same name as Fullerton's rival high school. He and Joanne bought the house in 1987, when Marianne was nine and Joey seven. Out back, George put in a pool and added a master bedroom.

Someone else has been busy. The front of the house has changed, pillars added to the doorway as well as those new windows. But as was the case in Eatontown, where Jim Gurbisz grew up, there's always the internet, where the house was shown for sale. Like the Miller place in Stoneboro, the old Emigh house in Fullerton is long and low. There's a compact kitchen and chairs around a coffee table and a big television in the corner. The pool out back is circular with an attached hot tub. There's lush foliage to screen it all and seats in the shade.

Joe Emigh's older sister Marianne is a mom herself now, to two girls in San Luis Obispo, a few hours north. As George drives, Marianne organizes sports practices and games from her phone. At some point there's even a trade. Marianne remembers her own sports-mad childhood. A softball win against the odds in the California Interscholastic Federation playoffs, 1994. She was just fifteen months older than her brother. They followed a simple rule. Do your schoolwork, play your sports, and Mom and Dad will take care of the rest. It wasn't a spartan existence, but it had a sort of rigor that extended to only having basic cable and no games console. Echoing Zac Miller, Joe Emigh called himself "Nintendo-challenged."[5]

"Our friends were at our house all the time," Marianne says,[6] "for a soccer party, a basketball party, football or whatever. Just to hang out. I had a friend, we'd finish school and have some time before softball practice or whatever, and she wanted to hang out with my mom. She wanted that comfortable environment. One of Joey's really good friends, David Brookman, he was six foot four and ended up playing football at Brown. My mom was like, 'Okay, David, are you hungry?' She'd get him and the rest of us food. She'd keep him happy, keep him well set."

Nik Wybaczynsky was even bigger than Brookman. He wasn't a friend—he played football for a rival school in Sonora. Emigh knew him as "Alphabet" and made plans to bring him down. But Wybaczynsky would know Emigh at West Point, and like others would be welcomed to Sunny Hills Road.

Wybaczynsky said, "With Joey being a running back and linebacker and me being an offensive and defensive lineman, we matched up a few times, most memorably our senior year. Our quarterback got hit as he threw and floated a ball right into Joey's hands. I tried chasing him down as he juked some of my other teammates and weaved his way down the field, only to barely touch his jersey as he crossed the goal line for the game-winning touchdown.

"All that for this: in plebe year at West Point, we were home for Christmas break, and I was headed to pick Joey up at his parents' house to head out with some other friends. Joey was a clown, and definitely got that from his mom, Joanne. I had met George and Joanne at the prep school but had never been to their home. I walked in, only to see Joanne tossing a videocassette across the living room to Joey. He popped the tape in, and it was perfectly cued to the point where Joey crossed the goal line as I failed to get to him in time. The three of them broke into laughter. The Emighs are the best."[7]

AT FULLERTON Union High, athletic director Joseph Olivas gives me a tour. Football is still big, the stadium looming to the north. There are other sports—Joe Emigh played basketball and baseball, there's a softball field, tennis courts, and a pool—but academics and theater are strong, and there's even a small farm. The school opened in 1893, modeled on Stanford University. A bell tower stands over Spanish-tiled roofs, and the mission-style buildings have arched windows and walkways mandated by the local historical society. As Olivas describes the diverse student body—"the richer kids from the hill, the poorer kids from the basin"[8]—students pour into the courtyard. In the shade of the Freshmen's Tree, a girl wearing an old-fashioned rugby shirt sits and laughs with her friends.

The school's badge and nickname are on prominent display. The badge is the head of a Native American chief, the nickname "the Indians." This is America in the early 2020s, a land of new sensitivity around race and identity, home to the Washington Commanders and the Cleveland Guardians. Over at the baseball field, standing on the husks of sunflower seeds chewed by players waiting to bat, Olivas says local tribes are offering counsel. He also tells of discontent among alumni, worried the Fullerton Indians may soon be consigned to history. It's fifty-fifty, Olivas says. The school has been this way before. In June 2020, a name was removed from the auditorium where Marianne and her brother once worked as ushers. Louis J. Plummer was a visionary superintendent. He was also a member of the Ku Klux Klan.[9] There's something in the air. At Disneyland in Anaheim, where George and Joanne took their children to see fireworks every Friday, they've covered up Jessica Rabbit.[10]

The Emigh kids should have gone to Sunny Hills High. But their parents wanted Fullerton, and that was possible by two routes: joining the Junior Reserve Officer Training Corps or studying Latin. Joe Emigh interviewed for ROTC, but Latin opened the door. He played sports and studied. He'd played basketball and baseball as a little kid, all buzz cut and bounce—soccer too—but George kept him away from football until he was twelve, the embargo eventually lifted so Joe could learn "how to hit and be hit."[11] He also ran for class office. He campaigned for sixth-grade president at Hermosa Drive Elementary, on a platform of getting air-conditioning installed. In high school, he aimed slightly lower, joining the ticket with a friend,

Jaimie King Schutze, when she ran for sophomore president. Jaimie had diabetes. One morning in 1996, when Joe was at football practice, Jaimie didn't wake up. Coach Smilowitz got word. He told Marianne. Twenty-five years later, the experience still hits hard. George still searches for the words.

"She'd expired. She'd passed . . . she'd died. And so that was a family tragedy."[12]

Marianne was seventeen, Joey sixteen. They "made the decision to get baptized together,"[13] Marianne says, as a way to remember Jaimie. In Fullerton, there are memorials. At the high school, there is a tree. At Loma Vista Memorial Park, there is a simple stone among many.

JOE EMIGH became class president sophomore year. He also became part of a football team Coach Smilowitz was hell-bent on improving.

"When I got to Fullerton in the spring of '92, we needed success. We were terrible."

Smilowitz had played on the offensive line at Brigham Young. Success meant hard work.

Emigh played linebacker on defense and running back on offense. It was commonplace for high school players to double up.

"You may start off at one position when you're younger because you're that size," George Emigh explained. "But as things progress and you grow and your body type changes, you end up at a different place. It gives you that overall understanding of the game. That's what we do with baseball, too, when you start at a younger age. And you know, if kids continue, the game gets better and faster, and they can adapt to it because they understand the game and how it's played."

When it comes to high school football in Fullerton in 1995 and 1996, Emigh is all over the newspaper archives. Two reports from the Orange County Register sum up his father's point about how he grew into the game. The first describes a crushing playoff loss in December 1995, to the Covina Colts, under Friday night lights, in front of four thousand fans, 34–0:

"One bright spot for the Indians was the running tandem of John Wilkie and Joseph Emigh. Wilkie, a 5-10, 193-lb senior, had 95 yards on 24 carries, and Emigh, a 5-10, 160-lb junior, had 52 yards on nine carries."[14]

The second, from September 1996, concerns a victory to open senior year, 14–12 over the Anaheim Colonists:

"Fullerton running back Joseph Emigh carried the ball 24 times for 119 yards . . . but it wasn't his running that helped the Indians to [victory]. The 6-0, 205-lb senior caught one pass, a screen from quarterback Justin Bruce, that went 35 yards for a touchdown. Then, with no time left, he blocked Fidel Rangel's field-goal attempt to save the Fullerton victory."[15]

In nine months, Emigh had grown two inches and put on forty-five pounds. Pictures show the transition. In one, he stands surrounded by girls, fourteen of Jaimie's friends. His neck is a pillar of muscle, his shoulders broad. In a prom photo, he has the ghost of a mustache and goatee. The facial hair has grown in a little in a baseball shot, Emigh in Indians red. In a football shot: Emigh chased by four defenders in blue and gold; it could be the touchdown in the Anaheim game.

"He was glad when people got in his way," Smilowitz says. "He would go out of his way to mash them."

Or to be mashed. Another picture: Emigh laid up on the couch, left ankle in a pot, contemplating his football helmet.

FOOTBALL WAS not only Joe Emigh's passion but a route to college with financial support. His dad could warn him about the dangers of such a plan: a bad knee injury in high school, the moment he realized, after four all-conference years in college, that he would not make the NFL. But as George says, "Joey was pretty good, obviously, and he got some interest. For two years, our summer vacations were based around touring colleges. One year, we toured all the colleges in California that Marianne and Joey were interested in. The next year we did some of the colleges in Arizona, in Colorado. And on that trip, we went up to the US Air Force Academy [in Colorado Springs] because they were interested in Joey. West Point came kind of late, when he was a senior. The second game, he hurt his shoulder a little bit. After we told Air Force that, they kind of dropped out. But Army stayed interested."

Recruitment was done through game film. The West Point coaches liked what they saw of Emigh as a linebacker, so George took him east "to watch one of their spring games and to see if he was interested. He got to meet some of the kids Army was trying to chase, in order to catch up to Air Force. One of the things they'd noticed was that Air Force had a lot of kids from California. So it ended up, there was a group Joey went to West Point with from southern California."

Nik Wybacyznsky, the "Alphabet" giant of Sonora, was among them. He's there in the newspaper archives, with Emigh, in a piece about a picnic for Orange County recruits:

> "We wanted them to meet each other so when times get tough there's someone to go to. Because it will get tough," said Bill Correia, president of Orange County's West Point Society. A cigar in one hand and trademark class ring on the other, Correia was among those dispensing advice to the plebes-to-be: "Work hard. Listen hard. And keep your mouth shut."[16]

That cheery social was in June 1998—close to a year after Emigh and Wybacyznsky graduated high school. They had been busy. West Point often sends football recruits for a year at its prep school. Emigh and Wybacyznsky flew out to Fort Monmouth, New Jersey. There, they worked at their books and played football and baseball. Emigh met and befriended Jeremiah Hurley and his girlfriend, Dawn Gasparri. One day, West Point Prep took a short trip into Eatontown to play baseball at Monmouth Regional High. The school had a standout football player, bound for West Point. Jim Gurbisz. He and Emigh chatted after the game.

Number 8 Dave Little and prop Jeremiah Hurley with matching black eyes.

Play

IN 2012, the novelist Ben Fountain published *Billy Lynn's Long Halftime Walk*, a satire of Iraq, America under George W. Bush, and football—"the *Catch-22* of the Iraq War," to some.[1] Like the NFL halftime show at the novel's heart, *Billy Lynn* is a performance: a relentless riff on militarism, consumerism, and the curdled American dream. At one point, Fountain sends his hero and the rest of Bravo Squad to run briefly amok in an end zone at Texas Stadium, home of the Dallas Cowboys. The soldiers pitch into "a loose game of razzle-dazzle, modified tackle-the-man-with-the-ball . . . just a bunch of guys tearing around the end zone, slamming into each other and laughing their asses off."

"And if it was just this," thinks nineteen-year-old Billy Lynn, "just the rude mindless headbanging game of it, then football would be an excellent sport and not the bloated, sanctified, self-important beast it became."[2]

Not every rugby player in the West Point Class of '02 thought of football that way. Not everyone thought of rugby as a "rude mindless headbanging game." But as Brian McCoy vividly described it ("I led with my head . . . and I fell in love"[3]), to many converts rugby *is* enticingly different. It is faster and looser. Every player can run with the ball and pass. Every player must tackle.

On Mike Mahan's watch, new players spent time down with the B, C, and D teams learning how to tackle, how to fall, how to ruck and maul, how to kick, how to pass sideways or backward with a spin.

Like rugby, becoming a rugby player while becoming a soldier could be messy and painful. Like rugby, it could be exhilarating too.

Brian Anthony, a scrum half, was club captain in 2000–01. After West Point, he was in Special Forces in Afghanistan and Iraq. After that he went back to California to write for film and television. He said, "In that Class of '02, the sheer number of guys that were able to fill in and contribute right away was what really made them stand out. Some big, muscular dudes from the classes of '98, '99 left us, and the team got smaller. But the 2002 class had incredible athleticism, grit, and toughness, and they had a level of talent. They were able to contribute in the pack, in the backs. None of the other classes had that number of people contributing."[4]

By September 2001, fifteen players from the Class of '02 were still with the program, from Andy Klutman at prop to Matt Blind at fullback. Blind was captain, but Jim Gurbisz was another leader from hooker.

"Jimmy was fearless," Anthony said. "He was relentless in his effort. You never saw him in pain, or if he was, he never showed it. Didn't back down from anyone including people on his own team. If he disagreed with you, he had no compunction about telling you that."

Thinking about Gurbisz and center Clint Olearnick, Anthony laughed. "Jim and Clint? They were little shits. I had to deal with all these degrees of leadership. Having to try to get them all to behave, or at least not get arrested. But you know, it always came in handy on the pitch. Nobody would be there to get your back quicker than those guys. Jim was a big dude and a big personality. He was not backing down for anybody. He'd be the first to put his nose in it if somebody was blowing up on teammates. Jim developed into an enforcer, both within the team and outside it. He'd probably punch you if he didn't like something you did. He practiced like he played too. It made no difference to him. He was going one hundred miles per hour, no matter what."

As Gurbisz's sister Kathleen said, her brother was "balls to the wall"[5] all the way. Anthony had to help Coach Mahan harness such energy and keep the team in order. It wasn't easy. Gurbisz and

Olearnick would pull some stupid shit. The kind of shit young men pulled. Sometimes up to the line, sometimes over it. Quite possibly appalling, seen from outside. But the shit they pulled had a point. It was a way to mark territory, to stake a claim to a place on the team. Like any team at West Point, rugby was highly competitive. Before the arrival of Women's Army Rugby in 2003, rugby was also very male. Every training session a pissing contest, every game a gang fight. If such energies weren't contained and directed, the superintendent would know. Flirtations with disbandment were common. Coach Mahan had withdrawn for a while when the drinking got too much. But he knew how to make rugby work for his players. He didn't squash the wilder side of the club but tried instead to channel it, to use the game as part of the cadets' education as well as an outlet for physical release. As George Orwell wrote, after all, serious sport is just "war minus the shooting."[6]

Mahan said, "I thought we should be using this vehicle to give cadets an advanced experience in leadership before they went out into the army, where they had to be a good leader, a platoon leader. Frankly, some of the experiences West Point throws out there as leadership examples are stupid. I mean, like collecting the laundry for people. You have somebody in charge and then you delegate. It's crazy. So, I went to the cadets, and I said, you know, 'We're going to train like a military unit, because that's what my experience was.'"

Training like a military unit has always meant training hard. In the Roman army, the historian Josephus wrote, training "lack[ed] none of the vigor of true war" and each soldier trained "every day with his whole heart as if it were war indeed . . . He would not err who described their exercises as battles without blood, and their battles as bloody exercises."[7] The Romans also knew what strategists of all kinds still preach: that training and combat is best done in small groups. "In modern infantry units," the historian Thomas E. Ricks writes, "squads are usually made up of eleven to thirteen people. Smaller than that, and the group becomes vulnerable when it suffers combat losses; bigger than that, and it is difficult to develop and maintain tight cohesion."[8] A rugby team contains fifteen players.

The US Army is rather bigger. From the ground up, units are organized like this: fire team, squad, platoon, company, battalion, brigade (or regiment), division, corps, army.[9] At West Point, from the top down, the corps of cadets is split into four regiments, each containing three battalions of three companies. It might follow that under Mike Mahan the West Point rugby team operated as a company within a battalion, the athletics department, which was itself part of a brigade, meaning the whole academy. Within the rugby team, the A, B, C, and D sides were platoons of fifteen men each, each split into two squads: seven backs and eight forwards. Within the squads, fire teams. Back three, centers, halfbacks. Back row, second row, front row.

Fifteen men started each game. There could be seven replacements. Often, substitutes for the A side, or those substituted, would then run out for the Bs; Kevin Lynch, a member of the Class of '03, told me that at Aldershot he played a full game for the Bs then ran over to finish the game against Rosslyn Park.[10]

Brian Anthony said, "The intelligence of the '02 class was something else. There was Slutman—that's what we called Andy Klutman—there was Morgan Greene, Matt Blind. Those guys . . . like their GPAs? They were definitely pulling the curve of the rugby team higher. I think we subverted a trope in that way. We were all pretty generally smart, but Klutman, he became a doctor. I remember him missing the kickoff of a final four game to go take the MCAT [the medical college admissions test], and then coming on at halftime. And he was physically huge. He was key to the team as a prop, a great athlete, but he was very intelligent as well."

There was also Jerrod Adams on one wing, quieter than Gurbisz and Olearnick, "much more like Coach Mahan, the speak-softly guy. I don't think I heard Jerrod raise his voice even once or get angry. In that chaotic time, at that age, an environment just drowning in testosterone? That really stuck out." Adams was the team poet, charged with writing toasts and roasts as well as game reports. There was also Matt Blind, the fullback, a quiet organizer on and off the field.

Up front there was big Dave Little, the number 8 from San Diego. Away from the play, his mood rarely rose above the horizontal. Sometimes, Anthony said, "I'd ask, like, 'Dave, are you here?' But then he would just *crush* people on the field. He would just be like, the most violent number 8 you'd ever seen in your life. And then he would just walk away."

Like Brian Anthony, Mike Mahan chatted through the Class of '02. Mahan is not just a coach. He's an airborne infantry officer and a professor of chemistry. When he thinks about something, it gets thought through. The day after we spoke, he sent me an email.[11]

"In those days, West Point allowed sixty-eight players on the rugby club. In fact, we often had ninety or more. We organized four sides, reordering every Monday based on performances at the weekend. I made it a priority to get all four sides a match (or at least a half) every weekend. To do so required West Point to register in two leagues. Our A and C sides played in the elite Eastern rugby league, which spread from Maine to Maryland. Our B and D sides played in the Metropolitan New York league. My agreement with Met NY was that the B and D sides could win it but would not represent it in post-season play. B and D routinely brought home the trophy.

"We'd often have the A and C sides (about thirty-eight players) on one bus heading north and the B and D sides on another heading into New York City. I always traveled with the A and C and usually had one or even two other coaches with me. That meant getting another coach to volunteer to accompany the B and D sides for a 'boomerang' day trip to NYC. The coach accompanying B and D was usually a young captain who had a kitchen pass from the missus for the day. Met NY teams often put on a party for the B and D, always with plenty of beer. West Point rules at the time allowed cadets of legal drinking age to drink, while those younger could not. This resulted in a very challenging assignment for the young captain in charge. For him, it was a 'bet your bars' assignment. If news of a scandalous nature were to reach back to West Point, punishment for the young captain (and the rugby team) would be severe. I was so concerned about this, I had to get the captain some help."

Zac Miller was a number 8 or a blindside flanker. Coach Mahan called him aside and asked if he would accept the ad hoc position of captain of the B side. "As such, he would travel with the B and D sides in support of the coach. This was a job very few cadets could have pulled off. Controlling fellow cadets with the temptations of NYC and beer was a huge task. Controlling without being scorned and abused was an impossible task for any other cadet. It also meant that Miller, who was second or third on the depth chart at number 8, would sacrifice possible playing time with the A side. Miller did not hesitate to accept. He pulled it off beautifully, sticking with the younger players, eschewing the beer, and was accepted as the rock star he was."

Mahan's tale chimes with those told about Miller back in Sandy Lake, Pennsylvania, where he was trusted from a young age. But Dave Little tells a story about Miller that also echoes tales from home—the ones that show his competitive edge.

In one of his first training sessions, Little fell on a ball knocked loose. It was his football training talking. That training also made him refuse to let go of the ball. In rugby, however, you have to.

"Zac? He gave me a nice smack in the face."[12]

Little let go of the ball.

TOM HIEBERT is a retired army colonel who commanded Second Battalion, 508th Parachute Infantry Regiment from June 2004 to May 2006, much of that time in Iraq, amid elections and spiraling violence. He's also a member of the West Point Class of 1987 and a driving force behind Old Gray, the rugby alumni program.

Tom's research for a history of Army rugby coincided with my research for this book, so he drove from his home in Chappaqua into New York for breakfast with me in Washington Heights. Neither of us needed to wear a carnation or carry a copy of *Stars and Stripes*. In hipster Manhattan coffee shops, retired colonels with high-and-tight haircuts, brisk military manners, and gleaming polished shoes tend to stand out from the crowd.

With Tom as my guide—and occasional driver from Peekskill station—I would go back to West Point repeatedly, touring the campus, watching games, surviving an Old Gray weekend in the raw Hudson Highlands spring, talking and drinking with colonels, generals, semi-retired Swamp Things, cadets, parents, and all. Thanks to Tom, I got hold of West Point's full run of results from 1998 to 2002.

It's a winning record, though for the A side it started on September 5, 1998, with a defeat at home to Penn State (35–10) on Daly Field, up by the Plain at the heart of the academy, next to Doubleday Field for baseball and Clinton Field for soccer. Pictures from the early 1920s show Army football on or near the future Daly Field, before Michie Stadium was built up the hill to the west.[13] The posts are the same as those used for rugby, H-shaped, placed on the goal line, not behind the end zone. A big crowd fills bleachers on either side of the gridiron, standing two deep at each end. To a rugby player's eye, it's a glimpse of what might have been, had American rugby taken its brief chance and supplanted football.

Elsewhere in the northern hemisphere, the rugby season runs from September to May. In the United States, where winters get properly cold, it's split between fall and spring. In 1998, the West Point A side went nine-and-three in the fall and six-and-four in the spring, including five games in California. They made the national final four, where they lost to Penn State (50–27) and Navy (44–22). Cal Berkeley was champion for the ninth time in a run of twelve.[14] The next season, 1999–2000, began with defeat at Towson, 33–29. The team picked itself up, finishing the fall with nine wins, two losses, and one tie. A spring tour to the UK brought defeat by Sandhurst and the Royal Naval College but victory, 32–31, over a British Army team. The A side made the final four, this time losing 49–19 to Cal before beating Indiana of Pennsylvania 43–20 for third.

Brian Anthony's season as captain, 2000–01, brought an eleven-and-zero autumn including wins over Penn State and Dartmouth. Spring opened with four games in California and a bad defeat by Navy, 52–12. The team made the final four, only to lose to Penn State and Navy. There were selections for a Combined Services All-Star

Team for a national tournament in June. Dave Birie, the fullback, made the All-American XV. There were honorable mentions for Anthony, Clay Livingston (a senior second row), Andy Klutman, and Jim Gurbisz.

All that meant that as 2001–02 rolled around, things looked promising. The junior classes had thrown up a crop of talent. Among the firsties, the only newcomer was Jeremiah Hurley, who had come from wrestling to complete a forbidding front row with Gurbisz and Klutman.

The players' various bloodings are all there in Tom Hiebert's records, from Brian McCoy's first run for the Bs at the Royal Military College of Canada (a 60–0 win, on September 19, 1999) to the game in the spring of 2001 when Bryan Phillips came on against Cal, who would put eighty-six points on Penn State in the championship game that year. On March 18, 2001, the cadets "only" lost 25–0. Other players had to learn just as fast as Phillips. All were focused on making their mark.

IN LATE August 2001, the rugby players returned to West Point for their senior year. None had spent much of the summer at home.

Jerrod Adams wanted to be a flier, so he took an internship shadowing a platoon leader in a cavalry squadron at Fort Hood, Texas.

"He was an OH-58 pilot, so I got to fly in the Kiowa with him, eat at the Waffle House after night missions, and sleep in my hotel room," Adams said. "Because the unit also had tanks, I was able to shadow a tank platoon leader in the field for a week, too, sleeping on the front slope of the tank under the stars."[15]

Diplomatically, Adams characterized conditions among the tankers as "different" from those enjoyed by fliers. It wasn't a hard choice to stay with helicopters. He went down to West Palm Beach, Florida, to the project to develop the RAH-66 Comanche—a light attack helicopter to succeed the Kiowa—which ended up getting scrapped a few years and a few billion dollars later.[16] Jerrod worked on computer simulations, "putting my aeronautics degree to good use," and watched test flights. There was also the West Palm nightlife—there was a strip club right in the hotel parking lot—and there was the motorcycle Adams bought with "no license, no training, just board shorts and flip flops riding in the rain." He only had two near-death experiences.

Scott Radcliffe was keener on armor. He went to Germany for a spell with One-Four Cav. Matt Blind went the other way, west to California and the Lawrence Livermore National Laboratory, where staff worked on the future and security of America's nuclear weapons.

"I'm still not sure what I did or was supposed to do," Blind said, "but they hooked me up with a sweet apartment, and I wore civilian clothes to work. I hung out in Santa Cruz and got so drunk I missed two days of work. No one noticed."[17]

Zac Miller was thousands of miles away, in a refugee camp in Azerbaijan, working with a group called Women Waging Peace, counseling kids and setting up a computer system. Miller didn't drink, but even if he had, there was only Coke because it was cleaner than the water. When Miller came home, he described the poverty he saw near Baku. He also told his mother not to pat his head: "I haven't showered in three weeks," Miller said.[18]

Bryan Phillips trained with the military police, learning SWAT team tactics. At six foot eight and three hundred pounds, he was first into any hostile zone, carrying the big shield, four or five normal-sized cadets behind him. Phillips also went back to West Point, where he, Blind, and others mixed business with pleasure as platoon leaders through R-Day and Beast.

"I was a basic training platoon leader," Blind said, "which was the easiest but most rewarding job I ever had to this day. I was the 'man in the red sash'—I remember new cadets reporting to me completely jacked up. I was laughing, remembering myself being so intimidated just three years prior. I smoked my platoon physically but didn't yell at them much, and they respected the hell out of me. I remember learning how important it was to lead from the front in PT, and that if I did the smoke sessions with them and looked to be unscathed, they would follow me anywhere. To this day, I have a letter in my lock box that a new cadet wrote to me and that I will remember for the rest of my life, explaining his experience and respect for his cadre in Beast. That was the experience that made me want to be an infantryman."

Matt and Bryan ran with their plebes, instructed them in the basics of weaponry, taught them academy rules. They presided over long marches in full gear, known as "rucks" in military speak—on the rugby field, the same word describes the fierce competition for the ball over any tackled man.

There were softer privileges too. Firsties could keep cars on campus. Most of the rugby team drove beat-up Hondas and Toyotas. Blind scoped out a spot to park, high on the hillside, near the chapel but far from the eyes of the other god, Lieutenant General William Lennox, the new superintendent. Blind put a keg of beer in his trunk. As term ground into gear, the rugby team went up to Blind's car and got down to work. As Blind saw things, as captain, it was a vital team-building exercise. Inevitably, the authorities found out, and Matt was given hours, walking off his sins in the barracks yard, rifle at his shoulder. When his hours were done, he drove into Highland Falls and bought another keg.

For firsties, the first major event of the year is Ring Weekend, when class rings are handed out and families visit for ceremonies, dining, and dancing.[19] In 2001, the big day, August 24, dawned brilliant blue. Wearing "India White" dress uniforms and red sashes, the Class of '02 marched to Trophy Point, over the glittering Hudson. Under yellow and black guidons, they formed ranks and were addressed by the commandant, Brigadier General Eric Olson. At his command they applauded their families. They received their rings, which contained gold from the rings of past classes and carried the motto "Pride in All We Do." The cadets put on their rings, cheered, and were dismissed. In pictures, Matt Blind smiles broadly, ring on his finger, arm around his sister. Zac Miller smiles with his parents, Rosalyn and Keith.[20]

The cadets marched back to barracks. Plebes were waiting to pounce for the ring poop, part of the absurd, enduring West Point liturgy. "Oh my gosh, sir!" they chanted, firsties surrounded and subjected to mock-fawning, pawing torture. "What a beautiful ring!

What a crass mass of brass and glass! What a bold mold of rolled gold! What a cool jewel you got from your school! See how it sparkles and shines? It must have cost you a fortune! May I touch it, may I touch it, please, sir?"

The chance for revenge came swiftly. After Ring Weekend—after Miller, his friends, and their dates took a cruise down in New York City, passing the World Trade Center at the tip of Manhattan[21]— there was rugby training, up at Stony Lonesome. Everyone ran up to H Lot. Most of the fresh faces were as eager as they were clueless. Coach Mahan imposed a kind of order, assistants working with him: Chris Starling, a Marine Corps major on exchange. Rich Pohlidal, once a player at Penn State, now working in West Point fundraising. Tony Field, the British exchange officer. In the way of club sports everywhere, players filled management roles. Mo Greene and Pete Chacon were in charge of admin, Clint Olearnick looked after the kit, Jerrod Adams was public affairs. Jim Gurbisz was social secretary.

The coaches picked teams for opening weekend. On Saturday, September 8, the A and B sides would go to Columbus to play Ohio State. The Cs and Ds were set for Kings Point, Long Island, and the US Merchant Marine Academy. Adams was detailed to write reports for the alumni newsletter. Nearly twenty years later, Matt Blind contacted the alumnus who ran the newsletter, Bill "Bull" Jackman, Class of '64, a Vietnam vet. Adams's reports were sent to me.[22]

On Friday, September 7, 2001, the A and B sides flew to Ohio. They spent a night in a cheap motel, and on Saturday they went to the game. The rugby field was dwarfed by Ohio Stadium, the hallowed home of Buckeyes football. That afternoon, "The Shoe" held more than one hundred thousand for a first game under head coach Jim Tressel, a 28–14 win over the Akron Zips. Some football fans might have cast a glance at their sport's unruly cousin. They might have been intrigued.

There were no pads or helmets, other than thin rubber scrum caps some forwards wore to protect their heads and ears. The players wore cotton shirts, shorts, and socks, all black for the cadets, red and white for the Buckeyes. They wore mouth guards and leather boots with cleats. Some strapped joints with medical tape. There was one referee, similarly dressed, carrying only a whistle. Substitute players ran the sidelines, raising a flag when the ball went out. Coach Mahan patrolled one sideline, the Buckeyes coach the other. The goalposts were padded at the base. Lines were marked with chalk. Ohio State kicked off. Army dropped the ball.

In any game of rugby, wingers spend a lot of time watching, tracking forward and back, waiting for ball or man. Jerrod Adams's Ohio report is detailed. He recorded how Joe Emigh scored the first three points of the season, with his second penalty kick at goal, after an attack mounted by Brian McCoy, Mo Greene, and Brent Pafford, a sophomore starting at prop. The first try came from another Pafford run, like others described by Adams as a "punch," a hard run onto a short pass—tiring to keep up but punishing as hell to defend. On this punch, Pafford "broke free and passed to Clint Olearnick in support, who ran over two defenders for a 20-meter try." Emigh missed the two-point conversion, leaving the score 8–0. The Buckeyes came back strong, scoring two converted tries to end the forty-minute half leading 14–8. Shannon Worthan, the junior at scrum half, scored the first try in the second half, taking a penalty quickly and darting over the line. Emigh missed the kick again, and the Buckeyes scored twice more to lead 26–13.

"Army didn't fold," Adams wrote. "We drove back down the field after the restart and McCoy scored on a two-meter punch for 26–18. But the OSU backs countered with a 10-meter run to finish the game with a final score of 33–18."

The As then watched the B side play. Or most did. Though he had come out of the A game injured, Pete Chacon played eighty minutes for the Bs, scoring twice. Army won 20–0.

For the A side, the season had begun in defeat. But there were promising signs, and the bars of Columbus were open. The Buckeyes and their friends shared a beer, or seven. The party went late. On Sunday, Jerrod Adams woke up on the roof of a bar. He ran for the bus to the airport, a beer box balanced on his head against the spitting rain.

The World Trade Center in March 2001 as seen from
a West Point training plane.

September

O NE MORNING in March 2001, Jerrod Adams climbed into the back of a Cessna 182 and clipped himself into his seat. Another cadet, Kevin Andreson, sat in the front of the plane beside the pilot, Major Todd Dellert, an assistant professor and their instructor for Introduction to Aerodynamics.

Like the pilot and his two twenty-year-old passengers—Adams a stocky Texan, Andreson from somewhere in the Midwest—the plane belonged to the United States Military Academy. There were black and gold stripes down the white fuselage and crests on the doors. The tinny voice leaking from Dellert's headset came from the tower at Stewart International Airport, about forty miles north of West Point, up past Storm King Mountain. Adams was majoring in mechanical engineering and aeronautical systems, Andreson in aerospace engineering. This was their first flight lab, one of three to learn about climbs and descents, drag factors and stall speeds and, tantalizingly, angles of attack.

"Everybody had to choose an engineer track," Adams said, of the academic demands that two years before had nearly sent Scott Radcliffe, his fellow rugby player, to the exit.[1] "Even if you were an arts and philosophy major, you had to minor in one of the engineering courses. Nuclear, environmental, chemical, civil, and mechanical. So I was on a mechanical engineering track with an aeronautical focus. The majority of my major classes were with the guys who did power trains or built cars or something like that. We took five or six electives that essentially made up an aeronautical track. One of them was learning how airplanes fly."

Adams already had a call sign, J-Rod, but that was for rugby, so he knew when to come in from the wing and sprint onto a pass. Bryan Phillips, in the second row of the scrum, was B-Phil. Brian McCoy, the openside flanker, was B-Mac. J-Rod could've taken himself to the West Point Flight Club, up at Stewart, building his hours in the Cessna. Because of rugby, he didn't have time. Instead, he ran drills, lifted weights, and got on the end of moves begun with possession won by B-Phil and B-Mac.

The Cessna taxied, bumping on wheels clad in white aerodynamic fairings like a military policeman's gaiters. Major Dellert eased the yoke and the plane accelerated, lifted, and flew. Up above Newburgh, Dellert turned south. Sunlight moved through the cabin in slats. No clouds, brilliant blue everywhere, trees bare on round brown hills over the blue-green river. Soon, to the west, West Point. Adams and Andreson used cheap digital cameras to rattle off shots. The flat expanse of the Plain, the barracks areas, the granite mass of the Chapel, the reservoir behind. Daly Field, marked for rugby. Trophy Point, Battle Monument. You could even pick out the statue of John Sedgwick, the general from the class of 1837 who died at Spotsylvania in 1864. As legend had it, struggling cadets could earn luck in exams by dressing in full uniform and spinning the spurs on his boots.[2]

Major Dellert flew south. Adams and Andreson gazed down at whitecaps and pleasure boats, riverside towns, the gray prison at Sing Sing. The first part of the lab was about getting used to flight. The George Washington Bridge passed below, a great gray span between Revolutionary War redoubts, Fort Lee on the Jersey side, Fort Washington, now a children's park, at the highest point on Manhattan. Further south, Riverside Park and Grant's Tomb to the east, to the west Weehawken, where Aaron Burr killed Alexander Hamilton in 1804. On the New York side at West 46th Street there was the USS *Intrepid*, an aircraft carrier turned museum. Adams thought "how cool it was, looking down and seeing the SR-71 Blackbird," a sleek black spy plane, looming dark on the deck.

Off the tip of Manhattan, Dellert rounded the Statue of Liberty, and there they were to the east, looming in the petroleum haze of a downtown morning, casting the Hudson shore into shadow, 110 stories high: the twin towers of the World Trade Center.

SIXTEEN YEARS later, on a hot August Saturday, Major Jerrod Adams was on his way to Afghanistan with the Third Infantry Division. From a transit lounge in Kuwait, waiting for a ride into Bagram, he spoke to me via Skype. America had been at war so long that someone had invented the videophone.

Adams took me through his career. In 2008, he completed a tour in Iraq, based in Baghdad, flying Apache helicopters. He went to Korea, then spent two years back at West Point, teaching math and serving as a rugby team liaison. He worked on drones for a while, and now came this tour to a war in its sixteenth year. He would be part of HQ for Operation Freedom's Sentinel, yet another idealistic rebranding of the attempt to beat the Taliban.[3] He was due to drive a desk, but he was hoping to fly. He was in his late thirties, had a shaved head, and wore combat fatigues and a look of tired anticipation. He had just spoken to his wife and daughters at Fort Stewart, outside Savannah, Georgia. He shifted in his seat, took a slug of water—"All the free H_2O you could want, courtesy of Uncle Sam"—and rubbed his jaw.

"I remember at the time thinking like, 'Holy Cow,' you know? You can see in some of the pictures I took that we were well above West Point, we were well above the bridges. But flying down to Manhattan, those skyscrapers were so tall, we were below the top stories. There was an incident where a small fixed-wing aircraft flew into one of those skyscrapers. That entered my mind."

He could be thinking, in fact, of a crash in 2006, in which a small plane piloted by the Yankees baseball star Cory Lidle hit a building on the Upper East Side.[4] He could be thinking of the time a B-25 bomber hit the Empire State Building in 1945.[5] Time plays tricks.

In March 2001, Jerrod Adams and Kevin Andreson had watched the World Trade Center loom alongside their little plane. Jerrod took a picture, the twin towers stark in the morning blue. Major Dellert flew north. At White Plains, Dellert landed, and Adams and Andreson swapped seats. Adams was up front.

"On the way back to West Point is where we actually took our lab data," Adams said. The cadets "tested stall speeds at different air speeds, what angle of attack we get before we get stall speed indicators, things like that. We plotted our stuff to produce basically a drag chart. We were kinda verifying results that were already published in the aircraft operator's manual. Learning about how they come up with those things. Had to write up a report after the flight, do some equations, figure out the length and drag curves for the Cessna."

It wasn't all dry math. In clear airspace, Dellert let Adams hold the yoke. For the first time, he was—sort of—flying. There was also an instructor's trick: Adams and Andreson placed their pencils flat in the palm of one hand. Dellert pulled back on the yoke, putting the plane into a steep climb. Airspeed reduced until at sixty knots Dellert pushed the yoke hard forward, forcing the nose of the aircraft down. "Zero-G pushover." For two or three seconds, as the plane tipped, the cadets' pencils appeared to float. So did their stomachs. Somewhere above Peekskill and the Indian Point power plant, Andreson threw up. He hit Adams on the back of the neck.

JERROD ADAMS'S junior year finished three months later. He spent his summer in Texas and Florida, and then went back to West Point. Three days after the Ohio State game, Tuesday, September 11, 2001, dawned bright and clear.

Adams was up before daybreak, limbs another day less sore from the game and the party. The rest of the four-thousand-strong corps of cadets were up too. In uniform, they hurried to breakfast formation. On the parade ground, they formed ranks by the statue of George Washington then marched into Washington Hall for breakfast. They hurried to first class, "first hour" in academy speak, 7:30 a.m. Some were in science, some were in finance. Some were in history, getting their minds around the revolution, the Civil War, D-Day, Vietnam. History was about to change.[6]

At 7:59 a.m. eastern time, two hundred miles to the north, a commercial airliner took off from Boston Logan. It was American Airlines Flight 11 en route to Los Angeles LAX.

At 8:14 a.m., another plane ran down the same runway and took off for the same destination. It was United Airlines Flight 175.

Somewhere over Massachusetts, American 11 was hijacked. At 8:19 a.m., a flight attendant made contact with ground control.

At 8:20 a.m., at Dulles airport outside Washington, American Airlines Flight 77 took off for Los Angeles.

At 8:24 a.m., a hijacker on American 11 broadcast a message intended for passengers but picked up by ground control in Boston: "We have some planes. Just stay quiet, and you will be okay. We are returning to the airport. Nobody move. Everything will be okay. If you try to make any moves, you'll endanger yourself and the airplane. Just stay quiet."

At 8:27 a.m., the hijacked plane turned south.

At 8:30 a.m., at West Point, the cadets transferred to second hour. For Jerrod Adams it was mechanical engineering. For Matt Blind it was money and banking, dreaded by almost everyone.

"Taylor Hall is between the Plain and the Hudson," Blind said, "and I seem to remember looking out the window and seeing the river and realizing how close we actually were. I remember that we had an exam scheduled after lunch that I was unprepared for. I was really screwed."[7]

Scott Radcliffe had completed an hour on the principles of fluid dynamics and now had a break till lunch, time to catch up on work missed when he'd stayed an extra day in Ohio, at home with his parents.[8]

Adams was in class, but his mind was half on rugby. He had to write up the Buckeyes game for the Old Gray newsletter, which was emailed to bases across the United States, to Germany and Korea, to the Pentagon and Capitol Hill, to Wall Street and Silicon Valley. There was also training that night, the run to Stony Lonesome.

Coach Mahan would be waiting. Under his eye, they would prepare for UMass on Saturday.

American 11 followed the Hudson. It flew over West Point, south to New York City, the same route Jerrod and Kevin Andreson had taken in the Cessna six months earlier. Any cadets allowing their minds to drift might have heard the 757 fly past. The roar of its two Pratt & Whitney engines. Not that the sound would've seemed unusual.

At 8:38 a.m., American 11 went into a rapid descent. Air traffic controllers thought it was heading for JFK, out in the steppes of Queens. A flight attendant was in contact with American Airlines headquarters.

At 8:42 a.m., United 175 was hijacked. American 77 was in the air, flying west over Virginia. In Newark, New Jersey, another plane took off for San Francisco: United 93.

American 11 flew down the Hudson to New York. At 8:44 a.m., a flight attendant said: "Oh my God, we are way too low."

At 8:46:40 a.m., American Airlines Flight 11 crashed into the North Tower of the World Trade Center. All seventy-six passengers and eleven crew members were killed. In the tower, in an instant, an unknown number perished.

AT WEST Point, the cadets and their tutors learned what had happened just fifty miles south the same way most people did: they saw it on television. Officers walked into classrooms and labs and whispered to teachers. Televisions were wheeled in or uncovered. Everyone sat, stunned.

Jerrod Adams said, "My mechanical engineering instructor heard the news from another instructor and turned on the TV in the classroom. It was before smartphones, so we were all fixed on the CNN anchor. I remember thinking at first it must have been a small, private plane with a terrible student pilot at the controls."[9]

Scott Radcliffe ran into a football friend, Jared Churchill. He broke the news. Like Adams, Radcliffe assumed an accident. A few hurt. Back in his room, he switched on his desktop iMac and its video function, a luxury extended to cadets that summer. He sat there, staring. In classrooms, cadets stared too. The world watched in gathering dread.

Sometime after 8:51 a.m., somewhere over West Virginia, American 77 was hijacked. A minute later, calls from passengers on United 175 reached the world below. They had been herded to the back of the plane. What the hijackers wanted, no one knew. United 175 flew south, a wider loop than American 11, flying over New Jersey and Pennsylvania before turning toward New York.

At 8:54 a.m., above Ohio, American 77 turned away from its course. Indianapolis air traffic control couldn't contact it. Nor could American Airlines. American grounded all flights nationwide.

At 8:58 a.m., United 175 approached Manhattan. It began to move erratically. At 9:03:11 a.m., the plane crashed into the South Tower of the World Trade Center. All fifty-one passengers and nine crew members were killed. So were an unknown number in the tower. The world saw it live on TV. Explosions bloomed. The towers burned. America was under attack.

At 9:27 a.m., United 93 made its last routine communication. At 9:32 a.m., the control tower at Dulles observed radar of a fast-moving plane approaching Washington from the southwest. It was American 77. At 9:34 a.m., the Federal Aviation Authority Herndon Command Center in Virginia advised that United 93 had likely been hijacked. At 9:37:46 a.m., in Arlington, Virginia, American 77 crashed into the western side of the Pentagon. All fifty-three passengers and six crew members were killed. In the Department of Defense, 125 were killed.

From United 93, as from American 11, an instruction to passengers was again broadcast to the ground in error. There was a bomb on board, the hijackers said. The plane was heading back to the airport.

THE WORLD knew what had happened in New York and Virginia. The government knew a fourth plane was heading for Washington— for the Capitol or the White House. The passengers on United 93 were connected to the ground by phone. They decided to fight. Among them were two rugby players: Mark Bingham, who had played for Cal Berkeley and was part of the gay rugby scene with the San Francisco Fog, and Jeremy Glick, who played at the University of Rochester. Both were number 8 forwards. Both were thirty-one years old.[10] At 9:57 a.m., someone on United 93 said, "Let's roll." Bingham, Glick, and other passengers tried to storm the cockpit.

At 9:59 a.m. in New York, the South Tower collapsed. More than six hundred people died. The world watched.

The struggle on United 93 was broadcast to ground control. Screams, shouts. The plane turned belly up. At 10:03 a.m. the plane came down in a field near Shanksville in Somerset County, Pennsylvania. All thirty-three passengers and seven crew members were killed.

At 10:28 a.m., the North Tower fell. More than one thousand four hundred perished.

More than four hundred emergency responders were among the dead.

In less than two hours, 2,977 people were killed. Thousands more were injured.

AT WEST Point, some professors tried to keep teaching. They gave up. Everyone stared at screens. Occasionally, cadets went to walk the corridors. Conversations were whispered, heads shaking. In minutes, life had changed. Clint Olearnick remembered a grim irony: because he was majoring in military science, his first class that morning was on counterterrorism.

"It was taught by a Special Forces major. And the last thing he said to us before we left class was, 'It's only a matter of time before someone attacks the United States.' I go back to my room. I turn on the TV and I see it. I was floored."[11]

Families watched too. Rosalyn, Zac Miller's mother, described the awful thought that West Point might be a target. She took "repeated phone calls from Nina Landgraf, the mother of Zac's roommate, Jay. The Landgrafs lived in Ridgewood, New Jersey. Nina was a librarian at the local elementary school. Many of her students' parents worked in New York City, a number of them at Cantor Fitzgerald. In an attempt to keep the frightening news from the children, all televisions and radios were turned off. Nina called me regularly: 'Had we heard from Zac? Were the cadets okay? What was going on at the World Trade Center?' It was all so surreal and unbelievable."[12]

Cantor Fitzgerald, a financial services firm, had offices on the 101st to 105th floors of One World Trade Center, the North Tower: 658 staffers died.[13]

Cadets contacted loved ones, friends, anyone with any connection at all to the hell in New York City, the gaping wound in the Pentagon, the burning field in Pennsylvania. Jim Gurbisz reached his sister, Kathleen, at her office in Manhattan.

"I was in a cubicle," she said, "and my cell phone didn't work, and I think he called the office. He was making sure I was okay, and he was, like, 'We're all fired up already. We're ready to go.' They were twenty-one-year-old kids."[14]

Some cadets did not find reassurance. One, whose brother worked at Cantor Fitzgerald, was seen weeping with the chaplain.[15] The television said the president had been taken to safety. He had not spoken to the people. All was smoke and confusion. Eventually, Matt Blind decided that as captain of the rugby team he would volunteer his men for the fray.

"I felt hopeless watching," he said. "So I spoke to Colonel Adamczyk, the brigade tactical officer, to volunteer the rugby team to deploy to Manhattan and help."

Joseph Adamczyk was a fearsome presence. A stickler for discipline. A warrior monk, nicknamed Skeletor by the cadets. He told Blind, "The right thing to do was to let the rescue teams and first responders do their job, to stay out of the way until they need us. It was the right call, but it left an empty feeling."

Blind spoke for his team. So did Coach Mike Mahan. September 11 was a Tuesday. Tuesday night was rugby night. As Pete Chacon remembered it, up at Stony Lonesome, "Coach pulled us together and said, just calmly, 'Hey, we all know what happened today. And if anybody doesn't want to practice, we totally understand. We are a team.' He said, 'My opinion is that the best way to honor people is for us to go on with our lives and stay strong and keep being ourselves and not give in to fear.' As a team, we decided we were gonna have practice. And so we got to it, but it was a silent, somber practice, like, guys running and tackling with no talking. It was a very sobering type of thing, that you just never see, where your people are just, like, quietly going about an intense rugby practice. It was weird."[16]

It made sense as much as anything did. The cadets wanted to mount up and barrel down the river, to join teams scouring the pit for remains. They wanted to serve the country that had spent three years preparing them to do so. They were denied. The authorities stood firm.

Chris Starling, the Marine Corps major and rugby coach on exchange, remembered that "a few people had to go [to Manhattan] from the hospital" up on Washington Road, at the top of campus. "A few people that had specific skill sets. Four guys. We all envied them. They got into a little convoy that headed down there to Ground Zero. We wanted to beat the guys that did this. We wanted to do something."[17]

No matter. West Point went on lockdown, double guards at the gate. Leave canceled. Airspace closed. An attack on the academy would threaten four thousand officers-in-training. It did not happen. West Point stayed silent, stunned, and sad. When lockdown lifted, Joe Emigh and some friends chanced a trip to New York. It turned out, said Eddie Johnson, another former football player, that there was nothing they could do.

"We wanted to do what we could to help, in any way we could. But we just couldn't get close enough. I think the closest we got was eight, nine, ten blocks north of Ground Zero. I remember the smell. That stuck with me. The combination of the building, the structure, the bodies. It was just sickening. I remember feeling completely helpless. We came all the way down here. We're so close, but we can't do anything. The police and firemen were doing everything they could to prevent access, for safety reasons. We got it."[18]

Everyone at West Point had plenty of time to think. They knew their lives had changed. Peacekeeping? America's supposed role in the post–Cold War world? Kosovo and Bosnia? Over. Anything that fell under the inevitable acronym, OOTWA, Operations Other Than War. Over. Graduates were going to war.

SIXTEEN YEARS later, I sat with Matt Blind in a harborside bar in Duxbury, Massachusetts. Like the town, a few miles down the South Shore from Boston, the bar was tony and gleaming, the kind of place where they served drinks in jam jars and most of the guys wore boat shoes. Waiting for a plate of oysters, Blind took a sip of his beer.

"We all knew right away that it was on," he said. "We knew we were going to war."[19]

He worked in Boston, in investments. He'd taken the day off for golf. A decade before, he had married Erin. Now they had three kids, a dog, and a boat. Blind wore Ray-Bans and a golf shirt, the West Point crest on the breast. Fifteen years before, he had left West Point. Two years after that, he'd been sent to Iraq.

Mosul. Heat, dust, fear. Patrols, ambushes, firefights. Bombs. Blind survived. Kept his platoon intact and came home. Two years later, five years' service done—the price of that fabulous, free West Point education—he decided to get out. He went into the corporate world, spent a while selling Jell-O, then found his niche with Fidelity. He'd made vice president. Twelve years had passed since Mosul. As we talked, Iraqi and American forces were fighting to take the city from Islamic State, the terror group that rose amid the ashes of the US occupation. Blind took a deep swig of his beer, then placed the jar on the mahogany counter.

"I can't say anyone would have been able to exactly predict the extent to which our lives would change," he said, staring into the polished wood. "But we were already thinking about our brothers in the field. The big recruiting pitch from when we showed up in '98, that America hadn't been to war since Vietnam, that we could get a free education, play sports, serve our country, and move on? That was suddenly null and void. It was time to grow up."

Team huddle before Army versus Rosslyn Park
match in March 2002.

Brothers

On D-Day, June 6, 1944, on Omaha Beach in Normandy, American soldiers fought their way ashore. Nearly sixty years later, on March 26, 2002, West Point rugby came to visit.

"It was low tide," said Brian McCoy. "Me and Joey Emigh walked all the way out to the waterline, where you couldn't go any further, and then we turned around. Just seeing the vast amount of beach that had to be covered, and looking at the pillboxes and what a disadvantage we were at? That is something I will never forget."[1]

The players collected stones from the beach.

McCoy said, "When you get thirty-four rugby players together, in Europe, the memories sorta . . . pass by. After the socials, you know. But Normandy? That is one spot. We studied American history, world history, military history. We were well versed in the tactics and everything behind it. But when we got there, we were standing in the pits where the bombs fell, where our ships just pummeled that coast. And then the cemetery there, how well done it was. How respectful. Walking through it all, with the guys you know are going to do the same sort of thing . . .

"We watched *Band of Brothers* constantly. Any bus trip we went on. I could quote Easy Company for you. Normandy was certainly outstanding."

The HBO miniseries *Band of Brothers* followed one company of the 101st Airborne Division from D-Day to Hitler's Alpine retreat. The title came from the speech in Shakespeare's *Henry V*, which gave West Point rugby its creed: "For he today that sheds his blood with me shall be my brother." *Band of Brothers* premiered on September 8, 2001.[2] Three days later, America was at war once again.

The cadets would have watched war movies anyway. In 1998 there was *Saving Private Ryan* and in 2002 came *We Were Soldiers* and *Black Hawk Down*. There was always *Platoon*, the film Jim Gurbisz badgered his dad to watch, and countless other movies about Vietnam. But *Band of Brothers* came in weekly shots. The players were hooked.

"I had to tape *Band of Brothers* and send it up to West Point," Ken Gurbisz said.[3]

"*The Sopranos* too," said his wife, Helen, "because believe it or not, Jim and Clint and Pete, they didn't have TV up there at the time in their rooms. So we would tape *The Sopranos* and *Band of Brothers*, and they'd take it to their community room and watch."

"*Band of Brothers*," Ken repeated, with a smile. "The greatest generation. And then at West Point, they're all going airborne all over again. They're going to helicopter school. They volunteer for light infantry."

ON OCTOBER 7, 2001, the United States invaded Afghanistan.[4] At home, someone was sending letters laced with anthrax. Five people died. Hawkish politicians pushed a connection to Saddam Hussein.[5] They urged Bush to hit Iraq.[6] Cadets were desperate to do their bit. A rumor spread: the Class of '02 would graduate early, like some in World War II, and go east to fight. The rumor came to nothing. But in November, as the Taliban were defeated at Mazar-i-Sharif, Branch Night came along.[7]

Every September, firsties name the branch in which they want to serve, making ranked choices. Two months later, on Branch Night in Eisenhower Hall, they discover their fate. There are remarks from a graduate and the commandant.[8] In November 2001, Brigadier General Eric Olsen said, "It is freedom that works miracles in America. And it is freedom that is being threatened, that is under attack. It's freedom that you are sworn to defend. And tonight you take another decision on the path to serve this nation, to defend that freedom."[9]

Then the first captain, the highest-ranking cadet, barked, "Open envelopes." The envelopes contained branch insignia. As David Lipsky put it, "Infantry has two crossed rifles, which, because the work is very hazardous, the cadets call 'idiot sticks.'"[10] In November 2001, a lot of cadets, a lot of them high on *Band of Brothers*, hoped their envelope contained idiot sticks. Among those on the rugby team, those who wanted their idiot sticks found them.

"I think Coach Mahan was particularly proud that we all went combat arms," Pete Chacon said. "There was a group of us that were all kind of the higher rank in our class, like Mo, Blinder, myself, Zac. Jimmy and Klutman were in the mix too. We all went straight infantry. We weren't going into finance or something."[11]

Jeremiah Hurley and Clint Olearnick chose infantry too. Scott Radcliffe chose armor. Jerrod Adams and Brian McCoy chose flight school. Joe Emigh wanted to fly but didn't have the grades, so he chose field artillery. Bryan Phillips, Nic Wybaczynsky, and Dave Little chose air defense.

Fired up by 9/11, more than two hundred members of the Class of '02 made infantry their first choice. The army took them all, thereby "bumping ROTC [Reserve Officers' Training Corps] cadets around the country into field artillery and military police."[12] West Pointers are sometimes resented as "ring knockers," a favored few pushed to the front of the queue.[13] Among West Pointers, it comes with the turf. Among West Point rugby players, there are relentless turf wars. Kevin Lynch, Class of '03, told me of an email sent by Jim.

"He listed every senior on the team and their branches. It read, 'infantry, not infantry,' next to each name, like that. And he didn't just send that out to the team, I believe he sent it out to the whole rugby network. To anyone that wasn't infantry, it was basically saying, like, 'You don't matter to me.'"

Lynch laughed. "Jimmy always had to play *Band of Brothers* on the damn bus rides. He was just so pumped to be infantry."[14]

True to its cherished outsider status, the rugby team does not feature much in *Surviving West Point*, the documentary Daniel Christman commissioned from *National Geographic*. But on Post Night, in

February, when the cameras followed Brian Clymer, the top-ranked cadet, into Eisenhower Hall, Mo Greene, another classroom high-flier, was with him. According to academic rank, the plum assignments—Italy, Germany—went first. After that, the postings nobody wanted. Fort Polk, Louisiana. Fort Sill, Oklahoma.

AFTER THE Ohio State game a few days before 9/11, things went according to plan for West Point rugby. On September 22, West Point beat Amherst 80–0 on Daly Field. Rugby being a brutal business, the only drawback was a concussion for Jim Gurbisz, who, Jerrod Adams noted, "did manage to send several others to the sideline." Kevin Dagon, a junior, came on at hooker. In the backs, another junior, Tim Lawton, replaced Adams on the wing, and a sophomore, Eric Stanbra, came on for Joe Emigh at center when Joe hurt his ankle. Rugby is attritional. Squad size counts. So does player safety. In 2002, though, West Point operated with a trainer and little else. Players often played injured. A week after Amherst, the A side went to Rhode Island, where it beat Brown, 43–5. As Adams wrote, Gurbisz, playing a week after a concussion that would usually carry a mandatory three weeks' rest, "lowered his head and bulldozed his way across the line for a try."

At the start of October, the University of Connecticut was beaten 29–8 at home. Mo Greene got a try from fly half, and Trent Geisler, a dynamic sophomore who had pushed Clint Olearnick from flanker to center, got two. Bryan Phillips—all six foot eight and three hundred pounds of him—got the other try. "Lineout to maul on the five-meter line," he recalled years later. Second row forwards remember their tries—even those scored by helping push a maul, the contest for the ball held off the ground, slowly over the line.

"I think every try I scored in college came from that maul. I was always the one coming around to cover up the ball. I was too big to lift. Coach Mahan wanted me driving the maul. And then all I had to do was look down and see the line and then fall down on the ball. I could do that."[15]

The stiffest tests of the autumn came from Norwich, a military academy in Vermont, and Dartmouth in New Hampshire. West Point beat Norwich 10–5, Dartmouth 33–29. Reporting the Dartmouth game in the *Old Gray* newsletter, Adams described "a beautiful fall afternoon, the sidelines packed with supporters." My future sister-in-law, a rugby player who made a US squad, was there among the crowd. She remembers a sharp edge to the game, including Vietnam-era catcalls—Army players derided as "baby killers," no less—but also post-match drinks in nearby bars.

By then, Nik Wybaczynsky was out for the season with an injured ankle, and Mo Greene had hurt his shoulder. Fly half was the fulcrum of the team. Next man up was a plebe, Liam Marmion. He had an advantage: born in the United States but brought up in Ireland, he'd played rugby at school. Back in the United States, he enlisted as an Army Ranger, planning to do three years before going back to Ireland to study law. Instead, he applied for West Point and spent a year at the prep. In Beast, in the searing heat of June 2001, Marmion had to do what Jeremiah Hurley told him to do. Hurley, himself a convert from wrestling, told the plebe with the Irish accent that he should come play rugby. Marmion started out at fullback, but Matt Blind, the captain, played there. So Marmion switched to fly half just as Mo Greene went down.

"Mo was the general," Marmion said, "probably the most tactically knowledgeable in the group and a brilliant, brilliant dude, like one of the smartest students I've ever seen."[16]

He was also ferociously hard on the man now wearing his shirt.

"He bullied the shit out of me. All year. I thought he hated me. I don't think he did, but I never had a pleasant time with him, until the point on our tour when I scored a try against the French team. Shannon Worthan [Liam's partner, the scrum half] set it up. He did the work. And Mo came over, like, *ran* over to me, and he's like, 'Brother, you did it.' And I saw then that maybe there was a purpose to how he drilled me."

Every practice a gang fight. Every passing drill a pissing contest. Every drinking session fraught with pitfalls. All of it meant—most of the time—to work for the good of the team.

"They all treated me like a little brother," Marmion said. "Overall, they had my best interests in mind, for development and looking after. But I would still avoid the hell out of Jim Gurbisz, unless I had a good reason to be anywhere near him in practice. He was an awesome dude, but I knew my main job with him was to obey."

Bryan Phillips was happy to try to explain: "One thing that's ubiquitous, and I guess it carries on to this day, is the people we like the most, we tend to bust their balls the most. Liam was a fantastic rugby player—and Mo and Jim were like that with everybody. It wasn't unique. Probably, in a way, Mo was a little threatened by Liam. The kid who's backing you up is pretty damn good. How do you react to that? Couple that with the fact that it's Mo, who's got three Brahma bulls' worth of testosterone running through his veins? It's always going to be interesting."

Mo Greene started as a wing, moved to center, then became fly half in junior year when the first choice blew a knee. Greene injured his shoulder away from the rugby field, "the summer between my junior and senior year, and then it just kept getting dislocated."

As for driving Liam Marmion hard, he was quite clear why: "At West Point, there are tribes of people that are cut from the same cloth. And the rugby team was definitely my people. The thing it gave me, for better or worse, was an escape from the academy life . . . a place to go. A place to be with your brothers. A tribe to pour yourself into, emotionally and physically. Absolutely draining practice, or a game? That was what kept me going, made me able to persist through the drudgery of academy life."[17]

If Greene couldn't play, he was going to make damn sure the man who could played well. He was going to play *through* him, to be as hard on Marmion as he would be on himself. And as Marmion was a plebe, life wasn't easy anyway.

Bryan Phillips said, "I talked to Liam five or six years ago. He came to town when his old roommate, Tyler Stegeman, got married. And Liam still tells stories about me, quote-unquote, 'hazing' him in the mess hall. One of my favorite games to play was Mystery Cupcakes. We had ten people at the table, and we'd get two packages of six cupcakes, so we'd have extra. So I would cut the tops off of the cakes and fill them with random condiments, and make the underclassmen play, you know, cupcake roulette. Every once in a while, you get a cupcake filled with honey. Another time, you might get it filled with No. 1 hot sauce. To me, that was pretty low-stakes stuff. But to hear Liam tell it, you know, I was really giving him the run-through. Tyler hasn't let go of that story either, for the record. But at the end of the day, at least from my perspective, we wanted to look out for those guys. I mean, we didn't want to take anything away from their 'cadet experience,' but there's an expectation that you kind of take care of your own. And Liam and Tyler ended up kind of the stars of the '04–'05 rugby team, so . . ."

Job done.

ON OCTOBER 3, 2009, in Afghanistan, the Taliban launched an all-out attack on Command Outpost Keating, a remote US base. The battle passed into legend in large part thanks to *The Outpost*, a book by CNN anchor Jake Tapper.[18] In the Hollywood adaptation, Scott Eastwood (son of Clint) plays Staff Sergeant Clinton Romesha, who won the Medal of Honor.[19] In 2016, Romesha published *Red Platoon*, his own account of the battle. He described how his platoon came together: "Civilians often harbor the impression that a platoon consists of a 'band of brothers,' but that's almost never the case. Any time that you throw nineteen or twenty young men together, not all of them are going to get along. And in the army, that tendency is further torqued by the fact that not everyone is a badass. The upshot is that you tend to wind up with a tight nucleus of insiders who like and trust one another, orbited by a scattered cluster of loners who never seem to fit in."[20]

For *platoon*, read *rugby team*.

To call any of the West Point players in the Class of '02 loners would be to overstate the case, but as in any team there were those who did not sit at its heart. There were those who were not first choice. There were those who did not drink, or drank less. There were those who sometimes took the brunt of the ball-breaking.

"I doubt anybody's really said much about me," Scott Radcliffe said.[21] "But I kind of do my own thing. And that doesn't fit in super well, in the army. I was kind of in the middle of things in football, and I kind of ended up like that in rugby too. They stuck me in the second row because I was tall but then they figured out I could run a little bit, so then they put me at number 8. But I played all over the place. I played flanker, a little bit of center, in desperation I played on the wing. A lot of the time, I was around the margins. At a dinner, around graduation, Coach Mahan said something that really touched me. He said, 'I wish I'd found a spot for Scott,' or something like that. He didn't know what to do with me, I think. And so I was kind of stuck on the B side for a lot of the time. Or on A side, I would get in for the last bit of the second half or whatever."

Radcliffe had his chances when Bryan Phillips or Dave Little were hurt, but "they didn't get hurt very much." The B side or the C side, Radcliffe said, could feel "like the land that time forgot." Zac Miller was down there too. He didn't mind so much. As captain, he had a job to do for Coach Mahan and for those he led. It was all part of an education Miller took very seriously indeed. But though he was a math genius who never saw a scholarship he didn't like, he had a sense of mischief too. R. J. Johnson, with Jay Landgraf one of two soccer players who became Miller's closest friends, said, "He sat behind me in our room. One day I'm sitting there working, and the icons on my desktop start moving around. And I'm like, 'The hell?' And I hear snickering. What's so funny? And Jay's laughing like hell. 'Man, like, what's going on?' And Zac's controlling my desktop. He was hacking the West Point network, just to mess with my computer."[22]

At any college, mischief often goes with chances to drink. Zac Miller didn't drink, and he wasn't the sort of cadet who ran his mouth off in bars. But he was there when someone did, one Saturday in early 2002 at Colgate University in Hamilton, New York, 160 miles northwest of West Point.

Jay Landgraf said, "We left the bar, and sure enough, like, the entire Colgate football team jumps out of a clown car. There's twenty of them. Like, oh my gosh. Someone throws a punch. I fall on the ground. I look up and Zac is pulling some guy off me. And then he gets kind of sucker-punched, and in the end he has to get stitches. The great follow-up is that he's walking around school with a black eye and stitches and one of the professors looks at him and says, 'Zac? Rhodes scholars don't get in bar fights.'"[23]

Zac Miller won the Rhodes, and with it two years at Oxford, in December 2001. It superseded the Truman scholarship he had also won and the Marshall scholarship for which he applied.[24] He wasn't the only star in the class. Rob Smith and Erica Watson also won Rhodes scholarships[25] and Anne McClain, the future rugby international and astronaut whom Zac had known in Pennsylvania, was one of three Marshall scholars.[26] But Miller's brilliance was clear. It wasn't that he didn't have grades below A—there was a B in history, first term '98–'99, even a B-minus in unit fitness three years later—but you had to hunt to find them. Conversely, in his scholarship applications, you didn't have to look hard to find reference to rugby. The Truman form asked for "additional personal information." He wrote, "My name is Zac Miller, and I am a rugby player. Contrary to popular belief, the statement above is not step one of a twelve-step process. I consider myself supremely fortunate to be part of the Army Rugby Team. For the past three years, I have learned so much from my teammates—not so much lessons about rugby but lessons about teamwork, dedication, and devotion to a cause greater than one's self."

Miller also made reference to rugby cliché: that it was a sport "described as everything from 'organized mayhem' to 'elegant violence,'" that most people believed "rugby players must be somewhere between slightly crazy and certifiably insane." He also quoted *Henry V:* "'For he today that sheds his blood with me shall be my brother.' To most people, that quote is little more than the antiquated words of Shakespeare, written centuries ago. For my teammates and me, those words represent a way of life. 'Brothers' is the motto of Army Rugby; it is something that permeates the team, written on our jerseys and shouted before every practice and before every game."

Miller told the world too—or the part of it that watched CNN. Broadcasting from West Point on March 15, 2002, the day before the academy's two hundredth birthday, Anderson Cooper interviewed Miller and Libby Haydon, another high achiever.[27] Both described how life had changed since 9/11. Both described their plans. Cooper asked Haydon what it was like to be a woman at West Point. Of Miller, who towered over him, broad shouldered and smiling, Cooper asked what had been the hardest part of West Point.

Miller said, "Probably being on the Army rugby team and being around a group of individuals that strives for excellence every year. Doing that, going out to practice every day, being challenged by your teammates to work hard. That's probably the hardest things I had to do here, and one of the most rewarding."

The comment caught the attention of the superintendent. Rosalyn Miller said[28] that Lieutenant General Lennox collared Miller at the Russian Tea Room in New York City that night, at a celebratory ball. Lennox said he hadn't been shocked at all. "I thought it was funny as heck he would do that. You know, we go after scholars, athletes, and leaders, and he was all three."[29]

Professors gave references. Their letters followed a pattern: descriptions of academic brilliance, slight bemusement about rugby. Recommending Zac Miller for a Marshall scholarship, Thomas Lainis, professor of physics, described an ability to "measure the terminal velocity of coffee filters using linear regression techniques." He also described watching Miller "motivating players, organizing plays, and reinforcing the coach's instructions."[30] Also for the Marshall, David A. Nash, assistant professor of electrical engineering and computer science, described "the most extraordinary student I have encountered during ten years of undergraduate teaching," a "natural leader . . . not in the least bit self-absorbed" who "puts me in mind of scholars like Descartes." He also noted that Miller "would often appear in class after a weekend's rugby tournament with spectacular bruises and cuts."[31]

Among scholarships, the Rhodes is the brightest prize. In October 2001, Miller was part of a group of potential scholars who went down to Harlem to meet Bill Clinton, who won a Rhodes in 1968. The former president, Miller told his hometown paper, was "down to earth and displayed a good sense of humor."³² Like Pete Dawkins, the great Army football star, Clinton played rugby at Oxford.³³

In mid-October, two majors wrote to Dr. Vishwajit L. Nimgaonkar, a Rhodes administrator at the University of Pittsburgh. Major Donovan D. Phillips, chief of institutional research and analysis, described Miller's work on complex problems, including a project that won first prize from the Society of Industrial and Applied Mathematics, and his frustration over an A-minus in his first term, which remained his only math score below A. Phillips wrote, "More impressive than what he has *done* is his *approach* to learning. Nothing is ever quite finished . . . it can always be improved."³⁴

The other letter was from Chris Starling, who helped Mike Mahan coach rugby. Starling, who had the buzz cut and bark of a true Marine, described his time with Miller through practice, games and "long hours on planes, buses, or in hotels outside college towns." He described how Miller managed a thirty-eight-thousand-dollar budget and built a website and marketing plan. He described how Miller led the lower sides, managing younger cadets, looking after visiting teams. He described how Miller applied himself to the game. Starling wrote that he "first noticed Zac as a player with great potential, one who would be great at rugby if he could unlearn American football. One of my first distinct memories as a coach was watching Zac on a particularly hot fall day during a grueling series of contact drills. The intensity in Zac's eyes reflected his physical determination to get the most out of himself during ladder sprints . . . a sadistic version of wind sprints in which hundred-yard sprints are combined with varying quantities of push-ups and sit-ups . . . From then on, I kept my eye on Zac."

Rhodes scholarships are awarded after rounds of interviews. Zac Miller was grilled in Pittsburgh and New York. Rosalyn Miller said that when her son showed up in Pittsburgh, he recognized kids he'd seen in advanced classes and weekend courses from the seventh grade on.

"He was trying to calm everybody down and telling them they would do a good job. These were his competitors, and yet he was rooting for them. So anyway, the next weekend they had interviews in New York, and then the Rhodes people deliberated. And then they came in and announced the scholarships in front of everybody. So four people that were chosen would be elated, and all the ones that were not would be heartbroken. We knew Zac would call us. We were both on the phone. I just said, 'Well?' And he goes, 'You're talking to a Rhodes scholar.'"[35]

Miller had promised his roommates that if he won a Rhodes he would drink one beer in their company. He made good on the deal.

A FEW months later, on the flight to Europe in late March 2002, some rugby players had more than one. There are various versions of what happened on the plane from New York to Paris. Chris Starling tells one of them. He wasn't on the flight, having traveled ahead, but he did have to smooth things over after touchdown.

He was familiar with such work.

Starling was there on the bus leaving Ohio State in September 2001, watching Jerrod Adams's mad dash not to be left behind: "He had on his head, like, a twelve-pack container, like a helmet, and he came running up. It was freaking hilarious. By the grace of God, I never reported any of those things. I had to laugh about it. You know, I'd try to scare them a bit. 'You're a goddamn idiot, Adams!' You know, make him think I was gonna write him up or do something. But I never did."

The New York to Paris situation was of a different order. This is how Starling remembers it.[36]

"So what happened was on the flight over, there was a flight attendant, and the cadets were kind of mocking this person's voice. And the person got annoyed. And while that person was asleep, some of the cadets went back to the drinks cart and they had a discussion. Like, 'Well, a cadet must not lie, cheat, or steal. But if the booze is free...' So they took all those little bottles and drank them. And that person woke up, I guess, and the booze was gone. The plane captain wrote this letter to the superintendent that said, 'I had these guys, they were rude to the flight attendant, and they drank the plane out of liquor.' And he said, 'I always thought service academy people were supposed to have the highest levels of decorum and discipline and behavior. From my experience in the Air Force, and ever since I've left, I found the opposite to be true.'

"I had to go have an appointment with the superintendent, Lieutenant General Lennox," Starling recalls. "I said, 'Sir, I have written a rebuttal of that letter.' I said, 'This guy obviously has a bone to pick with service academy graduates. The last part of his letter betrays that he has something stuck in his life from somebody from the Air Force Academy or the Naval Academy, and he's taking it out on us.' I said, 'You know, if the cadets had a couple of extra drinks on the plane, as soon as they got on the ground we were training because we were there to win games, not to get drunk.' And Lieutenant General Lennox, he was good with it. He just let it go.'"

It was a long flight. Starling shared pictures, shot on a digital camera, in the dawn's early light, somewhere over Europe. The images are grainy, low-res, as if seen through jet-lagged eyes. Cadets sleep. Zac Miller, unconscious in a neck pillow. Scott Radcliffe, head back, Brian McCoy passed out beside him. Clint Olearnick and Jim Gurbisz, slumped together askew. Pete Chacon, out cold in a middle seat. Not surprisingly, memories differ.

"So, what actually happened," Chacon said, "was we were drinking *with* the flight attendants. Blinder and J-Rod and me, we were in the back there, and the drinks ran out. They have, like, those little seals on drinks carts that you're not supposed to break. Who knows what the rules were. But they had these little, like, zip ties on. So Blinder passed out, J-Rod passed out, and I was, like, the last man standing, just bullshitting with these flight attendants like friends at a pub, waiting at the back of the plane. Well, they broke the seals. I didn't know any different. And we just kept drinking and kept having a good time, and eventually I went back to my seat. Apparently the pilot came back and was pissed because someone broke into the drinks carts. And a flight attendant totally blamed us, sold us out to cover their own ass. They were the ones that actually did it."[37]

Chacon also remembers a more immediate problem than a letter to Lieutenant General Lennox. The pilot, he said, radioed the Paris police.

"I was like, 'I didn't do anything! I literally did nothing.' I wasn't doing anything inappropriate. I was hanging out back there with them. I was like, 'What the hell?'"

Olearnick remembered "walking off the plane and seeing the captain standing there with his arms crossed, just shaking his head as we disembarked his plane. And I thought, 'What's this guy all frustrated about?' And I didn't think anything of it at the time."[38]

Starling grabbed Chacon. "He was totally organized. It was like an efficient plan. I got off the plane, and we just hauled ass through the airport. We got out and into a taxi. We went to the US embassy and then met up with everyone at the hotel later, when we were sure they weren't showing up there with the cops. So it was kinda funny..."

The tour was off and running. The squad was thirty-five cadets strong, eleven non-playing tourists too. There was Mike Mahan and his wife, Dorothy, and Chris Starling and his wife, Suzanne. There were the Carters, Bob and Marge, Bob a retired major general, a professor of behavioral sciences and rugby club chairman. There was Steve McCullough, a captain, assistant officer-in-charge, and his wife, Julie, and there was Kim Cokeley, the trainer. George and Joanne Emigh, Joe's parents, paid their own way to support their son.

The cadets were billeted at Satory, near Versailles. Starling's pictures show the barracks, the palace, and its gardens. A meal with wine. George Emigh bearded, Joanne beaming. A bar. Cadets smile, jet-lagged. The next morning, the Americans took a bus into Paris and Les Invalides, the gold-domed military hospital that houses Napoleon's tomb. The cadets wore suit jackets in boxy early-2000s cuts, button-down shirts, ties, and pleated chinos that billowed in the Parisian breeze. In a report for the Class of 1975, which helped finance the tour, Starling described how the governor of Les Invalides, General Bertrand Guillaume de Sauville de La Presle, "gave a moving overview and words of support for French and US efforts in the war on terrorism." The general is there in the pictures, with an aide in a pillbox hat.

On a bus tour of Paris, half the team lost the battle with jetlag. The camera caught them. Joe Emigh, passed out against a window. Jeremiah Hurley, yawing into the aisle. Jim Gurbisz, alert in a sea of sleepers, looking sharply out the window.

One picture shows Jason Williams, a big prop, held up by seat-belt alone. Like the fly half Liam Marmion, Williams was a plebe. The tour meant both missed Recognition, the ritual by which plebes are welcomed as full-fledged cadets. The team staged a ceremony in Europe.

They saw the Eiffel Tower, Notre Dame, the rest. The evening was free. This was Paris. There were bars. The next morning, the drive west to Brittany, flat French farmland a blur. Players passed out again. Zac Miller's glasses caught the sun. Clint Olearnick and Mo Greene, the lords of the back seat, were out cold. At a road-stop lunch, Brian McCoy dared eat andouillette, sausage made from tripe, the lining of a cow's stomach. At École Spéciale Militaire de Saint-Cyr, the cadets put on dress grays for a tour. They saw Napoleon's hat.

THE NEXT day, at last, there was action. Two games against Saint-Cyr. Jerrod Adams wrote the reports. The B side played first and scored first, Zac Miller securing a turnover to launch an attack, which ended in a try for Mike Ziegelhofer, a sophomore wing pushing Adams hard for a place in the As. The other wing, Tim Lawton, scored a second try, but the more experienced French team, officers reinforcing cadets, finished strongly to win 15–10.

On the same field of rough green grass, the A side dressed in black shirts, black shorts, and black socks to face a French team in blue. There was an early try from Dave Little. Photos show the pack at work. Jim Gurbisz, collar tucked in to deny opponents a grip, punches the ball up for the hit. His two props, Jeremiah Hurley and Andy Klutman, support. Bryan Phillips and Al Bairley—his second-row partner, a tall junior—head into a ruck to clear Frenchmen off the ball. Joe Emigh kicks for goal. Clint Olearnick plays with socks rolled down. Mo Greene looks on. Liam Marmion, Mo's project player, picks himself up from a hit. Jeremiah got a try, Shannon Worthan another, Pete Chacon three from the wing. The French scored a couple, but the Americans won 48–12.

Not a bad start to the tour.

Ceremonies followed. A meal and speeches. Mementoes presented. Old allies toasted.

Twenty years later, in the heat of a New York summer, I went out to Long Beach to meet Kevin Lynch, the 2003 grad who played second row for the Bs at Saint-Cyr. We went to a place with a deck out back, the Atlantic shallows below, Manhattan far off in the haze.

"Maybe Saint-Cyr was near the western front or maybe it wasn't," Kevin said, laughing, casting the scene back to the trenches of the First World War. "But they had all these old helmets on the wall. German, French, British, American. Typical post-match. Everyone's getting drunk. And soon guys are putting those helmets on and headbanging each other. I never knew there was a friendly way to headbutt, until that night. Clint was bleeding from his head, because he decided to get hold of the German one, with like the spear on it, and kind of headbutt things with that."[39]

The bleeding was stanched, the *pickelhaube* put back, the cadets rounded up. Next morning they were back on the bus. In Normandy, at Pointe-du-Hoc above Omaha Beach, the sky was a mournful gray.

German gun emplacements lay ruined, grown with yellow gorse. The cadets stood in contemplation, in ones and twos and threes. On D-Day, Army Rangers came up these cliffs under raking fire. In front of a shattered German position, the team unfurled a banner, the Class of '75. The cadets filed past American graves. Clint Olearnick wore a beret. It hid the gash from the headbanging. The cadets walked down to the sea. Olearnick, Dave Little, Joe Emigh, Jerrod Adams, Pete Chacon, and Mo Greene (right arm in a black sling), took a photo crouched at the edge of the dunes. In front, Jim Gurbisz sprawled in a parody of a firing position, grimacing monstrously. Infantry, not infantry. *Band of Brothers*. Out on the beach, Bryan Phillips put stones in his backpack.

The bus to Le Havre. A motorway sign. *Tout droit*, a clothing store called Twickenham, named for the home of English rugby. A male model in a shirt and tie with a black eye made of rouge. A ferry across the Channel to Portsmouth, home of the Royal Navy, great gray ships berthed next to HMS *Victory*, Lord Nelson's flagship. There was more drinking on the crossing.

Bryan Phillips: "Um . . . we drank a lot of Newcastle Brown, fully knowing that we had practice later that day at Sandhurst. And a couple of guys didn't show up for practice."

This time, Coach Mahan was angry. The no-shows "were told they were not allowed to drink any more on the trip," Phillips said. "And I can personally vouch for it: they did not drink again on the tour. What they did do was slam about thirty Red Bulls every time we went out, which led to its own version of intoxication. But they did not drink any alcohol, for sure."

THE TEAM was billeted at Sandhurst, the Royal Military Academy, in the heathland south of London. On the first morning, Thursday, March 28, the players got back into dress gray for a tour. The Americans saw the chapel with its lists of British dead. India, Africa, World Wars I and II. Stone columns glowed in the sun. There was light practice and yet another bus ride, due south to Aldershot. The Bs would play the Oxford University Officer Training Corps, and the As would face Rosslyn Park.

I was there in the Rosslyn Park changing room as the cadets prepared next door. I put on my red-and-white hooped shirt, my blue shorts and socks, my gray scrum cap, and my black boots with metal cleats. I taped up my wrists, and I taped up my thighs for my prop to grip to lift me. All these years later, thanks to Chris Starling, I can now see what I could then only hear in the room next door.

Bare walls, magnifying the sound of cleats on concrete and the stretch-and-tear of tape. Zac Miller making the rounds, ears taped, talking to his players, to Jason Williams and Brent Pafford, his props, to Chris Starling, who wears a Marine Corps jacket. The Bs wear gray, the As yellow. Al Bairley and Bryan Phillips change. Rugby teams breed mini-brotherhoods, fire teams within squads, squads within the platoon. Lock forwards stick together. Equipment bags say "Brothers" on the side. Clint Olearnick listens to music, head wound smeared with grease.

Proust had his madeleine dipped in tea. I have the smell of Vaseline or Deep Heat, a cream for pain relief. One part per thousand in the air, and I'm back there, in the changing rooms, psyching up or limping in.

On the field, under the lights, Matt Blind gives a team talk, players huddled 'round. Scott Radcliffe listens, wearing a tracksuit, a replacement yet again. Olearnick and Chacon stand stone-faced. Years later, in Blind's study in Cohasset, I asked what he told his team at such times.

"You kind of have to let people be themselves and do their own thing," he said. "And you also need to recognize that if you're always the guy that's out there screaming and telling everybody what to do, then eventually, nobody's gonna listen to anything that you say."[40]

The players lift their arms, their fists above the huddle. West Point teams still do it. Almost twenty years to the day after Aldershot, I saw it on Old Gray weekend, up on the banks of the Hudson, before the A side beat Central Washington. At Aldershot, the camera got close to Jim Gurbisz. Collar tucked in, eyes closed, head bowed, a bruise by his eye.

The shout: "'Brothers' on three! One, two, three, 'Brothers!'"
Kickoff.

There's a reasonable chance I caught it. If so, I would have been hit by Al Bairley or Bryan Phillips, or maybe Brian McCoy, Dave Little, or Trent Geisler, running faster. West Point scored first, in Jerrod Adam's words sending in "three phases of punches" before Jeremiah Hurley "pounded through three defenders for the try." Chances are, one of those flattened tacklers was me.

Rosslyn Park scored from a quick penalty, tying the score 5–5, then ran in another, a backs move from a lineout. Maybe I won the ball, jumping in the middle. Another try, Park "executing continuous play well," according to Adams's postgame report. That would be music to the ears of our coach, Bob Fisher, a disciple of flat passes and moving the ball from contact, a fast game that took me by surprise when I came down from Yorkshire, where rugby was slower, big forwards spending happy time in mauls. At Aldershot, the score was 19–5 in Rosslyn Park's favor when Liam Marmion dropped a goal, the loudly celebrated score that had Park confused, given it only made it 19–8. We scored again before Shannon Worthan ran his own quick penalty from scrum half for a try. Halftime: 24–13.

By Adams's account—given from the sideline, Mike Ziegelhofer having ousted him from the team—the teams swapped tries in the second half. Worthan won a penalty try when Park repeatedly failed to retreat ten meters after infringing. Chances are, that was me, half drunk with fatigue. But Park "finished off the scoring with a penalty kick and a try off a stolen scrum to make the final score 41–20." In my diary, I had it down as 41–25. Whatever.

In Chris Starling's pictures, the game goes by in a blur. A West Point move breaks down, a scramble and sprawl of limbs, Matt Blind unsure whether to commit to the ruck. A lineout throw clears Al Bairley, lifted by Jeremiah Hurley and Andy Klutman, and the Rosslyn Park number 5—me—turns to watch a teammate catch the ball at the back. The ball goes wide. The forwards chase. I'm in step with Klutman while Clint Olearnick runs from the frame, off to reset his defense.

Another play: Jim Gurbisz smashes the ball up, shadowed by Jim Ryan, our pitilessly hard number 8. Another Park forward braces to take the hit. A West Point scrum, ball at the back with Dave Little, front rows rising but keeping their bind. Joe Emigh moves the ball, missing Olearnick to hit Blind at pace. Me again, stage right, mouth open, scrum cap knocked askew.

After the game, the cadets huddle again. Jim Gurbisz looks like he's in the mood for murder, his face rubbed raw in the scrums. The two teams pose together, with the banner from the Class of '75.

"I remember being very disappointed we didn't win," Bryan Phillips said. "I mean, we held ourselves in pretty high regard. And I think what it led to, honestly, was that there were different versions of *who* we actually played. We came home, and I remember some guys saying, 'Oh, we played this professional team over in England.' And then, you know, to come to find out it's, like, a men's club team? Much, much more experienced and well organized than any American equivalent, yes, but that's kind of a blow to the ego. So, I think the reputation of Park kind of got inflated when we got home."

In his tour report, Chris Starling called Rosslyn Park "a semi-professional team." Not so. Strictly amateur. But some of us had played on the fringes of the professional game—incredibly enough, me included.

West Point's Bs lost at Aldershot, too, 15–14 to the team from Oxford. In the bar, Blind and Miller presented shirts to the opposing captains. I talked to Phillips. He gave me a shot glass. Rosslyn Park players went back to London, the cadets back to Sandhurst.

THE NEXT day, the cadets got back into their coats and ties. First stop, Westminster. I was about twenty minutes north, in the *Rugby News* office on Capper Street, getting the May issue done. Outside parliament, a protester. A banner: "Genocide of Iraq infants, innocents! USA/GB—Stop Now!" The invasion was a year away, but Bush had decided on war.[41] The cadets walked north. Horse Guards Parade. In Trafalgar Square, Brian McCoy and Joey Emigh sat on a lion. In the afternoon, a tour of Twickenham. A few days before, in front of seventy-five thousand, England had beaten Wales 50–10. I was in the press box.

For the Sandhurst game on Saturday, the Brits put on a show for the visiting Americans. There were dignitaries to meet and a band in bearskin hats. The Bs played first. Tired out, they went down 43–0. The As came out all in black. The Brits wore red. The teams lined up for the anthems. In the Sandhurst team, all these years later, I spot a familiar face, Will Mawby, an Australian flanker two years behind me at Durham. A seriously good player, compact and hard, a real openside, linkman for forwards and backs. He's still in the British Army. He remembers the cadets had "awful mess dress compared to ours" and were "always going on about *Band of Brothers.*"[42] Brian McCoy fondly remembers a hit quite possibly dealt by Will: "I don't know the name of the guy who picked me up, but I'd know him if I saw him today. He said, 'Good pass,' and I said, 'Great hit,' and we got on with the game. My ribs could have been broken, but I was having the time of my life."[43]

The cadets lost 30–20, but not without a fight. McCoy scored first, diving for the line with two tacklers on him. It was 5–5 at the half, and after fifteen minutes of the second period the Americans were up by ten points, after tries by Andy Klutman and Shannon Worthan. But Joe Emigh couldn't add the conversions, and as Sandhurst came back hard, their kicker slotted one, putting them up 17–15. A penalty made it 20–15, another added three, and as the Americans tired, Sandhurst ran in a try for 30–15. A consolation: Trent Geisler scored the last try of the tour.

There was one last drink-up. A heroic one. The cadets wore dress gray. Their hosts wore black, their officers red. The room was lit by candles. Dinner. Speeches.

Back at the bar, collars were loosened. The camera kept clicking. Joe Emigh, with his parents. Matt Blind, listening to a British officer. Eric Stanbra, Liam Marmion, and Al Bairley, pints in hand, jackets off. Jim Gurbisz with Jason Williams, looking intense. Brian McCoy holding two pints of Guinness. Captain McCullough in a British cadet's jacket, the British cadet in his. Clint Olearnick, shirt off, drinking a beer on a table. Olearnick drinking a beer from a shoe. A line of pints. The shoe. A British officer, up on the table, Olearnick shouting at him, full-throated. Olearnick's werewolf tattoo. Olearnick and two British cadets, completely naked, downing pints. The end.

The tour was over. The team flew home. Chris Starling kept taking pictures. The Sky Map. The plane over Newfoundland. Clint Olearnick's head wound. The bus back from JFK. A dark sally port, the barracks yard beyond.

*The West Point Rugby team with Bob and Marge Carter
at graduation in June 2002.*

Finals

ALEXANDER R. NININGER was a member of the West Point class of 1941. In January 1942, he was awarded a posthumous Medal of Honor for his actions against the Japanese on Bataan.[1] At West Point in 1964, when all but a fraction of the old Central Area barracks were demolished, the remaining nineteenth-century structure, a square crenellated block with an elegant porch, was named Nininger Hall.[2] Today, it hosts the William E. Simon Center for the Professional Military Ethic, the hearing room for cadet disciplinary cases, and displays of cadet quarters through the years.

In 2006, the West Point Association of Graduates initiated the Alexander R. Nininger Award for Valor. The first recipient was Major Ryan Worthan, an infantry officer, rugby player in the Class of '97 and brother of Shannon Worthan, the scrum half who played at Aldershot in 2002.[3] Worthan was recognized for his part in a fight at Shkin, Afghanistan in late 2003. Accepting the award, he described the actions of soldiers, including First Lieutenant Craig Mullaney, the Rhodes scholar from the Class of 2000, and Private First Class Evan O'Neil, who was killed. Worthan also held up a rugby ball signed by that year's West Point team.

He said, "I believe West Point's fields of friendly strife do prepare cadets for combat. I believe this is true of all the sports you play here at West Point. Rugby is the sport I know best and has surprising similarities to combat. Rugby is eighty minutes of pushing yourself beyond your limits with little rest. Before a game ever starts, the game plan is briefed and all decisions after that are made on the fly by the players on the field. There is no visible clock, so there is no definite end in sight. You simply have to grind it out, shedding the anger, the pain, the exhaustion, staying focused, and trying to see the field develop, find your opponents' weakness, and then exploit it. On the rugby field and in combat, team members draw confidence and inspiration from leaders who are calm and upbeat even in the worst circumstances. You will find that your soldiers will not quit on you, as long as they see you pushing yourself and keeping your own spirits high."[4]

At West Point, there isn't much debate about whether rugby is useful for training officers. Coach Mike Mahan said, "There's no other sport like rugby. You're playing hurt, usually, you're exhausted, you have to make decisions on your own. There's not ten coaches talking to you, and headphones [as in football]. Every person, despite their differences in size, ability, speed, whatever, they all have their jobs, and you depend on them to do their job, and they depend on you to do your job. And that's the essence of what the military unit is. It's the fog of battle, all that stuff. It's just so apropos, except when you leave this field, you're not carrying away your dead and wounded. Well, you may carry away some . . ."[5]

You may carry them to Nininger Hall. That was where, one May morning in 2002, the rugby firsties gathered to fulfill a tradition. They all wore gray uniform jackets, and most wore kilts, a tartan of Army yellow and black. Pete Chacon and Jerrod Adams carried sabers. Adams carried a rugby ball. So did Joe Emigh, Clint Olearnick, Mo Greene, Jeremiah Hurley, and Brian McCoy. Striking mock heroic attitudes, they posed on the hall's steps and porch.

Pete Chacon centers the picture, sitting on the third step, leaning on his saber, looking off to his right. Standing around him are Adams, Gurbisz, Emigh, and Olearnick. Gurbisz has one hand in his jacket, as though seeing Napoleon's tomb and hat on tour in France had made a lasting impression. Gurbisz, Emigh, and Olearnick are barefoot. Chacon wears shoes. Adams wears cleats and rugby socks. All gaze into the distance.

Andy Klutman stands stern and square, the only cadet looking straight at the camera. Scott Radcliffe leans on a railing, looking away to his left. Jeremiah Hurley mirrors him, gazing up to the sky. Mo Greene holds a ball in his good arm while Zac Miller sits on the balustrade, hands in his lap, lifting his face to the sun. Matt Blind and Brian McCoy stand on the rails of the porch of Nininger Hall, Blind at attention, arms to his sides, one shoulder braced against a column, McCoy holding a ball in one hand and a column with the other. Behind them all, at the apex of the composition, a sheer wall of a man: Bryan Phillips, looking down, his face a pattern of shadows.

The photographer printed the picture in sepia, enhancing its willfully archaic tone. In May 2015, when I went to West Point the first time, Coach Mahan put the picture out on his desk. I would work out that two players were not there: Nik Wybaczynsky, who'd barely played because of injury, and Dave Little, who barely made it anywhere on time and simply missed the photo shoot.

Mahan was preparing to step down from a job he'd filled for nearly thirty years. We were surrounded by cartons and cases. He pointed to three players. Less than four years after the picture was taken, all three were dead.

IN SPRING 2002, a month or two before their dramatic senior photo, the team returned to the field. On the first weekend of April, they went to the Cherry Blossom Tournament hosted by the Washington Rugby Club on the National Mall. In shortened games, the cadets beat Georgetown and Le Moyne on Saturday, Virginia Tech and Penn State on Sunday. They lost the final to Navy, 12–5. The next weekend, the national Sweet Sixteen tournament was at West Point. On Saturday, the cadets beat Virginia Tech 37–7. That booked a Sunday quarterfinal against Saint Mary's from Palo Alto, California.

"The sun was shining," Adams wrote to the Old Gray. "Six members from the West Point Sport Parachute team landed on the midfield line with the game ball, and senior cadet Josephine Holmon performed a beautiful rendition of the national anthem to set the tone for the match."

The Internet Archive yields pictures. Shannon Worthan kicks to touch as Jim Gurbisz, Jeremiah Hurley, and Andy Klutman look on. Joe Emigh runs toward his center partner, Clint Olearnick. Worthan runs a penalty close to the visitors' line. Defenders rush forward. Worthan has faked a pass to Brian McCoy and run past Jim Gurbisz and Andy Klutman. Dave Little is closer to the camera, obscuring Jeremiah Hurley and Trent Geisler, the big flanker who is about to take the ball from Worthan and crash over the line for a try. Years later, at Matt Blind's place in Massachusetts, when plenty of drink had been taken, Hurley looked at the picture and laughed.

"No one could match that move," said the Special Forces lieutenant colonel, full of bourbon, bravado, and bullshit—a very rugby cocktail. "Everyone was scared of us."

"We weren't," I said, full of the same, recalling Rosslyn Park at Aldershot.

A moment of silence. Laughter.

Against Saint Mary's in the Sunday quarterfinal, Liam Marmion scored twice and the game finished 30–13. The cadets had made the Final Four alongside Utah, Wyoming, and Cal. Cal—the Golden Bears from the University of California, Berkeley—had won eleven titles in a row, eighteen since 1980. Nobody wanted to draw Cal in the semi. Army did.

The finals were played over two days at the Virginia Beach Sportsplex. Saturday, May 4, was wet. The field would cut up, which would favor the huge Cal pack. Still, as Adams wrote, "Army fans were in the stands cheering on the Black Knights as they kicked off" the game. Again, the Internet Archive yields pictures. Army forwards in black watch Cal take a lineout unopposed. The two packs contest the resulting maul. Wearing blue, gold, and white hoops, Cal set up a drive. Andy Klutman has worked his way through the Cal pack, toward the ball at the back. Jeremiah Hurley waits to make a tackle or join the maul. Shannon Worthan and Jim Gurbisz stand off. The referee, in green, tells Army to stay onside.

Shortly after this picture was taken, barely two minutes into the game, Gurbisz's world changed forever. As he ran, his cleats caught in the grass, his knee turned, and he fell to the ground in pain.

Coach Mahan said, "It was obvious immediately that Jimmy's injury was severe enough to remove him from the match with seventy-eight minutes left to play. I had a qualified replacement who was almost as skilled as Jim"—Kevin Dagon, a junior—"but was half his size. As he ran onto the pitch and Jimmy was helped off, you could feel the air come out of the team. His departure foretold the result."[6]

Cal's forward pack was huge. A couple of players, a prop and a flanker, had already played for the Eagles, the US national team. For the cadets, an uphill climb grew steeper.

Mike Ziegelhofer, the sophomore wing, scored a first-half try, intercepting a pass. But at halftime the cadets were down 17–5 and creaking under the strain. They gave way. Adams's report deals with the horror in one terse paragraph. The match ended 59–5.

Coach Mahan said, "Through the clouds of my memory, one picture is crystal clear. Jim sitting on the sideline, tears running down his face as one teammate after another sat with him and embraced him, oblivious to the action on the field."

History turns on moments. What-ifs. Jim Gurbisz's left knee had been a problem in high school. He'd had surgery. At West Point, said his closest friend, Clint Olearnick, "He'd had trouble since the first year. Just watching him, you could tell he was in pain, constantly. But he was always fighting through. He would go until he couldn't. That was his MO. He would give you 110 percent until he couldn't. And that was it. He was done."[7]

"It was his ACL," said his dad, Ken. His anterior cruciate ligament. "He tore it. They said it wasn't that bad, but it never really healed properly."[8]

In a split second, Gurbisz's Army rugby was done. His band of brothers, the cause that kept him going through four brutal years. Done. He would never wear the shirt again. But a darker thought hovered. In a month or two, Gurbisz was due to report to Fort Benning to become an infantry officer. To live his dream. To swap one band of brothers for another. In the infantry, second lieutenants need a lot of things. Working knees are one.

Gurbisz's girlfriend, Tori Richardson, had driven down to Virginia from Jersey.

"I was coming down for the after-party," she said. "I pulled up, and he's waiting outside on crutches. And I'm like, 'What?' He's basically just like, 'Damn, my knee went completely backwards.' And I went on a bit of a tirade about not taking care of his body. 'I can't believe you've injured that knee again, and you already had knee surgery. How can you do this? You haven't even made it to like, twenty-two yet, and you've got multiple terrible injuries from playing sports! How is this all worth it? You're getting hurt!'"[9]

Tori had dealt with Jim's injuries before. The knee. The day she skipped a high school Thanksgiving football game and he called from the hospital to say, "Someone put their helmet right into my chest, and I thought I broke my heart." Now, though, she looked ahead.

"It was pretty much known that after graduation, at some point, they're all going to war. So I mean, of course, part of me was like, 'Yeah, sure. Hurt yourself enough that you don't have to go.' On the one hand, it's like, 'Oh no.' But if it's really bad? Desk job. You know, headquarters company, just keeping track of things. Taking inventory. On-base things like that."

That was Jim Gurbisz's greatest fear. He wanted infantry *bad*.

The loss to Cal stung. On Sunday, the cadets would play for third. On Saturday night, Mike Mahan imposed a curfew.

The coach said, "The team had not reacted appropriately to Jim's injury. On Saturday evening in the hotel and on Sunday before the game, we discussed how in combat, sometimes you lose a particularly good fighter or a good leader. Your team must be prepared to fight all the harder when that occurs. Others needed to step up. We decided that in Sunday's game, the last for the class of 2002, we would all step up. Wyoming were tough and gritty, but every member of the class of 2002 would play, regardless of his place on the roster. The team had to turn around from the disaster on Saturday."

As Jerrod Adams wrote, all the seniors "knew it would be their last game and fiercely wanted to go out with a win." It turned out to be a fierce fight, a real forwards' struggle. Kevin Dagon, Gurbisz's replacement at hooker, scored the first try after eighteen minutes, "trudging his way across the goal line after multiple rucks." Before halftime, Wyoming mauled the ball over the line for a try of their own. The game stayed level at 5–5 until, "with only five minutes left to play, Army found themselves deep in Wyoming territory and senior prop Andy Klutman powered his way through four defenders for the go-ahead try, scrum half Shannon Worthan converting the kick." Wyoming had to be repelled one last time. The brothers held firm to win, 12–5.

One of the B side players who got to play his part was Zac Miller. He got stuck in with the rest.

Coach Mahan said, "I remember Zac coming off with a huge smile on his face. He was almost delirious with joy. It was incredible. The class of 2002 finished the year as number three of some five hundred men's collegiate teams. I am very proud of that team."

That Sunday night, the team went out for a drink.

In 2015, Matt Sherman succeeded Mike Mahan as West Point coach. But in 2002, Sherman was Cal's fly half. On Sunday night in Virginia Beach, he got separated from his team.

"I ended up in a place with a bunch of Army guys," he said. "I remember Joe Emigh. I hung out with him. We spent a good hour drinking and talking. And I remember that the Pennywise song came on. 'Bro Hymn.' The Army guys went *ballistic*. There I was, looking around, thinking, 'Wow, I'm the only Cal guy around. I probably need to go find my people.' But I had a good time with those guys, just hung out."[10]

Pennywise is a punk rock band from Hermosa Beach, California, not far from where Joe Emigh grew up. "Bro Hymn" was written in 1991, in memory of friends who died young, two in motorcycle accidents, one by drowning.[11] Among the lyrics: "If you're ever in a tough situation / We'll be there with no hesitation / Brotherhood's our rule we cannot bend." It wasn't Shakespeare. It wasn't even System of a Down. But in the summer of 2002, to cadets facing the end of their rugby team and the start of life in an army at war, it had intense appeal.

There was one last bit of rugby business. The Old Gray game, which Jim, as social secretary, had spent a year preparing. Some alumni had a good reason for missing it: deployment. It was played in the traditional spirit. The commandant, Brigadier General Eric Olson, suited up for five minutes on the cadets' team. The Old Gray fielded grads from 1964—Bull Jackman, one of the originals—to 1994. Major Field, the British exchange officer, refereed the first half, then played against the cadets in the second. After the game, two old grads gave a presentation about plans for a permanent home for Army Rugby, then focused on Stony Lonesome, the rough spot used for training. Then the cadets came together, under the posts, for a final photo.

It was a blazing day, trees in full leaf, sky brilliant blue. Brian McCoy and Jim Gurbisz held an Army Rugby banner. Like Mo Greene, whose shoulder was still a problem, Gurbisz was in civilian clothes. A rugby shirt and jeans. Clint Olearnick placed a hand on his shoulder. Four cadets held another banner: "We few, we happy few, we band of brothers, for he today that sheds his blood with me shall be my brother—Shakespeare, *Henry V*." Nik Wybaczynsky was there, having put his boots on at last. Bryan Phillips draped an arm around Zac Miller, who stood with Joe Emigh, arms round shoulders, smiling ear to ear.

EVERY YEAR, before graduation, West Point hands out awards. On May 31, 2002, in Eisenhower Hall, Zac Miller won a sackful. He was frustrated to finish eleventh in the class—Mo Greene was fourth—but he would graduate with honors, Phi Kappa Phi, Upsilon Pi Epsilon. He won the Colonel Herbert Bainbridge Hayden Memorial Award for the highest standing in basic sciences, and he won prizes named for two famous grads: the Robert E. Lee Memorial Award for core mathematics; the Ulysses S. Grant Memorial Award for core science. Lee was a southern aristocrat, Grant a northern bulldog. The Lee prize was a ceremonial sword, the Grant a pewter tray. Twenty years later, Lee's name was removed from his prize.[12] But his name is still engraved on the case that holds Miller's sword on the wall of his bedroom back in Stoneboro, Pennsylvania. Miller also won an award given by West Point professor Bob Carter and his wife Marge Carter for academic achievement within the rugby team.

There were celebratory dinners, including an evening back in Pennsylvania. In pictures, Miller towers over his parents. His brother Nate, friends, relatives, and teachers all beam with pride. Keith and Rosalyn Miller had a video made, commemorating all the graduation celebrations, soundtracked by the national anthem, West Point songs, and other patriotic tunes.

Graduation day dawned hot. George W. Bush was coming to speak. By the time Michie Stadium opened, many family members were sweating. As Keith Miller said, "The problem of having the president doing the speech is that when he moves, nothing else moves."[13] Worse: a bus with handicapped access, which Rosalyn needed, hadn't shown up.

Rosalyn said, "The buses park way up on the hill. Keith said, 'If you can get your foot on that step, I'll get you on the bus.' And so he did, and we were on one of the first buses down to the stadium. We got in on time. But the bus John and Nina Landgraf were on, it stopped. And the driver wasn't going to let them off. And they were like, 'Our children are graduating from West Point, there's no way you're going to keep us here.' And so they all ran right down the hill."

The other parents—George and Joanne Emigh, who brought Marianne; Ken and Helen Gurbisz, who came with Tori; the Blinds, Olearnicks, Radcliffes, and the rest—were there too. Some attended a Friday night banquet addressed by Rudy Giuliani, recently stepped down as mayor of New York, a national figure since 9/11. On graduation day, news crews filmed. When the cameras panned away, you could see families hurrying into the stands.

West Point graduates are known as the Long Gray Line.[14] The cadets about to join that line filed into Michie Stadium. They wore white caps, gray jackets with gold buttons and white belts, white gloves, a red sash at the waist, and white uniform trousers. They carried sabers. They were a thousand, give or take. On film they form a long gray sentence punctuated by dark exclamation marks: Secret Service agents on the president's route to the dais.

Zac Miller and Mo Greene are part of the last group of cadets to enter: academic stars, those in command positions. All stand to attention. Lieutenant General Lennox introduces dignitaries. George Pataki, Republican governor of New York. Congressmen and congresswomen. The commandant of Saint-Cyr. The secretary of the army. Finally, the president and his wife, Laura, the president introduced as "grandson of a World War I artilleryman"—quietly sidestepping his father George H. W. Bush's time as a navy flier and Bush Jr.'s time in the Texas Air National Guard, during the Vietnam war.[15] Bush began with reference to Lee, the "perfect West Point graduate" and Grant, who "said the happiest day of his life was 'the day I left West Point.'"[16] The president, who enjoyed drinking and rugby at Yale,[17] had to restart his payoff—"During my college years, I guess you could say I was a Grant man." He made reference to the other classes' mocking nickname for the Class of 2002, the Golden Children. Then he switched to the meat of his speech.

In 2020, the historian Andrew Bacevich, a West Point graduate whose son was killed in Iraq in 2007,[18] published *The Age of Illusions*, a study of US foreign policy from the Cold War to Donald Trump.[19] In June 2002, Bacevich pointed out, a post-Taliban government was named in Afghanistan.[20] As Bush spoke, the future seemed bright. But Bacevich lamented the failures that followed. It is clear now that Bush's West Point speech was a key moment on the road to war in Iraq.

As described by Bacevich, Bush outlined his view of the supremacy of American values, which he defined as "the rule of law, limits on the power of the state, respect for women and private property and free speech and equal justice and religious tolerance." The message: after 9/11, no other values or challenge to those values would be allowed. To Bacevich, Bush threatened to "[wage] war on behalf of righteousness itself" as a "self-assigned global peace enforcer." The war on terror would "not be won on the defensive," Bush said. The United States, he continued, would "take the battle to the enemy, disrupt his plans, and confront the worst threats before they emerge. In the world we have entered, the only path to safety is the path of action. And this nation will act."

The speech laid out a Bush doctrine of preventive war that would be put into practice in March the following year. Al-Qaeda had found shelter in Afghanistan. Iraq, however, did not strike America. Nor did it threaten to do so. Bacevich wrote, "International law had hitherto condemned preventive war, the Nuremberg tribunal calling it the 'supreme crime.' Bush now exempted the United States from such prohibitions."

In Michie Stadium, on that hot first day of June 2002, the cadets and their families knew what Bush was saying. Rosalyn Miller said, "In my mind, it was like, 'Oh my God.'"

The cadets were going to war.

SOMBER REFLECTION could wait. Bush was applauded. The cameras showed Zac Miller and Mo Greene in their front-row seats. When the speech was done, Joe Da Silva, the class president, gave Bush a sword of his own.

"Thank you, sir," Da Silva said. "And Beat Navy."

Bush presented diplomas to the distinguished cadets. When Greene stepped up, the camera caught the president's words: "Congratulations, great job." It didn't pick up what he said to Miller. As the rest of the class came forward, Bush stayed to shake each graduate's hand. It was a nod to tradition, of sorts. Presidents used to be closer to their public. John Tyler was once so bruised by shaking hands he "could not hold a spoon for days."[21] Abraham Lincoln wore gloves to lessen the pain. Herbert Hoover reckoned he shook nine thousand hands a year.[22]

The rugby players took their places in a long gray river, flowing down both sides of the dais. Jim Gurbisz shook hands with Bush. The president nodded, and Gurbisz exited, stage left. Clint Olearnick was next, then Brian McCoy. Nik Wybaczynsky towered over the president. A cadet grabbed Bush for a hug. Ekky Stiller, the goat—bottom of the class, heir to George Armstrong Custer, the recipient of a dollar from every other cadet—earned a big cheer and a long word from Bush. Matt Blind, Peter Chacon, and Andy Klutman followed, a chant of "Klutes!" ringing out. Dawn Gasparri, soon to be Dawn Hurley, collected her diploma before Jeremiah. Dave Little. Scott Radcliffe. Jeremiah Hurley, Joe Emigh. As Jerrod Adams came up, the camera cut to the waiting line. This is what Chris Starling, the Marine officer and rugby coach, said was happening on the dais:

"This is frickin' great. President Bush is shaking hands with every cadet . . . there's a thousand of them to go through. And the president's kind of moving them along. But Jerrod had told me he's from the same hometown as Laura Bush, as the president's wife. Well, all of a sudden, it's like an accordion. It all backs up because Jerrod stays and shakes the president's hand longer than anybody else. And all these guys are bumping into each other. We call it 'asshole to belly button,' right? And Jerrod's standing there, having a conversation with the president. All of a sudden the president stops, kind of cocks his head to the side and turns and walks Jerrod over to Laura and introduces them. Everybody clapping and cheering, right? He got to meet Laura Bush right there and disrupted graduation doing it. It was hilarious. I just laughed so hard. That's just frickin' great. You know?"[23]

It is great. Except the video doesn't show it happening.

Nor does the video align with Clint Olearnick's memory of the day, which he shared with me when we sat with a beer at Matt Blind's house one summer afternoon.[24] Olearnick said Bryan Phillips "actually grabbed President Bush, in, like, this giant bear hug and lifted him off the ground," and that "these two Secret Service guys like come rushing out from behind him, and you can see President Bush just look back over his shoulder and like, nod them away, and then Brian sets him back down on the ground."

Being bullshitted? I took it as a compliment. All part of the game, the rugby thing. And if a story isn't true—if it's just inspired by Adams's cheekiness or Phillips's size—it doesn't mean it can't be told and retold.

The ceremonies concluded. The cadets raised their right hands, repeated the commandant's words, and were second lieutenants at last. There was a final ritual. The first captain, Andrew Blickhahn, shouted, "Class dismissed." A thousand new officers threw their hats in the air.

Olearnick couldn't remember much of Bush's speech, he said, in part because "it was very hot" and the day went by in a blur. He did remember sitting in Michie Stadium with Jim Gurbisz, with whom for four years he had "eaten together, slept in the same room, hung out, done everything together."

Later on graduation day, Olearnick and Gurbisz went through their pinning ceremony together, too, receiving the shoulder bars which marked them as second lieutenants. Bob and Marge Carter, rugby team supporters, had the whole team and their families over to their house for the event. Zac Miller's mother pinned one bar to the shoulder of her son's new green army uniform, his father the other. Miller took his first salute from his grandfather, who fought in North Africa and Italy. The family "met general after general after general," Rosalyn said. "My father-in-law, God love him, he said to one of them, 'I served in the war for four years, and I saw more generals today than I saw in all that time.'"

At the Carters' house, it wasn't Dave Little who was late. Bush's speech had made Scott Radcliffe's mom cry, so his family went for a restorative meal. That meant Radcliffe "got over to the rugby party very late and missed when everyone else pinned."[25] Fortunately, a rugby player on the West Point staff, Major Walt Kennedy, was there to conduct the ceremony. In a picture taken by his father, Radcliffe stands in his new green uniform in dappled shade, next to the Stars and Stripes. He raises his right hand, Brian McCoy standing with him. Jim Gurbisz walks behind them, arms by his side, full military order. Family members mill. Children wear the white caps the cadets had tossed in Michie Stadium.

There's a team picture, too, apparently taken at the British exchange officer's house, given the Union Jack in the background. Matt Blind pulls in Bob Carter while Marge Carter sits in front.

Bryan Phillips and Nik Wybaczynsky form their own back row. Zac Miller stands between Dave Little and Mo Greene, one arm reaching Andy Klutman's shoulder. Joe Emigh is at the other side, next to Clint Olearnick. Brian McCoy, Pete Chacon, and Jerrod Adams squat in the front row. Jim Gurbisz kneels—on his one good knee.

THE DAY after graduation, Jeremiah Hurley and Dawn Gasparri joined the long line of West Pointers who marry shortly after graduation, in large part because the army does not recognize unmarried couples and will happily post one half to Georgia and the other to Alaska.

"We had the Sheraton in Mahwah," Dawn said, two decades, five children, and many deployments later.[26] "And then my parents hired West Point tour buses to get everybody to the Catholic chapel on West Point," down the hill from Michie Stadium, "and pretty much the whole rugby team were the saber-bearers at our wedding, and then they stayed for the party, and by the end Jerrod Adams was swimming in the Sheraton fountain."

Dave Little would marry, too, to his high-school girlfriend, Lindsay, back home in California. Alone among the cadets, Zac Miller surrendered his precious time off. The day after graduation, he traveled with four other new lieutenants to Fort Benning, to attempt to pass Ranger School before heading for scholarships in Europe. The rest of the players would head for San Diego. As they left West Point, however, something at the heart of the team was amiss: at some point over graduation weekend, fueled by drink, Clint Olearnick and Jim Gurbisz fought. And unlike other times they'd wrestled or thrown a few punches, they did not make things right. A deep friendship splintered.

Gurbisz's sister, Kathy, was the first to mention the fight to me.[27] She didn't know what caused it. I asked around. Dave Little said, "I just sort of interpreted it as brothers fighting, because the two of them were more like brothers than anyone else in the group. They had a really unique, tight bond throughout the academy. It was sad to hear they'd fallen out, but I didn't believe it was long-term. I just thought, 'They're both fiery humans, big emotions and big aggression. I assumed it was just one of those things that happened.'[28]

Ken Gurbisz said Olearnick threw the first punch. I asked Olearnick.

"I forget what happened. We were down drinking somewhere and got in a big fight. Just over something stupid." He and Gurbisz made it through Dave Little's wedding, he said, and then "just sort of lost touch."

As the author Sebastian Junger points out in his book *Tribe: On Homecoming and Belonging*, the "energy of male conflict and male closeness" is closely linked. Junger "once asked a combat vet if he'd rather have an enemy in his life or another close friend." The vet looked at Junger like he was crazy.

"'Oh, an enemy, a hundred percent,' he said. 'Not even close. I've already got a lot of friends.' He thought about it a little longer. 'Anyway, all my best friends I've gotten into fights with—knock-down, drag-out fights. Granted we were always drunk when it happened, but think about that.' He shook his head as if even he couldn't believe it."[29]

To Olearnick's and Gurbisz's rugby brothers, the fight has long ceased to matter. Until they spoke to me, Olearnick's parents, Jan and Clem, didn't know it had happened. I also spoke to Gurbisz's girlfriend, Tori. She said, "Clint, he was not my biggest fan. For sure."

Cadets who come to West Point with partners from home—or the prep school, in the Hurleys' case—rarely leave with the same partners in tow. As the Association of Graduates defines it, "Another romance tradition at West Point is the Two-Percent Club, which refers to high-school sweethearts who remained committed to each other during the cadet's time at West Point."[30] Distances—physical, to and from the rock over the Hudson; emotional, between civilian and military—simply become too great. But Tori lived on the Jersey Shore, and some weekends she came to West Point to visit.

"The guys wanted Jim to go out and hang out with them, but sometimes I was kind of like, 'Hey, you know, I drove over two hours, got a hotel room, to come up here. Like, you can spend some time with me.' I'm sure to Jim there was definitely that, like, 'Hey, don't do just the girlfriend-type thing,' you know? I don't know if it was me in person, but, like, you got Jim, you got the girlfriend. And the guys were like, 'Let's go get wasted.' We weren't complete enemies all the time, but I know sometimes Clint would be, 'Don't listen to her.'

"It was weird, too, because I had my Jim and then there was rugby Jim . . . it was really hard if you weren't in it. And in the academy too. It's hard to understand all the weird inner workings. I remember the first time he told me, 'Yeah, we have a bar we can go to.' And I was like, 'Why? Why did they have a bar there for you?' I couldn't talk to him for two months at a time, and now he could go to a bar? I'm sure they have to do that to keep them from going crazy."

Cadets who drink too much can go a little crazy too. Clint Olearnick and Jim Gurbisz drank too much and they fought. But life went on. Jeremiah Hurley got married. Dave Little's wedding neared.

"I was pretty pissed off that we didn't get engaged right away," Tori said. "Like, 'Excuse me? Everyone else got married. What are we doing?'"

The tab earned upon completing the grueling, two-month-long Army Ranger School.

Ranger

THEY FOUND Zac Miller's body on the Tricolor Road Land Navigation Course at Fort Benning on Monday, July 1, 2002, at eight o'clock in the evening.[1] He had been missing for six hours and twenty-one minutes.

It had been a brutally hot day, above ninety degrees, heat category five, when the army recommends that hard work of any kind be limited to ten-minute increments and that 1.5 quarts of fluids be consumed every hour. Miller was last seen on a dirt trail on top of a wooded berm. He left the trail, dropping his map, his cap, and his glasses as he came down the slope. When he was found, he was still carrying a whistle—to attract attention if in trouble—and half a quart of water. He was lying on his back, across a fallen tree, his right arm stretched from his side. Sergeant Scott, the senior medic assigned to the Seventy-Fifth Ranger Regiment, found no pulse or breathing. Scott returned to his van, retrieved a cardiac monitor, and ran back down the berm. He cut away Miller's T-shirt, placed electrodes on his chest. There was no cardiac activity. At 10:00 p.m., the regimental surgeon confirmed Scott's assessment. At 11:00 p.m., in the thick darkness of a summer night in Georgia, police officers arrived. Military police and paramedics followed. At 11:45 p.m., Zachariah R. Miller, age twenty-two, was pronounced dead. At 1:00 a.m. on Tuesday, July 2, his body was driven away.

At 1:45 a.m., hundreds of miles north at West Point, Brigadier General Leo Brooks, the new commandant, was awakened by a call.

Brooks had played rugby at the academy himself.[2] He knew all about Miller, the rugby-loving Rhodes scholar.

Brooks said, "I was still in the guest house. I hadn't even moved into my quarters. I hadn't been there a week. A guy named Joe Votel was the commander of the Seventy-Fifth Ranger Regiment. I served in the regiment myself. I got a phone call from Joe to tell me one of the brand new graduates just died. And so I called the superintendent, Lieutenant General Lennox."[3]

Lennox was "devastated."[4] At 3:00 a.m., a call was made from Fort Benning to Fort Meade, the military personnel headquarters near Washington. At 3:30 a.m., a casualty report was sent to Fort Meade, West Point, and Fort Jackson, the combat training center. At 6:20 a.m., in Stoneboro, Pennsylvania, a casualty assistance officer notified next of kin.

Nearly twenty years later, I sat with Rosalyn and Keith Miller in the same house where they received the news of their son's death.

"Keith was doing summer work," Rosalyn said, referring to the construction her son helped with in high school, a role his brother Nate had come to fill. "I was sleeping. Keith hadn't left yet. I don't know what I would have done if he had left and I didn't know where he was working. And you know, the army man knocked at the door."[5]

Nate remembered hearing a car on the driveway as he walked to the bathroom.[6]

Rosalyn looked at her husband.

"I can remember you telling me that you opened the door and you knew why he was there but you didn't want to believe it. Keith came back. He opened the door and he said, in a tone of voice I'll never forget, 'Get dressed.' And I just got up, to go out in my pajamas, out to the living room. And he said, 'You can't go out there. There's a man out there.' I looked at him in shock and disbelief as I started to comprehend. I said, 'It's not Zac?' I knew from the expression on his face that it was."

Rosalyn went to the living room. A man was there, wearing a green army uniform. The Millers sat down. The soldier read a statement.

"All he could do was read the statement and tell us about the assistance we would be receiving," Rosalyn said. "At some point,

I guess the soldier left. You know, you just don't understand what happened."

IN HIS memoir of West Point and Afghanistan, *The Unforgiving Minute*, Craig Mullaney describes why, two years before Zac Miller, he put himself through Ranger School before going to Oxford.

Ranger School, he writes, was established at Fort Benning "during the Korean War . . . to build combat leaders, mimicking the stresses of combat through severe food and sleep deprivation. Between mock ambushes and raids testing tactical knowledge, students marched insane distances under heavy rucksacks in order to test their stamina and will."

After the Ranger Assessment Phase, a short and brutal introduction, the test has three parts: Darby, Mountain, and Swamp. Stragglers are either dropped or "recycled," allowed to repeat a phase. Passage without recycling takes nine weeks. The prize is a crescent-shaped black and gold tab, attached to the shoulder. Mullaney adds: "For an infantry officer, the Ranger tab was an unspoken prerequisite for respect and promotion. For all practical purposes, Ranger School was mandatory. Many commanders refused lieutenants who arrived at their first units without one, telling them in the fashion of the Spartans to return with a tab or not at all."[7]

Andrew Exum is another rugby-playing officer who fought in Afghanistan.[8] He went to Ranger School after the University of Pennsylvania. In his own memoir, *This Man's Army*, he describes his motivation: "Only trigger-pullers need apply for admission. The school is designed to simulate the stress of combat on the soldiers who actually fight the nation's battles, not the support personnel and desk jockeys who comprise the majority of the military."[9]

Exum and Mullaney both won their tabs before 9/11. Miller was one of the first West Point graduates after it. He was one of more than two hundred in his class who chose infantry—who chose to be the trigger-pullers. Most would go through Ranger School after officer basic training, also at Fort Benning. Many rugby players did.

But for Miller, as for Mullaney, the Rhodes scholarship changed the calculation. In an alumni email sent on Valentine's Day 2002, Coach Mahan described how another predecessor faced such a challenge: "John Barker '01, our scribe and A side winger last year, won a Marshall scholarship and is currently studying at the University of Edinburgh in Scotland. John is an infantryman. He was told the only way he could go to Ranger School was if he gave up his graduation leave, reported to Ranger two days after graduation, and was neither injured nor recycled. He reported for Ranger, passed without any injury or recycle and reported to grad school before the summer was out. Hooah!"

David Brooks of the *New York Times* defined "hooah"—spellings differ (hooah, hoo-ahh, huah, etc.), as do definitions[10]—as "the romantic warrior code of George S. Patton put into verbal form."[11] Brooks was reviewing David Lipsky's *Absolutely American*. In a chapter titled "The Theory and Practice of Huah," Lipsky defined the word and its place at West Point like this: "*Huah* is an all-purpose expression. Want to describe a cadet who's very gung-ho, you call them *huah*. Understand instructions, say *huah*. Agree with what another cadet just said, murmur *huah*. Impressed by someone else's accomplishment, a soft, reflective *huah*."[12]

In his final months at West Point, Miller was not feeling soft or reflective. Afghanistan had fallen. Miller and the other young officers could not know what lay ahead—of the invasion of Iraq in March 2003, of years of hell in Baghdad, Mosul, and Fallujah, of new fights in Afghanistan. But they wanted to see combat. To Zac, it seemed, that meant getting a move on.

"This guy was brave," Leo Brooks said. "Even though he was a Rhodes scholar, he wanted to be an instrument, to be tough, to do all the good, hard things that young, hard-charging graduates want to do. And one of them is to go to Ranger School."

In April 2002, West Point told the Ranger Training Brigade that five lieutenants would report to Fort Benning in June. Ken Wainwright, a historian who won a Marshall scholarship and would finish second in the class, was among them. So was Rob Smith, another

Rhodes scholar. The five trained together. Miller's friends watched. R. J. Johnson said, "I believe Zac did things that he thought he needed to do in order to get to where he wanted to be. Like, Zac was *not* a career infantry guy. He was never going to be a general. That would have driven him insane. But he was doing all the other things that the world thought were important résumé builders."[13]

For the summer of 2002, after Ranger School and before Oxford, Miller had lined up an internship with Arlen Specter, a Pennsylvania Republican senator.[14]

Johnson said, "This is hard. It's like, we were telling him, 'Man, Ranger School is gonna be crazy. Like, why are you doing it? Take a little time, go to school. You can do Ranger School whenever.' And he was like, 'No, I want to do it now.' And because he could get whatever he wanted as a Rhodes scholar, it was like, 'Okay, you're gonna get it.'

"The last months at West Point were definitely a different Zac. He had stuff on his mind. I remember saying goodbye after graduation. It was just weird. I was like, 'Are you gonna go?' And he said, 'See you later, man.'"

R. J. Johnson and Jay Landgraf were Zac Miller's closest friends. In their room, Miller and Landgraf took the bunks, Johnson the single bed. They worked, ate, and partied together. By the end of their fourth year, Johnson thought Miller wanted "to go do, like, more than anybody else was doing. He was kind of dating two girls in secret, at the end. Like, 'What are you doing?' He just started . . . dating. He wouldn't tell me and Jay. He was just very secretive about all that stuff, because he didn't want anything to weigh him down. I think he was nervous about going to Ranger School. That was definitely on his mind. But we didn't talk during that period after graduating. He kind of went off. It was like, 'All right, man, see you when you graduate from Ranger School, talk to you then. Good luck. You know, break a leg.'"

Johnson conceded that he doesn't know "everything that was on Zac's mind at the end. But I don't think he graduated as high as he wanted to. He was working pretty hard to graduate like first or second, and I think it really pissed him off that he didn't."

Miller finished eleventh in a class of 957. In a letter to his parents after his death, Erica Borggren, another Rhodes scholar, wrote, "Zac loosened up a lot last semester." He "checked out of the whole deal once he won the Rhodes" and "enjoyed himself so much more." If that were the case, R. J. said, Zac might have come to regret it. "Zac could get pissed. Like, he was a nice guy, but he had an angry side, which, I mean, going back to rugby, you have to have that to get through it or else you cannot survive. You have to have that mental toughness, and he clearly had that."

That echoed Dave Little, who remembered the smack Miller gave him when he held the ball on the floor. It echoed Keith Miller, who fired and rehired his son after any number of summertime rooftop bust-ups.

Even after nearly twenty years since Miller's death, R. J. Johnson's voice wavered:

"When I found out that he died, I was like, 'You fucking asshole. Like, just, tap out and go back another day.' But he was so, so tough mentally that he was like, 'No one else is doing this,' and he would push himself really hard. I mean, in the end, I don't know. It's all kind of a blur. But I definitely remember it weighing on his mind, all the things that were happening and what he was going to become. Remember, this was post-9/11. We were in a weird spot. That was our senior year, and we were on lockdown that whole year. We didn't know what was gonna happen. It would not have been crazy for Zac to think, 'Well, I could go to Ranger School and they could definitely deploy me first. I don't know where I'm going.' That was on our minds. We just didn't know. I can see Zac being upset that he had to go to school, that he couldn't go fight, that he would be behind his classmates. And being behind in a thing was less than desirable for Zac."

I WENT to visit former West Point superintendent Lieutenant General Daniel Christman. In his office on Lafayette Square, near the White House, Christman was courteous and funny, as delightedly bemused by the rugby team as in his days at West Point. Zac Miller, he said, "Was strange and unusual, in an entirely positive way. He had physical prowess and he had excellence academically, the kind of cadet I wanted to identify, encourage, and drive. The academy tries to spot plebes who have all-round gifts and attributes and will be competitive in international awards and scholarships, and Zac was in that group.

"I probably met him when he was a cow—a junior—in his 'critical thought' classes, which sought to give these cadets training in international relations, in the profession of arms, in leadership, and so on. He was tremendous. And then in athletics, on the sports field, he was not a barnburner of a rugby player, he seemed very within himself sometimes. But we don't get many Rhodes scholars at West Point, you know, so he was special."[15]

When he learned Miller had died, Christman was angered and dismayed. Talking to me in his office, he grew animated, jabbing his desk with a finger.

"It was a push-up test fail, that's why he was where he was. We have lost academy graduates through callousness and disregard of basic safety standards. Some APFTs [army physical fitness trainers] there would single out 'egghead' cadets and try to make them work harder. I called West Point to try to get Zac's last APFT results. He was doing a Pre-Ranger course, he wasn't in the school yet, that was why he was out doing night navigation and solo land navigation there. It was outrageous, an athlete like that."

I asked the US Army Safety Center at Fort Rucker in Alabama for its official report. It provided a copy, heavily redacted but including witness statements. The Millers gave me the Seventy-Fifth Ranger Regiment investigation and the autopsy, both unredacted. They sent pages from a notebook Miller kept at Fort Benning. And so, in reconstruction, what happened was this:

On June 2, 2002, the day after graduation, most of the rugby players attended Dawn and Jeremiah Hurley's wedding at the Catholic chapel at West Point and the Sheraton, Mahwah. Zac Miller did not. He and four other new second lieutenants traveled south to Georgia.

At 5:00 a.m. on June 3, all five reported to the Ranger Training Brigade at Fort Benning. The Ranger School handbook describes what awaited. Zero Week "tests the student's physical fitness, endurance, and some basic field skills. Training days usually start at approximately 0400 and last until 2300–2400. All training events are back to back allowing minimal or no time for rest and recovery."[16]

There was a problem. Four of the lieutenants—Ken Wainwright, Robert Padgett, Kenton Justice, and Rob Smith—were missing required sickle cell test results. The only one with the correct information was Zac Miller. He could start Ranger School as planned. But his attempt did not last long. According to the Seventy-Fifth Ranger Regiment, on June 8, "Second Lieutenant Miller failed Ranger School Zero Week APFT (push-ups)." The Army Safety Center report also says Miller failed the APFT but does not give a date. It says, "On day one of the course, Second Lieutenant Miller failed to meet the minimum standard for the sit-up event."

According to the Ranger Training Brigade, the five lieutenants were given a second try, starting June 10. Smith and Justice passed the APFT, but Miller, Wainwright, and Padgett failed. The Ranger report does not say which part Miller failed. The Army Safety Center does not mention a second attempt. Maybe the attempt it mentions, the sit-up fail, *is* the second attempt. Either way, Zac Miller and two others could not start Ranger School.

Remembering Lieutenant General Christman's anger, I asked Rangers-turned-authors Craig Mullaney and Andrew Exum if Miller might have been treated unfairly. They said no . . . and yes. Miller would have been treated harshly, sure. Unfairly, *possibly*. Because he was an egghead? *Maybe*. But the point of Ranger School was to be treated harshly and unfairly. Cadre—instructors—were equal-opportunity assholes. The point was to see if students would crack. When I spoke to Ken Wainwright, he said the five lieutenants spoke among themselves of "Ranger roulette—an inability to control what the instructor or the assessor is looking for."[17]

According to the Ranger School manual in use in 2002, the fitness test required fifty-two push-ups and sixty-two sit-ups, a two-mile run in fourteen minutes and fifty-four seconds, and six chin-ups to finish.

But, said Exum, those were just numbers. "It's ridiculously hard. They try to weed you out. Guys who go in able to do like eighty push-ups get dinged for not locking out the arms exactly. You just have to exaggerate it and do more. Do sixty-six, do eighty-six, doesn't matter. You're gonna do the official amount. So, the game is, you go and you just do very deliberate push-ups and you do your number and get out."[18]

Pete Chacon completed Ranger School after Officer Basic. He echoed Exum. Failing push-ups or sit-ups was "shockingly easy. Whatever the minimum number is, the instructors don't just count. Sometimes they're just messing with you, just to see that you have some mental errors too. It's like, 'One . . . one . . . one . . .' They'll stop you when you hit the minimum, but you actually may have done like eighty or ninety. It's this whole weird thing. There's always hazing too. Like, in Ranger School, you can't wear contact lenses. So you have to wear the dorky army glasses. And guys that were in glasses tended to get graded harder. Just, like, their physical bearing and demeanor was an attraction to the instructors. They're looking for, like, a Ranger image, so little biases creep in."

Zac Miller wore glasses.

Chacon said, "There was a lot of pressure on Zac because he couldn't be recycled. He had to go through, true blue. A lot of pressure when you can't fail."[19]

Miller and the two other lieutenants arranged to attend Pre-Ranger, with the Seventy-Fifth Ranger Regiment, a course used to prepare men from active units. They were not required to do so, but they decided to use it for training, as Wainwright put it, "to give us the best chance of success."

"We knew that the guys coming out of Ranger Regiment, the young specialists and PFCs and [those already] in [the] Ranger Regiment who needed to get the Ranger tab to become a sergeant, were going to run the best version of Pre-Ranger to prepare us for Ranger School."

The next Pre-Ranger started on June 17 and ended on July 3. The next Ranger School started twelve days later. Miller still had time to try again and go to Oxford with his Ranger tab. Before Pre-Ranger began, the young officers were given six days' leave. Miller went home to Stoneboro and told his parents he thought he'd had no chance.

"According to what we remember Zac telling us," Rosalyn said, "by the time they came to his push-up test, the next Ranger class had been filled. As he did his push-ups and the instructors counted, they got to a point where they counted 'Forty-eight, forty-eight, forty-eight, forty-eight.' The number never increased, and Zac 'failed' the push-up test. I honestly can't believe Zac failed the push-ups . . . he had just graduated from West Point and was in terrific shape; he would have known the standard for push-ups and would have been ready for the test."

At least Miller was home for Father's Day. As it turned out, Rosalyn said, June 16 was "the last day that we actually saw him. Keith took him to the airport in Pittsburgh. I didn't go. I said goodbye here at the house. I figured it was Father's Day, I would like Keith and Zac to have that time together themselves."

Pre-Ranger began the next day. Miller failed sit-ups again but continued in a class of thirty-six. The first week, the students took lessons, including learning how to write operation orders, "opords" for short. On June 23, they moved out to Cole Range, a remote area, for eight days in the field. The first four days were spent training. The next four, the Safety Center says, were filled with "continuous operations," focused on "raid, reconnaissance, and ambush."

Out in the hot woodland, under the thin Georgia pines, the sandy soil concealed snakes and spiders. "If bit by a snake," the students were told, "attempt to kill it so it can be identified." There were also ants and flies. The heat was infernal. Where he could, Zac Miller sought respite. Chancing a seat on a log, he took out a small notebook.

"It's not that bad here," he wrote, early in the week. "It's actually a lot more chill than I thought it would be. We've been in the field since early Sunday, when we ruck marched out to the training area.

We did some classes, learned some stuff (supposedly) and then went to bed early because it was raining."

On June 24, they were up at 3:00 a.m. for night-into-day land navigation. Miller completed the course and returned "just in time to have the cadre hand me a cell phone and tell me to call the Comm."

"So there I was, holding my breakfast plate in one hand, cell phone in the other, trying to dial up [Brig.] Gen. Eric T. Olson. He just wanted to call to let us know that everyone at West Point had heard of our plight, and that everyone was still very proud of us. Definitely a unique experience for the other guys around, they had a pretty good laugh at my expense. Ken Wainwright didn't believe me that the Comm actually called, but then when he heard the message he believed."

Next there was day-to-night land nav, students using compass and map to find marked "points," six each to collect. Miller found three. The darkness made it "impossible," he wrote. "Or at least that's my story and I'm sticking to it."

On June 25, he was put in a command role, giving an opord. "It went pretty well, especially since it was the first one. We didn't execute the mission but it was a good practice if nothing else." Miller also wrote that he didn't eat lunch, because he was simply too busy. Later, Sergeant Schmid, the instructor in charge, noted that Miller was given an "excellent" rating, "something the cadre never do but 2nd Lt. Miller had done an outstanding job."[20]

On June 26, the students executed a mission, Miller in the pack as a "regular Joe." He was "quite impressed with my ability as a pace man." He was "thankful that my math major is being put to good use." He drew a small smiley face.

On June 27, he wrote of going "out of the wire for the next few days" to practice a platoon ambush, adding, "We should get back for land nav on Monday, clean weapons on Tuesday, and hopefully kick out on Wednesday." He felt "out of touch with the real world" but realized the world "does indeed revolve without your presence." It was "really humbling to be out here, without all that many people who know you well, and have to prove yourself all over again. It's also nice to be quasi-anonymous and not have so many expectations of you."

There, sometime on Thursday, June 27, 2002, Miller's notebook entries ended. Two days later, he paid a brief visit back to the real world. He had been treated for rope burn earlier, but according to the Safety Center report, "at some time leading up to Saturday 29 June, 2nd Lt. Miller came in contact with poison ivy" on one of his thighs. Some trainers thought it could be cellulitis. The medic, Sergeant Scott, decided to take Miller to Martin Army Community Hospital, where he saw a civilian doctor. According to the Seventy-Fifth Ranger Regiment report, Miller received two injections, one of Rocephin and one of Decadron, and was prescribed "several topicals including Bacitracin, Silvadene Bactroban, Neosporin, and Tetrahydrozoline." Then he was taken back to barracks and allowed a shower and a change of uniform. He also called his parents.

Rosalyn said, "He was supposed to come home for the Fourth of July weekend. Some leave time. So we were making arrangements to get him at the airport. Keith and I were on extension phones. The last thing we said to Zac was, 'Love you, bud,' and he answered, 'Love you guys.'"

Back in the field, Zac Miller was "not in a student leadership position," the Safety Center said, "but he did carry a simulated Anti-Tank 4 filled with cement." AT4s can be carried with a strap or on the shoulder.[21] They weigh six to eight kilograms—roughly thirteen to seventeen pounds—without being filled with cement. The report said, "Several students commented that 2nd Lt. Miller was 'smoked' after carrying the extremely heavy weapon for the entire mission, and the student patrol leader tried to give 2nd Lt. Miller a break by putting him in an observation post."

The following day, June 28, brought "several tasks over a long period of time" but finished at 5:00 p.m. The students were briefed about the next day's challenge, solo land navigation, then sent to rest. None reported medical problems. On Monday, July 1, they were awakened at 6:40 a.m.

Among witness statements regarding what happened that day, two stand out for their closeness to Miller. One was by Second Lieutenant Ken Wainwright, the Marshall scholar from West Point. The other was by Ranger Morges, one of the many enlisted men who made up most of the Pre-Ranger class.

Wainwright told investigators that he had come to know Miller through competition for a Truman scholarship, in study groups "in which 2nd Lt. Miller would take charge. He was always a take-charge kind of guy. He played on the rugby team and he stood out from the other players, even from behind, because of his wide shoulders. Wainwright thought of 2nd Lt. Miller as being 'strong as an ox.'" Wainwright also said that as far as he knew, Miller did not top up that strength with any dietary supplements, which were banned at Ranger School. Wainwright described how the new lieutenants came to be in Pre-Ranger. He described "a mindset that they needed to succeed the first time around."

Ranger Morges described becoming Miller's roommate and "Ranger buddy," detailed to look out for each other. "They talked a lot about their career goals and [Zac's] experiences at West Point." Miller told him "about being on the rugby team at West Point." Morges thought Miller was "in good physical shape, and whenever 2nd Lt. Miller was put into a student leadership position, such as platoon leader or platoon sergeant, 2nd Lt. Miller did an outstanding job." Morges knew about Miller's APFT failure. He thought it was push-ups.

In the second part of the time on Cole Range, Wainwright said, everyone in the class had two to two-and-a-half hours' sleep each day. He mentioned Miller's trip to the hospital. He described the last day of field operations—Sunday, June 30—and the ambush in late afternoon. "It was really hot. Three-fourths of the class was 'smoked.'" Trainers told the class to add salt to their water. Lights out was 9:00 p.m., wake-up ten hours later. There was a foot check. Wainwright "commented about 2nd Lt. Miller taking all of the prescribed medications." There were buses to the Tricolor course, which the Seventy-Fifth's Pre-Ranger had used only twice before. There was some confusion about the chow. Hot food didn't show. The students ate rations, meals-ready-to-eat, MREs. Morges said he and Miller sat together, both eating a full MRE and drinking two canteens of water.

There was a briefing. The students would have four hours to collect a minimum five points out of seven and return to the start. They were told to carry four quarts of water and to keep drinking. There was a water buffalo—a mobile 400-gallon water trailer—at the points for start and finish. Morges and Miller filled their canteens together.

Maps were issued. The confusion over the chow delayed the start by nearly half an hour. The heat was rising. By late morning it was already category five, the highest level. The students were told they could unblouse their boots, remove T-shirts and caps, and roll up their sleeves. They were told not to use roads or trails unless they ran out of time. If that happened, they were to go to the nearest roadway and wait to be picked up. The class split into four groups. Miller was in the second, start time 9:45 a.m. His Ranger buddy, Morges, was in the third, start time 10:00 a.m. They moved out.

Two hours later, out on the course with map and compass, Ken Wainwright had collected four points. He was "smoked and did not want to become a heat casualty," so he decided not to go for all seven. He tried to run. He couldn't. After collecting his fifth point, he "thought he was not sweating as he should be, so he sat down in the shade for about 20 minutes and made it back as slow as he could. Some of the other students stated they saw 2nd Lt. Miller at his fifth point and 2nd Lt. Miller looked OK. They said 2nd Lt. Miller said he was going to get all seven points. Another soldier saw 2nd Lt. Miller at his seventh point and said 2nd Lt. Miller did not look OK, he looked to be exhausted."

Around 1:20 p.m. or 1:30 p.m., Morges felt "as if he was suffering from heat exhaustion and was 'smoked.'" He ran into his Ranger buddy. Miller "told Morges that he had located all of his points. Morges did not know if that meant he had his minimum required five out of seven points or if that meant he had all seven points. Morges was unsure where they met. He did recall that they met at an unimproved road and decided to return to the finish together.

"On their way back they saw a point, which was point 42. They did their individual plotting. At that time, Morges thought 2nd Lt. Miller had about 30 minutes" to complete the course. "Morges also said he was 'smoked and things were fuzzy in his head.' He decided not to take the trails back. He said he was going to 'bust brush, shoot a straight azimuth, hit the hard-ball, and come out right on the shack.' 2nd Lt. Miller said he was going to 'play it safe and take the trails because he did not feel like busting brush anymore.' Morges said 2nd Lt. Miller was smoked and did not seem like himself. 2nd Lt. Miller's reactions seemed delayed; he was late in responding to Morges' questions and his body language indicated to Morges that 2nd Lt. Miller was not himself. The last thing 2nd Lt. Miller said to Morges was that he was taking the trails back. They moved from point 42, and as they started moving, Morges looked back and saw" another student.

In the Safety Center report, the student's name is redacted. It appears to have been Ranger Latting. In his statement, Latting said he caught up to Morges and Miller after realizing he would not be able to complete the course. It is not clear who gave who a "head bob and moved out," as Morges put it, but Latting appears to have told Morges that Miller then "changed his mind" and said he would "bust brush for 900m to hit the finish line instead of taking the trails." Latting said he and Miller got up together then split, Miller heading into the woods.

Morges said, "Most of the students thought 2nd Lt. Miller should not have been participating in the training because of 'all the medication he was taking'" for what was either poison ivy or cellulitis. He also said he heard an instructor telling another "how upset he was about 2nd Lt. Miller being out on the land navigation course and the cadre not knowing 2nd Lt. Miller was taking medication." Sergeant Scott, the medic, was "asked about the significance of the medication" Miller was taking. "He replied: 'It makes you sleepy.'"

Morges did not make it back to the shack. Assessing himself a heat casualty, he "went into the woods, took off as many clothes as he could, then passed out for two hours." He woke when he heard a vehicle passing. "Before passing out [again], he remembered to take off what clothes he could and thinking he was going to die.

"He knew that he and 2nd Lt. Miller were alike in that they were going to do whatever it took to complete the training."

Ken Wainwright said there was no pressure to collect all seven points. He said the lieutenants knew they "were going to go to the Ranger Course if they passed or failed" Pre-Ranger. They were there on a voluntary basis.

Zac Miller was due to finish by 1:39 p.m. That he did not was not unusual. At 2:10, two instructors went out to resolve a disputed point and look for three students. At 2:30, Latting appeared at the shack.

At 2:40, vehicles went out, looking for both Miller and Morges.

At 3:00, a full search was mounted.

At 4:00, Range Control was notified. At 4:20, military police were called. They went to the wrong place. Then they turned out not to have dogs and to be driving a sedan, which meant they had to stay on the trails. At 4:30, Morges was found, given salts and water and placed in front of a fan. At 5:15, the students joined the search for Miller. A medevac helicopter was called to scan the woods from the skies. Thunderstorms delayed it. It arrived at 6:50. At 7:50, it was called away. At 8:00, Sergeant Schmid and another instructor "went near point 42 where 2nd Lt. Miller was last seen and started trying to figure out how 2nd Lt. Miller might have returned to the start point from that location. They walked a short distance down the trail. Schmid thought that by cutting through brush he would have been on the most direct route, so he started to walk down the hill.

"At that time, he saw a map. Ten more meters he saw a patrol cap and another 10 meters he saw 2nd Lt. Miller."

MORE THAN twenty years later, Ken Wainwright was still in the army, commanding First Battalion, First Special Warfare Training Group. He thought back to when he was a new first lieutenant in the woods at Pre-Ranger, waiting for his friend to come back.

"We were beat-up. But there was the usual joshing back and forth, talk about officers not being able to land-navigate. That's an army thing, as a lieutenant. 'You can't spell 'lost' without 'Lt.'" The reality is that generally speaking, we were, in the infantry at least, pretty good. I remember sitting around, waiting, I remember hearing they were going out to look for him. And I remember moving out to look for a little while. I remember it got dark. They put us into the LMTVs, which is a light medium tactical vehicle. Essentially, it's a truck. And we were singing songs. We just assumed that they had found them, they wouldn't be sending us back out to look. We assumed that Zac was okay. But they hadn't found him, until they did. So it was just a shock. When they called me in to tell me, the battalion commander or the captain or whoever was in charge told me Zac had died. It was just . . . it was a huge shock."

"THEY FLEW him into Pittsburgh," said Rosalyn Miller. "You go to a special hangar. Scott Black, the funeral director, took us down. They unload the casket, and it has a flag over it. There was a maintenance person there. He stopped working while they brought the casket off the plane and put it in the hearse. That was July 5. And then I remember asking Scott if he thought he was going to have him ready for family viewing that next day, and he didn't. I don't remember why."

Rosalyn looked to her husband, Keith.

"He had trouble getting the coloration right. Zac had been out in the heat."

Rosalyn continued, "I didn't really know what had happened. I can remember Scott telling me that he looked Zac over carefully to see if there was a bug bite or, you know, *something*. And I remember saying to Scott, 'Are you sure it's Zac?' And he said, 'Yes, Rosalyn, it's Zac.'"

Keith said, "Since he came from down south, they have split caskets, which we don't have up here."

Rosalyn said, "Just the top opens up, and I didn't like that. So Scott made arrangements to get us the casket we wanted, which had an army seal on it. And then Scott said that they can't sell caskets that have been used, but they can use them for homeless people or people worrying about what they have to take care of. So it didn't go to waste. And then we had a family viewing on the seventh and the general viewing on the eighth and the funeral on the ninth."

The funeral was at Sandy Lake Wesleyan Church, much larger than Sandy Lake Presbyterian, which the Millers attended. The *Record-Argus* of Greenville described "an overflow crowd of several hundred."[22] Another report put it at more than five hundred.[23] To Jay Landgraf, who spoke, it seemed like "a couple thousand."[24] R. J. Johnson spoke too. So did Coach Mike Mahan and Lieutenant General Lennox, as well as Lynn Charlton, Miller's first-grade teacher, and Jeff Engstrom, his math teacher and coach.

Landgraf made people laugh. He told a story about "how unassuming Zac was. Because I'm from close to West Point, Ridgewood, New Jersey, we went back to my house a lot just to get away. It was our sophomore year. There was a party. It's a bunch of other college kids, and they're talking to Zac. Zac had huge shoulders, and he had this deep voice. He would just talk to you like a regular person, but because of the deep voice and his physical stature, one of my friends came up to me and said, 'Hey, Jay, like, who's the meathead you brought home?' I just laughed. I was like, 'Dude, you have no idea about this kid. None.'"

Lynn Charlton remembered the super-bright little boy who chewed the cuffs of his shirt, the teenage babysitter who staged epic Nerf Gun battles. Jeff Engstrom said, "Zac wanted to be like everyone else. That's ironic because everybody wanted to be like Zac." R. J. Johnson talked about how Miller won the Rhodes. Coach Mahan said he could not remember who had won various West Point awards five years before, but he would always remember Miller, "one of the special people who enter your life for a short period of time and then never leave."

Lieutenant General Lennox said, "The toughest thing a commander does is say farewell to one of his soldiers. In my thirty-one years of active duty, this hasn't changed. It tears my heart out." He called Miller a "leader of character," a potential chief of staff. "But when I think of Zac, I don't think of potential. Potential is overrated. When I think of Zac, I think of what he accomplished."[25]

Then, Rosalyn said, "Jay and R. J. and the rest of the guys took the casket to the grave and lowered it into the ground."

Matt Blind and Brian McCoy, rugby captain and vice captain, brought up the rear. Shots were fired over the grave. A bugler sounded taps.

Most of the rugby team was still in California, where Dave Little had married Lindsay, his girlfriend since high school, two days before. At the wedding in San Diego, Jerrod Adams gave a speech and a toast. After the wedding, Jim Gurbisz proposed to Tori, quietly, on a cliff top over the ocean.

Mo Greene, who had been a distinguished graduate alongside Miller just a month before, said, "That was a super tough time. Because apart from the birth of my daughters and my wedding, that was probably one of the greatest times of my life. Like, we were graduates from purgatory, we were getting paid, and we were on almost two months of vacation. And Dave was getting married. And then we heard about Zac. It was kind of the highest of highs and the lowest of lows, come together. You know, I drank a lot of Jack Daniels then."[26]

Coach Mahan told the *Old Gray* the news. "I wish I could embrace him once more," he wrote, "and tell him, 'Well done.'" Players still at West Point, many of whom Miller led in the B side, tried to comprehend. Charlie Erwin, the second row, said the news came when cadets were on summer assignment, precluding any chance "to come together and grieve."[27]

Matt Blind had been closer to Miller than most. He remembered the church in Stoneboro, speeches about "all the things everybody wants to hear at a funeral. But I think the moral of the story, that Jay delivered, is that all Zac's achievements, while really impressive, he's not going to miss any of that about Zac. What he is going to miss is his friend. I will never forget that. When Jay got to the end of his speech, which was very funny and witty, he said, 'I guess I just miss my friend.' Zac wasn't always out with the rest of the guys. But Jay and R. J. kind of made it real that Zac was a really good friend, maybe the best friend.

"I also remember being around Zac's little brother. He was really dejected. I didn't know if he fully understood what was going on. I knew he was going to struggle."[28]

TWENTY YEARS later, Nate Miller was living a few towns away from his parents, awaiting the birth of a child. He remembered the day the soldier came to his family's home.

"By the time I got out and got dressed, my dad told me to come to the living room because he had something to tell me. And so I sat there, and my mom was there. They give you, like, a paper that kind of has a brief explanation, that he passed away at so-and-so time or whatever. And my dad just read it. I remember him reading off the sheet of paper like he was reading a grocery list, because obviously he was in shock. He just read it like he was reading the phone book, that Zac died yesterday. And it was just the most surreal moment in my life. I couldn't compute. It did not make sense. But I remember one of the first things I felt was, like, 'I knew something like this was gonna happen.' At certain points in my life, I just felt like Zac was too good to be true."

For Rosalyn, the days after her oldest son's death were "an out-of-body experience." She felt she was "offstage watching a horrendous tragedy, only to realize it was my life." Nate remembered his dad going to tell his own parents. Keith's father had been "extremely close" to his grandson. Rosalyn "felt the news might kill Grandpa." But her father-in-law "grabbed me by the arms, looked me straight in the eye with tears in his eyes, and said, 'You and I have a job to do. We have to raise Nate.'"

Nate said, "That day is kind of a blur. I had two grandparents pass away before I was born. I had nobody I was close to that died. I'd never been through an experience like that. All my close friends came over, and we were all just sitting around. So what we did was we went to my one friend's house and played video games for a while. And then we went and played, like, Wiffle Ball or something, just to keep ourselves busy. I was in shock. I cried a lot. But there were times

I would not be crying. I would just be playing Wiffle Ball. It was such an odd experience."

Nate didn't speak at the funeral. He didn't want to. He remembers "shaking all these hands. A lot of people you don't even know. It was so bizarre to me. Having to watch my parents greet all these people. My mom, she's a much more emotional person than my dad. Still to this day, I've never seen my dad cry. It's not to say that he didn't cry after my brother died, but he never let anybody see it. I remember feeling, like, 'We just lost everything, and he's shaking people's hands and smiling?' Not like there was nothing wrong. But I just thought, like, 'Why? Why are you doing this? Your whole life, your everything, everything we based our life on is gone,' and we're shaking people's hands that we barely knew. It was just so bizarre."

Rosalyn and Keith Miller did not see their son put into the ground. R. J. Johnson, who did, said, "At the very end, it was like, 'Well, do you want to put the dirt on the coffin?' And I was like, 'Uh, not really.' And Jay was like, 'I'm not fucking putting dirt on my friend.' So I was sitting there. I was like, 'I feel like I should.' And so I did, and I was like, 'The wrong person died. The wrong person died.'"

Miller's friends felt anger toward those who had sent him to Georgia. Toward those who ran Pre-Ranger. Johnson said, "Jay, he was ready to cuss up and down. Like, the superintendent came to the funeral. Lieutenant General Lennox. Jay was like, 'Get him the fuck out of here.' I was like, 'We're lieutenants, we're not talking like that.' I had to pull him away."

Lieutenant General Lennox flew away, back to West Point and up the hill to the chapel for another memorial to Miller, the same day as his funeral.

"Jay has fire," Johnson said. But Miller? He was "a star that should not have gone out."

AFTER THE funeral, silence. The visitors left. The flowers wilted. At Zac Miller's grave, on a gentle slope in Oak Grove Cemetery, a black granite cross bears the West Point crest. Among its inscriptions, "G-3: Jay and Ryan, Brothers Army Rugby."

And then, on August 1, 2002, the army came back to Stoneboro.

"It was right after 9/11," Rosalyn said. "Zac died mysteriously.[29] He was a high-profile graduate of the academy. So initially they were trying to rule out foul play. They were considering everything. There was a big investigation. They did a big report. And then they came to bring us the results. Lieutenant General Lennox came to our house. We met out here on the porch. And the man that was in charge down at Fort Benning came"—Colonel Joseph Votel—"and the officer from Fort Campbell, Kentucky, who did the autopsy." Colonel Eric Berg MD.

"I can remember telling Keith, 'They're coming.' And he said, 'I don't want to hear what they have to say.' And I said, 'You don't have a choice, they're all in the air, they're coming from three different places to be here.' They handed us a mustard-yellow covered folder and went over the various items in the report. It was like a house of cards. Everything that could possibly have gone wrong, went wrong."

Colonel Berg performed the autopsy at Martin Army Community Hospital, Fort Benning, on July 3, Captain Henry Bell MD and Major Robert Wenzel MD assisting. They listed the medications Miller was given for "cellulitis of the skin of his anterior thighs and probably also antecedent poison ivy exposure," and how they were administered. Miller's body showed evidence of the rope burn to his left wrist and bites from ants. Toxicology, negative. Miller was "alarmingly dry."

Opinion: "This 22-year-old white male, Zachariah Robert Miller, died of exertional hyperthermia (heat stroke). The manner of death was accident."

There was one final jolt. The autopsy showed Miller had "mild early atherosclerotic cardiovascular disease." The beginnings of a heart condition.

Lennox, Votel, and Berg told Rosalyn and Keith their son "probably didn't suffer or know he was dying and couldn't get help." That he "undoubtedly became disoriented and quietly slipped away."

"I want to believe that," Rosalyn said, "because the alternative is too painful to contemplate."

The pain was fierce. So was the anger. A reporter from the *Columbus Ledger-Enquirer* asked why Zac was out on his own.[30] A spokeswoman for Fort Benning said Tricolor land navigation was "the only training exercise where an individual goes out by themselves."[31] There was the question of risk management. In the fierce heat, should instructors have changed their plans? In February 2002, Major General Paul Eaton, commanding Fort Benning, distributed a memorandum about risk management policy that was included in the Safety Center report. In a handwritten note, he wrote, "Let common sense prevail. If your intuition tells you something is unsafe—act to preserve life and limb and eyesight." Eaton also signed a memo about heat injury prevention: "We owe each soldier and employee our best effort in ensuring their safety. Follow me, safely!"

The report also included a summary of the "human factors investigation," which said that the students on the Tricolor course on July 1, 2002, had suitable equipment and that communications were "functionally intact." A "subject matter expert" walked Miller's route and found nothing amiss. The buffalo of water and ice was deemed placed correctly, where students could see it. Statements from twenty-one witnesses, the report said, "generally corroborate the sequence of events." Under "accident survivability," though, it said, "The heat injury was survivable."

Other conclusions were redacted.

The Seventy-Fifth Ranger Regiment Investigative Summary Brief, which was in the mustard-colored folder the officers gave the Millers, is not redacted. It says investigators found "no evidence to conclude simple or gross negligence by either the Ranger Training Detachment cadre or the chain of command." It recommends improvements to procedures and posits questions and answers.

The first is this: "Why is the [land navigation course] conducted individually?" The answer: "The ability to land-navigate is a critical individual task required of all leaders and especially infantry leaders. Individual land navigation is trained and tested on Fort

Benning at all leader courses . . . the land navigation hands-on test is a graduation requirement for most of these schools. The ability to navigate is a confidence-building event for leaders and [it] is extremely important leaders possess this skill when they join their units in leadership positions."

The officers who came to Stoneboro, Rosalyn Miller said, "Told us they were going to make some changes based on what they had found out. And I just thought they were giving us lip service, to appease us, and didn't figure that anything would change. And yet, they did make some changes."

On April 22, 2003, nearly a year after Zac Miller's death, Major General Eaton wrote to Keith and Rosalyn Miller. As a result of their son's death, he wrote, Fort Benning had "formalized much more aggressive procedures for locating missing soldiers in the training area [and] to account for extreme environmental conditions." One of the changes dealt with "the conduct of individual land navigation training during the hours that are qualified as an extreme heat category." From here on, Eaton said, if such training had to be conducted in extreme heat, "one of the risk mitigating factors must be to modify training to reflect the method of training as buddy teams."

Under such rules, Miller and Morges would have run the Tricolor course together.

Any student taken for hospital treatment, Eaton wrote, would require a doctor's written permission to return to training. Students would wear orange vests for daytime land navigation and carry chemical lights at night. "Likewise, we are investigating options to procure an individual electronic tracking system for use on all individual land navigation courses."

Rosalyn said, "I was sad that Zac would have been the one to design a computer chip or something to have on their equipment, so they could be tracked."

Eaton wrote, "Nothing can take away the loss of your son. His death was a tremendous loss to your family, to the Infantry and the Army, and our Nation."

There were hundreds more letters.

Anderson Cooper, the CNN anchor who had interviewed Miller in March, wrote that he had mentioned Miller "to several of my friends, saying something like, 'You would not believe this kid I met at West Point, he's done everything . . . he's going to be president someday.'"

Libby Haydon was interviewed by Cooper alongside Miller. In her letter, she remembered "how confident and proud Zac was of who he was and where he came from," how he "spoke very fondly about the rugby team and the challenges he faced." Haydon wrote about being with Miller that summer, "with all the scholarship winners before they went to Ranger School." She described picking Miller up after Zero Week, when he failed the fitness test. He calmed the others' nerves, she said.

"He settled Rob, Rob, and Ken by using his easygoing manner and sense of humor. He told stories of intimidating Ranger instructors and physical exertion in a manner that made the others believe that they were capable of accomplishing their goals."

In Stoneboro, on the porch where the generals once sat, Keith and Rosalyn Miller finished their coffee and cake. Keith hadn't spoken much. But he did say this: "Of all the cards we received after his death, we had one that had a verse in there. 'Why good people pass, why would God let this happen.' And it was, 'Perhaps because God knew what was coming.' That this would be better than what was coming.

"And that's the one thing that I have in my mind that allows me to accept that Zac died. That there could have been something far, far worse to come."

Sunrise at Lake Conroe, Texas.

Conroe

IN THE box at MetLife Stadium in New Jersey, Eddie Johnson is one retired linebacker among many. It's a wet December day, and Army versus Navy has come to town.[1] More than eighty-two thousand are in the stands, many of them cadets and midshipmen in gray and black; about fifty people are wedged into the box. Johnson is forty or so, solid, six foot, dark hair short and sprinkled with gray. His LinkedIn page details a sales career, but his first job is there too: Platoon Leader, Fort Hood, Texas, and Baghdad, Iraq.

There are other former football players in the stadium box, as well as wives and kids and clients. Most wear "Go Army" sportswear. Talk is of college, war, business, football. Some of the men, such as Brian Zickefoose, a solid West Virginian in baseball cap and hoodie, played in the game below, in his case captaining Army in the first such game after 9/11.[2] Others, like Bryan Phillips, who looms over the cold cuts and Coors Light, were cut from football but found new purpose in rugby.

"They tried to get me to do it, and I just didn't have the guts," Johnson said, with a laugh.[3]

But he did become close friends with Joe Emigh. Johnson was from Florida, and he met Emigh from California at the prep school in New Jersey in summer 1997. In 1998, they went to West Point to play football. They got cut together. That hurt, and Johnson felt a little jealous when Emigh found rugby, a new target for his ambition and drive. But losing football hurt less, Johnson says, after 9/11, when every cadet seemed to "sit up in our chairs a lot straighter."

187

"I remember, thinking back, shortly after 9/11, thinking, 'Why was I so upset about not playing football? Like, *this* is why I'm here.' I had to focus on graduating. Although I was near the bottom, ten percent of the class were gone at that point. I think all of us who were left, our attitudes got incredibly serious. A lot of the football team, the rugby team, and all these athletes for the most part had shunned a lot of the military side of the culture. Then 9/11 happened, and eighty percent of those guys branched infantry, the most hardcore thing to do. But I remember talking to Joey, and he was like, 'Nah, we're still going artillery.' We both put artillery number one on our list. That was what we decided."

In February 2002, Johnson, Emigh, and every other firstie gathered for Post Night, to select where they would serve. Johnson sat with Emigh, "both pretty low-ranked in the class . . . I was, like, number eight hundred ninety out of, like, nine hundred seventy-five or nine hundred fifty, and Joey was, like, eight hundred eighty-something. Right in front of me."

In his book *In a Time of War: The Proud and Perilous Journey of West Point's Class of 2002*, Bill Murphy Jr. outlined how the cadets were thinking: "Why go to Fort Hood when you could head for the beaches of Hawaii, or pack up for Italy or Germany and spend every long weekend in Paris or Prague?" When the process began, "the first-ranked cadet in the room stood up. 'Germany,' he said, to cheers and groans, and an army officer crossed off a slot on an overhead screen. One by one, the firsties picked their stations, and soon the glory posts disappeared."[4]

Johnson and Emigh watched "in this big lecture hall, with giant projectors showing all the duty stations, the number of slots, where people are ranked, where you're going to select, and we're just seeing all the attractive duty stations get filled up. But we expected that. We expected what was left at the bottom of the barrel. We're comparing notes. Like, 'All right, so if Korea is available, let's both go there. Right, we'll be roommates and help each other out. So if Korea is not there, like what's next. Maybe Fort Sill or Fort Polk or whatever.'"

Fort Sill, eighty-five miles from Oklahoma City, was founded on Apache land by Philip Sheridan, the little general with the West Point demerit for football, during the Indian wars of the late 1800s.[5] In 2002 it was a hub for artillery, but it was still far away, flyblown, and flat. Nor was Fort Polk, in hot and swampy Louisiana, a particularly sought-after posting.

"So it gets down to Joey's turn," Johnson continued. "He's selecting right in front of me. And there's only one slot left to go to Korea. And he looks at me. He's like, 'Well, I'm not going to Korea without you.' And I say, 'Okay. I appreciate that. I mean, if you want to do that, we can certainly still support each other from afar.' He said, 'Nope, nope, nope, nope. We made a handshake agreement. I'm going to go with you.' So he chose Fort Sill, Oklahoma. So I'm up next. I'm like, 'All right, it's Fort Sill for me too.' That was just an insight into Joey. He was such a great buddy. He didn't have to do that for me. Fort Sill or Fort Polk? Those are two of the worst first duties. Korea is exotic. It's overseas and exciting. He could have done that. We would have been fine. I would have supported him. Okay, I would have been a little bummed, frankly. But no, he didn't. He was just cool. There was a big, life-changing decision, career-changing decision, and he chose to go down the path with me. I was really touched by that."

After exams and graduation, after summer break and the hard shock of Zac Miller's death, Eddie Johnson and Joe Emigh and the rest of the Class of '02 went to their posts for training. The rugby players split up. Mo Greene, Jeremiah Hurley, Jim Gurbisz, Clint Olearnick, Pete Chacon, Matt Blind, and Andy Klutman headed for Fort Benning in Georgia for basic training and Ranger School. Scott Radcliffe went to the cavalry at Fort Hood in Texas. Brian McCoy and Jerrod Adams went to learn to fly helicopters at Fort Rucker in Alabama. Dave Little, Bryan Phillips, and Nik Wybaczynsky went to Fort Bliss in Texas for missile defense.

The rush to war in Iraq was gathering pace. Consider just one day nearly a year after the 9/11 attacks, Monday, August 5, 2002:

As the now scattered rugby players studied books or weapons or marched or ran themselves into the ground, in Washington, the chief of Central Command, General Tommy Franks, briefed George W. Bush on the plan for invading Iraq. "It was a hit," the historians Michael T. Gordon and General Bernard E. Trainor would write. "After a long odyssey, the administration thought it had settled on a plan."[6] That evening, the rugby players finished training, came home, opened a beer, ate pizza. At the White House, Bush dined with his national security adviser, Condoleezza Rice, and his secretary of state, Colin Powell. It was the dinner at which Powell, a revered general, famously told Bush of Iraq: "If you break it, you own it."[7]

Bush would break it. Thousands of his soldiers—and hundreds of thousands of Iraqis—would be broken too.

But as August 2002 wore on and White House meetings continued, young officers had new lives to lead. Even after Zac Miller's death, even amid training in an army already at war, they had youth, fitness, and freedom. They felt invincible.

Brian McCoy said, "Flight school was the first time we were really on our own. We didn't have anybody looking over us. We were adults, notionally. What we really were was freshly graduated and suddenly picking up a paycheck. We had some responsibility, but we had fun too."[8]

McCoy and Jerrod Adams rented a house with a couple of other West Pointers, all determined to make the most of their relative freedom.

"Jerrod and I were stick buddies," McCoy said. "We were in the same class, learning how to fly helicopters together. He was a whiz kid. I would study all night, he would pass out on the couch. I'd wake him up at 4:00 a.m. He'd say, 'Oh, we have a test.' And he would study for five minutes and make a ninety-five. And I'd make a ninety, and I studied all night. We became close. We got in an accident once, on the way to the flight line one morning. We were in his tiny little car, took a little back road, might not have been supposed to be there, it was a little wet, we hit a tree and flipped. Both of us had our seat belts on, and we walked. I had zero scratches. To this day I don't know how. Jerrod had a bloody nose from the airbag, which I didn't because in that car I didn't even get an airbag. And somehow, that was it.

"It wasn't too much longer I got married to Denae, and when I did, Jerrod got pretty emotional. Because, you know, he remembered that less than a year ago, we'd been sitting upside down in a car. You know, we stuck together."

So did Johnson and Emigh. Before Fort Sill, around Dave Little's wedding, there were parties at Bryan Phillips's place in Bakersfield, California, and at Joe Emigh's on Sunny Hills Road in Fullerton. At the Emighs', Johnson was both impressed and a little envious.

Johnson said, "Joey's parents were just incredible. I remember seeing his home and his bedroom, all of his football memorabilia and homemade stuff on the shelf. And I just remember thinking like, 'I don't know this.' I didn't. My family wasn't really like that. I came from a broken home. And, like, my dad was not sentimental. We didn't have a lot of pictures and like, kind of trinket things. I remember looking at that, thinking, 'Man . . .' I was kind of jealous of how Joey grew up. It seemed so tight. His mom and dad were so supportive and sweet. I remember feeling really happy for him. And then, okay, there was that little bit of drama over a girl . . .

"I don't remember exactly where and when everything happened. That crew was just heavily alcohol-fueled. It was a fun time. But there was some drama. I remember Joey getting a little ticked off at a particular female that Lucas Welch"—another 2002 grad—"had shown some attention to, and, uh, Joey didn't seem to like that. Joey was really attached to that particular girl. Joey was drunk and learned that she had, like, kissed Lucas or something. And Joey just started throwing chairs around the backyard. And we were like, 'Let's go find a quiet space, until he sleeps it off . . .' Lucas and I went to sleep in the back of Joey's truck. He had a covered truck. He found us. Somehow he got away from his family, who were trying to corral him and put him to sleep, and he ended up fighting us. Well, we just kind of ran off into the dark. It was weird and dramatic. Joey was really attached to that girl."

It was a booze-soaked, emotional moment, but Johnson and Emigh had careers to begin at Fort Sill. They rented a house on Kincaid Avenue in Lawton, the town outside the base. It was almost completely unprepossessing: brick, one story, garage, gabled roofs, parched lawn out front, the shade of a single tree, a small yard out back.

Every morning, the young officers went out for physical training. Some officers were doing extra, preparing for Ranger School or because they were going to light artillery. Johnson and Emigh were looking at six months at Fort Sill, training to fire heavy guns. They chose not to push themselves too hard, too soon—the mental workouts were tough enough on their own.

"It was the schoolhouse there," Johnson said, "because it's incredibly math-intensive to be able to calculate manually how to fire artillery, you know, twenty kilometers away, with accuracy. Even though we had all this technology, we had to learn the old-school way in case something broke or whatever. So there was a lot of classroom work, and then we'd go out into, quote-unquote, 'the field.' We'd go to these ranges and sit on an observation point with binoculars and watch artillery land in this field, landing on old school buses and cars. I remember sitting on a little stool we were issued, next to Joey, going through these exercises. He was really good. He was smart. He would excel at that stuff. But it was boring. It *sucked*. And, you know, we would party just as hard as before."

Johnson, Emigh, and anyone they could round up went into Oklahoma City, "this little place called Scooters, it had penny beer night. I guess the beers in Oklahoma, legally, at the time anyway, were watered down to three-point-four percent. So they would just have these penny beer nights, where quite literally you just put a coin on the board and they gave you a beer. You opened a tab to close it with a tip, but we would just have fistfuls of coins in our pockets. We'd literally drink thirty beers and be just fine for competing in the morning."

Between classes, physical training, and field work, Johnson and Emigh lived like "typical bachelors just out of college. The most gourmet meal we would cook was pasta and meat sauce. And I'm just loving the sauce that I would make. I'm just like throwing stuff in it, acting. I'm tweaking it. Joey got so excited when I told him we were gonna make that for dinner."

There's a picture from the house in Lawton. Johnson and Emigh, standing in front of a metal fireplace set in a brick wall, bare except for a tacked-up poster, a cartoon, a mustachioed man in a sombrero and the word *Zapata!* Emigh is wearing sneakers, sweatpants, a yellow T-shirt, and a cap turned backwards. He is barrel-chested and broad. Johnson is taller and slimmer, smiling and holding a beer. Emigh's eyes are closed—"typical Joey"—he has one foot on the coffee table next to what might be manuals or notebooks, and he is making a sort of "ta-da!" gesture, arms out. The thing he's showing off is the mantel over the fireplace, which is lined with empty beer bottles, two deep.

"That's one of my favorite pictures," Johnson says. "Joey loved Corona."

ROUGHLY 350 miles south of Fort Sill, a straight shot on Interstate 45, lies Lake Conroe in southeast Texas. The lake is man-made, built in 1973 by damming the San Jacinto River to provide water to nearby Houston. Far from the biggest reservoir in Texas, it's big all the same: twenty-six miles long, six miles wide and seventy feet deep in the river channel; a ninety-foot lighthouse was built in 1977.[9] The Sam Houston National Forest, home to bald eagles and alligators, covers much of the north shore. Much of the rest of the shoreline is dotted with houses, docks, and bars. Like any stretch of water, Lake Conroe can be dangerous. In 2014, the *Houston Chronicle* called it the deadliest lake in Texas: twenty-two fatalities in fifteen years.[10] In most, alcohol played a role.

In the plains, summer gets hot. At Fort Sill, one hundred degrees Fahrenheit came and went. On Labor Day weekend of 2002, Joey and Eddie went south to Lake Conroe. A West Point classmate, Nathan Hekimian, had a lake house and a Glastron GX225, the kind of boat you'd use to pull a water-skier, benches at the bow and the stern. Another classmate, Rob Stoffel, came too. The young officers had a typical lake weekend, hanging out and drinking and taking the boat for spins.

Johnson said, "Nate knew this little sports bar where there were some volleyball courts. We trusted him to drive the boat back. He stopped drinking. He was fine. But the rest of us? We just got hammered."

In the early hours of Monday, September 2, the four friends set off back to the house.

"It was probably thirty minutes back," Johnson continued. "I remember Nate pointing ahead, saying there was a certain signature of lights on the bank that meant we were getting close. I was sitting at the back of the boat, on the bench at the right. Joey was back left. Nate was driving and Rob was sitting in front of Joey, in, like, the captain's chair. It was really loud, with the wind. We couldn't really talk. So we were just kind of sitting there, just trying to sober up. And I remember looking over at Joey, and he was just looking at me. And he just kind of smiled, like he was up to something. And then he stood up and jumped out of the boat."

He wasn't wearing a life vest.

Johnson thought, "Fuck me."

"So I stood up, slapped Nate on the shoulder and shouted to turn around: 'Joey's fucking around, we got to go get him.' And we turned around."

The boat idled in the dark, water lapping the hull.

"I was like, 'Well, I think this is where it is. Go a little further up.' We're all scanning and calling his name. 'Come on, Joey. Stop fucking around.' And a couple minutes passed. Rob was the first to like, kind of start *shaking*. He got anxious, 'Like, what the fuck is happening? Where's Joey?' I was like, 'I don't know, man. Like, he just jumped out. I don't know what to tell you.'"

Hekimian took the boat in circles. Johnson and Stoffel swept the dark water with flashlights.

"We couldn't find anything. We were pretty upset. We go back to the house, we make some calls. I think Nate kind of took charge. His dad came over. I don't remember. It's kind of fuzzy after that for me."

Someone called Joe Emigh's parents, waking them at the house on Sunny Hills Road. Marianne, Emigh's sister, was in college in Colorado. At six in the morning on Labor Day, her mom called.

"She wanted to make sure I had a friend nearby. I did. She just said, 'Hey, remember how your brother was going to a lake this weekend with some friends?' And then she told me he was missing. And they'd been searching. It was the hardest thing I've ever experienced."[11]

Joanne Emigh flew to Boulder to be with her daughter. George Emigh flew to Houston and drove to Lake Conroe to search for his son.

"When somebody drowns," George said, "the body gets heavy. It won't float for a few days, until the gas is built up. I stayed at the house, and there was a helicopter flying around the lake, looking."[12]

He waited.

Police scoured the lake. On the second day, Tuesday, September 3, past noon, they found Joey. Johnson and George Emigh were out on the dock.

Johnson said, "I remember seeing this nervous activity. The search boat stopped. And we're like, 'Oh shit. Are they finding something?' This happened a few times. I'm watching them through the binoculars, and George is next to me. I looked over to George. I said, 'I think they just pulled him up.' Joey was wearing a maroon T-shirt. I remember that. I remember seeing what they pulled out was the same. I looked over to George, and I said, 'I think they just found him.' I handed him the binoculars. He was very quiet. He looked at me, and said, 'Yep.' He handed me those binoculars back, and he turned and walked away."

They found his son, George said, "probably a couple hundred yards from the dock. They took me out on the lake. It's hard to imagine what happened, but throughout the lake there were buoys with lights on them. And I was just thinking, 'If something happened, you could see one of those, you could swim to it and hold on.' But . . . I don't really know. That's just what goes through your mind. A parent's worst nightmare."

Why? That was the question. Why did Joe Emigh jump?

George said, "We had a swimming pool. So Joey was in the pool a lot. We had the ocean. When the children were younger we had a ski boat, and he skied and he was around boats and lakes and swimming and life vests and all that kind of stuff and safety issues around water. And yet, that's what happened. I'm still not sure *what* happened. But that doesn't really matter. It happened. It was just a terrible accident."

According to the *Houston Chronicle*, it was the seventh death on Conroe that year.[13] In April, a canoe overturned. In May, a teen was swept away in a storm. In June, a man drowned while swimming. In July, a man and a woman crashed their boat into a bridge; that same month, a man jumped from a boat to cool off.

Johnson will never forget the look on his best friend's face that dark night in the boat. "It was just very typical Joey, like, 'I'm about to fuck up this night in a fun way.' He smiles and he jumps. He was a strong swimmer. An incredible athlete. I wasn't concerned. I'm not an experienced boater. We were going pretty fast. But I'm thinking, 'Well, Joey wouldn't have jumped out if he thought there was some risk.' But he was hammered. So I don't know. When he jumped and hit the water, I didn't keep my eyes locked on him. I just slapped Nate on the shoulder and gave him the universal turn-around thing, with my hand, just spinning it round. I say, 'Joey jumped out. Fucking turn the boat around.' My recollection is he jumped head-first, like into a pool. There was a lot of speculation about why we couldn't find him. There was the current, and the wake from the boat had the water churning. And it was black night. He may have swam down. He may have hurt his neck, his head, on entering the water. We don't know."

According to the medical examiner in Harris County, Texas, Joe Emigh was found in Atkins Creek, in the southern part of the lake, at 12:40 p.m. on September 3, 2002. He was a "well-nourished 229-pound white male" and he was wearing a "burgundy T-shirt and green, lime, turquoise, and white shorts." He had been drinking. Every finding accorded with freshwater submersion. He did not break his neck. Cause of death: asphyxia by drowning. Manner of death: accident.

He was twenty-three.

♦   ♦   ♦

MARIANNE EMIGH had a part-time job, nannying two small girls. The Tuesday after Labor Day, the second day of the search, her mother went with her to help.

"And that is when we got the phone call from my dad. Basically, he said, 'The helicopters are circling. I think they found his body.' That's when we knew he was truly gone, not just somewhere on an island, drinking a piña colada. It was your worst nightmare. And so much of it. The hardest thing was watching my parents. Watching my mom suffer."

Some of Emigh's rugby teammates were at Fort Rucker in Alabama with Brian McCoy and Jerrod Adams. George Emigh called.

"I remember taking the call," McCoy said. "I remember the house we were at. Most of us were probably drunk, just sitting around in sorrow."

Some felt flashes of anger. At West Point, as captain, it had been Matt Blind's job to know his players. He knew Emigh.

"Joey was kind of like right on the edge," Blind said. "He'd be sitting back and we'd hear nothing from him, and then all of a sudden he would start screaming, you know? All of a sudden, the dude becomes the center of attention. And then he'd completely go back into himself. I can just picture Joe in that boat. Sitting there, relaxing, then saying to himself, 'You know what? It's time I shake this up a little bit. I'm gonna do something funny as shit.'"[14]

Coach Mike Mahan said Emigh would "walk into a room and the whole room would light up. He had that little grin on his face. Like he knew a secret. But I am still so angry at him for doing that silly thing. I don't know what else to say. It was just an awful, awful time."[15]

The news reached West Point. Charlie Erwin, the second row, was starting his senior year. Shannon Worthan, the scrum half, was captain. Though rugby players, including Worthan's brother Ryan, had seen combat, Charlie said, "We weren't expecting to lose any of our teammates, and suddenly in two months we'd lost Zac and Joe. They called us to the rugby pitch. The Catholic priest pulled us all together. He said, 'You are going to see their parents. And I would encourage you not to feel awkward about it. Because they will want to hear stories about their boys. They will want to hear stories about their sons. Because these guys lived their lives here with you. And you have stories they will not know. They will want to know them, because they will want to know their kid was loved.'"[16]

The team held a memorial service—first planned for Zac Miller, now to include Joe Emigh too.

Eddie Johnson took Emigh's truck and drove back to Oklahoma. At the rented house in Lawton, his friend's possessions lay where he left them. At Fort Sill, "some slap-dick captain," said Johnson, started an investigation. Bewildered, scared, Emigh's friends gave statements. The investigation was dropped, the young officers left alone with their grief.

Marianne Emigh remembers getting home to Fullerton and "seeing the devastation" as her parents attempted to make sense of their loss.

"There was a service shortly after my brother died, at Fort Sill. My family didn't go. I have a recording. I have the book where everybody signed their names. I believe we have a flag and maybe a couple other mementos. And then we did the service in Fullerton in an unconventional way. We did it probably three weeks after my brother was found. I think a lot of the wait was denial. You know, my parents weren't gonna get to be a part of a wedding or any of those amazing experiences with my brother. So they wanted to make sure his funeral was perfect. So one of the things they did was they adjusted the date, because the two pastors had sons that grew up with him and played sports with him, and one couldn't make the day we were planning.

"The pastors, neither thought they could do it without the other because it was so close to home. One of the dates we had, I think Jeremiah Hurley might not have been able to make it. That was a deal-breaker too. You know, because the army is the army and they had lost one of their own."

Jerrod Adams had been close to Joey at West Point, playing outside him, wing to center. He arrived in California first. He helped confirm the funeral and the burial plot. When Emigh was sixteen and his sister was seventeen and their friend Jaimie had died in her sleep, they chose to be baptized together. Emigh's family planned his funeral for the same church. But, Marianne said, "some of our close friends looked at my mom and they said, 'The church is not big enough. We need to do it at EvFree," the First Evangelical Free Church of Fullerton. "They were right. The big church in town was full. So many people were there."

EvFree is on North Brea Boulevard, about halfway between Emigh's home and school. Palm trees line the road in, parched hillsides rise behind. It's a huge church, holding six thousand. Its architecture, like so much in Fullerton, is midcentury modern. The red-tiled roof rises to form a slab, a sort of obelisk that glows in the sun.

On Saturday, September 21, 2002, so soon after Dave Little's wedding brought the rugby players to southern California—and so soon after Zac Miller's funeral took some back across the country to western Pennsylvania—the brothers gathered again. Little, Brian Phillips, and Nik Wybaczynsky drove through the night from Texas. Little took his shift at the wheel. Otherwise, he sat in the back, in "disbelief and shock."

"Joey was one of the folks I identified pretty well with," he said, "because he was from southern California too. We roomed together. We bonded over action, sports, and music."[17] The obituary in the *Orange County Register* spoke of such things, of Emigh's love of the sun, of sports, his easygoing nature. It also registered that he was little more than a kid. At the house on Sunny Hills Road, his room was, "let's face it, a mess."[18] Little said, "It was hard to lose someone I felt bonded to on a different level. It was just disbelief, trying to figure out what really happened. But the next step was, 'Okay, we all need to get support to the family. We all need to get something together.'"

The funeral was tough. George Emigh can't remember much of it. He was "just trying to get through the day." Little remembers one small awkward moment caused by the young officer's cluelessness over simple dress protocols. It seems, in retrospect, very Joe Emigh.

"I didn't know much about anything. I hadn't been in the real army yet. And so my buddy and I were getting into our dress blues for the funeral, and we didn't know what to wear, the tie or the bow tie. And we both agreed that you should just wear the highest level, so we both wore the bow tie, which is in hindsight ridiculous because bow ties are for celebratory events. And we're the only ones that wore a bow tie to that funeral. I felt pretty self-conscious.

"But it was gut-wrenching to see Joey's family and the impact it had on all of us. It was hard. There were a lot of tears. Especially as we were carrying the casket out. That was a powerful, powerful moment. We all felt we needed to get up there and at least touch the casket."

Farshid Karamzsukh, a schoolmate, spoke about his friend. Jerrod Adams and Mike Mahan spoke too. Within months of graduation, the coach had seen two players die. George and Joanne Emigh had been close to the team, traveling to Europe, standing on sidelines back home. At Zac Miller's funeral, Coach Mahan had paid tribute to a class vice president, a Rhodes scholar who had loved rugby fiercely. Now he spoke for Emigh, a key part of the A side, inside center and kicker, a natural athlete ahead of Zac Miller on the field but a long way behind in the classroom.

"They were all so different," Mahan said. "But deep inside, their character was the same."

Players were pallbearers. So were Farshid Karamzsukh and David Brookman, the big Fullerton football player, and Brandon Rosenthal, another friend. The three Fullerton grads wrote a eulogy for the West Point alumni magazine. They would not forget Emigh's "boyish exuberance and good nature that touched so many people." He was a "truly genuine individual who loved his family, his friends and his country." And they adopted his voice, his southern California drawl.

"Heeey Dude," they wrote. "We'll miss you."[19]

Joseph J. Emigh was buried at Loma Vista Memorial Park, on a green lawn, a few graves away from Jaimie, his friend who died at fifteen. His grave marker is a small rectangle, flat to the ground. Under his name, Lieutenant Joseph John-Lyle Emigh, and his birth and death dates, a high school photo and his West Point graduation picture are set in stone. The verse is Matthew 5:9: "Blessed are the peacemakers."

George Emigh isn't quite the strong, silent type, but he chooses his words with care. It's not surprising: he was born among the Republicans of Orange County and played football there and in Colorado, both hard schools. He got a job, married well, had kids and watched them thrive. Then his son died. George has been through the mill. In 2016, Joanne died of cancer. She was only sixty-one. At Loma Vista, she is buried next to her son. Come time, George will lie there too.

He said, "When it comes to losing a child, what you try to do is just put it back there someplace. So you can just get through the day, the week, the year. It was tough. Because I was a salesman, I'd call on customers and have very good relationships. I knew their family, they knew my family, what was going on. And you know, that was a difficult thing. Just to get back to work. And to see people that knew Joey. He would go out golfing with some of my friends. You know, it's a struggle. Every day is a struggle. It was just his birthday. Last Friday."

Marianne told me a story about her little brother. When he was at West Point, his mom would send T-shirts made by Hurley, a surfing brand, to Emigh's big teammate Jeremiah Hurley. It became a thing, a joke between the two of them, and Hurley became as close to the Emighs as anyone. When their son died, the Emighs delayed his funeral to make sure Hurley was there. And then, years later, Joanne got cancer. She had major surgery. George and Marianne were warned she might not be able to speak. But, Marianne said, "The first thing she saw was 'Hurley' on this physical therapist's shirt. She lifted her hand and pointed and said, 'Jeremiah Hurley.'

"She had just come out of traumatic brain surgery. And the first thing she went to was that connection to rugby, to my brother and to his good friend. Jeremiah."

In Fullerton, Marianne and George showed me an album of pictures of Emigh, from little kid to West Point cadet. Eddie Johnson was there, the party at Sunny Hills Road, summer 2002, Emigh on his shoulder in goofy space-age shades. A girl, too, a blonde; it seemed better not to ask. In other shots, Emigh kicked a rugby ball and stood, arm-in-arm in sweat-soaked quartered shirts with Brian McCoy. Below that, Emigh and Hurley sat pitchside in Virginia after their final Final Four, each with a beer in hand.

One swampy summer night at Fenway Park, opposite the Green Monster, the stadium's fabled left-field wall, amid a sea of braying Bostonians, I sat with Jeremiah Hurley. He was a bearded father of five, a Special Forces lieutenant colonel with multiple tours behind him but on the brink of retirement. He was with his rugby brothers for the first time in a while. We were all a few beers to the good. I told him Marianne's story.

"I don't cry," he said, contemplating his drink. "But that story . . . I don't know, man."[20]

He tried to say something else, only to be drowned out by a home run. When the roar subsided, he said, "Joanne and George, they were like extra parents to me. Hearing she remembered me on her death-bed? That she pointed at the Hurley shirt? It's a thing, man. It's a thing."

Hurley wasn't the only player who told me he thought, and that George and Joanne had thought, that if Emigh had been with his rugby brothers on Lake Conroe he might not have made his fatal mistake. Mo Greene said so too. But like Hurley, Greene conceded that when they were together, and drinking, the team could always find trouble.

When any of the players talked about Emigh, they laughed sadly, with a shake of the head.

Joey Emigh, man. "Heeey, Dude."

At Fenway, Hurley looked into his beer. Then he looked away, and up, into the bright white lights over the deep green field.

The "Follow Me" statue at Fort Benning, known to many soldiers as "Iron Mike."

Benning

ORT BENNING was, in a way, like Casablanca. It wasn't the climate, which runs hot and wet—or cold and wet—not dry like the North African desert. It was more like Rick's, the bar that Humphrey Bogart runs in the movie: sooner or later, until very recently, everybody came to Fort Benning.

It straddled the southern Georgia-Alabama border near Columbus, Georgia, and was home to one hundred twenty thousand servicemen and women and their dependents. It was founded during the First World War, near the sites of camps for soldiers who fought Creek Indians, and by the 1920s was home to the infantry school.[1] It was named for Henry Lewis Benning, a slaveholder and Confederate general. In May 2022, in the long aftermath of the murder of George Floyd, the Pentagon decided to rename Fort Benning for Hal and Julie Moore.[2] Hal Moore commanded at Ia Drang, a 1965 battle in Vietnam made famous by his 1992 memoir *We Were Soldiers Once . . . and Young*, and the film adaptation. Julie Moore helped reform the way the army informs families of combat deaths.

Officer basic training was at Fort Benning and is now at Fort Moore. So is Ranger School. In the summer of 2002, like Jim Gurbisz and Pete Chacon, Mo Greene was heading for the 101st Airborne. He "drove to Georgia from Pennsylvania at the beginning of August. Blinder and Jeremiah would have already been there. We were all there in various states, trying to figure out what the hell we were doing. That course is about four months long. Andy Klutman had to play the All-American thing in South Africa."[3] The big prop was the sole Army selection for the collegiate national team, for three games in Cape Town and Stellenbosch. Klutman asked Greene what he should do. Greene told him, "'Go play, and then get to the October class at Benning.' We were all excited, and we wanted to be together. And so Andy did that. I think Clint voluntarily went to the October class. Blinder too. And so we graduated in mid-December, took Christmas leave, then Ranger School was at the start of January. Jimmy ended up going to the October class too. I don't remember how he got there. I think it was something to do with his knee."

It was. Jim Gurbisz's injury would be a problem. As Greene put it, new lieutenants spent "one week in a classroom environment, one week in the field, all on small unit tactics, forms of the offense and defense, urban operations." Outside of that, there wasn't much to do but drink—which was fine with Greene.

"People say, like, 'There's nothing in Columbus. It sucks. It's a shithole town.' But Columbus is a town of one hundred thousand, and I grew up in a town without a stoplight. In Columbus, you can find just about everything you want. Restaurants, bars, some bad parts of town. Victory Drive is the main drag that's known to be shady.[4] Every military post attracts tattoo parlors and pawn shops, places for cashing checks. But I kind of liked Fort Benning. I met my wife there in 2005. We made friends outside the fort, Columbus natives, some of the greatest humans I've ever met. We still go down there. People hated Fort Benning, but I kind of fell in love."

Tori Richardson? Less so. By the time Jim Gurbisz went to Benning, they were engaged to be married.

"We were in La Jolla outside San Diego," Tori said, of the trip to California for Dave Little's wedding in June, after the Hurleys married at West Point. "It was kind of like, 'If this doesn't happen . . .' I mean, it wasn't an ultimatum. But I was just like, 'I haven't stuck with you through four years of insanity for you to just string me along at this point.' Now I'm just like, 'Oh my gosh, it's so silly to be like that.' But when you're watching everyone else get married? You're like, 'What the heck, man?' We'd been together seven or eight years. I was just, like, 'Whoa.' It was pretty much expected. He knew I'd been to California before. He knew I liked La Jolla.

"And he did a good job. It was very nice. Sunset, on the cliffs. The ocean, the seals. It was beautiful. Everything was perfect. But, yeah, it was definitely at that point where I felt like for both of us, the clock was ticking. Because it was one thing when he was at West Point, a couple hours away. Sure. I can see you occasionally. But if you're in Georgia, then wherever else? I had a full-time job in Jersey. I couldn't fly to Georgia every week."[5]

Tori and Jim were young: twenty-one and twenty-two. But in the army, that's often just how it is. They planned to marry in Vegas at Christmas. Tori would move to Columbus. But then things went wrong at Benning.

Ken Gurbisz has told the tale many times. He told it when we first talked, and he told it in Eatontown seven years later, on Memorial Day, under the stone doughboy by the lake at Wampum Park. When his son went to Benning, he knew his knee wasn't right.

"He went through all the training. And the last day is a two-mile run. And he didn't make the time. He missed it by thirty seconds. And an officer said, 'I'm thinking hospital, something's not right. This is not like you.' And sure enough, they took him to the hospital, they saw he had microfractures on his femur. So he had surgery and six months recovery. Meantime, they profiled him. He couldn't go infantry. He was devastated."[6]

Greene said, "For whatever reason, around senior year, maybe my shoulder injury, maybe the fact we were going infantry and the 101st, Jimmy and I grew pretty close, to the point where I spent time with him and Tori. Tori had some mixed feelings about the rugby personalities. A lot of women do. But Tori and I got along pretty well, or at least I felt like she liked me. And so after we graduated, I drove down to Jim's house in Jersey. We went to a concert together, Jim, Tori, and I. We were at Fort Benning too. He picked me up on my break from Ranger School and took me to get some food. He was having his knee issues still, and lots of new issues too. I graduated Ranger School in March '03. Jimmy was still at Fort Benning, with no end in sight."

The Iraq War began on March 20, 2003, with missile strikes at Saddam.[7] Everyone had known it was coming. On the same September 2002 morning that the rugby team held a memorial for Joe Emigh and Zac Miller, Secretary of Defense Donald Rumsfeld had told Fox News that Saddam was pursuing weapons of mass destruction.[8] It would turn out that Saddam wasn't, but the rugby players knew they were heading to war. Gurbisz knew he wasn't.

Another player bumped into Gurbisz at Benning. Pat McGinty was a blindside flanker from the Class of '03, a wrestler from Cleveland who found rugby and held on for dear life, one of those for whom the game became a way to get through West Point. He remembered Gurbisz and Clint Olearnick as "the ringleaders, not our official captains but the people that sort of ran the show, the people that made it fun. One or two pranks along the way, leading chants on the bus or giving someone a smack to the face unexpectedly. Sometimes you'd wish they'd leave you alone."[9] Gurbisz would chase McGinty "around H Lot with a stick. That was one of his things. Grab a big stick and chase us round the field until practice starts. Whack you with the stick, if he could catch you. Luckily, I was faster than him."

It was all fun and games most of the time, and McGinty became Gurbisz's "protégé," helping him "plan parties in hotels off post or when we went to Ohio State or Dartmouth." When McGinty ran into Gurbisz at Benning—at the start of an infantry career that would take him to the Sunni "Triangle of Death," south of Baghdad—he was startled by the change in his friend.

"I was in officer basic from July '03 until December. I walked into the little headquarters building, and he was sitting behind a desk. 'Jim? What the hell?' He wasn't in a great place. He was really pissed. He wasn't the same Jim Gurbisz. We got to talking, and that's when I got the whole story about being hurt and not being able to go infantry. They had him in some bullshit desk job there, an admin position where he was at the beck and call of leadership, making copies, running things here and there. He was really angry about that."

Ken Gurbisz remembers his son being relegated to "going around with the vendors as they emptied the soda machines."[10] For the young officer who lived and breathed infantry, who obsessed over *Band of Brothers*, who yearned to lead men in combat, it was a completely miserable time.

"We met up once or twice for dinner or a drink," McGinty said. "Purgatory is a good word for what he was in. You could tell it was weighing on him. It was affecting his happiness. I will always remember coming away from it, like, 'Man, that's not the same Jim Gurbisz.'"

There was a respite in December 2002, when Tori and Jim got married. Tori said, "I was like, 'Hey, let's just go to Vegas. That'd be so easy. We can just bring my parents, your parents. It'll be awesome. Fun.' Jim was like, 'Okay, cool.' So we drove to the airport on Christmas."

It wasn't a West Point wedding like the Hurleys', lieutenants forming a guard, sabers raised. It wasn't a hometown special like in San Diego, for Dave and Lindsay Little. Pete Chacon was the only player who came to the wedding chapel at the Rio, to stand as best man. But the small party from Jersey had fun.

Tori said, "We were all getting drunk the night before. They all got me very drunk. Helen [Gurbisz's mother] was definitely really upset with Jim because I was super green 'round the gills. They were very worried I was going to be vomiting at my wedding. But I pulled through. I ate some really greasy food, managed to not look like I was dying at my wedding. And then they had a rooftop restaurant where we had dinner and toasts and all of that. So that was a pretty good time."

But reality beckoned. In January, Tori, Jim, and his father packed a U-Haul and drove to Georgia. Jim went back to his desk job. Tori did her best to fit in. It was far from easy. She had never felt more of a girl from Jersey. The weather was "muggy and buggy and gross." The locals, particularly the other army wives, *didn't* curse like cab drivers at Newark airport. You couldn't buy beer on Sunday. Tori got "a terrible job at Bed Bath & Beyond. It was soul-sucking. Absolutely soul-sucking. You want to talk about stress? There was Jim with his knee. And then there was me, such high stress that I could not get out of bed in the morning. It was not our brightest moment. We made it through, especially once the army was like, 'Oops, here's ten thousand dollars we forgot to give you.' We opened our bank account one day, and we're like, 'What? Where does this money come from?'"

Gurbisz tried to save his career, petitioning the chain of command. Ken said, "He wanted his infantry status, he wanted the crossed rifles. What he said to them was that the two-mile run is not mandatory, it's just the final day. He passed everything that was required of an infantry officer. So they made him an infantry officer. He got his rifles."

But Jim Gurbisz couldn't get out of Benning.

To Tori, "it was pretty clear that active infantry wasn't going to happen. I mean, the doctors did a good job repairing his knee, but it wasn't going to be like he wanted it to be as soon as it needed to be. It was sad. We were just married, moved in together, but his recovery was really hard. He was doing physical therapy, but they couldn't give a hard date for recovery because the surgery was so major. He became really depressed. He was drinking a lot. He was not supposed to put any weight on his knee, but he would try to walk around without his cane while he was drunk and he would hurt himself, stuff like that.

"I remember one night yelling at him. Like, 'You know what? Your knee is never going to heal. You're never going to be able to pick up your kids.' And he was like, 'I don't see myself making it to thirty.' And I just remember being so pissed off at him. You know, 'How can you even think like that?' I don't know if he was just depressed or if he just had a bad feeling. But now I'm just like, 'Oh my God, why did you say that? Oh my God, were you psychic? Or were you just in a really bad place and pissed off and drunk? Just pissed off at your wife nagging you to use your crutches.'"

More rugby players cycled through. Charlie Erwin, the second row forward from the Class of '03, remembered that "Tori would cook these great Italian meals and we would go to Publix, which was the grocery store, and get six-packs of beer and get a DVD and head back to their house and just drink beer and eat great meals and watch terrible movies. It was wonderful. They were great because they lived in an apartment. They had a dog. They were living like adults, where I was living in the officers' quarters, just one room and a bathroom. At Jim and Tori's, it was like going home again."[11]

Tori has fewer fond memories of Benning.

"I didn't retain a lot from that time because I didn't want to remember it. I hated my job. Jim hated trying to figure out what was going to happen to him. So, yes, it was like purgatory. We just had to wait it out and see what the army was going to do. That was the only choice we had."'

IT SEEMED that newlyweds Jim and Tori Gurbisz would never escape, when all of a sudden they did. It was April 2004.

Ken said, "Long story short, he gets a call from this lieutenant colonel who was a rugby player in transportation and asked Jim if he wanted to come on board."

Helen said, "This colonel, he'd been to West Point too. He says, 'What team did you play on?' And so Jimmy said, 'I played on the A team.' And the colonel had only played on the C team."[12]

Gurbisz was a West Pointer, near the top of his class, in an army at war on two fronts, eager for manpower. He was a big fish to be hauled in. A deal was done. Gurbisz became a transportation officer with Twenty-Sixth Forward Support Battalion, Second Brigade, Third Infantry Division, based at Fort Stewart on the Canoochee River in Georgia.

Gurbisz would have done "anything to get out of Fort Benning," Ken said. But he also knew his new battalion would soon deploy. "He knew that was why they were filling their ranks."

Tori was "selfishly glad. Transport? That's so much better than infantry. Like, okay, cool. We can work with this. It's not as scary-sounding as infantry. That was always the other side of the coin. Like, how dangerous is this going to be? And where's the base? For me those were the biggest concerns because I would be living by myself. Am I going to hate my life? Or is it going to be okay? We were definitely glad to go to Fort Stewart. It wasn't an arduous move."

The city around Fort Stewart is Hinesville. Like Columbus, it is home to all the sorts of businesses young male soldiers might decide they want. Young soldiers' wives, less so. So Tori and Gurbisz bought a house in Savannah, about forty-five minutes away.

"Jim basically was like, 'I don't want you living in Hinesville, especially alone while I'm gone.' In Savannah, you had normal neighborhoods. It was just like a normal city. Right before he left for Iraq, I got a part-time job with a friend who owned a couple UPS stores. I also had my own business, making candles and soaps. A side hustle before side hustles were cool. Our house smelled crazy. Candles in the garage, soap in the kitchen. Bars of soap curing, candles cooling. So I did that and I went and helped people mail packages a few hours a day. It was enough to keep me entertained and talking to people, because I definitely have hermit tendencies."

Gurbisz was quite the opposite. A big personality, relentlessly out-going—if not a ring-knocker (slang for military academy graduates who wear their large, flashy class rings), a confident and proud West Pointer. In transportation, he stood out. Better yet, there was a job for him to do—it involved improvised explosive devices: IEDs.

IN MAY 2003, Paul Bremer, head of the Coalition Provisional Author-ity in Iraq, made two decisions that would serve to throw fuel on the fire of the insurgency to come. Bremer ordered that members of Saddam Hussein's Baath party be purged from government jobs, and he disbanded the Iraqi army. In two moves, Bush's viceroy created a vast, embittered foe, with access to unsecured munitions.[13]

Soon, insurgents used such munitions to make bombs. Car bombs, suicide bombs, bombs in the roadside dirt.

In the summer of 2007, Rick Atkinson, the *Washington Post* reporter who wrote *The Long Gray Line*, the seminal book about West Point and Vietnam, published *Left of Boom*, an account of the role of IEDs in Iraq and Afghanistan and of attempts to lessen their toll. He described the first such blast, which killed four soldiers, a passerby, and the bomber, on March 29, 2003, just north of Najaf in

Iraq. "Lt. Col. Scott E. Rutter, a battalion commander who rushed to the scene from his command post half a mile away, saw in the smoking crater and broken bodies on Highway 9 'a recognition that now we were entering into an area of warfare that's going to be completely different.'"[14]

By the time Atkinson wrote *Left of Boom*, IEDs had "caused nearly two-thirds of the 3,100 American combat deaths in Iraq, and an even higher proportion of battle wounds." In 2007 alone, "through mid-July, [IEDs] also resulted in an estimated 11,000 Iraqi civilian casualties and more than 600 deaths among Iraqi security forces."

The bombers took aim at mosques and marketplaces, at lines for gas, food, or aid. They hit American checkpoints and vehicles.

At Fort Stewart in the summer of 2004, the Twenty-Sixth Forward Support Battalion (26 FSB) knew convoys would form the bulk of its work in Iraq. It needed a security platoon, outriders to watch for attacks and bombs. Jim Gurbiz saw his chance.

Ken said, "He went in to the company commander and said, 'I'm the best qualified for the job. I've been through officer basic.' So they gave him the platoon, and he started training them."

Tori saw a "huge turning point. The security platoon was a new lease on life. It was like, 'I get to do what I want to do. What I thought I wasn't going to be able to do and now I get this specialized new role.' So he was super excited about that."

Gurbisz's path to the security platoon echoed his path to the West Point rugby team. As his father put it, the security platoon was formed of "cast-offs."

"You know, when they say to other officers, 'You have to give two people to security,' they're not gonna give the cream of the crop. Maybe not the worst, but the lower-level people. But Jim trained them, and it became a platoon everybody wanted to get into."

At West Point, the rugby team were proud outsiders, cut from football, drifted over from lacrosse, wrestling, or track. A ragtag bunch, training on a rocky field at the shitty end of the campus. At Fort Stewart, 26 FSB's security platoon found the same sort of spirit.

On 9/11, Nate Hadd was a senior in high school in Michigan. When

America went to war, he joined the Marines. But he hurt his shoulder and couldn't ship out, so he joined the army instead on a waiver. He "wanted to be infantry but chose to be a tank mechanic as that was the only thing available. So I went to basic training in May '03 at Aberdeen Proving Ground in Maryland, and then my very first unit was the Twenty-Sixth Forward Support Battalion."[15]

When Hadd learned that 26 FSB would deploy to Iraq, he was told he would be going "to a place called a FOB, a forward operating base. And one of the things that the unit was doing was using support soldiers to secure supplies. So they were looking for thirty-five volunteers. I wanted to be part of combat, and I wanted to tell my children that. So this was my opportunity."

Zach Pamer was from Michigan, too, his dad a Marine who had served in Vietnam. He ended up with 26 FSB by a similar roundabout route, and one day his sergeant called him over and said, "'Hey, fucker, you still want to do some cool shit?' And I'm like, 'Yes, first sergeant.' He said, 'All right, go over to fucking headquarters company.' So I just packed up my gear and went."[16]

Hadd said, "I think there were maybe seven or eight of us off the original volunteer list. Everyone else that was assigned was kind of the misfit children. People who had disciplinary problems. People who were kind of nonconformist. So to say we weren't a very well-respected platoon right off the get-go was an understatement. We had cooks, medics, mechanics, everything you could imagine that was not a combat soldier."

Pamer trained as a medic under Staff Sergeant Robinson, an older soldier Pamer came to revere and call "the Enigma. He'd been busted down four times. Old Army Ranger guy. He had a mouth on him. But he knew what he was talking about. He forgot more than I will ever know about military medicine. It was insane. He was a little insane himself. But he taught me everything from how to give IVs to tourniquets and everything else. I just tried to learn from him, mimic him, down to always eating beef jerky. I soaked up his knowledge like a sponge."

The security platoon came up with a name: Top Flite. It sounded serious, but to those who knew, it was not. It came from *Friday After*

Next, a cult stoner comedy starring Ice Cube, released in 2002:[17] "We Top Flite Security of the world, Craig."

Tori saw that "they loved it. They loved that it was their own inside joke. It was kind of like a game. No one really wanted to go transport. These guys were the misfits among the misfits. Nowhere else to go, kind of thing. But the security platoon gave them purpose, something to hold on to, something to make them feel good."

Hadd said, "Summer '04, we have this platoon, we show up every day, we do basic medical training, stuff of that nature, but we really don't have a very good plan. But one of the things the army started doing at that time was they started to do a rotation to the Joint Readiness Training Center at Fort Polk, Louisiana. Down there, basically you throw everything into a blender and you get ready to go to combat. We had some cultural training, some awareness training, and we did specific convoy operation training.

"The very first thing Jim did was he explained to us all the standards and discipline of this platoon. How we were going to be different. We are gonna be the standard bearers for 26 FSB. He trained the shit out of us, man. There were some very, very long nights. We did runs daily, we did physical fitness. He took us from just honestly a bunch of shitbags to being ready to roll."

Randall Mullally joined the army at eighteen, out of high school, wanting to do "something" in the wars after 9/11. The military bureaucracy lost him, he said, somewhere on his way to airborne school.

"I found myself in this communications shop, totally out of place. And so there I was, waiting to go back to school, to get back on track for Special Forces, and then they decided to make this Top Flite platoon. I met with Jim and I was just like, 'This is exactly what I want to do.' I canceled all my plans and stuck with them. We absolutely loved him. He kept all of us there. He was amazing to the team. He used to pick up trash and cigarette butts, tidy up the place as he went about his work. To this day, I will pick up trash and cigarette butts and put them in my pocket. Jim didn't have garbage cans everywhere, so his pockets were full of trash."[18]

Zach Pamer remembered the cigarette butts, too, and the cigarettes Gurbisz would smoke himself sometimes, which he carried in a Ziploc bag. Early on, Pamer was detailed to be Lieutenant Gurbisz's driver, Van Torres his gunner. Torres was a mechanic who joined up to escape his small hometown in northern Colorado. He said Gurbisz "was the platoon leader, and everybody knew that, but he wasn't heavy-handed" when it might have been tempting to be so. "There were a lot of guys in the platoon for whom being there wasn't necessarily their idea. At times, it seemed like we were a bunch of rejects. But Jim went about things appropriately, ensuring that not only did we fit together but everyone was family. We looked up to him for his leadership ability, but he wasn't one of those people that had to tell everybody, 'I'm in charge.' He just knew he was. But he was also a joker, you know. He liked to have a good time."[19]

According to Pamer, Gurbisz used his joking as a leadership tool. He saw that "me and Van were a little on edge because we were two young guys trying to be hard-asses, to establish who was the best. It was very competitive. But then Jim would just calm us down: crack jokes, get us laughing, just get our heads right."

Alejandro Michel was a sergeant with combat experience in the Iraq invasion of 2003. He was "working in the motor pool, and then here comes this hot-shot lieutenant. These West Point guys? You can smell them a mile away. He was a different breed. He was in charge and everybody knew it, but he was real easygoing, real easy to talk to. He was a kind of charismatic guy. People wanted to be around him."[20]

Gurbisz organized trips to Fort Polk and to the National Training Center at Fort Irwin in California, out in the Mojave Desert. Randall Mullally said, "26 FSB had caught this big fish and they knew it. So they were like, 'Whatever you want, we're gonna make it happen. We were just gung-ho young guys who wanted to get the job done really well. We wanted to train with the best, so Jim stuck us with Special Forces guys down at Fort Polk, Louisiana. We trained with them as often as they would let us. We did a lot of interesting stuff. We didn't have a lot of time. We trained and trained and trained. One time at Fort Polk, Jim told us, 'Get these trucks stuck. So you can see what it means to get a truck stuck.' So we got a big truck stuck in six feet of mud and had to call wreckers to get it out. And he's like, 'That's what happens when you make a mistake out there. When you get a truck stuck, you're stuck. You're sitting ducks.' He knew what he was doing. He taught us a lot."

Gurbisz also tried to teach his men rugby. He had a ball, which often came out when he spoke about his days at West Point. The men had footballs, Mullally said, "but when Jim would play, it was underhand instead of overhead" passing. Most often, the games degenerated into rolling, laughing fights. Most often, Gurbisz was in among the scrapping. Most often, other officers chose to look away.

"I wouldn't say we had special treatment," Van Torres said. "But we were under a lot more stress than the majority of the people from the battalion because of what we were training to do. We knew we would be out there every single day in Iraq. And so we blew off steam, at times. It wasn't necessarily overlooked but it was understood. We knew we would be doing something other people didn't want to do. We knew we would possibly face our end, every single day. And if you're heavy-handed with people in that type of situation, the morale goes down. Morale was a big thing for us."

RIGHT AFTER Christmas 2004—the Asian tsunami in the news, storms over Fort Stewart—the time came to deploy.

Ken and Helen and Kathleen Gurbisz came down to see Jim off. Tori was preparing to be "completely by myself, taking care of the house, paying all the bills, managing everything from mowing the lawn and taking out the trash to making sure Jim's things were put on hiatus. His phone, things like that. It was a lot of work. Of course I was worried, but we were like, 'Hey, let's focus on what we can do, because it's coming no matter what. Let's do the stuff that's gonna matter, instead of just me freaking out every day until you've gone.'"

26 FSB flew to Kuwait. There was drama right after they landed, on the ride to Camp Virginia. A kid on Sergeant Michel's bus shot off his rifle by mistake, narrowly missing the driver. Gurbisz and his sergeant "got our ass handed to us by the brigade commander." Then Gurbisz got Top Flite to Udairi Range, a huge training facility Nate Hadd called "a shithole in the middle of the desert." In that shithole, also a vast boneyard of vehicles destroyed in Iraq, Gurbisz arranged practice convoys.

Pamer noticed that much of the training followed "a manual written during the seventies, the Vietnam War, and we were going into Iraq. We were just like, 'Really? Are you sure?' It seemed dumb." But in an army ill-prepared for a long occupation, for the kind of conflict that flickered and spat in 2004 and would cook up hellishly in 2005, imperfect training was common. Gurbisz, Pamer said, "would just tell us, like, 'We just gotta get through it. We'll just figure it out.'"

Hadd said, "There were a lot of soldiers that were pissed off at him. It was like, 'We're support guys. What the hell are we doing at three o'clock in the morning in the middle of the desert, shooting at camels and stuff?' Man, it was some hard training. But it ended up saving lives."

In the Iraq War, transportation was never an easy place to be. In convoy security, the job bore many hallmarks of what was required of infantry, but without anything close to the equipment, expertise, and support. Keeping spirits up was tough. Studies showed that transportation units had some of the worst morale in the entire American force.[21]

Gurbisz tried to keep his men sharp. When 26 FSB moved into Iraq, to FOB Rustamiyah in southeastern Baghdad, he divided Top Flite into three-man teams. Each of the platoon's High Mobility Multipurpose Wheeled Vehicles (HMMWVs, pronounced Humvees) had a driver, a commander, and a gunner, leaving one seat spare.

Michel said, "Jim was like, 'Hey, what do you guys want to do? Where do you guys feel most comfortable?' And I'm like, 'Sir, you can put me anywhere. Just don't put me as lead gun. I'm not good at navigating.' So, naturally, Jim put me as lead gun truck to navigate through Baghdad. And I'm like, 'Okay. Thanks, guy.'

"I was a little pissed off to begin with. But then I realized he'd seen something in me, and that made me a little bit better. And I learned to navigate real quick."

Cpt. Scott Radcliffe in a helicopter over Iraq in 2007.

War

IN EARLY August 2003 in northern Iraq, soldiers of the First Battalion, 508th Parachute Infantry Regiment moved north of the Little Zab River.

The "Red Devils"—a nickname acquired in the Second World War—had been dropped into hostile territory in March, securing airfields for troops to follow. At Erbil, the capital of Iraqi Kurdistan, they worked with Kurdish fighters to overrun Iraqi army positions. After that, they were in Kirkuk, and by July they were in Hawija, a hub for a growing insurgency fueled by Sunni Arabs once loyal to Saddam Hussein. The insurgents withdrew north. The Red Devils followed.

In the green and rocky landscape, their opponents used rocket-propelled grenades (RPGs) and small arms against poorly armored Humvees. The Red Devils' commanding officer decided the equipment was not the only thing lacking. He thought "pre-Iraq training was not adequate for reacting to ambushes. . . . The 'Kosovo' mentality of operating in a low-threat environment in which soldiers returned fire in a very limited manner was also not working." Therefore, "procedures were unhesitatingly modified to reflect a more traditional infantry approach in which known, likely, and suspected enemy locations were immediately suppressed." In other words, the Americans hit back hard—and "the number of killed and wounded enemy increased."[1]

The commander was Lieutenant Colonel Harry Tunnell, West Point Class of '84, a rugby number 8 whose aggression on the battlefield would earn a kind of renown.[2] One of his junior officers was

Andrew Klutman, the All-American prop from the Class of '02. As Tunnell described it, on August 3, 2003, Second Lieutenant Klutman led Third Platoon, A Company on an ambush patrol:

"The platoon set up on one of the roads near the company patrol base on the northern side of the Little Zab River. . . . During the early morning hours a three-man enemy RPG team packed up from its own ambush position and walked down the road into the platoon's planned kill zone. The paratroopers engaged the RPG team, killing one outright and wounding another (who died of his wounds later on). The platoon also captured three RPG launchers (two were loaded and ready to fire), six additional rounds of RPG ammunition, and one AK-47."

According to Tunnell, intelligence indicated that the man killed had fired the RPG that had killed twenty-year-old Specialist Justin Hebert, the Red Devils' first fatality.[3]

There were more.

On October 18, First Lieutenant David Bernstein, twenty-four, was killed on patrol near Taza. He was a West Pointer, fifth in the Class of '01, a swimmer nicknamed "Super Dave." Shot in the leg, he died for lack of a tourniquet.[4] Private First Class John Hart, twenty, was killed on the same patrol. Alarmed at the Americans' exposure to ambush, Hart had predicted his death to his father. He was shot in the neck.

Later, Lieutenant Colonel Tunnell was shot through the leg. Surgeries saved the limb. Lieutenant General H. R. McMaster, once a West Point winger, has described how "the orthopedic surgeon who did those surgeries was our scrum half in junior year, Tim Kuklo."[5]

There were rugby players everywhere.

After the campaign described by Tunnell, Andy Klutman came home from Iraq. Later, he deployed to Afghanistan, where he "mentored, trained, and assisted the Afghan government officials, police, border police, and national army in a province along the Pakistan border." After that, studying to be a doctor, he became student senate president at the University of Nebraska Medical Center. His time in an army at war, he said, taught him "not to sweat the small stuff."[6]

Other rugby players ended up in Iraq, sweating problems of every size.

Jeremiah Hurley ended up with the Seventy-Fifth Ranger Regiment. Mo Greene went to northern Iraq with the 101st Airborne, then switched to Special Forces. In 2003, the 101st took Pete Chacon and Clint Olearnick to Mosul, not far from Erbil and Kirkuk. In 2004, Matt Blind fought in Mosul with Third Battalion, Twenty-First Infantry, the Gimlets. Scott Radcliffe went into armor, One-Seven Cav, and deployed to Baghdad. Jim Gurbisz went there, too, of course, with Twenty-Sixth Forward Support Battalion, Second Brigade, Third Infantry Division.

Other players saw action later or not at all. Bryan Phillips, Nik Wybaczynsky, and Dave Little went air defense artillery. The Taliban didn't have ballistic missiles. Saddam did. Phillips arrived in Saudi Arabia in February 2003 "to provide missile defense for some airfields," but he "wasn't there very long. Once the threat was neutralized—Saddam fired missiles at Kuwait but never at Saudi[7]—we were among the first to come back."[8] Phillips spent three months in theater. Little manned Patriot missiles at Camp Virginia in the sands of Kuwait. Soldiers thanked him for shooting down Saddam's Scuds, never mind that it happened before he arrived. His battalion was sent to work the ports. Little "basically loaded ships for a month. Docks and ports and cramming all the redeploying units and their equipment into massive ships. I think we loaded five."[9] After that, Little spent a lot of time in Korea, where missile defense is key, then left the army after fifteen years.

Enforced multitasking was common. Eddie Johnson, Joe Emigh's close friend, stayed in field artillery after Emigh died. In Iraq, there was no one to fire howitzers at. Johnson ended up filling fourteen months in western Baghdad with jobs meant for engineers or infantry, "route clearance or guarding outposts," and leading "field artillery soldiers that had no idea how to kick in a door and to pull a trigger."[10] A small mercy: the area was quiet.

Jerrod Adams and Brian McCoy were fliers. In the first years of the 9/11 wars, Adams was based in Germany, flying Apache helicopters. In 2008, five years after the Iraq invasion, he went in. When we spoke in 2017, he was deploying to Afghanistan.[11] After that, he came back to Fort Rucker, Alabama, and was made lieutenant colonel. Among the Class of '02 rugby players, Adams was last man out of the army.

West Pointers serve five years on active duty. Brian McCoy followed that path. In 2003 he went to Italy to fly helicopters with the 159th Aviation Regiment. He was flagged for Iraq—then unflagged. He "went to Romania to do some joint task force stuff, then ended up in Korea."

When I first spoke to the brothers of '02, I asked each how they felt about the 9/11 wars. In particular, I asked about Iraq, the war that turned out to be built on sand. Not for nothing is the West Point motto "Duty, Honor, Country." Each player volunteered to join the army. Each went through four tough years to get there. Their political beliefs varied but debate was rare. The same went when I asked, "Iraq, right or wrong?" Brian McCoy spoke for them all:

"If it's a question of right and wrong, and did we do the right thing, I would say the answer was yes. But there was enough political uncertainty to last for the rest of my life."

Out of the army, McCoy lived in Texas with his family, worked a job in oil.

"I take my time, and I spend it with my wife and daughters," he said. "If I see a formation of Black Hawks, I stop and gaze at it for a while. At least my daughters know I used to fly them. I'm okay with that for now."[12]

MO GREENE met Becca Rae in Nashville in May 2004. He was back from Iraq, based at Fort Campbell in Kentucky with the Third Brigade, 101st Airborne Division, a storied outfit known as the Rakkasans, a derivation of the Japanese word for "parachute."[13] She was an aspiring country singer, performing at a bar in Printers Alley. For Greene and a bunch of other officers, "this was our starting bar. On Friday or Saturday, we would roll in around nine o'clock and just start buying buckets of beer. It was twelve dollars a bucket. And we were all like, quote unquote, 'rich lieutenants.' We would just give the waitresses twenty dollars, so these girls were making eight dollars in tips on a bucket. But the singers would bring around tip buckets too. And so that's how we met."

Becca was blonde, fine-featured, as slight as her voice was powerful.[14] Greene was still the pocket dynamo who played fly half, the iconoclast who chafed at West Point order and ritual but still finished fourth in his class.

"I left a bar napkin on the stage with my number. She called and we ended up going out. I was already smitten. I was in her car, and she had a key chain that said '2003.' And I was like, 'Oh, 2003, is that when you graduated from college?' She's like, 'No, high school.' I was like, 'Oh shit.' She was in high school when I was in combat. She's, like, five years my junior, which was a little bit weird at the time because that made her about to turn nineteen when I was twenty-three. But it was too late. It was already done."[15]

So was Greene's first tour. Around the time of the Iraq invasion, he went to assignment at Fort Campbell. There was nobody there. Greene submitted to a battery of vaccinations, including smallpox because "everyone was terrified of Iraq and chemical weapons," and sat through a briefing about "how to interact with the Muslim world, apparently." Then he was told to go home and wait for a flight. Eventually, someone saw his Ranger tab and made him "chalk leader"— the officer responsible for loading and managing the plane.

"So I've done nothing in the army at this point. But now I'm in charge of getting probably a couple hundred replacements from Fort Campbell to Iraq. My God. I got majors, I got captains, I got NCOs, I got privates. I got to figure this out."

He figured it out. Some of the 101st Airborne were in Saudi. Some were in Iraq in Tal Afar, an ancient city with a castle up near the Syrian border, a place full of trade and foreign fighters. Mo Greene didn't know where his brigade was.

"I ended up crawling around Saudi Arabia, trying to figure out, like, 'Are you my dad?' I had no idea. I remember climbing on a C-130, flying from Saudi Arabia to Baghdad, and they let me sleep in a bunk behind the cockpit, which was cool. I got shuttled over to some other air transport and they landed me in Mosul, and then I got on a truck and they took me west to Tal Afar, where I sat on the airfield for several hours, waiting for somebody to pick me up.

"They took me to the battalion headquarters, and I met my battalion commander. Lieutenant Colonel Chris Pease. Big, hulking guy. Looked kind of like Shrek. Put that in the book, he'll probably come back and fucking bite me. He was very sensitive about the fact he looked like Shrek. He was probably about six foot four, a wrestler.[16] He did the standard greeting. You wear your Ranger tab on your left shoulder. So when you shake hands with your right hand, sometimes you can't see the Ranger tab. So we call it the tab check. You shake hands with your boss and he kind of gives you a little spin to make sure you have your Ranger tab. If you're wearing it, in the infantry as a second lieutenant, you're going to be all right. And then he's like, 'Come on in.'

"He's like, 'Hey, normally I'd give you a rifle platoon, but I don't have any of those. And so you're gonna go to the anti-tank company and take a platoon.' He's like, 'I'm really glad you're here. It'll mean a lot to the guys. But, you know, this thing's over and we're gonna be going home.' I was like, 'Oh, that sucks. I missed the war.'"

But he didn't.

Based out of an "old, bombed-out fort just outside Tal Afar, a few miles down the road towards Mosul," Greene spent a lot of time on patrol. At Fort Benning, he had trained in tactics for dismounted rifle platoons. In Iraq, his anti-tank company had four Humvees with mounted fifty-cal or MK19 machine guns, TOW missile launchers too. Greene had to learn fast, not least how to bolt steel onto the floors of the Humvees to try to combat IEDs, but also how to stack sandbags on top of the steel, which in the already cramped trucks made Greene glad he'd never grown tall. He was "kind of pissed at not getting a rifle platoon, but it worked out great. I had free rein of a 240-square-kilometer sector."

The commander of the 101st Airborne was Major General David Petraeus, "the father of counterinsurgency tactics." Greene applied himself to learning the "human terrain." Getting to know villages and villagers, trying to figure out who was in charge and if they would work with Americans. Every day three platoons went out, one mounted base defense, and one rested.

The quiet did not last.

"It was late summer when the insurgency stuff started happening. The first thing was we lost some mortars. I don't know if that platoon was shot at, an ambush, or an IED explosion. I had one instance when I was leaving battalion headquarters and an RPG went flying over the hood of my truck. But the insurgents, they were ghosts. We couldn't find anybody. And then our headquarters got hit with a suicide vehicle-borne explosive. Somebody drove a vehicle into a checkpoint. It was the M249 SAW gunner that mowed them down, prevented a bigger mess. The main casualties came because our commander—and I don't blame him—didn't want our headquarters to look like a bunker. So he had glass windows installed. When the suicide bomb happened, flying glass created kind of shrapnel. That was the big attack in our sector."[17]

The Sunni insurgency grew, but Petraeus was determined to work with the Iraqis. Most of the time, Greene "didn't do combat patrols. Most of my stuff was interacting with locals and contracting for schools and buses and water and trying to establish legitimacy in northern Iraq. It was interesting, but if you read the annals of Tal Afar, it became quite a hotbed, especially for H. R. McMaster just a couple years later.[18] Tal Afar was a place where some one of my buddies earned a Silver Star. It turned into a pretty nasty place for a minute."

SECOND LIEUTENANT Mo Greene left Iraq in early 2004, relieved by Stryker battalions that included his old friend, Second Lieutenant Matthew Blind. Foreshadowing Blind's exit a year later, Greene and the Rakkasans drove south to Kuwait without a single attack. As Greene said, "Talk about timing and luck." Iraq soon burst into flames. Petraeus gone, hard-charging commanders in place, the Strykers faced a fierce fight in Mosul.

Back at Fort Campbell, Greene had to borrow his sister's truck to get home. "And that night, there was a dusting of snow on the road. So I'm driving this little red Chevy, old-school, and I'm kind of relearning how to drive. I hadn't driven in nine months. Officers don't spend a lot of time driving. I'm spinning out a little bit, fishtailing on the road, realizing I missed almost an entire year in America. I got home to my apartment. Clint and I were roommates. Clint was home. We went on thirty days' leave. We started training plans in terms of marksmanship and whatnot. But really what ended up happening is we spent a lot of time in Nashville. And that's when I met my wife."

Clint Olearnick would also meet his wife, Diane Molstad, in a bar. She worked in a joint near Fort Riley in Kansas. But in spring 2004, like Greene's transfer to the Ranger Regiment and on to Special Forces—with whom he would return to northern Iraq[19] to join the hunt for Abu Musab al-Zarqawi[20]—that was yet to come.

At Fort Campbell, Olearnick's main preoccupation was his return to the rugby field. US Army bases are often home to teams, many founded in the 1960s and 1970s,[21] enlisted men and officers scrummaging down together. Standards vary. Jeremiah Hurley said he tried playing when he went up to Alaska the first time: "I was posted there, and it was honestly the hardest thing I ever did—they weren't very good and it was dangerous. You were at risk of blowing out a knee or whatever. People were not in control of their bodies. Emotionally it was draining too. Within a year I went from playing on one of the best teams in the US to this scrub team. It was pretty rough, so I just stopped."[22]

Hurley focused his energies on the Ranger Regiment, Joint Special Operations Command, and deployments to Afghanistan and Iraq. Olearnick played on, through three tours in Iraq. Out of Fort Riley, with the Kansas City Blues,[23] he was selected to the All-Army team and the US Eagles player pool. He didn't win an international cap, but he got closer than any of his old teammates. He and Bryan Phillips, who shunted the scrum for Houston Athletic, played on the longest.

Olearnick's first deployment began in June 2003 with the 101st Airborne. It was a division easily large enough to include his old West Point rugby teammates Mo Greene and Pete Chacon in the same part of Iraq without the three friends ever running into each other. The 101st is a storied division. Second Lieutenant Olearnick joined First Battalion, 327th Infantry Regiment, the Bastogne Bulldogs, nicknamed for a battle fought by the Band of Brothers in the Second World War.

Olearnick said, "We started in this little town called Makhmur, spent a few weeks there, then once the Qayyarah air base got up and running, there was an oil refinery there and we kind of took that over. We stayed out of the building. It was just too hot inside."[24]

Olearnick was proud to get his platoon home. He called it a "great deployment," but there was fear and danger too. "IEDs were starting to become a thing. There was a guy in one of the other companies that got killed by an IED. My boss wanted us to do all these patrols, driving on the routes. And I said no. 'We're not going to do that. Why would we go out and just drive around? What you want to do with the 101st is fly out in a helicopter and then walk the route back down. And we'll walk off the road. That way we can see the road. We can see if there's anything on there. And we'll make sure it's clear, that it's good to go. Let's do that.'

"My company commander was a great dude. He fully supported that idea. So that was how I ran the remainder of my deployment. We had a weapons platoon attached to us, which was led by my buddy Joey Da Silva, my West Point class president. We'd rotate. One was our quick reaction platoon, we had a bridge traffic control point we had to man, and the other platoon would patrol or provide force protection."

There were different ways to detect IEDs. Walking the roads was one. In December 2005, south of Baghdad in the Sunni "Triangle of Death," Ben Britt, a rugby player from the West Point Class of '04 with the 502nd Infantry Regiment, 101st Airborne Division, walked over a huge IED. Britt was from Wheeler, Texas.[25] A talented scholar and relentless athlete, he learned to play hooker under the equally relentless Jim Gurbisz, inspiring a saying, "Britt Never Quit," that ended up on the weights machines at Anderson Rugby Complex.[26] They found his body in a canal. He was twenty-four. William Lopez-Feliciano, a specialist from Quebradillas, Puerto Rico, died too. He was thirty-three.[27]

Another way to try to counter the IED threat was to get Iraqis to tell you where they were. That was what Scott Radcliffe did. He went to Iraq in 2004 with One-Seven Cavalry, a regiment founded in 1866 by George Armstrong Custer and known as Garryowen for the Irish song it adopted. As it happens, high kicks in rugby are called garryowens, after an Irish club.[28] Garryowens are also known as "bombs," because they drop from the sky. The catcher must defuse the bomb while being rushed and hit. In Iraq, one of One-Seven Cav's jobs was to hold important routes, including Route Irish, the Baghdad Airport Road, one of the most bombed roads of all.[29]

Radcliffe said, "We had two platoons—a tank platoon and a heavy cav platoon—and we ran missions with them in and around Fallujah, Najaf, and Baghdad."[30] In Fallujah on March 31, 2004, four American contractors were killed by a mob, two bodies strung from the struts of a bridge.[31] The Marines went in. The fight was brutal. It looked like One-Seven Cav would go in, too, but orders changed. They stayed in Baghdad, Radcliffe said, "working the granular platoon level of, 'Hey, you go meet with the sheik' and this, that, and the other, and patrolling Route Irish every day." The Iraqis called it "Death Street."[32] But Scott had an advantage. In his tank, he felt "a hell of a lot more safe than I would have if I were a military policeman or if I was in transportation, just running convoys through random areas, across hundreds of miles. I was out there every day. I could tell when a box looked out of place. Those other guys couldn't. They might never have been there before. That, to me, was always a hell of a lot more dangerous than patrolling Route Irish all the time.

"I developed sources. There was one that saved my life. There was a family that lived around a curve in the road that goes from the south and then turns towards the airport, right around the interchange before you got to the Green Zone," the heavily fortified area where the Coalition Provisional Authority was based. "There were a bunch of shacks that were kind of like up around that bend. When I transitioned from my tank platoon to my scout platoon, and we were patrolling the sector, on one of the first patrols I was out there, my platoon sergeant introduced me to this family they developed a relationship with. And there was this girl who was just the sweetest thing. So anytime I got packages, I would save some cookies or whatever else to give her and some of her brothers. At one point, they flagged us down. Like, 'Hey, there's something over there.' And they were right. There was a big IED that I would have definitely run through and potentially not come back from. And that was because I developed sources for my platoon over time."

Radcliffe completed his tour. In the late summer of 2005, he deployed to New Orleans after Hurricane Katrina. After that wet hellscape, the army sent him back to a dry one: Tal Afar and then Anbar, southeast of Baghdad. It had been a hotbed of the Sunni insurgency, but it became a launching point for the Sunni awakening, a United States–supported effort during the troop surge of 2007 that helped turn the tide against al-Qaeda. Radcliffe became a staff officer and speechwriter to General Ray Odierno, who later commanded all US troops in Iraq.[33] When Scott left the army, he ran for Congress in Ohio.[34] After that, he went into IT security. He now lives in Austin with his wife, Mandie, and their three young girls.

THE MOST direct way to discover an IED is to run over it. That was what happened to Pete Chacon in December 2003 in Mosul.

Months earlier, in May, George W. Bush had infamously announced "mission accomplished" in Iraq while standing aboard the USS *Abraham Lincoln*.[35] But Mosul, the big city straddling the Tigris, ethnically diverse with Sunni Arabs dominant but also sizable communities of Assyrians, Turkmen, Kurds, and other minorities, would not burst into open warfare until the end of 2004. The president was wrong.

In the summer of 2021, I spoke with Pete Chacon at Matt Blind's place in Massachusetts.[36] Pete thought back to December 2003, when he was, "you know, flying down the roads with Humvees with no doors. With no armor on our vehicles. Nothing. And it was a miracle I survived.

"We would get these little flyers, intelligence reports about enemy tactics. 'This happened in this city down here. This is what the enemy did. Apply it to your training.' I was a pretty badass platoon leader, so we got a lot of missions. The sexy jobs, if you want to call it that. Kicking in doors, air assault into some random village, finding a gunrunner, doing snatch-and-grab on some VIP. My guys were really well trained. When everyone else was off sleeping or playing video games, I would make my guys rehearse in the compound.

"So we get this flyer about these fucking roadside bombs. So we need to come up with a plan. What we're going to do if this happens to us, if we get hit hard. What's our response going to be? I have to admit that in retrospect, what we came up with was a very bad plan. But it was the best we could do at the time.

"Our genius plan was this. The intelligence said the bomb would be hardwired. And if you find the line and follow the line, you find a trigger, right? It's got to be within so many feet, because they have to see you and push the button to detonate. So we came up with this plan: if we got hit, we wouldn't treat casualties right away. We would trust that we had the 'golden hour' for first aid. We would get out, set a perimeter and arrest everyone we could within like a fifty-foot radius of where the detonation happened. That was our logic.

"So we drive over the IED. And it was a miracle it didn't blow me to the moon because it was a massive IED. I got lucky, in that they"—those who planted the bomb—"inadvertently tamped it down. They paved it into the road. The concrete above it was denser than the concrete below it. So the blast went down and everything that hit me was ricochet. But it was a fucking six-foot hole. It was amazing how deep it was. I couldn't believe it. When I saw it, I was like, 'I can't believe I survived this.' They waited till it was underneath my seat. It exploded underneath me. It was nuts. It was guardian angel stuff. There's no other explanation. It was unreal."

Chacon laughed. "And so, anyway, the plan. So my guys did exactly like we trained. They set up the perimeter, they didn't worry about treating casualties. I was the only one anyway. My radio operator was unconscious for like thirty seconds max. And they arrested everyone within a fifty-foot radius. Well, it just happened that within a fifty-foot radius was the only Catholic mass in all of Mosul. It was just getting out. There were maybe a hundred people. So, all one hundred Catholics in Mosul were within a fifty-foot radius of the IED that hit me. So my guys arrested them.

"They were wiping them down. Doing gunpowder residue checks. I'm looking at this and I'm all bloody. I got shrapnel sticking out of my face. I'm a mess. I'm hobbling around. I'm just running off adrenaline. I'm looking at the people that were arrested, and they're terrified because I've got dust and blood all over. I'm all screwed up. My face looks like a porcupine.

"And I'm like, 'Hey, did you guys just get out of that building right there?' And they're like, 'Yeah. It's a church.' I didn't even know they existed in Mosul. And they're like, 'Dude. Sign of the cross.' They're pointing. So I turn to my guys. I'm like, 'I'm knocked unconscious for fifteen seconds and you arrest the only fucking Christians in the entire fucking city. These guys didn't plant bombs. They're hoping we take over. The one Catholic church in the *entire fucking country*, and you arrested everybody.' And my guys say, 'Well, that was our plan. We were gonna arrest everybody we saw.' And the Catholics, they were coming to see if they could help.

"I was like, 'This is insane. Somewhere else in the fifty-foot radius, there's a guy running around who just detonated this thing.' They're like, 'Oh yeah. We didn't think of that.' I'm like, 'Dudes, I get knocked unconscious for fifteen seconds and this is what happens.' It was very, very funny."

Less so when the adrenaline wore off.

"There was a battalion response. There's helicopters all over the place, trying to vector in on the triggerman. No one found anything. My company commander comes in to relieve me, I'm like, 'Well, I got to start pulling my machine guns back,' and he takes a look at me and is like, 'Whoa, dude. You need to sit down.' So I go back to the compound. We're walking through the front gate, we're clearing our weapons, I pass out right there. They carry me in. When I woke up, the medics had pulled all the shrapnel out of my face. Bits of concrete, stuff like that. And I was like, 'Nice, I can have a cigarette, I can drink.' And they're like, 'Well, you can have a cigarette.' It was nuts. A piece of concrete had flown and smashed my pinky finger against my rifle. Where I was holding the buttstock. Crushed it like a hammer. That's what it felt like. It fucking hurt.

"There was my eye too. I'd had my night-vision goggle down. Shrapnel just stopped in the eyepiece, lodged there. I was like, 'Yeah, if I lose my right eye, that's no big deal. At least I got my left eye still.' I knew I had one good eye. But I was still like, 'Man, my pinky hurts so bad.' It really hurt. I was like, 'Cut it off, man. If you have to cut it off, just do it. Just do it. I won't look.' And they were like, 'Dude, your hand's fine.' I was like, 'No, get rid of it, just get rid of it.' They didn't. And I was like, 'My leg kinda hurts a little bit too. I feel like I got a sting there.'

Chacon pointed to a scar on the back of his thigh.

"They found the piece here, a piece of shrapnel the size of a thumb tip. It traveled up my femur and lodged like an eighth of an inch from my femoral artery. The doctors said, 'We're not going to go get that because if we nick your femoral artery, you'll die in surgery. It's better to leave it.'"

In March 2004, Chacon went back to Fort Campbell. He deployed again, 2005–06, to Baghdad and Samarra. He felt the strain. The effects of the IED, a busted shoulder. He got out in 2007. He went to Oklahoma, got into oil. Losing the army was "really hard on the family situation. I'd lost my driving force." There was a divorce from the mother of his children. He married again.

Pete Chacon smiled, rueful. "I was just telling Blinder, a couple years ago I was shaving, I pulled out the last piece of metal in my face. So this in my leg is the last piece in me. The last piece of Iraq."

Front seat view from a Humvee in Baghdad, following the
First Cavalry Division in late 2004.

Baghdad

"ONE THING everybody who has ever been hit by an IED knows is that the first thing that happens is a flash of red and orange. Then black."

Eric Stanbra is in business now, president of Superior Fence & Rail in Palm Beach, Florida. He has a wife and two kids. Life is good. Over the phone, he sighs.

"I haven't thought about that in probably ten or fifteen years."[1]

Stanbra grew up in San Diego, went to West Point in 2000, and came to rugby from football. A running back, he ended up in the centers. Joe Emigh, the A side man at inside center, took Stanbra on as a project. Maybe it was because they were both from southern California. Maybe Emigh was just a nice guy. Either way, he taught Stanbra well. In late 2001, Emigh hurt an ankle. Stanbra replaced him. It meant playing outside Mo Greene, inside Clint Olearnick. Emigh taught Stanbra how to deal with those two, the alpha dogs with their demands for support and service. Like Liam Marmion, who took over at fly half when Greene hurt his shoulder, Stanbra survived, then thrived. Unlike Greene, Emigh took his place back. But Stanbra was set. He loved rugby, became an All-Army pick, and tried out for USA Sevens, the national team in the seven-a-side form of the game that plays on the world circuit. After Emigh died, Stanbra found that playing rugby the best he could was the best way to honor his friend. He never stopped telling Emigh about his progress on the field.

"I had his cell phone number. I would have conversations with him. Almost a year after he passed, just leaving messages after every game, sometimes when I was drunk, give him a call, leave a message. Call it crazy southern California stuff. But he and I had a bond."

By 2005, Stanbra had followed the 2002 team into the army— another second lieutenant fed to the gaping maw of GWOT, the Global War on Terror. In Baghdad, the occupation was heading into a third terrible year. As the *New York Times* put it, "Neither military campaigns nor political transition had calmed Iraq's violence."[2] There were elections, but the Americans were unable to install a strong central government. The occupiers were the true authority, but they were mostly clustered in forward operating bases, FOBs, behind concrete blast walls and guard towers, apart from the people, cocooned with some of the comforts of home but lethally exposed when rumbling out in Humvees or Bradleys to patrol or guard lumbering convoys.[3] The heat rose. Casualties climbed. Sectarian conflict flowered. Civil war loomed.

Stanbra joined the US Army Corps of Engineers. They sent him to Camp Taji, an old Iraqi base about twenty miles north of Baghdad, and put him on route clearance. That meant patrolling "a stretch on MSR Tampa, the main supply route that ran north and south through Iraq. About ten to fifteen miles, to the north of Baghdad. My job was to go and look for bombs."

Deployed by Sunni and Shia, by resistance cells, militias, and terror groups tied to al-Qaeda, IEDs caused 60 percent of American injuries and deaths.[4] Not that they were new. One bloody example: for much of the twentieth century, IEDs were used in Northern Ireland against troops and civilians. As in Belfast, in Baghdad there were car bombs, too, known as "vehicle-borne improvised explosive devices," VBIEDs for short. The first lethal bomb of the Iraq War was a VBIED, more than one hundred pounds of C-4 plastic explosive hidden in the trunk of a taxi on Saturday, March 29, 2003—day ten of the invasion—at a checkpoint on Highway 9 north of Najaf. A witness described "a huge white blast." Four soldiers from the Third Infantry Division and one bystander were killed. The driver, too, apparently a suicide bomber.

In a popular imagination fueled by reportage and dramatization, from the *Washington Post* series *Left of Boom*[5] to Kathryn

Bigelow's Oscar-winning film *The Hurt Locker*,[6] the IED became a weapon "as iconic as the machine gun in World War I or the laser-guided 'smart bomb' in the Persian Gulf War of 1991."[7] Buried in the road or hidden in roadside garbage, the bombs hit patrols and convoys. They were homemade, cheap, and simple, used to crippling effect against the most expensive force in history.[8] They were often made of artillery shells from ammunition dumps abandoned by Saddam's army but not destroyed by the Americans. There would be a shell, a mortar round, or a mine, maybe two, connected to battery and blast cap, packed with nuts and bolts for shrapnel.[9] The deadly contraption was detonated by a trigger man at the end of a long copper wire, or by a timer wrenched from a washing machine, or by pressure plate, or remote control. The first remote-controlled IED hit a convoy in Baghdad in November 2003.[10] Cordless phones, garage door openers, motion sensors from strings of Christmas lights. Any infrared device might do. The bombers were elusive, their targets vulnerable.

Eric Stanbra and his men were meant to find IEDs and defuse them. They were not best prepared to do so. They did not drive Cougars or Buffalos,[11] Mine-Resistant, Ambush-Protected (MRAP) monsters with heavy armor and V-shaped hulls to withstand blasts from below,[12] equipped with long mechanical arms to probe for death in the trash.[13] They did not even have Humvees. Stanbra and his engineers had M113 personnel carriers, tracked vehicles in service since Vietnam, with aluminum armor and a fifty-cal gun on top. Also, they had only two M113s, not the three prescribed for patrols. To go so light on force and protection needed special dispensation. It was duly granted. The engineers tracked slowly back and forth on their highway, day after burning day, watched by wary Iraqis, watching warily back, scanning the crowd and the road, not knowing who might be the bombers, their supporters, or their spies. When the Americans found an IED, they got out and dealt with it.

In 2004, at FOB Volturno outside Fallujah, the Irish journalist Patrick Cockburn spoke to a squad of sappers with the Eighty-Second Airborne Division—combat engineers who support the front-line infantry, their name derived from the French word for spade. Cockburn asked how the sappers worked.

"We look for wires," Staff Sergeant Jimmy Anderson said, "anything that seems out of place."

Cockburn described how they looked, "gently prod[ding] the sandy ground with short, silver-colored wands. The wands, eighteen inches long and looking like a conductor's baton, are made of titanium and are nonmagnetic. They are curiously delicate and old-fashioned and in a way symbolic of the war the US is now fighting in Iraq."[14]

Conventional mine detectors were no good because the roadside trash was strewn with scrap metal as well as waste and dead dogs. Sometimes the IEDs were hidden under the dogs. Or in them. Sometimes the IEDs were camouflaged as rocks. Often, there were booby traps too.

"Somebody has watched us at work," Anderson said.

Armor improved. So did technology. Back in New Jersey, at Fort Monmouth near Eatontown where Jim Gurbisz once proudly sat on a tank, technicians worked on scanners to jam frequencies used by the bombers. In Iraq, the bombers answered each move. A sort of infernal chess developed, each player searching for checkmate in rising heat. Wherever you played your part, however you played it, it was lethal. Where Eric Stanbra was, out on the roads of Iraq, it was tense, it was frightening, it was hell.

A little further north, in Balad, Brian Castner was an explosive ordnance disposal officer for the US Air Force. He has since written two memoirs of blasts and blood, of primal fear in mouthfuls of dust: *The Long Walk* and *All the Ways We Kill and Die*.

"There was still lots of hillbilly armor running around in '05," Castner said. "Not everybody had the right electronic jamming gear either. There was Route Irish"—the Baghdad airport road—"and other places not completely scoured of trash and debris. And so there were still hiding places for IEDs. The T-barriers [concrete blast walls, sardonically known as Bremers after George W. Bush's man in Iraq] were not everywhere yet. It was remarkable."[15]

Tactics would change, the "surge" of 2006–07 bringing more troops and attempts to work with the locals. But in 2005, when it came to dealing with IEDs, the military was still "flying by the seat of its pants," Castner said.

"I call that time, and lots of other people call that time, the bad old days. Before the surge, everybody was just waiting for the war to end. It was Groundhog Day. There was no plan. We would say, 'What does winning look like?' Nobody knew. It was just a grind."

Stanbra knew the feeling: "Who knows how many times I saw a disturbed piece of dirt. I could see it, sniff it out. But that wasn't every time. They would hit us. I got hit several times. Thankfully, I was able to bring all of my soldiers home. But we had no idea what we were doing. In my opinion, I'm lucky to be alive."

Lucky indeed. 2005 also brought a new threat. As with everything the US Army touches, the new threat acquired an acronym: EFP, short for "explosively formed penetrator." EFPs were based on technology used in the oil industry since the 1930s and had been used in battle before, if not in this theater.[16] By 2007, amid the surge, EFPs proliferated in Iraq. The United States accused Iran of supplying EFPs to Shia militia.[17]

The *New York Times* described them: "To make the weapon, a metal cylinder is filled with powerful explosives. A metal concave disk manufactured on a special press is fixed to the firing end. Several of the cylinders are often grouped together in an array. The weapon is generally triggered when American vehicles drive by an infrared sensor, which operates on the same principle as a garage door opener. The sensor is impervious to the electronic jamming the American military uses to try to block other remote-control attacks. When an American vehicle crosses the beam, the explosives in the cylinders are detonated, hurling their metal lids at targets at a tremendous speed. The metal changes shape in flight, forming into a slug that penetrates many types of armor."[18]

That same year, at FOB Rustamiyah in southeastern Baghdad, a *Washington Post* reporter, David Finkel, embedded with Second Battalion, Sixteenth Infantry Regiment, known simply as the Rangers, or the Two-Sixteen for short. In the award-winning book that resulted, *The Good Soldiers*, Finkel described what happened when an EFP hit an American patrol.

On April 6, 2007, Jay Cajimat, twenty, private first class from Lahaina, Hawaii, "was driving the third Humvee in a convoy of six, which was the one chosen by someone hiding in some shadow with a trigger in his hand. A wire ran from the trigger to another shadow, this one at the edge of the road. Almost certainly the man couldn't see the actual IED, but he'd lined it up beforehand with a tall, tilting, broken, otherwise useless light pole on the far side of the road, which he could use as an aiming point. The first Humvee arrived at the aiming point, and, for whatever reason, the man didn't push the trigger. The second Humvee arrived, and again he didn't push. The third Humvee arrived, and, for whatever reason, now he did push, and the resulting explosion sent several large steel discs toward the Humvee at such high velocity that by the time they reached Cajimat's door, they had been reshaped into unstoppable, semi-molten slugs.

"At most, the IED cost $100 to make, and against it the $150,000 Humvee might as well have been constructed of lace. In went the slugs through the armor and into the crew compartment, turning everything in their path into flying pieces of shrapnel."

Four soldiers made it out. Cajimat did not.[19]

EFPs were seen in 2003 but began to proliferate in 2005, used first against the British in the south, then spreading north.[20] In March, on Route Predators in eastern Baghdad,[21] Shia territory, an EFP took out an Abrams tank. The crew avoided injury, but their commander, Lieutenant Colonel Kevin Farrell of One-Sixty-Four Armor, would tell historians that EFPs were "the only thing that really worried us."[22] His superiors were slow to catch on. The commander of Third Infantry Division, Major General William "Fuzzy" Webster, tried to crack down on the networks that smuggled EFP components, the cells that put them together, and the men who placed them. Washington protested to Tehran.[23] Nothing worked.

Eric Stanbra remembers the first time he heard about EFPs. It was in a briefing, like almost everything in the army, given on

PowerPoint software. "I got a printout of what an EFP was. And after looking at the PowerPoint, I talked to the intel officer. He was like, 'Yeah, so if you get one of these, there's absolutely nothing we can do. You're pretty much fucked.' Like, okay. Thanks. Wish me luck now."

And out Eric Stanbra rolled again, to search for death in the dirt.

*Cpt. Jim Gurbisz and Spc. Zach Pamer with locals while
on patrol in Baghdad in 2005.*

Rustamiyah

"**R**USTAMIYAH WAS a very, very interesting place."

On FaceTime, from Michigan, Nate Hadd smiles. He's in his mid-thirties, sandy-haired, affable, still a soldier, a recruiter now, with a wife and kids and a dog.

"The first thing that comes to my mind is that it was situated between the number-one-producing oil refinery in Iraq, the Dora refinery, and the Baghdad sewage plant. So you got an interesting mix of oil and human excrement, just floating all over the place."[1]

Oil and shit. The Iraq War.

In late 2004, First Cavalry Division left Baghdad. The Third Infantry took over. Specialist Hadd and First Lieutenant Jim Gurbisz of the Top Flite security platoon and the rest of the Twenty-Sixth Forward Support Battalion, Second Brigade, Third Infantry Division were sent to FOB Rustamiyah. It would be their home for a year. In *The Good Soldiers*, David Finkel described the base:

"There was Iraq. There was Baghdad. There, marking the eastern edge of Baghdad, was the Diyala River. And there, next to a raggedy U-turn in the river, which to laughing nineteen-year-olds looked like something dangling from the rear end of a dog, was their new home. . . . Everything in Rustamiyah was the color of dirt, and stank. . . . The air caught in their throats. Dirt and dust coated them right away. . . . Soon after sunrise, a few soldiers climbed a guard tower, peeked through the camouflage tarp, and were startled to see a vast landscape of trash, much of it on fire."[2]

Eric Westervelt, a reporter for National Public Radio, was at Rustamiyah with 26 FSB.[3] He described the history of the base— once the oldest military academy in Iraq—and how the United States remade it. First it was Camp Muleskinner, then Camp Cuervo—not after the tequila, but in honor of Army Private First Class Rey D. Cuervo, who was killed in combat in Baghdad in 2003. In Cuervo's case, as in so many others, "combat" meant a patrol and a buried IED.[4]

Westervelt described FOB Rustamiyah as "a sprawling series of stern-looking, Soviet-era buildings," home to "some three thousand soldiers and contractors. . . . Army carpenters and engineers have tried to spruce the place up, but . . . the base is dilapidated. An old hospital and office buildings have been converted to sleeping quarters. Soldiers have taken over the Iraqi shoebox-sized barracks and made them their own."

Those barracks contained basic comforts many Iraqis lacked. There was electricity, which meant there was air-conditioning, and there were stereos and widescreen TVs. There were sandbagged bunkers for rocket attacks but also a gym and "nightly movies, pool tables, and other games in the air-conditioned Liberty Center." A soldiers' saying: "We're at war while America is at the mall."[5] It was profound in a military sort of way, but it could echo against itself. One soldier told Westervelt the chow hall at Rustamiyah was "kind of like a food court in a mall." There was seafood night and a coffee shop and there were donuts and ice cream. Eventually, the reliance on FOBs would be reduced, frontline soldiers sent among the population. But that was in 2006 and 2007, the years of the surge. If there was an official "Year of the FOB," it was 2005.

Westerveld said, "American contractors . . . keep the base running along with hundreds of laborers and cooks from India, Pakistan, and Sri Lanka. They live inside the wire . . . rarely if ever venturing beyond the thick, high concrete walls. Soldiers have nicknamed . . . anyone who never leaves the FOB, as Fobbits."

The word entered the language, not least thanks to a novel called *Fobbit*, a satire by David Abrams, an army journalist who was in Baghdad in 2005. Describing his fictionalized FOB, Triumph, Abrams wrote of "a small, rustic American city of tents, trailers, Quonset huts, and dust-beige rectangle-houses (leftovers from the regime), but a city nonetheless."[6] He compared FOBs to the camps that sprang up around railroads and mines in the American west in the 1800s, only populated with "supply clerks, motor pool mechanics, cooks, mail sorters, lawyers, trombone players, logisticians: Fobbits one and all."

Abrams also noted that unlike the REMFs—"rear-echelon motherfuckers"—of Vietnam, the Fobbits of Iraq were not removed from frontline hazard. They might be behind walls, but the walls were in a warzone where rules shifted by the hour. FOBs were attacked. In December 2004, when Matt Blind and his Strykers were recovering from the Battle of Mosul, a suicide bomber made it into the mess hall at FOB Marez. Twenty-three died.[7]

TORI GURBISZ can't remember much about the day her husband left Georgia, en route for Rustamiyah.

"I remember it was dark but I can't remember if it was late at night that they left or really early in the morning. . . . I remember being really sad. We did the joke, like, 'Are you sure you don't want me to, like, get your West Point pistol and, like, shoot you in the foot?' That kind of thing. 'Get you out of going.' Then we dropped them off, and they got on some buses and went."

Gurbisz's men were similarly matter-of-fact. His driver, Zach Pamer, said, "I told my parents, 'Like, don't worry about it, I'll be fine. You don't need to come. I'll be good.' Come the day, we sat there, I talked to Jim and Tori, and I was nervous, I was scared, but at the same time I was ready. It was time to start this new chapter. Just get this shit going. I talked to my girlfriend on my phone, and I was just like, 'We'll figure it out, you know, I miss you, I love you.' And I took my phone, threw it in the trash, and got on the bus."[8]

To Tori, "It wasn't profound. It was literally just, like, a bunch of people milling around in a parking lot with family members. It was very anticlimactic. Like, 'Okay, later,' you know? There wasn't any big send-off or anything."[9]

Tori and Jim Gurbisz parted like the kids from Jersey they were—the MTV generation, faced with the prospect of war.

"Most of the time, I just feel like I was pretty oblivious to a lot of things. He was just like, 'Dude . . . like, I don't feel like dealing with that. Let's just skip it.'"

So they skipped it. And 26 FSB flew out.

Back in Savannah, Tori learned to live on her own, to keep busy, to dial the anxiety down to a low background hum. She'd been happy, really, when her husband's knee problems had closed the door to an infantry career. But she'd also been happy when he got the security platoon. After the bad days at Benning, the pain, drinking, and doubt, she'd been happy to see him set out each day with purpose. But then she heard or read the news one day and suddenly thought to herself, "Oh shit, they're blowing up convoys."

"I'm just like, dammit. Out of the frying pan, into the fire, you know? But Top Flite was still a new lease on life for him. It was kind of like, 'I get to do what I want to do. What I thought I wasn't going to be able to do in any capacity, and now I get this specialized new role.'"

She paused. "So he was super excited about that."

In New Jersey, Ken and Helen Gurbisz faced the same fears. Years later, they sat on their porch and looked out over their lake, its fountain, its flotillas of well-fed ducks. It was a soft September day, nearly twenty years since their son went to Iraq. As they remembered their contributions to his life at Rustamiyah and their attempts to soften its edges, it was impossible to escape one overriding impression: many of the Americans at the FOB were very young indeed.

They did all sorts of jobs. They were mechanics, clerks, infantry grunts, and tankers. They came from all across America. Some were college graduates. Many just had high school or barely even that. Some were northerners and some were midwesterners and many came from the south. But most had two things in common with Lieutenant Jim Gurbisz. They were young, and they liked to be reminded of home.

"Pop Tarts," Helen said, smiling. "Those they thought were the greatest."[10]

"We used to go shop," said Ken, the logistics guy, "and buy, you know, stuff that's on sale. So you can get more stuff. Pop Tarts a dollar a box. Cases of hot dogs. We sent it all, and next thing you know we hear from Jimmy. He goes, 'Yeah, we had a late convoy, and we got in and the mess hall was closed. There was nothing to eat, and then we got the Pop Tarts.'"

Ken laughed. "Imagine, all these guys and girls walking around with Pop Tarts. Like little kids."

"We sent them popcorn for Halloween," Helen said. "We did the big canister. I had always gotten popcorn for the kids here. Popcorn. Those are the things to remember."

Ken and Helen tell stories like this, together, lines swapped with the easy humor of a couple married since 1973, two years after Ken came home from Vietnam.[11] When their son was in Iraq, they also sent him money for internet access, phone cards for calls. It was a bit like keeping a kid happy at Rutgers or Columbia, even at West Point. A bit.

"We were talking," Ken said, "it might've been October, and Jimmy yells, 'Leave that spider alone!'"

"Because they had to go up on the roof to try and make the phone calls," said Helen, "and they had these big poisonous spiders that would jump at them, or something."[12]

"So the spider jumps on Jimmy," Ken said, laughing. "And you hear this *scream*. And then he comes back on and he says, 'The spider jumped on me and I screamed like a little bitch.' I said, 'I don't blame you . . .'"

Tori sent stuff, too, often the products of her home business, soaps and candles. They spoke "pretty often, because he had at some point procured his own satellite phone. I mean, it was not his, but he kept it on his person. I would wait for him to call. He said, 'Don't call me, just in case I need the line.' There were letters and emails. I'd send him boxes, more smelly soaps and candles. He was my guinea pig. He must've had an extremely nice-smelling transport unit. Like, apples and cookies, piña colada."

Piña colada soap might've been tough to take, given that the army banned alcohol.

"We did joke, like, 'What if I dye some vodka blue and send it in a Listerine bottle?' We were kids. But most of the boxes just had random snacks, stuff like beef jerky. And I made him cards, sent little random knickknacks. Things from me and from home."

Some who were with Gurbisz remember packages from closer to camp, bottles of illicit "hajji hooch," a local spirit, strong as hell.[13] Some, thanks to Baghdad being home to thousands of feral dogs, also remember a pet.

"You weren't allowed to have any mascots or any dogs," said Dawn Hurley, Jeremiah's wife, who was also with 26 FSB. "But Top Flite found a puppy inside the camp. And they named it Rocket, and they got Captain Mattus, the company commander, on board. His wife was involved in animal rescue at home. She sent flea and tick medicine. So they had Rocket. They hid him. And when they left Iraq, they gave him to Special Forces guys at Baghdad airport."

There's a picture of Gurbisz holding Rocket. The dog, small and brown, nuzzles into his chest. Gurbisz smiles. Otherwise, he's every inch the American soldier: buzz cut, wraparound shades, desert fatigues. On his shoulder, the diagonal-striped insignia of Third Infantry Division. Lieutenant Gurbisz, leader of Top Flite security platoon.

Not much had changed since Top Flite formed back home. They were cooks and mechanics and misfits. Sergeant Alejandro Michel commanded one Humvee, usually the lead. Gurbisz rode in the second, usually driven by Zach Pamer. Each crew had a gunner: Colin Johnson for Michel, Van Torres for Gurbisz. Sometimes Gurbisz's driver was Nate Hadd, or it could be Dustin Yancey.

Yancey was a generator mechanic from Goose Creek, South Carolina, an army kid whose dad, a sergeant, went to Iraq too. Yancey was a good driver, so Top Flite made a good home. He had some discipline problems, Hadd said—like many others in the unit—but Lieutenant Gurbisz helped iron those out, and Yancey fit right in.

"He never wanted to see anybody upset," his dad, Tim Yancey, told me. "If he came across somebody who was upset, it was his goal to put a smile on their face, whether it was some of his antics, from reciting Monty Python or whatever card trick, or just playing some music. He was very apt with the guitar."[14]

Yancey was also, Hadd said, a sort of walking, talking "automatic cigarette machine. I've never seen a human smoke so much. The man loved cigarettes. He loved magic too. He was always doing stuff with cards. Whenever we would stop, when we had some time with the Iraqis, he would blow their minds with magic tricks."[15]

People who could help kill time were invaluable. If the US Army has an unofficial motto, particularly in transportation, it is "hurry up and wait." Logistics take time. Bureaucracy takes more. Randall Mullally, the radio specialist, remembered playing a little football to pass the time. He also remembered Gurbisz and "his funny white ball."

Mullally said, "There wasn't a lot of time for it because his focus was on keeping us alive, but we played a bit of rugby here and there."[16]

Hadd remembered the rugby and how mostly it "just ended up in fights." Zach Pamer remembered a scrum in Sadr City. Laughing, he said, "Jim would be like, 'New game! Steers or Queers!' And he would throw the rugby ball to me. Next thing I know, I'd have ten guys running after me, just trying to beat the shit out of me. I'm just running around, going, 'Oh Jesus Christ!' And then one time at a FOB, Camp Hope, up in Sadr City, we did a rugby scrum and Jim put me in the middle."

Pamer means hooker, Gurbisz's position, where he gained an All-American mention—the position you have to be a little bit crazy to play.

"Jim's like, 'All right, you're gonna be in the middle against me. Like, you put your arms on everyone's shoulders, they lift you up. And then when the ball gets rolled in the middle, you want to kick it back.' And I'm like, 'All right, cool. Yeah, I'll give it a shot.' He's like, 'All right, man, I ain't gonna take it easy on you.' I'm like, 'Whatever, dude, I ain't worried. You do you.' I knew he played rugby. I didn't know how good he was. So the ball rolls in the middle, and next thing I know, he kicks me as hard as he can in the shin. I'm screaming, like my shin blown wide open, and he kicks the rugby ball back. Then he throws it into me again.

"It was all good fun and games. He always told me, like, 'You're pretty good at throwing this thing.' I was like, 'Bro, I can skate twenty miles an hour with a stick. Controlling a little football? I could do that.'"

Van Torres said, "We blew off steam however we needed to. There were a lot of combat arms troops around the FOB, and it was nice that we were seen on a similar playing field with them, because of what we were doing. We went around raising our fair share of hell, at times. It was just because we were stressed."[17]

Members of Top Flite who did not want to be named, even so long after the events, described a couple of instances when things got a little out of hand. There was the time Lieutenant Gurbisz imposed discipline after a fight, having the guilty party do push-ups in a dress in the sun. Kid stuff. Rugby club stuff, if they'd known. There was also the day someone came back from Baghdad airport, BIAP for short, with some Starbucks coffee. Real beans, French Roast or Pike or whatever, a real prize out in the oil and the shit, better than the stuff they sold at Green Beans Coffee Co., a familiar sight on every FOB. There had been a warehouse at the airport, and the doors had been open, and on a day "hot enough to cook an egg on the hood of a truck," soldiers waiting for the drive back to Rustamiyah walked inside for the shade. And there they found the coffee, and the crates were open, so they took a bag or two, and all was good for a while, with good coffee, a taste of home, until someone complained and officers asked questions and the shit hit the fan. And Lieutenant Gurbisz smoothed it out.

Zach Pamer watched Gurbisz close as any.

"Have you heard the term 'ring-knockers'? Jim wasn't one. He cared, he listened. It was not his way or the highway. He would let me go off sometimes. Then he was like, 'All right, calm down.' In private it was, 'Say what you want to say, get it out, get it done.' But never disrespect him in front of other people. He's a lieutenant, I'm a private. If you ever disrespected him in front of another officer, an NCO or something like that, oh, you'd pay dearly. He'd give you an inch, but if you took a mile, he was gonna put his foot up your ass for the next three miles. You learned when and where you could talk to Jim. And how you talked to him. He'd get you ramped up, ready to run through a brick wall, and then one second later calm you down.

"It was hot as shit out there. But he made sure to get as close to us as he could. He slept apart because the officers did, but we went to chow together, talking, building that relationship, because we knew this was no joke anymore. People were dying. It was the real deal."

ANOTHER CALL, this time to the Washington suburbs. Dawn Hurley has recently moved north from Fort Bragg, North Carolina, with her five children and her husband, Jeremiah. Out of the army, he's shifted into the defense industry, as one does.

Back in the mid-nineties, Dawn was a Jersey girl who needed someone to pay for college, and so the army beckoned. Jeremiah Hurley was from Missouri, and they met at the prep school when it was at Fort Monmouth. At West Point, Dawn and Hurley stayed together. Hurley wrestled, switched to rugby. Dawn ran marathons. They got married and set out together in the US Army, to Maryland, Alaska, and Georgia. Dawn deployed to Iraq with fellow New Jerseyan Jim Gurbisz.

She ate the Pop Tarts, of course, but she also carried on running, seeking precious release. She "ran the perimeter. I want to say maybe I could get a mile when I ran the whole perimeter of our little camp."

"I was such a Fobbit," she said, with a laugh.[18]

Hurley was "a shop officer, in charge of fixing stuff for the battalion."[19] Randall Mullally described some of what was required:

"Every day, every night, I checked all the radios in all of our trucks. . . . A whole mission could get stalled half a day while you wait on some radio guy to come out with a little black box. I had thirty-three radios, or something like that, and they had this frequency encryption which drifted, so you had to check and recheck every day, perfectly good vehicles, go spend two or three hours reloading encryption so their time would be perfect."

Dawn supervised that sort of stuff, did a lot herself. And the job was *not* confined to Rustamiyah. She had an electronic maintenance cell outside the walls. She and Gurbisz grew close, eating together, providing mutual support. Come time to leave the FOB, Dawn rode with Gurbisz. The cell was about six miles north at Camp Hope, formerly Camp War Eagle—as a British adviser to a US general once observed, Americans tend to name things "without any sense of irony"[20]—and it was on the edge of Sadr City.

Sadr City is a vast slum in eastern Baghdad. A Shia area—Shia Muslims are the clear majority in Iraq, although Sunnis long ruled[21]—it was built by communists who named it al-Thawra, the Revolution, after the overthrow of the monarchy in 1958. In 1982, fourteen years after the Baathist coup, the area was renamed for Saddam Hussein. After Saddam fell, and with him the Sunni Arabs he had placed in power, the place was renamed for Mohammad Sadiq al-Sadr, a Shia leader Saddam killed in 1999. When Dawn, Gurbisz, and the rest of 26 FSB arrived at Rustamiyah in December 2004, Saddam was set for trial.[22] The man in power in Sadr City was Muqtada al-Sadr, a young cleric whose two brothers Saddam had killed.[23]

It was a place where Sadr and his followers decided what the law would be. In October 2005, the *Guardian* reporter Rory Caroll was kidnapped in Sadr City, an ordeal triggered by tensions between the Shia and the British in the south of Iraq. Carroll remembered what he had been able to see while held down in the back of a speeding car, a gun trained on him from the passenger seat: "Sagging power lines, crumbling houses, sheep grazing on rubbish, traffic."[24]

American soldiers who drove through Sadr City were able to take pictures. Gurbisz did.

Heat haze and dust clouds. Crumbling palaces on islands in dirty streams. Scrambled traffic, palm trees, Iraqi men looking back. Smog.

Gurbisz gave Nate Hadd a memory stick. Hadd sent me a Dropbox link. Gurbisz had a Fujifilm camera. In the photos, I can see Iraq through his eyes.

Often, the pictures are taken through a dirty Humvee windshield. Many show another truck ahead. Convoy commanders rode second. In one shot, the sky between low-lying smog and alkaline yellow clouds is a deepening evening blue. In the Humvee ahead, a gunner seems to aim at a white van. The barriers at the side of the road are rough and broken, the dirt strewn with rocks and garbage, dun-ochre, same as the American trucks. The Humvee ahead has identifying marks: 1-CAV. First Cavalry. A "left-seat, right-seat" drive, the short process by which Top Flite was meant to learn the lay of the land, troops about to leave showing the land to their successors. It's a still photo, but you sense the way the landscape spools by. There are light poles and palm trees and a grim unending sprawl.

Zach Pamer remembers the ride. "We were just like, 'Okay, okay, this is happening. I guess we'll figure this out.' We got shot at, nothing serious, and then One-Cav were like, 'All right. There you go.' You're just like, 'All right, so I guess we're thrown into the fire here.'"

More pictures. Back at Rustamiyah. Out of helmet and body armor, Lieutenant Gurbisz makes notes on a paper spread out on a Humvee hood. Behind him, a laughing Iraqi man in jeans and sweatshirt. A translator? Pamer's flak jacket is on the Humvee. In another picture, the same motor pool, a man looks over his shoulder, surprised midbriefing. Michel? A soldier behind him laughs. He's heavier-set, wearing a cap. Dustin Yancey? Zoom in. Nope. That tag says "US Army." It seems to be Pamer. And that seems to be Van Torres, Gurbisz's gunner, half-obscured to the left.

Another picture. Gurbisz, Pamer, and Torres sit on the roof of a Hummer. All three wear shades, Gurbisz is holding his camera case. The sky is clear blue: morning or midday. Pamer holds a bottle of Gatorade, livid orange. When I spoke to Torres, he laughed and said he had the same picture in front of him. It wasn't Rustamiyah, he said. "We were at a different FOB. That was War Eagle, outside of Sadr City." The pictures are not in chronological order. Gurbisz's hair is relatively long in the first, buzzed close in the second.

In another shot, Gurbisz is in full armor, glasses on, goggles up on his helmet. He's holding a clipboard, giving directions, wedding ring catching the sun, Pamer at his right. Others listen. Robinson, the medic who taught Pamer all he knew, the tough ex-Ranger sergeant, sucks a lollipop. Gibson adjusts his helmet. Behind them, a huge red drum is marked 'DiESEL' in spidery white letters, lowercase *i* an incongruous touch.

Then we're in Gurbisz's Humvee, close up, the picture taken from the driver's seat. Gurbisz is on the radio. There's barely room to move. At the right, a pair of legs in desert fatigues: Torres, the gunner.

The convoy moves out. Top Flite Humvees, fifty-cal machine guns swiveling, then the big rigs, more Humvees to the rear. Gun trucks pass blast walls and guard towers. Leaving Rustamiyah? Humvees drive empty roads, palm trees off to the left. Heading into Baghdad? A road fringed by irrigated fields, deep green, a building on a hill, some sort of castle or citadel, a man and a boy by the road, the man in a white robe, a hawk in flight above. The roadside slopes and crumbles.

A highway, an overpass, blue signs in English and Arabic. Left for Ramadi-Mosul, right for airport and city. The Humvee ahead carries a sign in Arabic, a warning to keep clear. Another highway. In the distance, fire and pluming smoke. The same fire closer. Flames fierce orange, smoke black, thinning to cancerous yellow-gray, drifting past power lines and trees. Eric Stanbra's words: "A flash of red and orange. Then black." It's not clear what was hit. It seems to have just happened.

In April 2005, Ann Scott Tyson of the *Washington Post* went out south of Baghdad with an American patrol. The commander was Colonel H. R. McMaster, the West Point rugby player who made his name in the first Gulf War.[25] Tyson described how McMaster's soldiers thought. They had "refined the deadly calculus of traveling Iraqi roads. They know the rear seat on the driver's side is the safest in a Humvee. They know the lead vehicle in a convoy is often the least likely to get hit. They have memorized the worst stretches of highway, and the twists in the road that leave them vulnerable by forcing them to slow down. They also understand that no matter how hard they try, any mission could be their last."[26]

Top Flite knew it too. For Randall Mullally, "Big engagements were not very frequent. But small engagements, like taking a couple pings off the truck? Probably every other mission. A lot of the time in 2005, the combat for a moving convoy was from a distance. Sniper fire, or somebody took a couple potshots then lay down arms. We didn't always fire back, because there was no point in shooting at unknown targets."

There were rules of engagement. But even when return fire was merited, Van Torres said, "not every gun truck in the convoy was able to participate, given how spaced out we were, what direction it was coming from, and if we had clear lanes of fire."

Soldiers yearn for combat. Mullally said he was "always jealous when somebody came back with shrapnel, because I didn't get any. Until I did."

Gurbisz's pictures show the results of contact. He's there, in reflection, lifting his camera to capture a bullet strike in a Humvee windshield. It's on the driver's side. Gurbisz again, reflected, wearing a soft sun hat, taking a shot of four strikes to the glass on his own side of the truck. In another shot, a bullet has done greater damage, spider-webbing the windscreen on the passenger side. Sunlight catches the cracks, glinting green and purple. There are shots of a green Humvee, one front wheel blown out on the passenger side. Three soldiers grin. The picture turns up on a Google search. Its caption: "Near miss."

"That was Nate's vehicle," Torres said. "We were, I think, going to Baghdad airport. But because of the contact we took, the damage on his vehicle, we had to detour to another FOB. Get some stuff fixed, you know?"

There is a picture of a medic applying a field dressing, tight to the knee of a man in civilian clothes who holds a bloodied dressing. A truck driver, maybe Pakistani or Indian or Thai. His hands have Henna tattoos. It seems a minor wound.

Gurbisz took shots of convoys in light traffic and heavy traffic and stuck still, among idling cars and trucks. Signs warn Iraqis to keep their distance. Many times, they can't. Tension, inside the Humvees, out among the Iraqis. Gunners swivel. Drivers grip their wheels. The Americans know their enemies are watching.

When they'd first arrived, Zach Pamer said, it had felt like Top Flite was under constant attack. "But then, as you've been there for a little bit, you start to realize, 'All right, somebody is shooting from four blocks over. It's not impacting us.' You just get used to it. You'd go through two weeks where you would see nothing besides nice kids giving you cigarettes and stuff. And then you'd go back into it. We had rocks thrown, we had mirrors broken, sometimes we'd have small IEDs that wouldn't do anything and other times we hit big ones.

"I roomed with this guy Chambers. And I remember one time we were on a mission, close to base, and his truck just got obliterated. The dust cloud was so big. Sergeant Robinson was in the vehicle. And all I could think was, 'Everyone in that truck is dead. I just watched some of my best friends and my mentor die.' They were thirty, forty yards in front. We couldn't get him on the radio. We stopped. And then they all got out of there. I'm like, 'How the fuck are you guys alive?' And Sergeant Robinson is like, 'My ass is sore. That shit blew up and the battery hit my ass.' And that was just how it was.

"Another day, a guy gets back and he looks at his Humvee and is like, 'Holy shit.' And there's a bullet hole in the little pipe that sucks in air so the truck can go through water. The snorkel. A bullet. It missed the driver by like, four inches. So that was either an extremely lucky potshot or we were under sniper fire and didn't know it. We would just laugh it off. Like, 'Holy shit, you know?' Just go with the flow. And that was every day for us."

The Americans were not the only ones under attack. One day, Top Flite found a shot-up truck. "And it's two Iraqi police officers in there," Pamer said. "I don't know how many bullet holes I counted. Probably twenty each. This was late October 2005, so we'd been there awhile. I was senior medic on the mission. One of the cops was alive. So I was just like, 'Okay, let me get some work going on here.' I probably worked on him for like twenty or thirty minutes, doing all I could. But he ended up passing. My uniform was covered in blood. I didn't have a single uniform anymore that didn't have blood all up and down. It was supposed to be an easy day. I look down, my knees down are soaked in his blood, my arms and elbows are soaked in his blood. And I just lost it.

"I started screaming, like, 'Goddammit!' I throw my aid bag. I run over, I grab two body bags out of my truck, I fling them at other Iraqi police, 'They're your fucking buddies, just roll them.' And Jim looks at me, he goes, 'Are you all right, man?' I go, 'I'm fucking fine.' And he goes, 'Okay.' Now I see I was breaking. I'd seen enough, done enough. I wasn't mentally good. And Jim saw that. And when we got back to the FOB, we sat in his room and had a long conversation."

And some hajji hooch. "He cracks open a bottle. I'm a specialist at the time. I'm just sitting there with my lieutenant—no, my captain by then—having a drink and talking. He talked me down. Gave me the next day off. Or tried to. I was like, 'No, I'm good. I'm good.'"

And so Top Flite rolled out again.

More pictures. Sadr City? Roadside stalls stacked with shoes and fruit, under awnings and umbrellas. Men mill about. In the distance, a refinery tower throws flame. By the side of the road, in slum housing, a man helps a small girl put on a vivid blue dress. On a slope to an overpass, three men walk, backs to the camera. One carries a green flag. On another overpass, a procession. Some men wear white robes, some carry flags of black or red. Others wear black. Some carry black flags with white Arabic writing. Some wear green headbands. A picture of Muqtada al-Sadr pasted to a road-side column.

From a base of power that was "less a district than a densely populated twin city to the rest of Baghdad,"[27] Muqtada led his militia, the Mahdi Army. The Shia had much to gain from the downfall of Saddam, a secular dictator who favored the Sunni minority. But in spring 2004, Bush's viceroy, Paul Bremer, decided to close Sadr's newspaper. One of Sadr's lieutenants relayed a message: "Either the newspaper is reopened or there will be hell to pay."[28] The paper stayed closed. There was hell to pay. In Sadr City on April 4, eight Americans were killed.[29] The fighting spread to southern Iraq and Najaf, the Shia holy city. The militia could not win. The Americans could not destroy the militia. In June, Sadr issued a ceasefire. In August, in Najaf, it broke down. Again, the fight was fierce. Again, the Sadrists were not destroyed.

By the time Dawn Hurley and Jim Gurbisz came to Rustami-yah, the United States had problems all across Iraq. Fighting Sunni insurgents and groups linked to al-Qaeda, the Americans pressed hard in Fallujah and Haditha. The Marines went in, the fight was ferocious, and problems bloomed elsewhere. Up north, insurgents in Mosul took advantage of American attention on Fallujah. Matt Blind went into battle. Further south, in Baghdad, Sadr City was relatively quiet. There were good days. At the end of January, millions voted in the first election post-Saddam, images of "smiling Iraqi women in black *abayas* emerging from polling booths" transmitted back to the United States by eager TV crews, the women "brandishing a purple finger that showed they had voted."[30] But there were warning signs, not least the recognition that in some areas barely 2 percent of Sunnis turned out. There were other attempts to get things working. In Sadr City, Shia "public order battalions" worked to improve sanitation and housing. Some crews drove Chevy pickups "adorned with placards featuring the figure of Muqtada al-Sadr against a backdrop of burning Humvees."[31]

The threat mutated. A new kind of bomb appeared. It "looked like a large coffee can with a wide and precisely milled copper disk at one end.... Some Mahdi Army fighters called the new bombs *kafa* ('jump-ers'), while others called them 'Persian bombs' or 'Nasrallahs,' alluding to a connection between the weapons and Iran."[32] The Americans called them EFPs.

AFTER THE election, as EFPs proliferated, *Stars and Stripes* came to FOB Rustamiyah.[33] To outside eyes, *Stars and Stripes* is a curious thing: a newspaper run by the Department of Defense but editorially independent. In March 2005, its man at Rustamiyah, Vince Little, spoke to members of Top Flite.

Specialist Van Torres, of Lupton, Colorado, said convoy work was "pretty scary at times, but I like it a lot. You don't just sit around the FOB and do nothing. We've always got a mission, and it's pretty important stuff."

Sergeant Alejandro Michel, of Amarillo, Texas, said, "It's a lot of fun rolling out with these guys. I won't say it's better than doing my [regular] job, but it's definitely more exciting."

First Lieutenant Jim Gurbisz, of Eatontown, New Jersey, said training back home had been "a real benefit . . . a chance to train together and blend all of our personalities."

Little wrote, "Since arriving in Iraq, the platoon has encountered some small-arms fire and dodged a few roadside bombs, none resulting in casualties. The switch to full-time security, however, is rejuvenating a few careers."

Among them, that of Jim Gurbisz. It seemed fitting to Dawn Hurley that "in September 2005, towards the end of the deployment, we got picked up for captain early. Our sequence number came up, because people were not staying in the military. And so we went ahead and we had a ceremony together at Rustamiyah," outside the small base hospital.

Top Flite was ready. Alejandro Michel, Gurbisz's sergeant, supervised the formation. "They read the official orders and all that. But we thought it'd be funny to fill some buckets full of, like, water, rations, ketchup, a real monster mash-up. I think we even threw somebody's dirty underwear in there."

Nate Hadd laughed. "It's not customary to have enlisted men congratulate officers. But we had taken, like, two big Gatorade containers and filled them with just all the shit you could find, MREs and more, for about two days. And we pinned Jim down and doused him in it."

Michel: "Naturally, we expected him to be mad. But he saw the funny side."34

Both Hadd and Michel mentioned how Gurbisz handled the less funny side of his role. Hadd approached him at Fort Stewart, back in Georgia, while having "really bad second thoughts about putting myself out in front." Gurbisz, he said, "sat down with me and explained the importance of, you know, being a man, and being honorable in telling someone you're going to do something to do it. And that really stuck with me."

For Michel, at Rustamiyah, it was the other way around. Gurbisz approached him. Michel had a daughter, born when he was just seventeen, and he and his wife were going through a difficult time. Gurbisz noticed. Michel's account of what happened next was a textbook example of male reticence and discomfort.

He "pulled me out of the sun and said, 'Hey, you need anything? Like, do you need money? Like, are you okay?' And I'm like, 'Yes, my God, you know, it's just like, you know, like, mostly like emotional stuff that I'm going through.' And he picked up on the fact that I was going through it, and he kind of put his hand out, you know, and helped me through that time. And once I come back from leave? He was very understanding. He's like, 'Hey, how did everything work out?' And I'm like, 'Well, you know, it's going,' or whatever. 'But, you know, thanks. Thanks for reaching out, thanks for kind of being there to listen to me whine about my personal problems.'"

There was also something rather less masculine, thanks to Tori back in Georgia.

"He's like, 'Hey, man, like, my wife sent these soaps, like, you know, you can kind of keep them in your room to, like, you know, so you have a little bit better home environment.'"

Michel laughed. "I never used it. It was just sitting there on my shelf above my bunk, more like ornament-type shit. But whatever. He gave me soap from his wife."

Gurbisz went on leave, too, in late summer, two weeks home with Tori. His parents came down to Georgia, his sister Kathy too. It wasn't easy.

"He was very secretive with me," Tori said. "He would talk openly about Iraq with my father, because he was in the navy. He talked with his dad about things too. But I'd come in the room and they'd all clam up. I was like, 'Don't do this to me. I know you're doing scary shit. I know it's scary over there.' I was very frustrated. I told him, 'Don't shut me out. I'm the one here, holding the fort by myself.'"

When Gurbisz did talk to Tori about Iraq, it wasn't always good.

"When we were just driving around town, he was like, 'You know, it's really hard, 'cause I see a rock or a plastic bag on the side of the road and it freaks me out.' He was seeing IEDs. We'd be driving around and he'd be trying not to look at the road."

Looking back, Tori sees worrisome omens everywhere.

"We were pretty much in the home stretch. We had September, October, a couple more months. We were almost done with it. We could taste the end of the thing. We were at the beach. And there was a hurricane out at sea. Not close, but enough to make it really choppy."

Gurbisz had to go back. Tori took him to the airport in Savannah.

CALEB HASTINGS, from Hartsville, South Carolina, joined the army after high school. They taught him to drive a big rig, a Heavy Equipment Transporter or HET, the kind of monster truck that can haul an Abrams tank.

"I'm gonna be honest with you," Hastings said, his shift at the paper mill done. "When I first got to Baghdad, I was nineteen, twenty years old. And it was mind-blowing. I was scared. Then I realized it wasn't like I could call home and tell somebody to come get me. I realized I was going to make it through this or I was not. When you realize that, you realize you just got to make the best of the situation—and often, it wasn't a good one."[35]

Death lurked out on the roads. Death came to Rustamiyah. Nate Hadd described the attacks, when insurgents would fire Katyusha rockets or decide to "mortar the shit out of us, at least once or twice a month." They knew the rhythms of American life. "Around the holidays, like Super Bowl Sunday? They were unrelenting."

When the sirens wailed and the shells exploded and the black smoke rose, everyone raced for the sandbagged bunkers or threw themselves down where they were. Nearly everyone.

Paul Rieckhoff was an infantry officer in Baghdad in 2003. In 2006 he published *Chasing Ghosts*, a searing memoir of heat, sweat, dirt, and fear, which is also a dissection of the motivations of those attracted to such an infernal role—as Gurbisz was before he injured his knee.

"'Follow me' is the credo of the infantry," Rieckhoff wrote. "Lead by example. Always."[36]

Lieutenant Jim Gurbisz was interested in that sort of advice. Rieckhoff also writes that "for soldiers, being the best isn't always the best thing for your survivability. I firmly believe that is why some soldiers do their best to stay mediocre. Stay out of the spotlight. It's what guys give you as the best piece of advice in basic training." Jim was less interested in that.

Back in Jersey, his father laughed.

"He told us one day they came back from a convoy, and as soon as they shut down their Humvees, an explosion put a hole in the wall. And so Jim gets his guys and they go to the wall. Other transportation guys are laying down, covering their heads. Jim's guys were at the wall. He calls the sergeant and says, 'We're just going to go there, check it out.' He says, 'No shooting unless you hear from me.' And he went out there. And then about two minutes later, the infantry guys come out and they ask, 'You getting action?' And someone says, 'Well, Lieutenant Gurbisz is out there.' And the guy goes, 'That figures.'

"So, yeah, that was Jim. He was pretty straightforward."

At Rustamiyah, when 26 FSB was close to the end of its deployment, Dustin Yancey turned his thoughts into words. His MySpace page is hard to find now, but his words are on Facebook, shared by his sister with a small black-and-white picture of Dustin in shades and army fatigues.

Yancey was proud of his work. As his dad described it, "He quickly was able to dissect routes through Baghdad and other areas as they did supply runs and troop retreats. He was able to find alternate routes when they encountered issues with road blockages or routes that were heavily attacked. So he was put into the lead convoy, often as the driver of the convoy commander, which would have been Captain Gurbisz. Or that lead driver position."

Nearly two decades after Yancey wrote it, his description of the work he did and the pride he took is as raw as it is honest and, in hindsight, terribly sad.

> "As the end of the deployment is inching ever so closley
> to us we are left to think back on everything we did here.

From the training we did for months before we left, to the
many, many, many missions that we have accomplished
in a short period of time. Because of my team we kept over
7,000 sloiders and contracters fed, about 1,000 vehicles
running, delivered litterally millions of gallions of fuel, and
that is just off the top of my head. We have driven hundreds
of thousands of miles, and we have the maintainace
records to prove it. We have been blown up several times,
shot at hundreds of times, made many detours, and with
the detours discovering new routes. All of that will end
when we get on that plane to go home. No one will be left to
say, Hey, remember those guys that were on the dangerous
streets of baghdad daily, sometimes 2 or 3 times a day, for
hours at a time? That what we do here is for the safety of
America, the freedom of Iraq, and ourselves. We do are
what others arent, and we do what others cant, not to say
we are better then them, but for them. You know how they
say less is more? Well i believe that. The less people we have
doing the dangous missions the more families back home
can rest easy at knight b/c they know that their family
members are safe. No long nights stairing at the celing
wondering what he/she is doing now, no late night phone
calls from the Red Cross in where they realize their worse
fear, none of that. So with that i end this little discussion
about everything and nothing. I do my job for everyone
and also for no one, because i take pride in what i do and i
doesnt matter who it is helping, as long as it helps, if only a
little, even if i am risking my life to take one person to the
soliders resort so they can rest up a little. It will make the
rest of their time here a little less difficult. I am proud to be
part of the 33+ solider group of people that may not seem
like it, but they are all elite people, fathers, sons, daughters,
wifes, husbands, brothers and sisters. We are the back bone
of our batallion, we are Top Flite Security, and we secure
the WORLD."

Cpt. Jim Gurbisz consults a map on the hood of his Humvee.

Convoy

O N NOVEMBER 7, 2005, the US Department of Defense issued a press release that, like so many others, announced the deaths of American soldiers.[1]

"They died in Baghdad, Iraq, on November 4, 2005, when an improvised explosive device detonated near their HMMWV during convoy operations. The soldiers were assigned to the 26th Forward Support Battalion, 2nd Brigade, 3rd Infantry Division, Fort Stewart, Georgia. Killed were: Capt. James M. Gurbisz, 25, of Eatontown, New Jersey. Private First Class Dustin A. Yancey, 22, of Goose Creek, South Carolina."

Some papers added color. In New Jersey, the *Asbury Park Press* said Gurbisz and Yancey were out on a scouting mission.[2] In Newark, the *Star-Ledger* got it right: they were part of a convoy security platoon.[3]

When I first reported Gurbisz's story in the *Guardian*, I simply repeated the official account. But when I looked more closely, it became clear that the Department of Defense release was a simplified version of what had happened in Baghdad.

The Pentagon said there was one IED. Those who were there say there were two. The Pentagon said one Humvee was hit. Those who were there say there were two.

But the press release was never meant to tell the whole story. As former army journalist David Abrams wrote in his novel *Fobbit*, such official accounts were the products of bureaucratic process and security protocol, meant to be both concise and opaque.[4]

In any fatality, there is an official investigation that produces a report known as a 15-6. Often, next of kin are given copies. In the deaths of Jim Gurbisz and Dustin Yancey, family members do not have them. Nor do those with whom they served. Nor could freedom of information requests induce the army to part with even a redacted version. However, one of the first official accounts of what happened on that Baghdad highway on November 4, 2005, a significant activity report (SIGACT) filed in the immediate aftermath, found its way into the public realm in October 2010 when it was included in the WikiLeaks release of more than 390 thousand Iraq War documents provided by the whistleblower Chelsea Manning to outlets including the *New York Times* and the *Guardian*.[5]

The SIGACT is heavily redacted. What is not blacked out is a knot of military acronyms. Unthread them, though, and what it records is clear.

Other than in Baghdad, the SIGACT does not say exactly where the blast happened. It does not clearly say when. It appears to have been filed at 3:30 p.m. and to say the explosion happened two hours before. No time zone is given. The first line, however, is stark. A vehicle from a FSB (forward support base) "struck a second IED almost simultaneously with the first." There were two IEDs.

The SIGACT for the first explosion is not in the WikiLeaks logs. But the SIGACT that is says the second blast caused two US casualties. There was "1X U.S. WIA" (wounded in action), a driver who "received non-life-threatening wounds." Dustin Yancey was a driver. He was killed. So by the logic of the SIGACT, he died in the first explosion.

The SIGACT also says that as a result of the second blast, "(TC) DOW AT FOB."

TC means "truck commander." DOW means "died of wounds." FOB, in this case, means Forward Operating Base Rustamiyah.

Captain Jim Gurbisz.

There's more: "There were a [redacted] number of ICE units in the patrol" but "1x [redacted] was disabled." Brian Castner, the retired explosive ordnance disposal officer who pointed me to WikiLeaks, told me what that meant.

"There was an odd jammer called ICE that almost no one had and didn't last long. Everyone thought it sucked, and people swapped to Warlock Duke about as fast as they could."[6]

Jammers were electronic devices designed by the Joint IED Defeat Organization to intercept and block radio signals used to detonate bombs.[7] Some jammers were developed at Fort Monmouth, back on the Jersey Shore where Gurbisz grew up.[8] On his final patrol, the jammers didn't work.

Scott Radcliffe, who patrolled the Baghdad Airport Road with One-Seven Cav, offered a note of caution. A SIGACT, he said, is merely a short report written right after the blast. And in Gurbisz's case, as so dreadfully often, "the person who should have been writing the report, Jim, couldn't do it. You need the first-person perspective. Those reports can be wildly misleading."

Radcliffe also had angry words for WikiLeaks. In Baghdad, he said, he used SIGACTS to try to understand terrible events. The time "a car bomb went off as we were handing out wheelchairs at a school. And then another one went off that was specifically designed to explode and have shrapnel come out, ball bearings, at around knee level. And it just shredded through some of our medics and folks like that."[9] Such reports are not meant to be read by the world.

Still, if you place the SIGACT about the blast that killed Jim Gurbisz next to witness accounts, it checks out. And it holds more. The IED that killed Gurbisz, it says, was on the right side of the road. As David Finkel wrote in *The Good Soldiers*, those who planted IEDs knew how Americans worked. They knew truck commanders sat in passenger seats. They knew convoy commanders rode in the second Humvee. And the Americans in the Humvees knew the insurgents knew this. Every ride became, as novelist Ben Fountain wrote, "an exercise in full pucker."[10]

So, on that Baghdad highway, an American convoy was hit with a practiced one-two punch. An IED hit the first Humvee. An IED hit the second.

The SIGACT also says what kind of IED killed Jim Gurbisz. It was precision-made. It contained four milled copper discs, an "array," on top of cylinders packed with explosives. It was an explosively formed penetrator, an EFP.

FRIDAY, NOVEMBER 4, 2005, began like any day. Top Flite was to provide security for a convoy to Baghdad Airport.

Nate Hadd described how such missions unfolded: "We would have anywhere from one to sixty vehicles. We had American truck drivers, we had Iraqi truck drivers. . . . We had the gamut, and we were just a large target, because we weren't able to go off of the main roads, the supply routes. We called them the MSRs.

"We took oil, petroleum, and then just other things, too, like mail, every once in a while. Or we would have a smaller convoy and we would take medical patients, non-urgent stuff, like if you broke your arm or something. Something that doesn't require metal. We would run those guys to the combat hospital in Baghdad. We would take people to a place called Freedom Rest, right in the Green Zone, where soldiers would be given two or three days off. We would take prisoners, we would take dogs. Anything. Any milk-run thing you could think of, our platoon did that."[11]

Caleb Hastings was usually somewhere in the line of vehicles guarded by Hadd and Top Flite. His massive heavy equipment transporter hauled "M1 tanks, Bradleys, cranes, anything."[12]

"Sometimes it would only be a three-vehicle convoy," Hastings said. "It might be me, Captain Gurbisz's vehicle, and one other vehicle. We might go pick up just one piece of equipment. It varied: sometimes Captain Gurbisz would have to escort civilian convoys too."

On November 4, 2005, Dustin Yancey drove the lead Humvee. Sergeant Alejandro Michel was truck commander, and Colin Johnson manned the gun. Captain Gurbisz commanded from the second vehicle, call sign Top Flite Six, with Zach Pamer driving and Van Torres on the gun. Major Geoff De Tingo, the brigade executive officer, took the spare seat in the back. Pamer was convoy medic, Hadd his backup, driving another Humvee. Like any convoy, this one was extensively briefed.

"They'd tell me the night before where I'd be going the next day," Hastings said, "tell me when the meeting time would be, who would be in command. Nine times out of ten it would be Captain Gurbisz. So then we'd get to the convoy briefing. Six in the morning, usually. Captain Gurbisz would brief us about what we had to pick up, what we had to bring back, how many people were in the convoy, what route we were going to take, alternate routes. Who was going to be where."

In April 2005, the Third Infantry Division's in-house newspaper, the *Marne Express*, described what 26 FSB did.[13] The mission was to "push essential supplies out to . . . soldiers all over eastern Baghdad with speed and efficiency." The paper also quoted Staff Sergeant David "Bones" Logan, about the "camaraderie" in Top Flite security platoon: "It's a high-stress environment, so you've got to know when it's okay to joke around and when it's time to put your game face on." And there was Nate Hadd in a photo. "Driving the big trucks through the traffic in Baghdad is a huge responsibility," Hadd was quoted. "You've got to be respectful of civilians while keeping yourself safe— otherwise you might make a new enemy."

Baghdad International Airport (BIAP) was southwest of FOB Rustamiyah. There were different ways to start the journey across the bottom of the city, but by any route you had to cross the Tigris and you had to deal with traffic. And whichever way you sliced it, you had to take the Airport Road.

The Americans called it Route Irish. Like Notre Dame's football team, the "Fighting Irish," it had a reputation. As the *Washington Post* reported the very day Top Flite set off for the airport, Route Irish was "the most dangerous highway in Iraq, five miles of bomb-blasted road. . . . A white-knuckle ride." The reporter, Jackie Spinner, described "military convoys roar[ing] past in a frantic attempt to escape the looming dangers of suicide bombers, grenades, rockets, and booby-trapped litter," as "insurgents' relentless attacks claimed a steady toll."

"To reach Baghdad or leave it," she wrote, "you had to survive the Airport Road first."[14]

In fact, the main part of Spinner's report described how a concentration on security had reduced the toll of Route Irish from thirteen Americans killed in April 2005"—around the time the *New York Times* said "Iraqis call it Death Street"[15]—to just one wounded in October 2005. But the *Post* headline still seems optimistic: "Easy Sailing along Once-Perilous Road to Baghdad Airport."

Iraqi highways were dangerous. But even in November 2005, two years into the occupation, American vehicles were not properly protected. Soldiers improvised, bolting on sheets of steel. As Brian Castner put it, "There was still lots of hillbilly armor running around in '05."[16] Worse, most highways were not like the Airport Road—secured, monitored, scoured of trash where bombs could be stashed and primed. Most were battlefields, where one side moved quickly and fired back hard, sometimes indiscriminately, and the other hid and pounced.

Accounts of the terror are legion. David Philipps, a *New York Times* reporter, described what the 506th Infantry Regiment endured south of Baghdad, in the Sunni Triangle: "The same scenario played out again and again: the quiet highway, heat swimming off the asphalt, the sleepy towns with their bizarre foot traffic of modern and ancient, the mind-numbing routine . . . then boom!"[17]

C. J. Chivers, another *Times* reporter, described a stretch of highway outside Fallujah that attained a dark cult status similar to that of Route Irish. The Americans who drove Route Chicago did not just endure the heat and the fumes of their cramped Humvees, their lurching trucks, their clanking tanks and Bradleys. They endured sheer torture, impossible stress stoked by "pointless routine and bloody lottery." They took precautions meant to lessen the effects of a blast from below. Mouths were kept hanging open, so eardrums might not burst. Hands were tucked in body armor. Feet were placed one in front of the other, so as to lose only one. They drove "coiled, waiting for the blast or the shot."

Chivers also describes a Marine Corps medic's surprise at advice from the man he relieved, advice that might have sounded familiar to Pamer and Hadd, medics for Top Flite: "Stock up on tourniquets and bleederkits, bro, and get ready to do your job."[18]

◆　　◆　　◆

FROM AN army base in Texas, Sergeant Alejandro Michel thought back more than fifteen years to November 4, 2005.[19] Top Flite escorted its convoy out of Rustamiyah at five or six in the morning. Not solely for operational reasons. As Napoleon or Frederick the Great or whoever else opined, armies march on their stomachs.

"We would always leave early just so we could get down to the heck of a chow hall they had at the airport. We would always try to get breakfast there. They had a good PX, too, so even though we knew the trucks weren't gonna be ready to come back till after lunch, we would always leave early, to go down there and relax a little bit."

Nate Hadd remembered the job included "picking up KBR drivers" —contractors for Kellogg Brown & Root, some American, cashing in, some from places like Pakistan or the Philippines, earning a lot less[20]—and "some lumber or something like that. It was a very routine trip. We went there, we got done extremely early. But on that same day, there was the suicide bomber that drove into an Abrams tank."

Among the WikiLeaks logs, the SIGACTS for Baghdad on November 4, 2005, do not reveal such an incident. A "local national van" did run into a US tank, but the SIGACT says it was an accident, three Iraqis killed, seven hurt. There were car bombs, too, injuring women and children. But that could have been pretty much any day in a year spent sliding toward civil war.

Either way, Hadd said, while Top Flite and the convoy idled, "all the routes were what we called black, because the air was too bad to fly. Whenever there's good air, helicopters can fly and provide security support. When there's some enemy activity, it's called red, and we'd sometimes go on red routes. But whenever there was no aviation support, and there was enemy activity, it was called black."

The convoy was stuck. In the yards at BIAP, 26 FSB fell into a holding pattern "for, like, seven hours," Hadd said. "We were just waiting to leave. We had nothing but time. We had simply nothing to do."

Hadd and friends passed some time "bullshitting with the Iraqi truck drivers, trying to see if we could bum some smokes off them, or just mess around with them." Random shit-shooting revealed that Caleb Hastings "was actually from the same hometown as Yancey," Goose Creek, South Carolina. Laughing about that passed a few more minutes. But Sergeant Michel was growing impatient.

"The routine once you got into BIAP was everybody had to go where they had to go. They had to run to some brigade headquarters to pick up something or go talk to somebody or go negotiate for this person or that person or go away on the logistics trucks, or whatever. That particular day, Captain Gurbisz had something to do. I think he was gone most of the day. I forget what the actual thing was. So we ended up meeting a little later in the afternoon at the truck yard, a little frustrated for sure."

Finally, Battalion headquarters sent orders. The route to Rustamiyah was still black. Didn't matter. Time to load up and go. Zach Pamer, Gurbisz's driver, didn't like it.

"I was like, 'You're telling me the route's fucking black and they want us to drive through that shit?' I'd always been vocal, but it was the dumbest shit I've ever fucking heard. I was like, 'That's the shit that gets people killed. For what? Why don't we take another route?' 'No. Battalion said we gotta go this way.' 'Okay, so we gotta go this way through a black fucking neighborhood.' You know, I'll never forget that. It's like, 'Because they say so. Because they think the intel's good.' And I said, 'We're the ones on the fucking street. They are not. How the fuck are they making that call? Like, they cannot make that call. So they're making a call with our lives on the line. We should have the final say in some things, you know?'"[21]

Top Flite did not have the final say. The convoy formed. As it did, Nate Hadd heard something.

"I heard Jim talking to my sergeant, and he was like, 'Yeah, you know, just talking to Tori, and you know I just took out an extra five hundred thousand dollar life insurance policy.' And we were like, 'Man, sir, like, what the fuck are you talking about? You can't say shit like that. Now you've just jinxed yourself.' And he's like, 'I don't believe in any of that stuff.'"

Hadd paused.

"So, you know, it was kind of weird that he said that."

Many soldiers are superstitious. Most are at least fatalistic.

Van Torres remembered Gurbisz saying, "Screw it. Tori will be taken care of." He also remembered thinking it was "typical conversation for us. You know, military guys. Dark humor. Whatever." Zach Pamer agreed, and demonstrated such dark humor: "We called our trucks the Death Squad. Sergeant Michel, [call-sign] Top Flite 2, and Top Flite 8, Top Flite 6 [Gurbisz's truck], we were the Death Squad. All the shitty missions. If it was crazy, we went. We always joked, 'Yup, we're gonna die here.' Whenever something's dumb, it's always our three dumb trucks. That was the job we had."

From BIAP, the job was simply to get back to Rustamiyah. Michel's truck had been having mechanical problems, Pamer said, which meant that others had recently taken the lead. But on this day, Michel's Humvee was running smoothly.

Hadd said, "Yancey and I, we were like, 'Well, who's going to lead?' And he was like, 'Well, I'll do it,' and I'm like, 'No, I'll do it.' And then we just came to a consensus. We were like, 'You know what? Let's just let Captain Gurbisz decide, because he has his favorites or whatever.' So Jim more or less was just kinda like that"—Hadd mimed a playground game, pointing one way and the other—"and he was just looking at us, and he was like, 'All right, Yancey, you can go ahead and lead it.' So Yancey ended up leading the convoy."

The convoy rolled out. Hadd reckoned he was "probably a mile and a half back from Yancey. Gurbisz was the second vehicle, and then I was probably like seven or eight vehicles back, but I had civilian truck drivers in front of me. We went on Route Irish. Man, that was a shithole."

But at the time a relatively safe one. As Pamer drove, Gurbisz kept talking and joking.

"He was pretty good at keeping the mood light," Pamer said. "We'd been down these roads almost a year. There were too many choke points, too many bad areas. I was just like, 'We shouldn't be doing this, like, the routes are black. This is a bad call.' But we were doing what we had to do, and Jim was trying to keep some humor for everyone, talking about life and everything after, and he's like, 'Yeah, I just took more life insurance, to make sure Tori's taken care of. I've learned, from everything we've gone through, I gotta take care of her. I gotta make sure that we're good.' And I was like, 'Yeah, that makes sense.' And we just talked a little bit."

Route Irish. No contact.

Next, Hadd said, the convoy "took another route around the Baghdad University, Route Senators [for the Ottawa hockey team], and then we ended up going on one of the most dangerous roads, it was called Route Brewers [for the Milwaukee baseball team]. And I mean, we usually just completely avoided this road because it was very, very bad."

Route Brewers was a major north-south highway to the east of the Tigris. Palm trees, trash, rubble and dirt, light poles, wires between them, barriers half down, ditches of dirty water. Iraqis watching. As Zach drove, he groused: "There were, like, Hesco barriers"—mesh baskets of rocks and earth—"blocking the side of it but with little gaps. I'd said so many times, 'They need to fix this shit. Like, it's too easy to hide shit. Not just there but like every other side of a road. Why don't we do something about this? This is ridiculous.' You know?"

He imitated his captain's exasperated sigh.

"Jim was just like, 'Shut the fuck up and drive, man.' And I said, 'Cool,' and he just tried to take my mind off it, like he always did, cracked a little joke, kept going."

Michel said, "Captain Gurbisz had two radios in his vehicle. He would monitor our frequency, and he would monitor the brigade frequency, so we could communicate with each other and with the battalion. He would be on the brigade net, monitoring the status of the routes and stuff like that."

Pamer said, "So we were doing all that when we got onto the ramp [to Route Brewers]. And next thing I know, I just see a massive blast go off."

Further back, Hadd "heard a boom, and then a boom. And we heard Jim scream. And then we didn't hear anything. The convoy just came to a rolling stop."

◆　◆　◆

THOSE WHO were in the convoy experienced what happened in different ways and remember it differently too. What they agree on is that it was pure, ghastly hell.

"I was in the lead truck, and we were on the ramp to get onto Brewers," Sergeant Alejandro Michel remembered. "We did our little procedure. The lead truck would take off and swing out once it got off the ramp and block any oncoming traffic so the rest of the convoy could get on there. And then the middle truck would relieve us, and we'd haul ass back to the front. That day, myself, Specialist Yancey, and Specialist Johnson, I believe we had the chaplain with us at the time, we accelerated to go lock off the road. And as we accelerated, Captain Gurbisz was not too far behind us. And then there was a pop.

"It wasn't a boom. It was just like a loud pop. I guess I kind of lost consciousness for like a split second. I opened my eyes. The truck filled with smoke. Yancey is slumped over in the driver's seat, and the vehicle's bouncing back and forth from the barriers on the off ramp. The vehicle finally comes to a stop. And Yancey, he's not doing too well. Myself, I just had some shrapnel wounds to the side of my face, some cuts from glass breaking and all that.

"So I get out of the vehicle to assess the situation. To see if it's on fire or anything. And then I look back, and I see Captain Gurbisz's truck is stopped and there's smoke coming out of it."

Pamer and Torres were inside.

Torres said, "Standard thing for us was when an IED goes off, you get over the net and say it three times. 'IED, IED, IED!' I want to say Jim might have been able to get it out twice before our truck was hit on his side. The one that went off on the truck in front of us? It was fucking huge. It was loud. Nothing but dust and smoke. And I'm up in the gunner's hatch. I remember I didn't want to be too high up in the turret. I'd dropped down a little bit. And I heard Jim say it over the net. 'IED.' Let everybody know. And I think by the time he was trying to get the third one out, was when we got hit."

Next to Gurbisz, Pamer was "out cold for a couple seconds. I wake up, I'm all cockeyed in the seat. I grabbed the wheel and tried to turn. But I couldn't do anything because the front of the truck was gone. And I'm just like, 'What the fuck?' Trying to get my wits about me."

Torres blacked out too. He came to "inside the truck, upside down, behind Zach. I remember this grit, this dirt or whatever it was, in my mouth. Like chewing on rocks. A mouthful of sand. And I've got what I'm assuming was, you know, vehicle fluid and who knows what else on me."

Pamer looked at Gurbisz. Gurbisz looked back.

"And he's fucking screaming, 'Oh God, my legs, my legs!' He's fucking screaming bloody murder at me, 'I'm fucked! I'm fucked! My legs! My legs!' And I'm still thinking, 'What the fuck just happened?' The truck bounces off the sidewalk a few times, we come to a stop. I don't remember anything about Van during that time. I don't remember anything about Major De Tingo. I just remember Jim screaming my name, screaming, 'I'm fucked! I'm fucked!' And I go to start trying to help him, and I can't get to him, and then the screaming stops."

Torres could see Jim was "pretty fucked up. But I popped back out the gunner's hatch because one of the things we're taught is an initial attack is followed by small-arms fire. And just north of where we're at is this neighborhood that every now and then we pick up a little small-arms from. So I'm kind of trying to compose myself enough to see if we're about to take fire."

Up ahead, Michel got back into his Humvee.

"I called over the radio. I'm like, 'Hey, I need some help. I need some help.' And I call Jim, to call sign Top Flite 6. There's no answer. And I get frustrated. I'm like, 'Isn't anybody on the fucking net? I need some help down here. I think my driver's dead, and I think Captain Gurbisz got hit too.' And at that point, the rest of the convoy is stuck behind us."

Hadd was back in the convoy. "So we drove up there. And I immediately saw Zach, and he's a medic. And I saw his hand, and it was just completely mangled."

Unable to reach Gurbisz, Pamer had climbed out of the truck.

"I couldn't grab anything," he said. "I had nerve damage in my right hand, one of my fingers was blown almost completely off, I had some fractures in the bones. But I just couldn't feel it."

Pamer was convoy medic. Hadd was Pamer's backup. Hadd thought, "'I'm gonna have to do my job as the combat lifesaver.' So I start grabbing all my stuff, and Zach's like, 'No, no, no, no! Wait!' He's like, 'Don't worry about me.' I'm like, 'What, what?' He's like, 'Go to Jim!' I'm thinking to myself, 'Man, if his hand is that bad, and his fingers and stuff were everywhere, Jim must be really bad.'"

Hadd could see Michel and Yancey's vehicle "maybe half a mile on. He had skidded down onto the railing on the highway. I thought maybe they just hit, got their bell rung. It looked to be okay. I went around to Jim's door. And I went to open it, but the force of the blast had sealed it shut."

From the top of the Humvee, Torres ducked back inside.

"I remember I cut Jim's seatbelt," he said. "And guys were trying to get his door open. And I don't remember what they asked him. But he said, 'I can't. I'm fucked up.'"

Hadd struggled with the door. Then, "that other guy I was talking about, Caleb Hastings, who I'd introduced to Yancey? He came out of nowhere."

From the cab of his heavy equipment transporter, Hastings saw Yancey's Humvee swerve, skid, and stop. He saw the smoke. He saw Pamer getting out of Gurbisz's truck, "and I remember I could see the top of Van Torres's head, and Zach's mouth was bleeding, and his hand was bleeding too. Major De Tingo got out of the vehicle. As I was getting out of my truck I could see Captain Gurbisz. I don't know if I saw him through the rearview mirror on the vehicle or if I saw him through the back-door window, but I could see him just slumped over. Not moving."

Hastings used a pry bar to wrench open the Humvee door.

"Jim was a big guy," Hadd said. "I undid his seatbelt, and I was like, 'Caleb, you're gonna have to help me.' So we went to go pick him up . . . and he just came right up."

Hastings said, "We pulled him out of the vehicle and laid him on the ground. And I mean . . . It was a bad day, man."

Hadd said, "What happened was, it hit right in the wheel well. You had the tire and the wheel. The EFP came right through it and hit Jim right at the kneecaps."

Pamer said, "Above the knee, on both legs, was gone. It was hamburger meat. Spaghetti. Whatever you want to call it. That was all there was. He's pale as shit, he's not talking to me anymore.

"We did so many CLS [combat lifesaver] trainings, we trained our nonmedics' asses off for this. I knew they would get to me. I was like, 'If I get fucked up, it's just you idiots. You think I'm gonna leave my life in you guys' fucking hands? No, y'all gonna learn this shit.' I taught them how to do tourniquets, IVs, the most basic stuff. If something really bad goes wrong, they can stop the bleeding for me, they can give me help.

"Sergeant Michel, God bless him, it worked, because he worked on Yancey. Yancey survived, you know. He lost his arm but he survived. He died in the hospital. He lived through the bomb. I like to say that was for him, the way we all just pushed each other to be better."

Dustin Yancey's mother, Anita, was told her son "never said a single word when he got hit. Shrapnel went up under his helmet. Until they tried to pull that shrapnel out, he was doing fine. But as soon as that shrapnel came out of the back of his head, that's when it went bad."[22]

On the road in Baghdad, behind Yancey's vehicle, Captain Jim Gurbisz lay in the dirt. Years later, Pamer's words came in a rush. His voice broke, recovered, broke again: "So, we got Jim out. And he's just laying there, and I'm looking at him. And I'm like, 'I can't use my right arm. I can't use my right arm.'"

Hastings could see Gurbisz was "still breathing, still had his eyes open. But he was not responding. Nathan was holding him the whole time. He was talking to him. I remember telling him to hang in there. 'Everything's gonna be all right. It's gonna be fine.' But I knew it was bad. No, it was really bad. And it just . . . I mean . . . I don't know."

When Hadd, Hastings, Pamer, Torres, and Michel all described that deadly day, it was more than fifteen years gone. Hastings said that talking worked like therapy, in a way. The horror was always there. But it was buried. It had to be. Hadd was an army recruiter in Michigan. Hastings worked at a paper mill in South Carolina. Pamer worked for the US Postal Service in Florida. Torres was a sheriff's deputy in Colorado. Michel was still in the army, stationed in Texas. Each day they went to work and came home. Some days, they thought about what happened on the ramp to Route Brewers in southeastern Baghdad on November 4, 2005. Most days they did not. Either way, they rarely spoke of it.

Pamer said, "We flipped Jim around, so he was facing downhill. You always want as much blood flow into the major organs as possible. You use the terrain. So I'm talking, I'm like, 'All right, you need to get this tourniquet up here, fucking take everything you have, *everything* you have and just cinch the fuck out of it. Everything you have, dude, I don't care if it hurts you, if it hurts him.' I said, 'Just go until you can't go anymore, that needs to be tighter than anything ever.' Just trying to stop the bleeding."

Hadd said, "I had to take Jim's tourniquet out of his vest, to take my tourniquet out of my vest, and I had to put them on his legs . . . but he was just unresponsive. He was in traumatic shock."

Pamer said, "I ended up getting two IVs in with my left hand, but, it's like, it didn't matter. Like, if there's no blood in there, I can give you as much fluid as you want but it actually doesn't carry oxygen. So you need to stop the bleeding, and that's why we did the tourniquets."

Hadd said, "I can remember trying to do some compressions, to give him some breath. I checked his airway to make sure if he had any teeth or anything in there, blocking his breath, and then I elevated his head and we tried to get it going. But his veins were so collapsed from the loss of blood, it was just not even happening. So we had maybe, maybe four or five minutes where I held his hand, held his head and just talked to him. 'Everything's gonna be all right, you're going to be fine.' Things of that nature."

Hastings looked on.

"I think about how blue his eyes were because that was the last thing I can remember. Looking into his eyes. He was staring like,

like, *through* me. I'll be honest with you. It was really bad. But just the way his eyes were: it was almost like they weren't in any pain at all."

Hadd described a similar, utterly indelible moment: "I could feel him die. He stopped breathing. I could feel him just relax, for maybe ten seconds. And then he was gone."

Michel was wounded but walking. He saw "an infantry patrol and Bradleys, running across the street. I guess they saw the whole thing happen."

Colin Johnson, the gunner in Michel's truck, had a leg wound. Torres had superficial wounds, shrapnel and rocks to the legs. The troops who rushed to the scene, Michel said, "took Torres and Captain Gurbisz and loaded them into their truck. And then the Bradley came next to me, and I loaded up Yancey and Johnson and they sped up and away."

Hadd put Pamer in his own Humvee. The wreckage was shunted aside. Hadd "got on the radio, and we started to move the convoy. We were maybe a mile and a half from Rustamiyah. I had them open the gates. We went directly to the hospital. I remember seeing Dustin for the first time. I remember seeing his TC, Alejandro Michel, and I remember seeing his gunner."

Yancey was hit in the head and the arm. Hadd said, "He didn't die until, I want to say, like three or four hours later, in Baghdad. They airlifted him out. They said he had died."

To this day, Dustin Yancey's family doesn't know much more than that. His mother, Anita, said, "We were just told that he was killed by an IED. That he was killed by a bomb. And what went through my mind was, 'Was he just blasted apart? Is there anything remaining? Do we have a body?' Days and days, I didn't know. Then we found out he was still alive in surgery. That he wasn't killed instantly. That he survived a surgery. We know he lost his arm but didn't know his arm had been amputated. I thought it had been blown off. He survived the amputation surgery. They had to do that to stop blood loss or something before they could move on to try to do anything with his head. That's when it went bad."

♦   ♦   ♦

NATE HADD remembers Jim Gurbisz dying in his arms on the road. Zach Pamer remembers him dying in the next hospital bed.

"No one ever died under my care," he said. "Jim did not die when I was working on him. He died in the hospital next to me."

At Rustamiyah, another medic pulled Pamer from Hadd's Humvee. Pamer remembers what the sergeant said, using a nickname: "Don't worry, Meat. I got you."

"I remember him looking down at me. And he goes, 'Oh shit.' And I'm like, 'What?' And he yells, 'We need fucking litters! We need litters! His fucking legs are fucked!' I'm like, 'What? *My* legs? I was walking a second ago.' I'm trying to figure it out. Apparently, there was so much blood it looked like my legs were blown off. But it was all Jim's blood and mine and everyone else's."

The medics got Pamer "taken care of pretty good. And medics, we make the absolute worst fucking patients ever. Because we know what's going on. We had a man, went on a bunch of missions with us, Tony Ortiz, Medical Corps officer. And he's in there working on me. And I see the tears in his eyes. And I'm like, 'What? Where's Jim? Where's Jim?' They told me he was in the next bed. I wanted to open the curtain. They wouldn't do it. I'm starting to get pissed off. They won't do it. And I hear them charging to shock him. You know, they're like, 'Two hundred sixty joules!' And I'm just like, 'Ah no,' and I start freaking out, I'm like, 'What do you mean, shock him?'

"I hear them shock him. I hear them shock him. And there's silence. And then Tony Ortiz was over there, peeking around. And he just turned around, and it went from tears in his eyes to bawling and he looked at me and said, 'Jimmy's gone.'

"I just lose it, I'm flying out of that bed, you know, and they get me to the ground, a couple guys, and they just knock me the fuck out. They just pump me full of shit. Someone told me about it. It happened and I don't even know."

Torres and Michel were walking wounded. Michel said they "went straight to the front desk to inquire as to the status of our battle buddies, Gurbisz and Yancey. And the nurse was like, 'Hey, you can have a seat back over there.' I was, like, 'Why do you want us to sit down? What's the problem?' She said, 'Just have a seat and somebody will be with you.' I'm like, 'Whatever, you know, I'm not gonna get irate, bro. Like, let me do what they say.' And then I see the chaplain come out. And he said, 'They're gone.'"

In 2003, Michel manned a gun on the march to Baghdad. He saw "all kinds of crazy violence, things eighteen, nineteen, twenty-year-old kids shouldn't have to see. I thought I was numb to that kind of stuff. All the other crazy shit we had seen just on the streets of Baghdad. But then to find out that your friends are gone? Man . . ."

Pamer was flown to BIAP. They told him about Yancey there. Then Pamer was flown to Germany. He had his arm fixed. Eventually, he went home.

Torres remembered walking back to his bunk at Rustamiyah, alone, "a complete mess, dirty and disgusting, slightly injured but just completely demoralized. Jim was our Ultimate Warrior. That's what we called him sometimes. The Ultimate Warrior. Not to take away from Dustin Yancey. But Jim, we were in the same truck the entire time. He was my TC. I saw him as an amazing leader. The last time I saw him, they were loading him in another vehicle. It was like, 'No, that's not really what's going on right now.' It was . . . a lot of disbelief. Actual pain. The pain in your heart."

Colin Johnson, the gunner from Michel's Humvee, was in the hospital too. "Part of his leg was gone," Hadd said, but it "felt good because he was screaming. That meant he looked likely to live."

Hadd himself wasn't hurt. But, like Pamer, he was covered in the blood of his captain.

Cpt. Jim Gurbisz on his Humvee's radio.

After

Tori Gurbisz was used to the empty house in Savannah. She was used to the fear and the worry. She'd been upset when her husband came home on leave and talked to his dad about what it was like in Iraq but went quiet when she walked into the room. She'd dealt with it and got on the best she could with her life.

In November 2005, Captain Jim Gurbisz's deployment was nearly done. The plane home was close.

Tori said, "Everyone was biding their time. Where I was kind of really dramatic and very worried about things before, now I was like, 'Don't think like that, don't have these inner monologues.' My friend moved down, my mom was down, and I was, like, all right. Better. More grounded. We were like, we're *there*. Just biding our time until it's time for the flight to leave."[1]

And then the car came.

Tori hadn't been feeling well, but she was "getting ready for a big show at the beach in Savannah, Tybee Island. I was absolutely busting my butt to make candles and soaps and all that stuff. I'd actually talked to Jim the day before and told him, 'I am so sick. Like, I'm scared of how sick I am.' It was just a really bad flu or something, but I was hugely anti-doctor, because, let's just say, the doctors on post were very condescending to military wives. Especially during deployments. But I remember the conversation with Jim. I promised I'd go on base, I'd go to the hospital, if it got any worse.

"My jeep was out in the driveway, and I had the whole garage as a candlemaking factory. It was still pretty warm. Savannah in

November is occasionally in the eighties during the day. And I was wearing Jim's C3 company shirt from West Point, because I was sick and I wanted baggy clothes on. And it was okay if I got candle wax on it.

"We lived on a cul-de-sac, still a few houses to the turnaround. And I saw a black Impala drive past my house, slow. Cars always go into a cul-de-sac and turn. But I stopped what I was doing. I just stood there, waiting for it to turn around and leave. But it stopped in front of my house.

"I knew instantly. I knew the military. There is nothing good about this car being in front of my house. I know it's here about Jim. It was just the weirdest moment of clarity that I've ever had. Something was terribly wrong. I debated not answering the door. Because I didn't want to hear what they had to say. And then I saw them get out. And of course there was a chaplain. The chaplain was a man and the other person with him was a woman. And they came to the door.

"And my house was an absolute mess. There were boxes and packaging for candles all over my living room. I didn't have any-where for them to sit. I'm like, 'Let me move these boxes.' I'm in Jim's shirt. It looks ridiculous on me. And they started telling me, and I wanted to say, 'No, it's not true.' But I'm like, 'You're not like that.' That wouldn't be a super cool thing to do. But I'm not a religious person either. And, you know, chaplains, they want you to pray with them. And I'm just like, 'Get out. Get out of my house. I don't want to pray with you right now. Because, you know, even if there is a God, I'm pretty pissed right now. So I don't think any god would want to hear what I had to say.'"

The chaplain didn't want to leave Tori alone. But her mother was close by.

"We're gonna call her," Tori said. "Just get out of my house, *please.*"

"I was absolutely terrible to them. I was like, 'It sucks that you're the bearer of bad news, but get the fuck out of my house. I'm done with you right now. You can leave.' And they did leave. And I waited. I mean, how do I call my mother and say, 'Hey, come over, because Jim died'? It was a super surreal situation. I pretty much lost it. I called her and said, 'You just have to come over now.' She knew I'd been very sick. She thought she needed to bring me to the hospital. But she came over, and she was like, 'Oh my God.' She knew right away. It was definitely, definitely rough."

Eventually, the army did take over—to do what it does with bereaved wives.

"After that was such a blur because of course they take me to post and they give me all kinds of anti-anxiety and antidepressants like Valium, like Trazodone, so I'm not a complete disaster and can actually sleep. So my memory gets even crappier here. But I remember when I talked to Kathy, Jim's sister. She just instantly . . . it's like falling. It was just so intense. That was that same day, later that evening. You're all feeling pain for the same person, but it's different. 'Oh my God, you lost your brother. Oh my God, you lost your son.'"

IN HIS Rutgers oral history interview, Ken Gurbisz described how he and Helen learned the news.[2] They'd last spoken to Jim on Columbus Day, October 10, by satellite phone. On November 4, they went shopping for a vacuum cleaner for Tori. A couple of hours after the army visited Captain Jim Gurbisz's wife in Savannah, Georgia, it visited his parents in Eatontown, New Jersey.

Ken said, "Helen was starting to get dinner together, and I was sitting, talking to my mother, and the doorbell rang and I opened the door. I saw the three officers standing in our front door, and I knew immediately it was bad—at least I thought I knew immediately that he had been killed, but they say they'd come even if he was wounded. They came in and I sat them in the living room and I excused myself and I got Helen. I just told her she's going to have to be strong, and then they came in and they started and they told us how he was killed, and they were very good. The one colonel started breaking up, and it was hard to keep control . . . From then, it was hard."

Kathy Gurbisz was working in New York. "My mom called, I want to say it was like 5:00 p.m. or 5:30 p.m. And I almost didn't pick up the phone. I almost was like, 'Oh, wait until I get home.' But something told me to pick it up. And, I don't know, I think I couldn't even understand what they were saying. People from my office took me home."[3]

BY NOVEMBER 2005, Gurbisz's rugby brothers were spread throughout the army. Matt Blind had left Iraq a month before, commanding a convoy from Mosul to Kuwait. He was in the Pacific northwest, resting and refitting. Dave Little and Bryan Phillips had been home a long time. Scott Radcliffe was just out of New Orleans after Hurricane Katrina. Jerrod Adams was an Apache helicopter pilot. Brian McCoy was flying choppers in Italy. He opened an email. It said Jimmy was dead. Brian read it "four or five times." He called for his wife and they cried.[4]

Four players were in Iraq. Mo Greene was out in the western desert, hunting Abu Musab al-Zarqawi. He didn't find out right away. Jeremiah Hurley was with Special Forces too. His wife, Dawn, had seen Gurbisz brought in after the bombing. Clint Olearnick and Pete Chacon were with their infantry units.

Olearnick was in Hawija, in Kirkuk province, "one of the birthplaces of Isis and a terrible deployment." Three years into the army and on his second tour, he was a battle captain. He and his roommate, Joe DaSilva, West Point class president 2002, "were the guys in the operation center managing all the units on the battlefield. And so we would switch night and day. And that was the time Joe came in and told me Jimmy died."[5]

Olearnick hadn't spoken to Gurbisz in years, since the fight at graduation. They never ran into each other or got around to a call. Now Clint knew he would never see Jim again. He borrowed a colonel's satellite phone and called his own parents, who had been close to the team.

"If they're getting a phone call from Iraq, they're thinking the worst thing ever. But I called and told my mom to grab my dad. I said, 'Jimmy died today.' And we all started crying. Maybe it was just as close as they were to him. I mean . . . we protected each other for four years, you know, at West Point. You know, it was . . . it was really hard."

Olearnick talked to me, remembered the hard news, sitting in Matt Blind's study, at the top of his house in Cohasset, Massachusetts. It was mid-August 2021, and the players had come for a weekend of talking and drinking, a party bus to a ballgame at Fenway, interviews with the British guy writing the book. Olearnick was shaven-headed, black-bearded, tattooed. He was wearing a rugby shirt and carrying a bottle for spitting his chew. He looked at the tape recorder on the table. He spat a gout of tobacco.

AT WEST Point, Pete Chacon was the third musketeer alongside Clint Olearnick and Jim Gurbisz, the other rugby player Kathy Gurbisz would find asleep in the living room in Eatontown, the other shaven-headed kid who sat around the kitchen table with Ken, eager for tales of Vietnam. Twenty years later, in Cohasset, Chacon played something of a mediating role, a bridge between the big dogs and the more contemplative souls. A wrestler who ended up on the wing, Pete is from hardscrabble Oakland, "gangland going on, pretty shitty."[6] He's dark, and his surname isn't Irish like Hurley or German like Blind or English like Radcliffe or Phillips. At West Point, inevitably, his nickname was "Mexican Pete." In Massachusetts, on Matt's boat on the way to lunch at Marblehead, he worked his way to the stern.

"Hey, Dave," he shouted to his big buddy, the number 8. "Guess what? You're more Mexican than me!"

True. The Chacons are French-Portuguese. The Littles, from San Diego, have their Anglo name, but via Dave's mother they also have a direct Mexican line.

Laughter. Beer. The reverent irreverence of rugby. The old everybody-gets-it shit, close to the line, not over it. This time.

Up in Blind's study, Chacon sat for an interview too. He wore a peach polo and cargo shorts, held a beer, and went barefoot. At West Point it was Chacon and Olearnick and Gurbisz, together all the time. When it came to rugby, it was Olearnick then Gurbisz then Chacon. One worked on the next to play. Gurbisz put the screws to Chacon during Buckner, summer training that follows plebe year.

"I got this great picture of us," Chacon said. "We got our shirts off, we got our dog tags on, we look like we've been starving for a week. We're all skinny and drawn and chewing huge dips. It's me, Clint, Jim, and this other guy too."

After Gurbisz was killed, Chacon got a call in Iraq.

"So, they walk in and they say my wife's on the phone. And so I have no idea why she's calling me. I mean, that was really uncommon. We had one phone once a week for like two hours, and we could rotate through the entire platoon and call our loved ones for one minute. And someone from time to time would get a sad one. And now my wife's on the phone. She was trying to help me out, but as soon as they handed me the phone I knew it was tragic news. And my mind was stateside. Was my son hurt? She said I needed to sit down. She said, 'I got some really horrible news.' I was like, 'Fucking tell me right now.' I said, 'I'm not gonna sit down. Just tell me the fucking news.' And she goes, 'Jimmy was killed.'

"I sat down. I felt so fucking guilty because I was just relieved that it wasn't my boys. I was mentally ready for, like, 'Your son got kidnapped,' or 'Your son got killed, a car backed over him in the parking lot.' Something terrible. And it was *Jimmy*. And first, I felt so much *relief*. It was terrible. Just terrible."

He found a way to try to atone. "Ken wrote me an email. He told me that they just weren't hearing anything. They were just being told Jim died in combat. That was it. No explanation. And Ken was like, 'Hey, look. I'm telling them I'm a veteran. I've seen combat, I've seen friendly fire. I've seen horrible things. You know what happened. Give me some information.' But the army was giving him nothing. He was very frustrated. He just wanted resolution, I think, instead of playing millions of different scenarios in his mind. And he brought up the Pat Tillman thing."

Tillman played football for the Arizona Cardinals until he left his sports career behind after 9/11 and enlisted. He became a Ranger and died in Khost province, Afghanistan, in April 2004, when another platoon mistook his for the enemy. A harsh truth, it was not immediately told.[7] Chacon said Ken Gurbisz told him, "I don't care. If that's how he lost his life, I just want to know."

PETE CHACON, Clint Olearnick, and Jeremiah Hurley went to Rustamiyah for a memorial to Jim Gurbisz and Dustin Yancey. When I spoke to David Finkel of the *Washington Post*, who lived there a year, he did not just describe the look of the place and the smell. He made me aware of the obvious: had I looked at YouTube? In 2005, soldiers in Baghdad didn't have iPhones, but they could shoot video. Finkel emailed a link: "In memory of SPC Yancey and CPT Gurbisz." Four minutes and six seconds. Posted by Pablogrone, July 8, 2007. Caption: "November 4, 2005. Camp Rustamiyah, Irak-3rd Infantry Division, 2BCT, 26TH FSB. We lost 2 of our brothers!"[8]

The video is edited, a mix of stills and moving images set to a sad song by Evanescence. It begins with a picture of Yancey sitting on a Humvee, helmet off, and one of Gurbisz in his truck, on the radio, in wraparound glasses and armor. There are stills of Bronze Stars and Purple Hearts. Each man's memorial: boots, rifle, dog tags, and helmet in front of flags and guidons.

There is a still of Lieutenant Colonel Michael Armstead, commanding officer, 26 FSB, then footage of him speaking. He stands at a lectern, leaning into a microphone as if in some conference room at a hotel: ceiling tiles, fans, strip lights, beige floor. If such hotels hosted men with high-and-tight haircuts and khaki fatigues. If every second guest carried a gun.

Dawn Hurley speaks, dark hair tied back, eyes downcast, turning to salute the memorials. The video cuts to the audience, men and women in desert gear, solemn, seats full, some standing at the back. Another speaker, his name tag too blurred to read. Back to the pictures, propped against the dead men's rifles. Specialist Yancey. Captain Gurbisz. The next speaker's name obscured by his rifle. The next speaker seems to be Captain Jethren Mattus, Gurbisz's immediate commanding officer. A shot of the helmets again, Third Infantry insignia affixed.

The audience again, standing to attention. A soldier wipes a tear. A man stands in front of the helmets, rifles, and boots. He has a pistol strapped to his thigh and he has white hair and he fingers the dead men's dog tags, looking down to pray. Stepping back, he crosses himself and salutes. The next soldier places something on each man's boots. He salutes. The next man salutes, places something by Gurbisz's right boot, and gently touches the left. He salutes Yancey too.

Fade. Yancey's picture behind three bullets. A guitar pick, a pack of Viceroy cigarettes, and a matchbook.

Fade. Three bullets in front of the picture of Jim. Two aces of spades, tucked into the frame.

The video stops.

Nate Hadd remembered the bugler playing taps, the roll call, Yancey and Gurbisz's names unanswered. Rifles fired in salute.

IN COHASSET, Massachusetts, Pete Chacon sat back in his chair. After the memorial, he said, "Clint had to leave right away. But I stayed for a couple of days, interviewing people, to get the stories so I could tell Ken and give him some something, some sort of resolution. I talked to Dawn, I talked to the medics, and I talked to some of the guys in the unit. I felt I got a pretty good understanding.

"One of the guys had the damn armor plate from Jim's vehicle when the projectile went through it. It came away from the vehicle, just split in half in the heat. You could see the round hole from the shape charge, and then you could see the rest of the steel plate fracturing right down the middle. And the guys, they had it in their little sleeping compound. They were like, 'This is it, it went through here and this plate split off and, you know, there's blood all over the vehicle. We couldn't get the damn door open.'"

That led Chacon to a theory: "There's this whole mess. They're trying to get the door open and they're worried about fire, and then they're worried about third and fourth charges going off. So that delayed things. And that was it. That was, I think, the thing the army was not wanting really to be out there, was that Jim's treatment was delayed. Because it turned into like, well, 'We need to slow down, we understand there's casualties and people are bleeding, but this could be much worse. There could be a total bait thing, like draw people in, a third bomb. This could just be like an ongoing ambush, you know.' There was a real concern.

"And so that little piece right there, I would call it a maybe fifteen-minute delay in him getting more than just the guys next to him treating him. That was the thing that I think the army was hesitant to disclose, because it's very possible that if someone would have come up, a trained medic, boom, *Okay, this is it?* Then possibly he would have lived."

Zach Pamer was a medic, but he had been hit in the hand. Nate Hadd was Pamer's backup. He held Gurbisz. He says he died in the road. So does Caleb Hastings, the Heavy Equipment Transporter driver. Pamer says Gurbisz died in the hospital, in the very next bed.

The house in Cohasset was silent, the other players drinking out back somewhere. Around us, the tools of Matt Blind's prosperity. The standing desk and the whiteboard, the computers and monitors, the kegerator, the chairs around the coffee table, the shelves of memorabilia from West Point and Ohio high school football. Around the room, airbeds, where in the small hours men crashed drunk to sleep. Chacon rubbed his chin and stroked his head and took a sip of his beer. The tape got it all. The sandpaper rasp of his stubble. The tap of the can placed on the table.

"I found out a bunch of stories too. About when they were wheeling Jim in, the stuff he was talking about, things he was saying. They said it was pretty amazing. It was *funny*, because his personality was there at the end."

Both Nate Hadd, who held Gurbisz, and Zach Pamer, who was next to him, said Gurbisz was in no state to talk.

Chacon continued.

"I told Ken the whole deal. I framed it the way I thought it should be framed, which was there was a detonation on this initial vehicle. I didn't mince words. Ken knows what an ambush is. They blew up the first vehicle, stopped the convoy, and then as Jimmy rushed up to help his fellow soldier, to help his boys, they detonated the second charge. I don't think the army would have ever framed it that way. They would have framed it as, like, this was just a complex ambush. You know, I framed it for Ken that Jim was rushing up to his brothers because that's how I saw it from everything that I've heard enough times."

This is how the story about how Captain Jim Gurbisz died got started.

THE WEST Point rugby players tell the story. So does their coach, who heard it from Gurbisz's commanding officer. So does Gurbisz's father. It has become part of team lore. Pete Chacon told it to me the first time we spoke, in 2015, and he told it again six years later, when Matt Blind's boat got us to Marblehead for lunch with Father Mahan. In Chacon's words, the story goes like this.

"There weren't too many guys like Jimmy. When he was, like, being carried into the hospital? When he was, like, bleeding out, right? He's sick. He's dying. And he's joking about how his wife is gonna get this great insurance policy. He's *laughing*. He's like, 'Man, thank goodness I signed up for extra life insurance.' He's *joking* about it. And that's just how he was."[9]

Told by Coach Mike Mahan, the story changes slightly.

"Jimmy was joking with the medics. They couldn't stop the bleeding. His legs were just, there were no veins to be found or arteries, but he was joking with them about, 'Oh, I needed to lose some weight anyway.'"[10]

Both men laugh, sadly, when they tell their versions of the story.

When Chacon first told me the story, it struck hard. But I didn't double-source it, and my article for the *Guardian* worked without it. As I got deeper into work for this book, the story came back to haunt me. I spoke to Nate Hadd, who told me he held Gurbisz as he died, out on the ramp to Route Brewers. He said Gurbisz was in no state to joke. I spoke to Zach Pamer, Gurbisz's driver, who saw Gurbisz scream and fall silent. But Hadd and Pamer also told me Gurbisz *did* joke, about life insurance, at Baghdad airport and on the way to Rustamiyah. Over lunch in Marblehead, when Chacon repeated the story, I made a note but kept quiet. Then someone ordered up a round of Irish Car Bombs (stout, Irish whiskey, cream) and, delighting in the grim irony, the brothers raised a toast to Jim.

The next afternoon, I sat down with Clint Olearnick. He brought up the story too. I told him what I knew. He chewed his tobacco and nodded.

"Joking about the entire situation was exactly what Jimmy *would* do," he said. "That was the kind of dude he was. You know, at that point, we all thought we were invincible. I wouldn't put it past the joker."[11]

I went back to New York. The players told a story about how Gurbisz died. It made sense if you'd known him. But according to the man who held Gurbisz as he died, and his driver, injured in the same blast, the story wasn't true. How to write that?

I met up with Nick Utzig, another West Point grad from the Class of '02. He flew Chinooks in Afghanistan and Iraq but was now studying Shakespeare at Harvard. We met on Stone Street in Manhattan, down in the old city, next to the Fraunces Tavern, where in 1783 George Washington said farewell to his men. I described the problem. Nick took a sip of his beer. Then he nailed it. Facts matter. But so do stories. The story about Gurbisz's last moments may not be true, but like all stories—like Shakespeare's *Henry V*, from which Gurbisz and his rugby brothers drew so much—it is *built* from truth. Gurbisz joked about life insurance. Gurbisz died. Not at the same time, sure, but, as Olearnick said, the story about Gurbisz joking *as* he died is true to Gurbisz in its way. So tell the story and tell the truth too. Both matter.

Then I called Dawn Hurley. Discussing life and death at FOB Rustamiyah, she explained Coach Mahan's version of Gurbisz's story.[12]

On the afternoon of November 4, 2005, Dawn waited for her friend to come back. She was in the maintenance shop when she "heard on the radio that people were being evacuated to a little hospital on our FOB. I had a meeting, so I said, 'Okay, I'll walk the long way by the hospital and go check it out.' And I was there when the vehicles came in.

"A crowd started forming up. Jim came in and then Yancey came in. When Jim got wheeled out, he was gray. And I remember . . . I'm a nervous laugher. And I said, to no one in particular, 'He didn't need those legs anyway.' Jim, he had bad knees. That's why he couldn't go infantry. And I was like, 'It'll be fine. He didn't need those knees.'"

She paused.

"And then, yeah. It turned into this nightmare."

The story about Gurbisz's jokes in the face of death was born in the pitch-black heart of that nightmare. Gurbisz didn't joke about his knees. Dawn Hurley did. The darkest possible joke, born in a moment of terrible shock. But fitting. *Like* Jim Gurbisz. And, in the telling—as Gurbisz's joke about life insurance shifted in time, from before the convoy to during it and then to after the blast—Dawn's joke got given to Gurbisz. For those who loved Gurbisz, the story about his death, in either version, simply became a way to cope with the horror.

And still the truth twists and turns. In New Jersey, by the lake and the fountain and the ducks, with Helen by his side and coffee freshly made, Ken Gurbisz spoke softly.

"We were called by Colonel Armstead, who said Jim didn't suffer. Which is not the truth. They actually transported him to the hospital, and he died on the operating table."

So Zach Pamer said.

Ken continued, "Matter of fact, the guys were saying they were amazed that here he is, all torn up, and he's joking with them. And Petey told me that."

Pamer didn't say that.

"You know," Ken said, gently, "it comes out in time. And I don't know how long he was on the operating table. They weren't even sure we'd get an open casket."

They did get an open casket. That was something. They coped, however on earth they could.

The SIGACT seems to agree with Ken and Pamer. It says Gurbisz died of wounds at FOB Rustamiyah. But Nate Hadd, who held Gurbisz, says he died out on the highway. Again, both versions can be true. David Abrams, the army journalist who became a novelist, explains it: No fatality was ever confirmed until a doctor did so, having tried every last way of revival. And doctors stayed at the FOB.[13]

The story about how Captain Jim Gurbisz died may evolve again, in time. But its essence is irreverence and endurance and that makes it fitting. Jim Gurbisz was the high school kid who would joke about anything, the yearbook class comedian. The West Point cadet who embraced the suck, who sat up all night in Beast, shattered, pissed on with rain, manning the gun for his team. The hooker Coach Mahan would send running around the posts and back ten times each training session for insubordination or trash talk or just trash play, and who would come back laughing for more.

Jim Gurbisz's irreverence was learned at home and at school in Jersey. At West Point, a very reverent place, he found the rugby team and added the zeal of the gleeful outsider. Training up at Stony Lonesome, smashing into others who swapped football for the game you play without pads. Drinking in the firstie club or on the bus from Ohio State or in shitty clubs in Jersey, New York, or Georgia. Partying at Dave Little's wedding out in San Diego.

It all helped.

It all helped get Gurbisz through four punishing years, through the pain of injury and missing out on the infantry and through the misery of Fort Benning.

And all of it, the experience and the irreverence, the frustration, the glory of rugby at West Point, he poured into taking the oddballs and misfits of 26 FSB and creating Top Flite Security, another bunch of happy outsiders. Sometimes, he tossed them a rugby ball too.

It's all good. It's all Jim Gurbisz. It's all, as Sergeant Alejandro Michel called his captain on a somber online tribute page, "Jim Hellwig from parts unknown, AKA Wrestling's Ultimate Warrior."

And so, among his brothers, among those who loved him, the death of Jim Gurbisz has become a tale to be told and retold, shaped and reshaped, with laughter and a sad shake of the head.

◆　◆　◆

IN COHASSET, Massachusetts, Pete Chacon continued.

"Now, at this point we had gotten intelligence that there were shape charges out there. And we had actually seen some and found some."

The first bomb, the one that hit Yancey and Michel's Humvee, was a regular IED, the sort that hit Chacon in Mosul in 2003. If you got lucky, like Chacon did, like Michel did, you could survive those. Get your bell rung. Fuck a shoulder up. Tweeze bits of Iraqi road out of your face for years. If you got lucky. If you got unlucky, like Dustin Yancey, you died. But the bomb that killed Gurbisz was different. In the words of Van Torres, who survived it, it was "molten hell."

Chacon thought for a moment.

"I think Jimmy was one of the first, second, or third to be killed by an EFP."

According to the US government, Chacon might be right. If he is, it might account for the army's reluctance to describe precisely how Gurbisz died.

EFPs came from Iran. In any year, that would be a very serious matter. But in November 2005, as Iraq fell apart, no US official would have been keen to tell the public that Iran was helping kill American soldiers. Close to twenty years later, relations with Iran are still very sensitive indeed. Why give a writer the 15-6 report?

On the other hand, the silence over the 15-6 might be simply bureaucratic; odds are it was.

Still, there are clues to be found. In summer 2015, Republicans opposed to the Iran nuclear deal pressed the Obama administration over Iranian responsibility for American deaths in Iraq. Citing Pentagon sources, Senator Tom Cotton of Arkansas, a veteran of Iraq and Afghanistan, put the figure at five hundred.[14] Experts thought that might be low. EFPs became common amid the troop surge of 2006–07 but were seen years before that.

Republicans kept up the pressure. Later in 2015, the Pentagon declassified documents that put the death toll from EFPs in Iraq at 196.[15] According to those figures, the first EFP attacks were in

July 2005. The first casualties, one wounded and one killed, were recorded in November. It maps. Zach Pamer, WIA. Jim Gurbisz, KIA. But the toll is not settled. In April 2019, the Pentagon blamed Iran for 603 American deaths. That figure came from the Trump administration, which wanted to justify scrapping the nuclear deal.[16] I asked the Pentagon if it still thought the first American killed by an EFP died in November 2005. It did not reply.

In 2018, the lawsuit Karcher v. Islamic Republic of Iran was filed in US district court for the District of Columbia by more than three hundred plaintiffs. The suit described eighty attacks with EFPs, which it defined as "short metal pipe[s] loaded with high-energy explosive and capped with a concave copper disk." It described what happens when "an EFP pierces even an up-armored Humvee, the slug dispers[ing] shards of the Humvee's steel and Teflon, potentially blow[ing] the vehicle's doors off of their hinges due to the pressure wave, and possibly ignit[ing] the vehicle's fuel." It described what EFPs do to people.

In the case that gave its name to the suit, Lieutenant Colonel Timothy Karcher was in a convoy "traveling south on Route Miller in Baghdad" on June 28, 2009.[17] "At approximately 11:28 a.m., a multi-array explosive from the west side of the street struck LTC Karcher's armored vehicle within the convoy. . . . The explosion that ensued sent slugs through LTC Karcher's armored vehicle's engine block and the front passenger door, severely injuring both of LTC Karcher's legs. . . . The Significant Activity report from the attack confirms the 'IED Type' as 'EFP' and contains a description of the device as a 'four array, copper-lined EFP.'"[18]

I am back where I started. The SIGACTs. The roads of Baghdad. Death in the dust down below.

Without an unredacted 15-6, I cannot know how the army says Jim Gurbisz died. The SIGACT, from WikiLeaks, only provides clues, not answers. I do not know why the army chose to describe Gurbisz's death, and that of Dustin Yancey, in the way that it did. But with work, and thought, and through so many hard conversations, I have arrived at these conclusions.

At my desk, on the phone or Zoom or FaceTime. On the road or the rails or a plane, staring out the window, thinking my way through the story. Whenever I try to picture what happened on the ramp to Route Brewers on November 4, 2005, whenever I think of Jim Gurbisz and Dustin Yancey's last moments, Eric Stanbra's words return:

"A flash of red and orange. Then black."

The headstone of Cpt. James Gurbisz in Section 60 of Arlington Cemetery.

Arlington

C APTAIN JIM Gurbisz lies in Virginia soil, in grave 8151, Section
60, at Arlington National Cemetery. On a burning day in September, I walked out to see him.

I left the visitors' center and turned left on Eisenhower Drive. At
the road named for the Civil War general George McClellan stood a
gate named for him, too, long passed by the bounds of the cemetery,
a lone red sentinel high over fields of small white stones. The humid-
ity of the Washington summer was gone, but it was still pitilessly
hot, shade giving way to naked tarmac, pans for the lasering sun.
Every now and then a groundskeeper buzzed past in a buggy. From
Chaplains Hill to the west I heard two renditions of taps, the bugle
call played at all US military burials, notes drifting down over fields
of stones. At Arlington, taps is played twenty times a day.[1] Back at
the center, a guide had instructed tourists about what to do if they
came across a funeral. Stop. Be respectful. Then continue, quietly, to
where JFK and the Unknown Soldier lie buried.

I walked on, past Section 59, which contains a memorial to 241
Americans killed in the Beirut barracks bombing of 1983. A plaque and
a Lebanese cedar. The further south I walked, toward the edge of the
grounds, where the Pentagon sits behind a wall, the more alone I felt.

The sky was uniform blue. To the north, the obelisk of the Washington Monument, burnt umber. Dusk was on its way. In the trees
that dotted the paths, shadows gathered. There was the wind, the
birds, and the rumble of DC traffic. A plane took off from Reagan
National Airport, south down the Potomac. Another.

I turned east down York, into welcome shade, used my phone to find the point to turn south again, out into Section 60, the right row of graves to walk down. Naked to the sun, the grass was dry and brittle. I loosened my tie, passed my jacket from arm to arm. I'd been to Lafayette Square, near the White House, to meet Lieutenant General Daniel Christman, the West Point superintendent when Gurbisz first arrived. Christman shared his name with the first man buried at Arlington: William Henry Christman, a Union private from Pennsylvania who was twenty when he died of measles in 1864.[2] He was the first of more than four hundred thousand. With him are three thousand eight hundred people once enslaved who died free in DC.

Section 60 is relatively small, fourteen of 624 acres.[3] Out where the Pentagon looms, new plots are ready. In time they will be like Section 60, which is just like any other. It goes on, rank on rank of small white stones. It opened in 2003. It is home to older soldiers, veterans of the Second World War, Korea, and Vietnam who lived to die in bed. But many of its graves hold men who died after 9/11, in Afghanistan and Iraq. Operation Enduring Freedom. Operation Iraqi Freedom. Those wars were controversial. When coffins came back, no cameras were allowed.[4] For a while, the army tried to keep the media out of Arlington too.[5]

The first American killed in the Iraq War and buried at Arlington, Captain Russell B. Rippetoe, lies in Section 60.[6] On April 3, 2003, near Haditha, he stopped a car. A suicide vest detonated. Two other soldiers died.

As I walked south, I walked back in time. These soldiers died in 2010, 2009 . . . 2006, 2005. I stopped at a grave with a rock placed neatly in the center of the white marble tombstone:

JAMES GURBISZ

CPT

U.S. ARMY

SEP 13 1980

NOV 4 2005

BRONZE STAR

PURPLE HEART

OPERATION

IRAQI FREEDOM

A bouquet lay on the grass, a week old, placed for what would have been Gurbisz's birthday. The red roses were wilting. The geraniums were still bright blue. A florist's card, edges curling, ink beginning to smudge. Addressed as if to a resident: "Capt. James Gurbisz, Arlington Cemetery, 1 Memorial Dr, Arlington VA." A message: "Happy Birthday Jim! Love, Mom and Dad, Kathy and Steve, Tashie and Tori."

Something flew past my ear like an arrow from a bow. A black cicada landed in a small birch sapling, a little to Gurbisz's left. I backed into the shade of the mature sycamore in front of the grave, read the names on the stones nearby.

To Gurbisz's right lay Major Jeffrey Philip Toczylowski, US Army, born August 26, 1975, died November 3, 2005, Iraq. The day before Gurbisz. He was from Upper Moreland in Pennsylvania, and he was on a Special Forces mission in Anbar province when he fell from a helicopter. He was posthumously promoted. His friends and family received an email, a modern-day letter "to be opened in the event of my death." Toczylowski had set aside one hundred thousand dollars in life insurance payout for a party in Las Vegas. It made the news.[7]

To Gurbisz's left, Lieutenant Colonel Thomas A. Wren, US Army. Born November 17, 1960, died November 5, 2005. The day after Jim. Wren was the twelfth lieutenant colonel to die in Iraq. A traffic accident in Tallil. Wren was from Fairfax County, Virginia, and he had also served in Afghanistan and Bosnia. He had just married a second time. He had four children in all.[8]

Gurbisz was a captain buried next to a major and a lieutenant colonel. Next to the lieutenant colonel there was a major from the Marines. Behind, a monument to a whole US Army Air Force crew, six men lost over Tunisia in 1942, found and buried in 2009. In front lay a twenty-one-year-old army corporal. Jimmy Lee Shelton, Iraq, December 3, 2005. He was asleep when his position in Baiji was mortared.

He was from Lehigh Acres, Florida.[9] Two graves to Shelton's right lay Dustin Allan Yancey, who died with Gurbisz in Baghdad.

Another cicada whirred past, another bird sang, another plane took off from Reagan. The shadows lengthened. Back toward the main gate, men who fought in Korea lay next to wives met in Japan. Gurbisz's widow, Tori, had married again.

I walked back along the graves. Most were bare. Some had small bouquets, one a pair of helium balloons tied to a twig, an echo of a rawer time in Section 60, when families and friends came to mourn young men lost in wars that still raged on. Mourners opened beers and bourbon, left bottles on the freshly covered graves, cigarettes, too, superhero toys, pictures of Britney Spears. Section 60 became a modern, chaotic memorial to two modern, chaotic wars.

Gurbisz's funeral was very Section 60. Tori, though, can't remember much about it.

"I don't even know how many different drugs I'd taken," she said. "There was an insane turnout from the rugby players that could make it. My sorority sisters came down, people we went to high school with. But a lot of this is almost secondhand, because I barely remember it. I do remember people commenting because I wasn't crying. And I was just like, 'You guys think I'm not mourning because I'm not crying?'"[10]

Ken and Helen Gurbisz remembered the long walk out, the speeches over the grave. The flag from their son's casket, folded and handed to Tori. Another flag, handed to them. The West Point rugby team was there. Coach Mahan spoke, as he had for Zac Miller and Joe Emigh. Brian McCoy flew in from Italy. Players carried the casket. Not all the brothers made it. Clint Olearnick and Pete Chacon were in Iraq. Bryan Phillips couldn't get leave. He asked his boss, Dan Karbler, to be there. Fifteen years later, Karbler was a lieutenant general, in charge of missile defense. He thought back, to a grim time for his army.

"I was at the Pentagon. I had to have gone to twenty-five funerals that year. Some I went to because, as in the case of Jimmy, someone asked me to go. Other times you go because you want an officer present. Other times you go because it's just the right thing to do. Because you're in uniform. And this is a fallen comrade."

When Jim Gurbisz was buried on November 14, 2005, Karbler thought the crowd "kind of felt like central casting. Jersey. Rugby too. I'm not a tight-ass or a stuffy officer, but I remember at one point thinking, 'Okay, gentlemen, it would be time for a little decorum right now.' But it was healthy. There was a reunion aspect, celebrating Jimmy's life. It was all good. At the right times, taps and all, they were good."[11]

Eventually, years later, Section 60 was cleaned up. Some of the keepsakes and tributes were tagged and bagged for history. Most went in the trash. Families protested.[12] In time, the fuss died down.

I noticed two women among the headstones, standing quietly over a grave. Both were in late middle age, dressed in slacks and tennis shoes, wearing visors against the sun. Stepping back into the shade of York Drive, I looked back, across the light-drenched field. The sycamore by Gurbisz's grave was a rich blazing gold, its leaves into their turn. The other trees were green.

I turned back up York, walked right along Eisenhower, past McClellan, Leahy, and King. Past row upon row of graves. I remembered other West Point rugby players killed in the line of service, during the wars in Afghanistan and Iraq:

Ben Britt, Class of 2004, IED, Iraq, December 2005

Ian Weikel, Class of 1997, IED, Iraq, April 2006[13]

Guy "Bear" Barattieri, Class of 1992, IED, Iraq, October 2006[14]

James Harrison, Class of 1981, shot by an Afghan soldier, May 2007[15]

Tom Martin, Class of 2005, firefight, Iraq, October 2007[16]

Dimitri Del Castillo, Class of 2009, firefight, Afghanistan, June 2011[17]

John Hortman, Class of 2004, helicopter crash, Fort Benning, August 2011[18]

At the visitors' center, the clattering chatter of life. A school party. Tourists. More family members, come to remember their dead. Out among the gravestones, silence reigned.

Clint Olearnick and James Gurbisz enjoy a rooftop drink at Cal Berkeley in 2001.

Clint

O N TUESDAY, December 21, 2021—as this book was being written—Clint Olearnick died. He was forty-two years old.

Three months before that, he met his brothers at Matt Blind's place in Cohasset, Massachusetts. They drank and talked and laughed. They raised toasts to Zac Miller and Joe Emigh and Jim Gurbisz, those who died too young. They threw a ball around and tackled each other, bear-hugged and wrestled, traded friendly insults. They talked about their wives and showed pictures of their kids. They talked about their jobs. They talked a lot about when they were soldiers once, and young.

At the kitchen table, Olearnick held court. He was big, shaven-headed, bearded, and tattooed. He chewed dip and spat. He picked up Blinder's *Wall Street Journal*. The headline was about Afghanistan. The American withdrawal, after twenty years of war.

"Looks like they fucking want us to fucking go back in there," he growled.

I needed to talk to him. About West Point and Iraq. About rugby and Jim Gurbisz. But he didn't seem eager. He was with his brothers, at the center of it all with the other big dogs, Mo Greene and Jeremiah Hurley, ribbing Pete Chacon and Dave Little and Matt Blind, laughing when Jerrod Adams fell asleep with Blind's actual dog, Archie, listening to Brian McCoy tell stories, Bryan Phillips too. Listening, as they always did, when Mike Mahan spoke.

Years before, when I was writing my *Guardian* article, Olearnick called me, Saint Louis to New York. It was a brief conversation. Wary.

I knew then he had been close to Gurbisz. I asked if he went to the funeral, at Arlington in Virginia.

"It was one of those army things," Olearnick said, with a sigh. "I wish I would've been able to make it . . ."[1]

Six years later, I feared I wouldn't land the interview. But then, late on the second day, Olearnick tapped me on the shoulder. "Let's do this," he said. And we did, for two hours. His Colorado childhood. Rugby at high school. Rugby at West Point. Rugby in the army. Three tours to Iraq. Jim. Yes, they fought, sometime around graduation. But Clint couldn't remember what about. Or didn't want to. He just missed his friend. He'd been missing him fifteen years and more. I turned the tape recorder off. We went back to the boys for a beer.[2]

Later, Olearnick's mother, Jan, told me, "He couldn't say enough about that weekend. He loved it. He thought it was just perfect."

His father, Clem, said, "That was the last time he actually felt good."[3]

A couple of months later, late October, I went to Washington to watch the US Eagles lose by a hundred points to the All Blacks.[4] In the parking lots outside FedEx Field, at the Army Rugby tailgate, I met Jeremiah Hurley and Dave Little. I'd expected to see Clint. Hurley and Little told me he was in the hospital. Cancer.

The obituary said Clint "left the military in 2013 as a Major in the Army. He played rugby for the Army, both at West Point and afterwards for the All-Army team and the All-Military team. He also played with the Kansas City Blues and others. The brothers he found on the pitch remained his friends to the end, and the experiences he shared with them took him around the world. It was his favorite thing to do."

There was no funeral. "When asked about services, Clint said he didn't want any of that sad bullshit, but would prefer those of us who remember him to do so with the exuberance and generosity he so capably embodied."[5]

And so, later, in October 2022, Olearnick's family, friends, and rugby brothers gathered again at West Point.

It was a blazing autumn Sunday, the end of homecoming weekend. In Highland Falls, the motels and bars were filled with the Class of 2002. The golden children, twenty years on, entering middle age. I walked down to Anderson Rugby Complex, to the far north of the post, past the water treatment plant and the parachute team on a run, boots slapping tarmac, cadets exhaling like breaching whales. On the banks of the Hudson, the trees were in their turn. Behind one set of rugby posts, a maple blazed orange, bright as a bursting flame. Before it, the field was endless green.

Matt Sherman, the West Point coach, was there with a dozen of his players. The cadets wore uniform—gray trousers, white shirts, white peaked caps—and carried themselves with care. Rich Pohlidal, Coach Mahan's assistant in 2002, was at the clubhouse too. So was Trent Geisler, in fall 2001 the big junior who won a starting spot at blindside flanker, pushing Olearnick out to the centers. Geisler was now a lieutenant colonel, back at West Point teaching math. Casey Olearnick, Clint's brother, was there with his wife, Sara. So were Clint's wife, Diane, and their daughter, Zosha.

Speakers told stories about Clint, the kind of tales his parents told me, delightedly, when we spoke by phone. Most involved post- or pre-match drinking. None of that sad bullshit. Well, some. Big Bryan Phillips read a message from Jan and Clem, who like Pete Chacon and Scott Radcliffe attended by Zoom from home. Phillips's voice broke. Brian McCoy read a poem, sent by Father Mahan. He struggled too.

Zosha listened. Diane stood to speak. She remembered her husband's final hours, how she tried to ease his pain. The sun had gone, the sky clouded over. Over the field, first one bald eagle then two swooped and turned, casing the grass, looking for prey between the twenty-two and halfway, lines marked for rugby. A poem came to mind. Like the red-tailed hawks August Kleinzahler described in "Anniversary," the eagles made "partnered loops, wheeling and diving, / enraptured by all they were, were able to do, / not as separate beings, but as two."[6] They came to rest on a floodlight.

When Clint Olearnick was in hospice care, he recorded a message for his brothers. Nearly a year later, at West Point, Brian McCoy used a Bluetooth speaker to play it. In the team room at Anderson, trophies lining the walls, Clint's voice was clouded by morphine.

His words were edged with pain. He loved his rugby brothers. He asked them to help others he loved. To walk Zosha down the aisle, come time.

"I love you all," Clint said. "I'll see you all in a better place."

The tape ended with a gasp of pain.

The brothers moved outside, to the bright green field of play. Matt McSweeney, a friend of the team, played the bagpipes as he had twenty years before, when sometimes he marched the brothers from bar to bar. Casey Olearnick carried his brother's ashes, handing out helpings to scatter. Cadets dropped ashes on the ten-meter line, in midfield, in the corners where box kicks land. Their predecessors, some wearing their game shirts from 2002, performed the same careful task. Over by the scoreboard, near the touchline where second row forwards do their lineout work, Bryan Phillips held his son and gazed at the Hudson hills. At the north end of the field, Andy Klutman stared at the grass. Once an All-American prop, he was now an ER doctor in Lincoln, Nebraska. Married to Laura, a father of three.

The mourners came together. They raised a toast to Clint Olearnick. Then, on halfway, they linked arms and sang a song long sung by West Point rugby teams. "Scrum of the Earth." Like most rugby songs, the lyrics aren't pretty. But they mean a lot to those who sing them. There was another ritual. Arms raised, fists together at the peak of the huddle. As captain, as he did twenty years before, Matt Blind called it.

"'Brothers' on three! One, two, three, 'Brothers!'"

There was one last thing to do.

Behind Anderson Rugby Complex there is a steep wooded bluff, sixty feet up on the way to Stony Lonesome, where the Class of '02 trained on the broken ground of H-Lot, amid the beer cans and bottle tops and sinkholes and condoms. Back when the team had nothing, when Anderson didn't exist. At the top of the bluff stands a wooden post and crossbar. On the post there is a bell. On the crossbar hang the dog tags of every West Point rugby player killed in the line of service.

There is no path up the bluff, just loose earth and tree roots and trunks. Regardless, all went up. Players, coaches, wives, and children. Diane and Zosha. Me.

It was brutal, a near-vertical scramble. There were missed steps, lost footholds, loose scree skittering off down the slope. But each climber reached the top, some with help from others. Before each one caught their breath, they rang the bell on the post.

The bell had rung often for this rugby team, this brotherhood. Too often.

I stood at the top of the bluff. I had stood at Zac Miller's grave, on a gentle hillside in far-western Pennsylvania. I had stood at Joe Emigh's grave, on a green lawn in California sunshine. I'd seen where Jim Gurbisz came from in Eatontown, New Jersey, heard how he found rugby and thrived, and how the game he loved brought an injury that changed his life and sent him out on the path to his death. I had stood at his grave in Arlington. Now, I had rung the bell for Clint Olearnick.

Zac. Joe. Jim. Clint. They came from places I had not known, accepted challenges I could not imagine, faced fears I would not face. But thanks to rugby, to a single game played nearly twenty years before, when we shed our blood together, I shared some small part of their bond. I knew what their brotherhood meant. I could write their lives.

At the top of the bluff, we stood a few moments more. Then we turned to go.

I had a cab to catch, to Peekskill Station, the Hudson Valley train, south along the river, down to New York, to my wife, to our three daughters, to school drop-off and pick-up, to playdates and cello lessons, to the subway, to morning conference, to the rush and din of breaking news and the silence of the newsroom when the story is done.

GLOSSARY OF RUGBY TERMS

Backs The seven players behind the scrum. Scrum half, who puts the ball into the scrum and distributes possession; fly half, the quarterback of the team, who decides whether to kick or pass the ball and run; two centers, attacking runners who also form the core of the defense; two wings, usually the fastest players, strike runners who operate wide out; a fullback, both last line of defense and a key runner on attack.

Blood replacement Any player bleeding from an open wound must leave the field of play and may return when treated and the blood flow is stopped.

Conversion The equivalent of an extra point, taken anywhere a line back from where the try is scored. Worth two points.

Drop goal A kick through the goalposts from the hand, the point of the ball hitting the ground at the point of impact by a player's boot. Worth three points.

Forwards There are eight forwards on a rugby union team: a front row, of two props and a hooker; a second row of two locks; and a back row of a number 8 and two flankers.

Halftime Rugby games, known as matches, are eighty minutes long, played in two halves of forty minutes, with a ten-minute interval.

Kick The ball may be kicked in open play, in any direction.

Knock-on A ball spilled forward from hand.

Lineout The means of restarting the game when the ball has left the field of play. Seven forwards from each team line up against each other. The ball is thrown in by the hooker, and jumpers are lifted to compete for possession.

Maul A contest for the ball in which play has not stopped, the player in possession of the ball being held off the ground while players from each team push against each other and attempt to free the ball.

Pass Rugby passes must travel laterally or backwards from one player to another.

Penalty goal The equivalent of a field goal, kicked from the point where a penalty is awarded for foul play or technical infringement. Worth three points.

Scrum (scrummage) A means of restarting the game, in which eight forwards bind onto each other in formation and push against the eight forwards of the other team, the hookers striking for the ball when it is put in by the scrum half.

Tackle Rugby tackles must be below the chest, with arms wrapped around the man, who may not be lifted from the ground and tipped onto shoulder, neck, or head.

Try The equivalent of a touchdown. The ball must be placed on the ground on or behind the opposing team's goal line. Worth five points.

Turnover When the ball changes hands, after a tackle, in a ruck or maul or if one team drops the ball.

Red card/sent off Permanent dismissal from the field, usually for foul play but can be for disrespecting the referee.

Ruck A contest for the ball when a player has been tackled to ground, in which players from either side must push over the ball to make it available to their scrum half.

Rugby union The fifteen-per-side version of rugby football, as distinct from rugby league, which is thirteen-per-side and has different rules, and sevens, the shortened form of union. This book is about rugby union, referred to throughout as rugby. In New Zealand, they call union "rugby" and league "league." I've always thought that a healthy arrangement, but . . . here be dragons.

Yellow card/sin-bin A warning for foul play or persistent technical infringement. A player sent to the sin-bin must spend ten minutes off the field.

ILLUSTRATIONS

Note: The vast majority of the photographs used to illustrate the chapter openings are old, print photographs, many of which were taken with low-quality (i.e., disposable) cameras. While the images are not crisp and professional, they certainly authentically convey the times and conditions in which they were made, which is the point.

Frontispiece. *Photo by Academy Photo. Courtesy of Cpt. Pete Chacon.*
Preface. *Photo courtesy of Maj. Dave Little.*
Introduction. *Photo by Ray Kachatorian, courtesy of H. R. McMaster.*
Shitsucker. *Photo courtesy of Lt. Matt Blind.*
Aldershot. *Photo courtesy of Marine Corps Maj. Chris Starling.*
Point. *Photo by Adam Jones, Global Photo Archive, 2002.*
Eatontown. *Photo courtesy of Gurbisz family.*
Beast. *Photo by Tim Engleman.*
Stoneboro. *Photo courtesy of Miller family.*
Rugby. *Photo courtesy of Maj. Dave Little.*
Fullerton. *Photo courtesy of the Emigh family.*
Play. *Photo courtesy of Maj. Dave Little.*
September. *Photo courtesy of Lt. Col. Jerrod Adams.*
Brothers. *Photo courtesy of Marine Corps Maj. Chris Starling.*
Finals. *Photo courtesy of Cpt. Scott Radcliffe.*
Ranger. *Photo by Maj. Karla N. Evans, South Carolina National Guard Public Affairs, 2022.*

Conroe. *"Sunrise @Lake Conroe" Photo by Koh Takahashi, 2017.*
Benning. *"Follow Me! – Iron Mike, Fort Benning Georgia" by Expert Infantry.*
War. *Photo courtesy of Cpt. Scott Radcliffe.*
Baghdad. *Photo courtesy of Spc. Nate Hadd.*
Rustamiyah. *Photo courtesy of Spc. Nate Hadd.*
Convoy. *Photo courtesy of Spc. Nate Hadd.*
After. *Photo courtesy of Spc. Nate Hadd.*
Arlington. *Photo courtesy of Martin Pengelly.*
Clint. *Photo courtesy of Maj. Dave Little.*
Acknowledgments. *Photo courtesy of Martin Pengelly.*

SOURCE NOTES

Preface

1. Earl Zukerman, "This Date in History: First Football Game Was May 14, 1874," www.mcgill.ca, May 14, 2012.
2. Martin Pengelly, "Say It's So, Joe: We Know Biden's a Rugby Fan, but Who Did He Play For?" *Guardian*, July 23, 2021.
3. Martin Pengelly, "It's in My Blood: How Rugby Managed to Unite America's Elite," *Guardian*, June 1, 2018.
4. Kurt Vonnegut, "Speaking of Sports: Mood Indigo on Upper Alumni, or, It Ain't Cricket," *Cornell Daily Sun*, May 1, 1941.
5. Figures from *Costs of War*, Watson Institute for International and Public Affairs, Brown University.

Shitsucker

1. Hamid Saeid Kachel, Azhar Mohammed Al-Khazali, Fenik Sherzad Hussen, and Ersen Aydın Yağmur, "Checklist and Review of the Scorpion Fauna of Iraq," *Arachnology Letters*, March 5, 2021.
2. Dana Priest and Josh White, "Before the War, CIA Reportedly Trained a Team of Iraqis to Aid US," *Washington Post*, August 3, 2005.
3. S. Lucas, "Hell on Wheels: The US Army's Stryker Brigade Combat Team," US Marine Corps Command and Staff College, 2005.
4. Jeffrey A. Lockwood, "Scorpion Bombs: The Rest of the Story," oupblog.com, December 17, 2014.
5. William Booth and Karen DeYoung, "Dozens of Decapitated Bodies Found at School Near Mosul," *Washington Post*, November 7, 2016.
6. Matt Blind, April 22, 2016.
7. Thomas E. Ricks, *Fiasco: The American Military Adventure in Iraq* (New York: Penguin Press, 2006), p. 228–232.
8. "Fierce Fighting in Mosul," aljazeera.com, November 16, 2004.
9. Lynn Brezosky, "Three Texans Reported Killed in Iraq," Associated Press, November 10, 2004; "Senior NCO from New York Killed in Iraq," Associated Press, November 11, 2004.
10. Susan Kinzle, "Silver Spring Man Is Killed in Iraq," *Washington Post*, November 13, 2004.

11. Michael R. Gordon and Bernard E. Trainor, *The Endgame: The Inside Story of the Struggle for Iraq, from George W. Bush to Barack Obama* (New York: Random House, 2012), p. 126.
12. Jeremy Redmon, "The Inside Story of the Deadliest Attack on a US Military Base in the Iraq War," TaskandPurpose.com, December 2, 2020.
13. Fred Minnick, *Camera Boy: An Army Journalist's War in Iraq* (Ashland, Oregon: Hellgate Press, 2009), p. 109.
14. "Illinois-Born Soldier Dies in Iraq," Associated Press, March 30, 2005.
15. "NY Soldier Killed in Iraq Left His Mark, Says Wife," Associated Press, August 15, 2005.

Aldershot

1. Andy Bull, "Barbarians 'Greatest Try' Against All Blacks Is Relived 40 Years On," *Guardian*, January 27, 2013.
2. Richard Williams, "Cliff Morgan: Obituary," *Guardian*, August 29, 2013.
3. Christopher Hitchens, "Fleet Street's Finest," *Guardian*, December 2, 2005.

Point

1. David McCullough, *1776* (New York: Simon and Schuster, 2005), p. 233–242.
2. James Trager, *The New York Chronology* (New York: Harper Collins, 2003), p. 3.
3. Philip Lopate, *Waterfront: A Walk Around Manhattan* (New York: Anchor Books, 2004), p. 193.
4. Niles Eldredge and Sidney Horenstein, *Concrete Jungle: New York City and Our Last Best Hope for a Sustainable Future* (Berkeley: University of California Press, 2014).
5. Washington Irving, *A History of New York from the Beginning of the World to the End of the Dutch Dynasty by Diedrich Knickerbocker* (New York, 1809).
6. Katie Rogers, "A Whale Takes Up Residence in the Hudson River," *New York Times*, November 22, 2016.
7. Lopate, p. 190.
8. Trager, p. 77.
9. David Rothkopf, *Traitor: A History of American Betrayal from Benedict Arnold to Donald Trump* (New York: Macmillan, 2020).
10. Charles Dickens, *American Notes* (London: Penguin, 2001), p. 221.
11. Lisa W. Forderaro, "A Series of Suicides Unnerves West Point," *New York Times*, February 21, 2009.
12. James Salter, *Burning the Days* (New York: Random House, 1997), p. 40.
13. Charles Dickens, *American Notes* (London: Penguin, 2001), p. 221.
14. Mike Mahan, January 7, 2021.
15. "How to Get Into West Point: 10 Ways to Get Your File to the Top of the Pile," blog.westpointadmissions.com, March 1, 2017.

16. Salter, p. 40.
17. Salter, p. 66.
18. Douglas R. Cubbinson, "Historic Structures Report Logistical and Quartermaster Operations at Fortress West Point, 1778–1783," New York, West Point Museum, February 22, 2006.
19. Martin Pengelly, "'This Game Is Under Attack': Rutgers' Chris Ash Uses Rugby to Tackle Football Safety," *Guardian*, September 30, 2016.
20. Michael Weinreb, "Harvard vs. Mcgill Set the Stage for the Growth of College Football as We Know It," *Athletic*, January 28, 2019.
21. Stephen E. Ambrose, *Duty, Honor, Country: A History of West Point* (Baltimore: Johns Hopkins University Press, 2000), p. 304.
22. Alex Goff, "West Point Rugby Programs to Go Varsity," goffrugbyreport.com, July 15, 2014.
23. Nicolaus Mills, "On NFL Guns and Concussion Problems We Should Consult . . . Teddy Roosevelt," *Guardian*, December 27, 2012.
24. Jim Caple, "Americans Took Long, Strange Trip to Rugby Gold in 1924 Olympics," espn.com, August 9, 2016.
25. Mike Schredl and Bill Kosco, *Establishing the Brotherhood: The West Point Men's Rugby Program* (independently published, 2021), p. 32.
26. "All-American Pete Dawkins' Rugby Progress Amazing," Associated Press, December 6, 1959.
27. Art Buchwald, "This Guy Even Tops Mr. Robert Taylor," *Miami News*, November 27, 1959.
28. Ibid.
29. Pengelly, "It's in My Blood."
30. Schredl and Kosco, p. 79.
31. Ibid.
32. "Pete's One-Handed Throw to Change Game of Rugby," Associated Press, December 10, 1959.
33. *Our Fallen Brothers*, oldgrayrugby.com.
34. John Alexander Hotell III, "A Soldier's Own Obituary," West Point, 1969.
35. Carl A. Posey, "How the Korean War Almost Went Nuclear," smithsonianmag.com, July 2015.
36. Douglas MacArthur, *Reminiscences*, 1964, quoted in Elizabeth D. Samet, *Soldier's Heart: Reading Literature Through Peace and War at West Point* (New York: Picador, 2008), p. 191.
37. Michael D. Matthews, Diane M. Ryan, and Richard M. Lerner, "Developing Military Leaders of Character: The Sample Case of Lt. Gen. Robert L. Caslen, US Military Academy Superintendent," *Journal of Character Education*, Vol 16, Issue 1, January 2020.
38. Brian Moore, "It's CRUNCH Time!" *The Guardian*, February 12, 2003.
39. Seymour M. Hersh, *Chain of Command: The Road from 9/11 to Abu Ghraib* (New York: Harper Collins, 2004).
40. Bryan Phillips, June 3, 2015.
41. Samet, *Soldier's Heart*.
42. Liz Samet, April 8, 2021.

43. Mel Gussow, "Literature Re-enlists in the Military; Pilot Project Is Send-ing Books to American Ships and Troops Abroad," *New York Times*, November 7, 2002.
44. Craig M. Mullaney, *The Unforgiving Minute: A Soldier's Education* (New York: Penguin, 2009), p. 326.
45. Mike Mahan, January 7, 2021.
46. Alex Goff, "Rugby Is Ground Combat: How D1A Win Resonates at West Point," goffrugbyreport.com, June 6, 2022.
47. Fred Lowrey, "Anderson Rugby Complex Dedicated at West Point," *Assembly*, West Point Association of Graduates, July/August 2007.

Eatontown

1. Jesse Bradell and Sandra Stewart Holyoak, "Interview with Kenneth Gur-bisz," Rutgers Oral History Archives, March 4, 2011.
2. Jon Hurdle, "The Wrecking Ball Targets a Former Army Base," *New York Times*, September 23, 2014.
3. Anthony Talerico, May 26, 2021.
4. Jay Medlin, May 26, 2021.
5. Andy Teeple, May 26, 2021.
6. Toby Stark, May 26, 2021.
7. Amy Davidson, "A Reporter's Life," *New Yorker*, December 15, 2002.
8. Kathleen Gurbisz Forte, August 2, 2021.
9. Lawrence Arnold, "Eatontown Church Unveils Sanctuary," *Register*, Jan-uary 23, 1989.
10. Ken Gurbisz, Helen Gurbisz, and Ted Jarmusz, May 26, 2021.
11. Anthony Bongi, June 9, 2021.
12. Tori Chapel, June 3, 2021.
13. Ken Gurbisz, Helen Gurbisz, and Ted Jarmusz, May 26, 2021.
14. Ken Gurbisz, July 22, 2015.
15. Ken Gurbisz. Oral History Interview, March 4, 2011, by Jesse Braddell and Sandra Stewart Holyoak. Rutgers Oral History Archives.
16. Ibid.
17. Frank Blazich Jr., "America's Kaiser: How a Pigeon Served in Two World Wars," National Museum of American History, December 4, 2018.
18. "Execution of the Rosenbergs," *Guardian*, June 20, 1953.
19. Michael Moran, "Fighting the Insurgency at the Jersey Shore," NBCNews.com, July 18, 2005.

Beast

1. Michael E. Haskew, *West Point, 1915: Eisenhower, Bradley, and the Class the Stars Fell On"* (Minneapolis: Zenith Press, 2015).
2. Robert M. S. McDonald (ed.), *Thomas Jefferson's Military Academy* (Char-lottesville: University of Virginia Press, 2018).

3. Bill Murphy Jr., *In a Time of War: The Proud and Perilous Journey of West Point's Class of 2002* (New York: Macmillan, 2009), p. 7.
4. Ed Ruggero, *Duty First: A Year in the Life of West Point and the Making of American Leaders* (New York: Harper Collins, 2001).
5. Daniel Christman, September 20, 2017.
6. David Lipsky, *Absolutely American: Four Years at West Point* (New York: Houghton Mifflin Harcourt, 2003), p. 113.
7. Lipsky, p. 188.
8. David Brooks, "Huah!" *New York Times*, July 13, 2003.
9. Lipsky, pp. xii–xiii.
10. Anton Myrer, *Once an Eagle* (New York: Harper Collins, 1968).
11. Elizabeth Becker, "Military Goes by the Book, but It's a Novel," *New York Times*, August 16, 1999.
12. Rick Atkinson, *The Long Gray Line: The American Journey of West Point's Class of 1966* (New York: Picador, 1989).
13. Lipsky, p. 188.
14. Ty Seidule, *Robert E. Lee and Me: A Southerner's Reckoning with the Myth of the Lost Cause* (New York: St. Martin's Press, 2021).
15. Salter, p. 40.
16. Craig M. Mullaney, *The Unforgiving Minute: A Soldier's Education* (New York: Penguin, 2009), p. 5.
17. Mike Mahan, January 7, 2021.
18. Lipsky, p. xi.
19. Ken and Helen Gurbisz, September 16, 2021.
20. Jon C. Malinowski and Eugene J. Palka, *The Spirit of West Point: Celebrating 200 Years* (New York: Black Dome Press, 2001).
21. Keith and Rosalyn Miller, July 22, 2021.
22. George Emigh, June 30, 2021.
23. Dave Little, August 30, 2021.
24. Clint Olearnick, August 14, 2021.
25. Pete Chacon, August 13, 2021.
26. Mullaney, p. 12.
27. "Bugle Notes: Learn This!" westpoint.org.
28. Gabrielle Bunton, "Lieutenant Colonel Reflects on Finding Purpose in Service," *College Heights Herald*, March 7, 2021.
29. John F. Burns, "US Strike Hits Insurgent at Safe House," *New York Times*, June 8, 2006.
30. Stanley McChrystal, *My Share of the Task: A Memoir* (New York: Penguin, 2013), p. 97.
31. Morgan Greene, January 14, 2021.
32. Matt Blind, October 6, 2021.

Stoneboro

1. Keith and Rosalyn Miller, July 22, 2021.
2. Tom Dart, "Can American Football Talent Become Rugby Gold? One Colorado City Says Yes," theguardian.com, January 31, 2021.

3. US Census Bureau, "Vintage 2020 Town and City Population Estimates," retrieved August 2, 2021.
4. Ronan Farrow, "A Pennsylvania Mother's Path to Insurrection," *New Yorker*, February 1, 2021.
5. Mark Scolforo and Claudia Lauer, "Feds Arrest, Charge Woman in Pink Hat During Capitol Attack," Associated Press, February 5, 2021.
6. Keith Miller, Rosalyn Miller, Denny Charlton, and Lynn Charlton, July 22, 2021.
7. Caleb Stright, "Seventeen Years Later, Few Have Forgotten Zac Miller," *Record-Argus*, May 21, 2019.
8. Rosalyn Miller, email, November 26, 2020.
9. Quoted by Nate Miller, speech, Lakeview Academic Hall of Fame, May 20, 2019.
10. Stright.
11. Chuck Lueckemeyer, "A Dutiful Mind," *USA Rugby*, May 2002.
12. Rosalyn Miller, July 22, 2021.
13. Zac Miller, personal essay, West Point application, 1997.
14. Woodrow Wilson, "Basis of American Foreign Policy: Address to the Gridiron Club at Washington," February 26, 1916.
15. George Bernard Shaw, *Man and Superman*, 1903.

Rugby

1. Rosalyn Miller, September 11, 2015.
2. Lueckemeyer.
3. Jimmy Byrn and Gabe Royal, "What Should West Point Do About Its Robert E. Lee Problem," Modern War Institute at West Point, June 22, 2020.
4. R. J. Johnson, February 17, 2021.
5. Scott Radcliffe, July 8, 2021.
6. Martin Pengelly, "H. R. McMaster on Rugby: 'The Warrior Ethos Is What a Good Team Has,'" *Guardian*, May 28, 2018.
7. "Twelve Young Veterans Running as GOP Candidates," Associated Press, February 26, 2008.
8. Dave Little, August 30, 2021.
9. Martin Pengelly, "Meet Phaidra Knight: Free Radical Flanker in World Rugby Hall of Fame," theguardian.com, November 4, 2017.
10. Jay Atkinson, *Memoirs of a Rugby-Playing Man: Guts, Glory, and Blood in the World's Greatest Game* (New York: Thomas Dunne Books, 2012), p. 7.
11. Pengelly, "It's in My Blood."
12. Craig Mullaney, March 31, 2021.
13. Mullaney, *The Unforgiving Minute*, p. 309.
14. Ibid., p. 199.
15. Mike Mahan, January 7, 2021.
16. Ken Gurbisz, July 22, 2015.
17. Clint Olearnick, August 14, 2021.
18. Vladimir Nabokov, *Speak, Memory* (New York: Knopf, 1999), p. 209.

19. Matt Blind, October 6, 2021.
20. Charlie Erwin, January 19, 2021.
21. Jay Landgraf, January 14, 2021.
22. George Emigh, June 30, 2021.
23. Bryan Phillips, June 3, 2015.
24. Brian McCoy, July 2, 2015.
25. Jeremiah Hurley, August 9, 2015.

Fullerton

1. Julian Smilowitz, December 8, 2021.
2. "Joanne Marie Emigh, 1955–2016," *Orange County Register*, December 31, 2016.
3. "How the County that Launched Nixon and Reagan Turned Democratic," *Times of San Diego*, August 11, 2019.
4. Gustavo Arellano, "When Did Ronald Reagan First Utter His Infamous OC Quote?" *OC Weekly*, November 18, 2008.
5. Robin Hinch, "A Life Story: Joey Emigh's Sunny Life Ended Much Too Soon," *Orange County Register*, September 19, 2002.
6. Marianne Emigh, June 23, 2021.
7. Nik Wybaczysnky, November 19, 2020.
8. Joseph Olivas, December 8, 2021.
9. Jesse LaTour, "School Board Votes to Remove Plummer Name from Auditorium," *Fullerton Observer*, June 17, 2020.
10. Brady Macdonald, "Disneyland Covers Up Sexy Jessica Rabbit in a Detective's Trenchcoat and Fedora," *Orange County Register*, December 9, 2021.
11. George Emigh, December 8, 2021.
12. George Emigh, June 30, 2021.
13. Marianne Emigh, June 23, 2021.
14. Jim Inghram, "Covina Charges Past Fullerton, 34–0," *Orange County Register*, December 2, 1995.
15. Bill Norris, "Emigh Blocks Field-Goal Try to Preserve Fullerton Victory," *Orange County Register*, September 13, 1996.
16. Susan Besze Wallace, "West Point Plebes Learn It's No Picnic After This," *Orange County Register*, June 15, 1998.

Play

1. Theo Tait, "*Billy Lynn's Long Halftime Walk* by Ben Fountain—Review," *Guardian*, July 6, 2012.
2. Ben Fountain, *Billy Lynn's Long Halftime Walk* (New York: Harper Collins, 2012), p. 163.
3. Bryan McCoy, July 2, 2015.
4. Brian Anthony, September 29, 2021.
5. Kathleen Gurbisz, August 2, 2021.

6. George Orwell, "The Sporting Spirit," *Tribune*, December 14, 1945.
7. J. E. Lendon, *Soldiers and Ghosts: A History of Battle in Classical Antiquity* (Yale: Yale University Press, 2005), p. 235.
8. Thomas E. Ricks, *Waging a Good War: A Military History of the Civil Rights Movement, 1954–1968* (New York: Farrar, Straus & Giroux, 2022), p. 41. It should be added that Ricks pointed me to J.E. Lendon and Josephus.
9. "How the United States Army Is Organized," chatter.vetfriends.com.
10. Kevin Lynch, August 5, 2021.
11. Mike Mahan, email, January 8, 2021.
12. Dave Little, August 30, 2021.
13. Malinowski and Palka, p. 52–53.
14. Alex Goff, "College Men Historical Champions," goffrugbyreport.com, December 24, 2014.
15. Jerrod Adams, August 27, 2017.
16. Renae Merle, "Army Scraps $39bn Helicopter," *Washington Post*, February 24, 2004.
17. Matt Blind, August 24, 2017.
18. Caleb Stright, "Miller Was Gifted in Academics and Athletics, but Those Who Know Him Talk About His Heart," *The Record Argus*, May 21, 2019.
19. Greg Cannon, "A Tradition Rings Out at Military Academy," *Times Herald-Record*, January 22, 2005.
20. "Ring Ceremony," West-Point.org, https://www.west-point.org/family/mem2002/ringweekend/.
21. Rosalyn Miller, email, September 11, 2021.
22. Rick Smith, "Whatever Happened To: Bill Jackman, Algonquin/West Point," *Milford Daily News*, February 1, 2009.

September

1. Jerrod Adams, August 4, 2017.
2. Keith J. Hamel, "West Point, A Changing Landscape," *West Point Magazine*, April 28, 2023.
3. Editorial Board, "The Tragedy of Afghanistan," *New York Times*, August 15, 2021.
4. James Barron, "Manhattan Plane Crash Kills Yankee Pitcher," *New York Times*, October 12, 2006.
5. James Barron, "Flaming Horror on the 79th Floor: Fifty Years Ago Today, in the Fog, a Plane Hit the World's Tallest Building," *New York Times*, July 28, 1995.
6. All times and descriptions are taken from the National Commission on Terrorist Attacks, *The 9/11 Commission Report: Final Report of the National Commission on Terrorist Attacks upon the United States* (New York: WW Norton & Co., 2004).
7. Matt Blind, email, June 6, 2017.
8. Scott Radcliffe, email, June 12, 2017.
9. Jerrod Adams, email, June 8, 2017.

10. Brian Vizard, *With You! Rugby Podcast*, United States Rugby Federation, October 25, 2021.
11. Clint Olearnick, August 15, 2021.
12. Rosalyn Miller, email, September 11, 2021.
13. Max Reyes, "Cantor Fitzgerald's 9/11 Tragedy: 'We Lost Them All,' CEO Lutnick Says," *Bloomberg News*, September 10, 2021.
14. Kathleen Gurbisz, August 2, 2021.
15. Lipsky, p. 258.
16. Pete Chacon, August 14, 2021.
17. Chris Starling, March 25, 2021.
18. Eddie Johnson, July 28, 2021.
19. Matt Blind, August 18, 2017.

Brothers

1. Brian McCoy, July 2, 2015.
2. Nancy Franklin, "Combat Fatigue," *New Yorker*, September 9, 2001.
3. Ken and Helen Gurbisz, September 16, 2021.
4. Donald P. Wright, James Bird, Steven Clay, et al., *A Different Kind of War: The United States Army in Operation Enduring Freedom (OEF) October 2001–September 2005*" (Fort Leavenworth, Kansas: Combat Studies Institute Press, 2010).
5. David Rose and Ed Vulliamy, "Iraq 'Behind US Anthrax Outbreaks,'" *Observer*, October 14, 2001.
6. Robert Draper, *To Start a War: How the Bush Administration Took America into Iraq* (New York: Penguin Press, 2020), p. 22–47.
7. Council on Foreign Relations, "The US War in Afghanistan, 1999–2021," www.cfr.org.
8. https://www.westpointaog.org/branchnotification.
9. Murphy, p. 32.
10. David Lipsky, *"Absolutely American: Four Years at West Point* Booknotes," C-Span, August 17, 2003.
11. Pete Chacon, August 13, 2021.
12. Murphy, p. 32.
13. Mark Thompson, "Academies Out of Line," *Time*, June 24, 2001.
14. Kevin Lynch, August 5, 2021.
15. Bryan Phillips, April 15, 2022.
16. Liam Marmion, August 30, 2021.
17. Mo Greene, January 14, 2021.
18. Jake Tapper, *The Outpost: The Most Heroic Battle of the Afghanistan War* (New York: Back Bay Books, 2012).
19. Glenn Kenny, *"The Outpost* Review: At War, in a Worst-Case Scenario," *New York Times*, July 2, 2020.
20. Clinton Romesha, *Red Platoon: A True Story of American Valor* (New York: Dutton, 2016), p. 49.
21. Scott Radcliffe, July 6, 2021.

22. R. J. Johnson, February 17, 2021.
23. Jay Landgraf, February 14, 2021.
24. Jim Fox, "Triple Triumph: Three Cadets Earn Trumans," *Pointer View*, April 20, 2001.
25. Jim Fox, "Six Cadets Selected to Further Eeducation in England," *Pointer View*, December 14, 2001.
26. Alex Goff, "Rugby to the Moon? Two Former Eagles Ready to Lift Off," goffrugbyreport.com, December 12, 2020.
27. Anderson Cooper, "Tomorrow, US Military Academy on Hudson River Will Celebrate 200th Birthday—Transcript of Interview with Libby Haydon and Zac Miller," CNN, March 15, 2002.
28. Rosalyn Miller, September 11, 2015.
29. William Lennox, January 20, 2021.
30. From documents provided by Rosalyn Miller.
31. Ibid.
32. Leslie Lauer, "Rhodes Scholar Looks Forward to Opportunity as He Heads to Oxford," *News-Herald*, December 10, 2001.
33. Pengelly, "It's in My Blood."
34. From documents provided by Rosalyn Miller.
35. Rosalyn Miller, July 22, 2021.
36. Chris Starling, March 25, 2021.
37. Pete Chacon, August 13, 2021.
38. Clint Olearnick, August 14, 2021.
39. Kevin Lynch, August 5, 2021.
40. Matt Blind, October 6, 2021.
41. Hersh, p. 229.
42. Will Mawby, August 5, 2021.
43. Brian McCoy, July 2, 2015.

Finals

1. Michael S. Bell, "Lieutenant Alexander R. Nininger's Medal of Honor," National WWII Museum, January 12, 2022.
2. "US Military Academy, Central Barracks, West Point, Orange County, NY," Historic American Buildings Survey, Library of Congress.
3. Jim Johnston, "The Association of Graduates Alexander R. Nininger Award for Valor at Arms," Assembly, November–December 2006.
4. Ryan L. Worthan, "Remarks, United States Military Academy Nininger Award for Valor at Arms for 2006," West Point, New York, September 27, 2006.
5. Mike Mahan, January 7, 2021.
6. Mike Mahan, email, January 7, 2021.
7. Clint Olearnick, August 14, 2021.
8. Ken Gurbisz, July 22, 2015.
9. Tori Chapel, June 3, 2021.
10. Matt Sherman, May 5, 2021.

11. Sean Irving, "The Sad Beauty of the Comment Section for Pennywise's Bro Hymn (Tribute)," acclaimmag.com.

12. Byrn and Royal, "What Should West Point Do."

13. Rosalyn and Keith Miller, July 22, 2021.

14. See Rick Atkinson, *The Long Gray Line*—and a thousand other books and films.

15. George Lardner Jr. and Lois Romano, "At Height of Vietnam, Bush Picks Guard," *Washington Post*, July 28, 1999.

16. George W. Bush, "Graduation Speech at West Point," georgewbush-white-house.archives.gov, June 1, 2002.

17. Pengelly, "It's in My Blood."

18. Guy Raz, "Son of Prominent War Critic Dies in Iraq," npr.org, May 15, 2007.

19. Andrew Bacevich, *The Age of Illusions: How America Squandered Its Cold War Victory* (New York: Metropolitan Books, 2020), p. 112–113.

20. Council on Foreign Relations, "The US War in Afghanistan, 1999–2021."

21. Jonathan L. Stolz, "Until the 1930s, Americans Lined Up to Meet the Nation's President on New Year's Day," *Virginia Gazette*, December 31, 2021.

22. Ibid.

23. Chris Starling, March 28, 2021.

24. Clint Olearnick, August 14, 2021.

25. Scott Radcliffe, June 4, 2017.

26. Dawn Hurley, October 28, 2021.

27. Kathy Gurbisz, August 2, 2021.

28. Dave Little, August 30, 2021.

29. Sebastian Junger, *Tribe: On Homecoming and Belonging* (New York: Twelve Books, 2016), p. 108.

30. https://www.westpointaog.org/romantic-traditions-at-west-point.

Ranger

1. "Description of Events Taken from 75th Ranger Regiment, Investigative Summary Brief," August 1, 2002, and Army Safety Center Report.

2. Ed Hagerty, "Leo Brooks, West Point Commandant," *Rugby Today*, April 4, 2004.

3. Leo Brooks, February 18, 2021.

4. William Lennox, January 20, 2021.

5. Rosalyn and Keith Miller, July 22, 2021.

6. Nate Miller, August 5, 2021.

7. Mullaney, p. 89.

8. Andrew Exum, "The Best Athlete Americans Have Never Heard Of," *Atlantic*, October 13, 2019.

9. Andrew Exum, *This Man's Army* (New York: Gotham, 2005), p. 26.

10. Sarah Sicard, "The Mysterious Origins of 'HOOAH,' The Army's Beloved Battle Cry," taskandpurpose.com, October 5, 2017.

11. David Brooks, "Huah!" *New York Times*, July 13, 2003.

12. Lipsky, p. 11.
13. R. J. Johnson, February 17, 2021.
14. Sheryl Gay Stolberg, "Arlen Specter, Pennsylvania Senator, Is Dead at 82," *New York Times*, October 14, 2012.
15. Daniel Christman, September 20, 2017.
16. https://www.benning.army.mil/mcoe/usmc/content/pdf/Ranger1.pdf.
17. Ken Wainwright, December 2, 2022.
18. Andrew Exum, March 12, 2021.
19. Pete Chacon, August 14, 2021.
20. All quotes are from witness statements taken from the Army Safety Center report.
21. "AT-4 Light Anti-Armor Weapon," Army-technology.com, July 30, 2018.
22. David Thompson, "Second Lt. Zac Miller Laid to Rest," *Record-Argus*, July 10, 2002.
23. Nancy Horn, "Area Again Overcome with Sadness," *Herald*, July 10, 2002.
24. Jay Landgraf, January 14, 2021.
25. William J. Lennox Jr., "Farewell to a True 'Leader of Character,'" *Pointer View*, July 12, 2002.
26. Mo Greene, January 14, 2021.
27. Charlie Erwin, January 14, 2021.
28. Matt Blind, October 6, 2021.
29. "Rhodes Scholar Army Officer Dies Mysterious Death," accesswdun.com, July 3, 2002.
30. John T. Reed, "*In a Time of War* by Bill Murphy Jr.," johntreed.com, November 28, 2015.
31. S. Thorne Harper, "Army: Heat Killed Soldier," *Columbus Ledger-Enquirer*.

Conroe

1. Katherine Fominykh, "Ex-Players, Veterans Return to See Navy Beat Army After Coronavirus Pandemic Forced Fans Out in 2020," *Stars and Stripes*, December 12, 2021.
2. "A Look Back at the First Army-Navy Game After 9/11," Navysports.com, December 15, 2011.
3. Eddie Johnson, July 28, 2021.
4. Murphy, p. 32.
5. Lance Janda, "Fort Sill," Oklahoma Historical Society.
6. Michael R. Gordon and Bernard E. Trainor, *Cobra II: The Inside Story of the Invasion and Occupation of Iraq* (New York: Random House, 2007), p. 80.
7. Draper, p. 167.
8. Brian McCoy, September 15, 2021.
9. "About Lake Conroe," lakeconroe.com.
10. John D. Harden, "Lake Conroe Is State's Deadliest Since 2000, Figures Show," *Houston Chronicle*, August 2, 2014.
11. Marianne Emigh, June 23, 2021.
12. George Emigh, June 30, 2021.

13. Sue Thackeray, "California Man Drowns in Lake Conroe," *Houston Chronicle*, September 3, 2002.
14. Matt Blind, October 6, 2021.
15. Mike Mahan, January 7, 2021.
16. Charlie Erwin, January 19, 2021.
17. Dave Little, August 30, 2021.
18. Robin Hinch, "A Life Story: Joey Emigh's Sunny Life Ended Much Too Soon," *Orange County Register*, September 19, 2002.
19. David Brookman, Braridon Rosenthal, and Farshid Karamzsukh, "Joseph J. Emigh 2002," Assembly, West Point Association of Graduates, October 2003.
20. Jeremiah Hurley, August 15, 2021.

Benning

1. "The Formation of Camp Benning," benning.army.mil.
2. Nick Wooten, "Fort Benning's Newly Proposed Name Honors a Famed Vietnam Commander and His Wife," *Columbus Ledger-Enquirer*, May 24, 2022.
3. Mo Greene, August 26, 2021.
4. Elliott Minor, "Off-Limits to Fort Benning Troops," *Washington Post*, August 1, 2004.
5. Tori Chapel, June 9, 2021.
6. Ken Gurbisz, July 22, 2015.
7. Rajiv Chandrasekeran and Thomas E. Ricks, "US Opens War with Strikes on Baghdad Aimed at Hussein," *Washington Post*, March 20, 2003.
8. Draper, p. 204.
9. Pat McGinty, May 31, 2022.
10. Ken and Helen Gurbisz, September 16, 2021.
11. Charlie Erwin, January 19, 2021.
12. Lieutenant Colonel Willie Williams commanded Twenty-Sixth Forward Support Battalion, Second Brigade, Third Infantry Division in the invasion of Iraq.
13. Michael Isikoff and David Corn, *Hubris: The Inside Story of Spin, Scandal, and the Selling of the Iraq War* (New York: Random House, 2007), p. 224.
14. Rick Atkinson, "The Single Most Effective Weapon Against Our Deployed Forces," *Washington Post*, September 30, 2007.
15. Nate Hadd, May 6, 2021.
16. Zach Pamer, August 16, 2022.
17. Roger Ebert, "*Friday After Next*," rogerebert.com, November 22, 2002.
18. Randall Mullally, November 1, 2021.
19. Van Torres, March 10, 2022.
20. Alejandro Michel, November 3, 2021.
21. For example, "Mental Health Advisory Team (MHAT) VI, Operation Iraqi Freedom 05–07, Final Report," Office of the Surgeon, Multinational Force-Iraq and Office of the Surgeon General, United States Army Medical Command, November 17, 2006.

War

1. Harry Tunnell IV, *Red Devils: Tactical Perspectives from Iraq* (Fort Leavenworth, Kansas: Combat Studies Institute Press, 2006), p. 34–35.

2. Luke Mogelson, "A Beast in the Heart of Every Fighting Man," *New York Times*, April 27, 2011.

3. Robert Burns, "In Iraq, Youngest US Troops Bore the Heaviest Toll," *Salt Lake Tribune*, August 20, 2011.

4. April Witt, "Fatal Inaction," *Washington Post*, June 18, 2006.

5. Pengelly, "H. R. McMaster on Rugby."

6. Karen Burbach, "Klutman Takes Over as Student Senate President," University of Nebraska Medical Center, January 21, 2010.

7. Iraq fired seventeen ballistic missiles at Kuwait. Rick Atkinson, *In the Company of Soldiers: A Chronicle of Combat* (New York: Henry Holt & Co., 2004), p. 108.

8. Bryan Phillips, June 3, 2015.

9. Dave Little, August 29, 2021.

10. Eddie Johnson, July 28, 2021.

11. Jerrod Adams, August 4, 2017.

12. Brian McCoy, July 2, 2015.

13. Joel Salgado, "Rakkasans Honor Past and Future," army.mil, February 25, 2014.

14. Matt Keeley, "Interview: Becca Rae," kittysneezes.com, June 17, 2008.

15. Mo Greene, August 26, 2021.

16. Esther Schrader, "Far from Ready for More War," *Los Angeles Times*, May 15, 2004.

17. Jane Arraf and Jamie McIntyre, "Iraq Attacks Injure 33 US troops, Officials Say," CNN.com, December 9, 2003.

18. George Packer, "The Lesson of Tal Afar," *New Yorker*, April 10, 2006.

19. Mo was still in Special Forces in 2015, which is why his name does not appear in my original piece for the *Guardian*. Years later, I asked about his role in the hunt for the leader of al-Qaeda in Iraq. He pointed me to General Stanley McChrystal's memoir, *My Share of the Task*. This note does the same.

20. William Branigin and Debbi Wilgoren, "Zarqawi Did Not Die Instantly, US General Says," *Washington Post*, June 9, 2006.

21. Martin Pengelly, "World Cups Bring American Rugby to the Point," therugbynetwork.com, May 18, 2022.

22. Jeremiah Hurley, August 9, 2015.

23. *Kansas City Blues Rugby Club 2013 Yearbook*, yumpu.com, p. 8.

24. Clint Olearnick, August 14, 2021.

25. Brent Walker, "And the Party Never Ends," in Cory Wallace (ed.), *The Strong Gray Line: War-Time Reflections from the West Point Class of 2004* (Lanham, Maryland: Rowman & Littlefield, 2015), p. 21–26.

26. Fred Lowrey, "Anderson Rugby Complex Dedicated at West Point," Assembly, West Point Association of Graduates, July/August 2007.

27. Jim Frederick, *Black Hearts: One Platoon's Descent into Madness in Iraq's Triangle of Death* (New York: Random House, 2010), p. 161–169.
28. Adam Hathaway, "Why Is a Garryowen in Rugby Called a Garryowen?" *Rugby World*, February 3, 2022.
29. Blake Stilwell, "Five Reasons Route Irish Was the Most Nerve-Racking Road in Iraq," wearethemighty.com, December 8, 2020.
30. Scott Radcliffe, July 6, 2021.
31. Jeffrey Gettleman, "Enraged Mob in Fallujah Kills Four American Contractors," *New York Times*, April 1, 2004.
32. John F. Burns, "On Way to Baghdad Airport, Death Stalks Main Road," *New York Times*, May 29, 2005.
33. Eric Schmitt, "Gen. Raymond T. Odierno Dies at 67; Oversaw Iraq Surge," *New York Times*, October 9, 2021.
34. "Twelve Young Veterans Running as GOP Candidates," Associated Press, February 26, 2008.
35. George W. Bush, "Remarks by the President from the USS *Abraham Lincoln*, at Sea Off the Coast of San Diego, California," https://georgewbush-whitehouse.archives.gov, May 1, 2003.
36. Pete Chacon, August 14, 2021.

Baghdad

1. Eric Stanbra, September 27, 2021.
2. C. J. Chivers, *The Fighters: Americans in Combat in Afghanistan and Iraq* (New York: Simon & Schuster, 2018), p. 127.
3. Eric Westervelt, "Base Life: Risk and Routine in Baghdad," NPR, June 20, 2005.
4. Jason Shell, "How the IED Won: Dispelling the Myth of Tactical Success and Innovation," *War on the Rocks*, May 1, 2017.
5. Rick Atkinson, *Left of Boom, Washington Post*, 2006.
6. Steve Rose, "Kathryn Bigelow: Back in the Danger Zone," *Guardian*, August 19, 2009.
7. Rick Atkinson, "The Single Most Effective Weapon."
8. Rachel Martin, "The IED: The $30 Bombs that Cost the US Billions," NPR, December 17, 2011.
9. Brian Castner, *The Long Walk: A Story of War and the Life that Follows* (New York: Random House, 2012), p. 76.
10. Gordon and Trainor, *The Endgame*, p. 32.
11. Eric Westervelt, "US Forces Employ 'Buffalo' to Battle Roadside Bombs," NPR, May 24, 2005.
12. Mary Roach, *Grunt: The Curious Science of Humans at War* (New York: Norton, 2016).
13. Rory Carroll, "Fear and Pride in Hunt for Weapons of Moderate Destruction," *Guardian*, June 27, 2005.
14. Patrick Cockburn, *The Age of Jihad* (London: Verso, 2017), p. 79.
15. Brian Castner, April 28, 2021.

16. Gordon and Trainor, *The Endgame*, p. 32.
17. Marcus Weisberger, "How Many US Troops Were Killed by Iranian IEDs in Iraq?" *Defense One*, September 8, 2015.
18. Michael R. Gordon, "Deadliest Bomb in Iraq Is Made by Iran, US Says," *New York Times*, February 10, 2007.
19. David Finkel, *The Good Soldiers* (New York: Farrar, Straus & Giroux, 2009), p. 20.
20. Michael R. Gordon and Scott Shane, "US Long Worried that Iran Supplied Arms in Iraq," *New York Times*, March 27, 2007.
21. Monte Morin, "US Soldiers Find that They're Targets on Route Predators," *Stars and Stripes*, April 12, 2007.
22. Gordon and Trainor, *The Endgame*, p. 151.
23. Gordon and Shane.

Rustamiyah

1. Nate Hadd, May 6, 2021.
2. Finkel, p. 17.
3. Eric Westervelt, "Base Life."
4. "Memorial Service Held for Fort Polk–Based Soldier Killed in Iraq," Associated Press, January 14, 2004.
5. Phil Klay, "The Warrior at the Mall," *New York Times*, April 14, 2018.
6. David Abrams, *Fobbit* (New York: Grove Atlantic, 2012), p. 48.
7. Jeremy Redmon, "The Inside Story of the Deadliest Attack on a US Military Base in the Iraq War," TaskandPurpose.com, December 2, 2020.
8. Zach Pamer, August 16, 2022.
9. Tori Chapel, June 9, 2021.
10. Ken and Helen Gurbisz, September 16, 2021.
11. Jesse Bradell and Sandra Stewart Holyoak, "Interview with Kenneth Gurbisz," Rutgers Oral History Archives, March 4, 2011.
12. In fact, not spiders and not poisonous. See Rod Crawford, "Myth: Too Many 'Camel Spider' Tall Tales," Seattle: Burke Museum.
13. Greg Kitsock, "Beer Lift for the Troops?" allaboutbeer.net, July 2007.
14. Tim Yancey, Anita Yancey, Kimberly Winter, Kelly Tennant, and Bobby Yancey, November 12, 2022.
15. Nate Hadd, May 6, 2021.
16. Randall Mullally, November 2, 2021.
17. Van Torres, March 10, 2022.
18. Dawn Hurley, October 28, 2021.
19. Anita Powell, "Support Unit's Behind-the-Scenes Work in Iraq Is Essential," *Stars and Stripes*, October 28, 2005.
20. Emma Sky, as quoted in Thomas E. Ricks, *The Gamble: General David Petraeus and the American Military Adventure in Iraq, 2006–2008* (New York: Penguin Press, 2009), p. 155.
21. Andrew Cockburn, "Iraq's Oppressed Majority," *Smithsonian Magazine*, December 2003.

22. James Bluemel and Renad Mansour, *Once Upon a Time in Iraq* (London: Penguin, 2020), p. 231–50.
23. Patrick Cockburn, *Muqtada al-Sadr and the Battle for the Future of Iraq* (New York: Simon & Schuster, 2008), p. 27.
24. Rory Carroll, "Gunmen Surrounded Us, Firing into the Windscreen. The Dreaded Moment Had Arrived: Kidnap," *Guardian*, October 22, 2005.
25. Pengelly, "H. R. McMaster on Rugby."
26. Ann Scott Tyson, "Horror Glimpsed from the Inside of a Humvee in Iraq," *Washington Post*, April 21, 2005.
27. Cockburn, p. 34.
28. Gordon and Trainor, *The Endgame*, p. 67.
29. John C. Moore, "Sadr City: The Armor Pure Assault in Urban Terrain," *Armor*, November–December 2004.
30. Isikoff and Corn, p. 380.
31. Gordon and Trainor, *The Endgame*, p.151.
32. Ibid.
33. Vince Little, "Rustamiyah Support Battalion Finds Security Within Its Ranks," *Stars and Stripes*, March 26, 2005.
34. Alejandro Michel, November 3, 2021.
35. Caleb Hastings, November 3, 2021.
36. Paul Rieckhoff, *Chasing Ghosts: Failures and Facades in Iraq: A Soldier's Perspective* (New York: NAL Caliber, 2006), p. 194.

Convoy

1. United States Department of Defense, "News Release No. 1159-05: DoD Identifies Army Casualties," November 7, 2005.
2. Keith Brown, "Eatontown GI Dies as Bomb Hits Humvee," *Asbury Park Press*, November 8, 2005.
3. Mary Jo Patterson, "Monmouth Soldier, 'A Great Kid,' Dies in Iraq," *Star-Ledger*, November 8, 2005.
4. Abrams, p. 6–7.
5. David Leigh, "Iraq War Logs: An Introduction," *Guardian*, October 22, 2010.
6. Brian Castner, April 28, 2021.
7. Clay Wilson, "Improvised Explosive Devices (IEDs) in Iraq and Afghanistan: Effects and Countermeasures," Congressional Research Service, August 28, 2007.
8. Michael Moran, "Fighting the Insurgency at the Jersey Shore," NBCNews.com, July 18, 2005.
9. Scott Radcliffe, July 6, 2021.
10. Fountain, p. 61.
11. Nate Hadd, May 6, 2021.
12. Caleb Hastings, November 3, 2021.
13. Ben Brody, "Challengers Keep Vital Supplies Rolling Along," *Marne Express*, April 24, 2005.

14. Jackie Spinner, "Easy Sailing Along Once-Perilous Road to Baghdad Airport," *Washington Post*, November 4, 2005.
15. John F. Burns, "On Way to Baghdad Airport, Death Stalks Main Road," *New York Times*, May 29, 2005.
16. Brian Castner, April 28, 2021.
17. David Philipps, *Lethal Warriors: When the New Band of Brothers Came Home* (New York: Palgrave Macmillan, 2010), p. 52.
18. C. J. Chivers, p. 127.
19. Alejandro Michel, November 3, 2021.
20. Ariana Eunjung Cha, "Underclass of Workers Created in Iraq," *Washington Post*, July 1, 2004.
21. Zach Pamer, August 16, 2022.
22. Tim Yancey, Anita Yancey, Kimberly Winter, Kelly Tennant, and Bobby Yancey, November 12, 2022.

After

1. Tori Chapel, June 9, 2021.
2. Jesse Bradell and Sandra Stewart Holyoak, "Interview with Kenneth Gurbisz," Rutgers Oral History Archives, March 4, 2011.
3. Kathy Gurbisz Forte, August 2, 2021.
4. Brian McCoy, September 15, 2021.
5. Clint Olearnick, August 14, 2021.
6. Pete Chacon, August 14, 2021.
7. Dexter Filkins, "The Good Soldier," *New York Times*, September 8, 2009.
8. Pablogrone, "November 4, 2005. Camp Rustamiyah, Irak-3rd Infantry Division, 2BCT, 26TH FSB. We lost 2 of our brothers!" Youtube.com, July 8, 2007.
9. Pete Chacon, July 2, 2015.
10. Mike Mahan, January 7, 2021.
11. Clint Olearnick, August 14, 2021.
12. Dawn Hurley, October 28, 2021.
13. Abrams, p. 61.
14. Andrew deGrandpre and Andrew Tilghman, "Iran Linked to 500 US Deaths in Iraq, Afghanistan," *Military Times*, July 14, 2015.
15. Marcus Weisgerber, "How Many US Troops Were Killed by Iranian IEDs in Iraq?" Defenseone.com, September 8, 2015.
16. Kyle Rempfer, "Iran Killed More US Troops in Iraq than Previously Known, Pentagon Says," *Military Times*, April 4, 2019.
17. Fran Mannino, "Lt. Col. Tim Karcher Injured in Iraq," *South County Times*, July 2, 2009.
18. Timothy Karcher, et al., Plaintiffs, v. Islamic Republic of Iran, Defendant. United States District Court for the District of Columbia. Civil Action No. 16-232 (CKK) (D.D.C. Jan. 14, 2021).

Arlington

1. Jari Villenueva, "All Is Well, Safely Rest," legion.org, October 24, 2012.
2. Michael E. Ruane, "Arlington Cemetery Wants to Change the Rules on Who Can Be Buried There," *Washington Post*, September 25, 2019.
3. Robert M. Poole, *Section 60: Arlington National Cemetery, Where War Comes Home* (New York: Bloomsbury USA, 2014).
4. Dana Milbank, "Curtains Ordered for Media Coverage of Returning Coffins," *Washington Post*, October 21, 2003.
5. Dana Milbank, "What the Family Would Let You See, the Pentagon Obstructs," *Washington Post*, April 24, 2008.
6. Annie Gowen, "Father's Salute to a Son with a Big Heart," *Washington Post*, April 11, 2003.
7. Gary Weckselblatt, "Green Beret and His Letter Remembered Ten Years Later," *Bucks County Courier Times*, November 3, 2015.
8. Tara Bahrampour, "Two Soldiers from Virginia Die in Iraq Within Days," *Washington Post*, November 9, 2005.
9. "Army Announces Deaths of Two Fort Campbell Soldiers in Iraq," Associated Press, December 2005.
10. Tori Chapel, June 9, 2021.
11. Daniel Karbler, January 13, 2021.
12. Greg Jaffe, "Cleanup in Arlington National Cemetry's Section 60 Upsets Families of War Dead," *Washington Post*, October 1, 2013.
13. Eric Whitney, "Colorado Loses 'Best and Brightest' in Iraq," NPR, May 10, 2006.
14. Mike Barber, "Ex-Seattle Police Officer, Green Beret Killed in Iraq," *Seattle Post-Intelligencer*, October 4, 2006.
15. "Colonel from Fort Leavenworth Dies," Associated Press, May 7, 2007.
16. Michelle Hillen, "Ward Man Killed in Iraq Exuded a Spirit of Service," *Arkansas Democrat Gazette*, October 17, 2007.
17. Kait Hanson, "How a Military Family Honors the Memory of Wife's Fallen First Husband," Today.com, November 7, 2019.
18. "Army Pilot Killed in Fort Benning Crash Hailed as Leader," *Augusta Chronicle*, August 11, 2011.

Clint

1. Martin Pengelly, "He Today that Sheds His Blood with Me: When West Point Rugby Went to War," *Guardian*, September 19, 2015.
2. Clint Olearnick, August 14, 2021.
3. Jan and Clem Olearnick, April 7, 2022.
4. Martin Pengelly, "All Blacks Run Up Three Figures, but It's Not All Doom and Gloom for USA," *Guardian*, October 24, 2021.
5. "Clint Olearnick," *Warren County Record*, January 3, 2022.
6. August Kleinzahler, *Sleeping It Off in Rapid City: Poems, New and Selected* (London: Faber and Faber, 2008), p. 71.

SELECTED BIBLIOGRAPHY

This is not an exhaustive list. It is a list of books I found most useful. Some cross categories (e.g., memoirs of life at West Point and service after) but are only listed once. Reportage, news stories, features, or interviews are cited in my notes. So are my interviews with the West Point rugby players, their loved ones, and those who knew them. —M. P.

West Point

Stephen E. Ambrose. *Duty, Honor, Country: A History of West Point.* Baltimore: Johns Hopkins University Press, 2000.

Rick Atkinson. *The Long Gray Line: The American Journey of West Point's Class of 1966.* New York: Picador, 1989.

Michael E. Haskew. *West Point, 1915: Eisenhower, Bradley and the Class the Stars Fell On.* Minneapolis: Zenith Press, 2015.

David Lipsky. *Absolutely American: Four Years at West Point.* New York: Houghton Mifflin Harcourt, 2003.

Jon C. Malinowski and Eugene J. Palka. *The Spirit of West Point: Celebrating 200 Years.* New York: Black Dome Press, 2001.

Robert M. S. McDonald (ed.). *Thomas Jefferson's Military Academy.* Charlottesville: University of Virginia Press, 2018.

Craig M. Mullaney. *The Unforgiving Minute: A Soldier's Education.* New York: Penguin, 2009.

Bill Murphy Jr. *In a Time of War: The Proud and Perilous Journey of West Point's Class of 2002.* New York: Macmillan, 2009.

Anton Myrer. *Once an Eagle.* New York: Harper Collins, 2000.

Ed Ruggero. *Duty First: A Year in the Life of West Point and the Making of American Leaders.* New York: Harper Collins, 2001.

James Salter. *Burning the Days.* New York: Random House, 1997.

Elizabeth D. Samet. *Soldier's Heart: Reading Literature through Peace and War at West Point*. New York: Picador, 2008.

Elizabeth D. Samet. *No Man's Land: Preparing for War and Peace in Post-9/11 America*. New York: Farrar, Straus & Giroux, 2014.

Ty Seidule. *Robert E. Lee and Me: A Southerner's Reckoning with the Myth of the Lost Cause*. New York: St. Martin's Press, 2021.

Cory Wallace (ed.). *The Strong Gray Line: War-Time Reflections from the West Point Class of 2004*. Lanham, Maryland: Rowman & Littlefield, 2015.

US Military & History

Daniel P. Bolger. *Why We Lost: A General's Inside Account of the Iraq and Afghanistan Wars*. Boston: Houghton Mifflin Harcourt, 2014.

Andrew Carroll (ed.). *Operation Homecoming: Iraq, Afghanistan, and the Home Front, in the Words of US Troops and Their Families*. Chicago: University of Chicago Press, 2008.

David Finkel. *Thank You for Your Service*. New York: Farrar, Straus & Giroux, 2013.

Sebastian Junger. *Freedom*. New York: Simon & Schuster, 2021.

Sebastian Junger. *Tribe: On Homecoming and Belonging*. New York: Twelve Books, 2016.

Jim Mattis and Bing West. *Call Sign Chaos: Learning to Lead*. New York: Random House, 2019.

David McCullough. *1776*. New York: Simon and Schuster, 2005.

Robert M. Poole, *Section 60: Arlington National Cemetery, Where War Comes Home*. New York: Bloomsbury, 2014.

Mary Roach. *Grunt: The Curious Science of Humans at War*. New York: Norton, 2016.

David Rothkopf. *Traitor: A History of American Betrayal from Benedict Arnold to Donald Trump*. New York: Macmillan, 2020.

Iraq

David Abrams. *Fobbit*. New York: Grove Atlantic, 2012.

Rick Atkinson. *In the Company of Soldiers: A Chronicle of Combat*. New York: Henry Holt & Co., 2004.

James A. Baker III and Lee H. Hamilton. *The Iraq Study Group Report*. New York: Vintage, 2006.

James Bluemel and Renad Mansour. *Once Upon a Time in Iraq*. London: Penguin, 2020.

Dana Canedy. *A Journal for Jordan*. New York: Crown, 2008.

Brian Castner. *The Long Walk: A Story of War and the Life that Follows*. New York: Random House, 2012.

Patrick Cockburn. *The Occupation: War and Resistance in Iraq*. London: Verso, 2007.

Patrick Cockburn. *Muqtada al-Sadr and the Battle for the Future of Iraq*. New York: Simon & Schuster, 2008.

Robert Draper. *To Start a War: How the Bush Administration Took America into Iraq*. New York: Penguin Press, 2020.

Nathaniel Fick. *One Bullet Away: The Making of a Marine Officer*. New York: Houghton Mifflin, 2005.

Dexter Filkins. *The Forever War*. New York: Vintage, 2009.

David Finkel. *The Good Soldiers*. New York: Farrar, Straus & Giroux, 2009.

Ben Fountain. *Billy Lynn's Long Halftime Walk*. New York: Harper Collins, 2012.

Jim Frederick. *Black Hearts: One Platoon's Descent into Madness in Iraq's Triangle of Death*. New York: Random House, 2010.

Michael R. Gordon and Bernard E. Trainor. *Cobra II: The Inside Story of the Invasion and Occupation of Iraq*. New York: Random House, 2007.

Michael R. Gordon and Bernard E. Trainor. *The Endgame: The Inside Story of the Struggle for Iraq, from George W. Bush to Barack Obama*. New York: Random House, 2012.

Michael Isikoff and David Corn. *Hubris: The Inside Story of Spin, Scandal, and the Selling of the Iraq War*. New York: Random House, 2007.

David E. Johnson, Agnes Gereben Schaefer, Brenna Allen, Raphael S. Cohen, Gian Gentile, James Hoobler, Michael Schwille, Jerry M Sollinger, Sean M. Zeigler. *The US Army and the Battle for Baghdad: Lessons Learned—And Still to Be Learned*. RAND Corporation, 2019.

Phil Klay. *Redeployment*. New York: Penguin Press, 2014.

Stanley McChrystal. *My Share of the Task: A Memoir*. New York: Penguin, 2013.

Peter R. Mansoor. *Baghdad at Sunrise: A Brigade Commander's War in Iraq*. New Haven: Yale University Press, 2008.

Fred Minnick. *Camera Boy: An Army Journalist's War in Iraq*. Ashland, Oregon: Hellgate Press, 2009.

Carl Mirra. *Soldiers and Citizens: An Oral History of Operation Iraqi Freedom from the Battlefield to the Pentagon*. New York: Palgrave Macmillan, 2008.

George Packer. *The Assassin's Gate: America in Iraq*. New York: Farrar, Straus & Giroux, 2005.

David Philipps. *Alpha: Eddie Gallagher and the War for the Soul of the Navy SEALS*. New York: Penguin Random House, 2021.

David Philipps. *Lethal Warriors: When the New Band of Brothers Came Home*. New York: Palgrave Macmillan, 2010.

Paul Rieckhoff. *Chasing Ghosts: Failures and Facades in Iraq: A Soldier's Perspective*. New York: NAL Caliber, 2006.

Thomas E. Ricks. *Fiasco: The American Military Adventure in Iraq*. New York: Penguin Press, 2006.

Thomas E. Ricks, *The Gamble: General David Petraeus and the American Military Adventure in Iraq, 2006–2008*. New York: Penguin Press, 2009.

Harry Tunnell IV. *Red Devils: Tactical Perspectives from Iraq*. Fort Leavenworth, Kansas: Combat Studies Institute Press, 2006.

James Verini. *They Will Have to Die Now: Mosul and the Fall of the Caliphate*. New York: Norton, 2019.

Joby Warrick. *Black Flags: The Rise of Isis*. New York: Doubleday, 2015.

Leonard Wong, Thomas A. Kolditz, Raymond A. Millen, Terrence M. Potter. *Why They Fight: Combat Motivation in the Iraq War.* US Army War College, July 2003.

Trish Wood. *What Was Asked of Us: An Oral History of the Iraq War by the Soldiers Who Fought It.* New York: Back Bay Books, 2007.

Evan Wright. *Generation Kill: Devil Dogs, Iceman, Captain America, and the New Face of American War.* New York: Berkley Caliber, 2004.

Afghanistan

Brian Castner. *All the Ways We Kill and Die.* New York: Arcade, 2018.

Andrew Exum. *This Man's Army.* New York: Gotham, 2005.

Vanessa M. Gezari. *The Tender Soldier: A True Story of War and Sacrifice.* New York: Simon & Schuster, 2013.

Sebastian Junger. *War.* New York: Hachette, 2010.

Clinton Romesha. *Red Platoon: A True Story of American Valor.* New York: Dutton, 2016.

Jake Tapper. *The Outpost: The Most Heroic Battle of the Afghanistan War.* New York: Little, Brown, 2012.

Donald P. Wright, James Bird, Steven Clay, et al. *A Different Kind of War: The United States Army in Operation Enduring Freedom (OEF) October 2001–September 2005.* Fort Leavenworth, Kansas: Combat Studies Institute Press, 2010.

9/11 and After

Andrew Bacevich. *The Age of Illusions: How America Squandered Its Cold War Victory.* New York: Metropolitan Books, 2020.

Steven Brill. *After: How America Confronted the September 12 Era.* New York: Simon & Schuster, 2003.

Jason Burke. *The 9/11 Wars.* London: Penguin, 2011.

Patrick Cockburn. *The Age of Jihad.* London: Verso, 2017.

Simon Cottee & Thomas Cushman (eds.). *Christopher Hitchens and his Critics: Terror, Iraq, and the Left.* New York: New York University Press, 2008.

Seymour M. Hersh. *Chain of Command: The Road from 9/11 to Abu Ghraib.* New York: Harper Collins, 2004.

Lindsey Hilsum. *In Extremis: The Life and Death of the War Correspondent Marie Colvin.* New York: Farrar, Straus & Giroux, 2018.

Bill Langewiesche. *American Ground: Unbuilding the World Trade Center.* New York: Macmillan, 2002.

Margaret MacMillan. *War: How Conflict Shaped Us.* New York: Penguin Random House, 2020.

H. R. McMaster. *Battlegrounds: The Fight to Defend the Free World.* New York: Harper, 2020.

National Commission on Terrorist Attacks. *The 9/11 Commission Report: Final Report of the National Commission on Terrorist Attacks upon the United States*. New York: WW Norton & Co., 2004.

George Packer. *Interesting Times*. New York: Farrar, Straus & Giroux, 2009.

Jean Edward Smith. *Bush*. New York: Simon & Schuster, 2016.

Rugby

Jay Atkinson. *Memoirs of a Rugby-Playing Man: Guts, Glory, and Blood in the World's Greatest Game*. New York: Thomas Dunne Books, 2012.

Mike Aylwin and Mark Evans. *Unholy Union: When Rugby Collided with the Modern World*. London: Constable, 2021.

John Daniell. *Confessions of a Rugby Mercenary*. London: Ebury Press, 2009.

Adam Hughes. *This Is Rugby: The Story, Culture, and Future of American Rugby*. Independently published, 2022.

Huw Richards. *A Game for Hooligans: The History of Rugby Union*. London: Mainstream, 2007.

Mike Schredl and Bill Kosco. *Establishing the Brotherhood: The West Point Men's Rugby Program*. Independently published, 2021.

Martin Pengelly and his father, Philip Pengelly,
in Melrose, Scotland in 1995.

ACKNOWLEDGMENTS

To my wife, Kate Super. I love you. To my all-daughter back row, Emma, Helen, and Frances. I love you too.

To my parents, Jean and Philip Pengelly. I miss my dad every day. This book was mostly written in New York City (and partially edited in Washington, DC), but bits were written in Leeds, England, in Mum's study. As long as the house on Davies Avenue doesn't collapse inwards under the weight of the books, it is home.

To my brothers. I watched Owen play rugby before I was old enough to follow, which I've been doing ever since. Robin, my best friend as a kid, helped me re-enact internationals on Soldiers Field, the great green space in Roundhay that now seems so appropriately named. To my brothers' wives and children. Rachel, Beatrice, Alice, and Ed. Nienke, Thomas, and Alastair. There are rugby players among you.

I also worked on this book in Duxbury, Massachusetts. Thank you to my American family. To Charlie Super and Sara Harkness. To Bruce, Maggie, Amelia, and Madeleine Church. To Betsy Super and Natalie Konopinski, to Sam and Ada Super-Konopinski. To John Super, Julie Meyer Super, and James and Claire Super. There are rugby players among you too.

Any list from my own days as a player is bound to be incomplete. There are too many good people—and quite a few bad people who nonetheless taught me to take a tackle or a punch. I will just thank my first coaches at Moortown, who set me out on the road. Mick Howard and Roger Pullan.

Considering my decade in and around rugby in North America, it seems safest to try for one list, expats and interviewees included. So here goes, with apologies to anyone inevitably missed.

Errik Anderson, Katherine Aversano, Bill Baker, Perry Baker, Malcolm Beith, Nic Benson, Calder Cahill, Phil Camm, Al Charron, Kisset Chirengende, Pat Clifton, Doug Coil, Alex Corbisiero, Sebastian Cray, Mark Cuban, Fred Culazzo, Tom Dart, Adam Duerson, Chris Dunlavey, Nate Ebner, Paul Emerick, James English, Scott Ferrara, John Fitzpatrick, Ben Foden, Allyn Freeman, Adam Freier, Mike Friday, Darren Gardner, Kaleb Geiger, Candace Gingrich, Ryan Ginty, Danny Glantz, Gary Gold, Alex Goff, Mark Griffin, Abby Gustaitis, Carille Guthrie, Pat Guthrie, Bryan Habana, David Hale Smith, Eleanor Holmes Norton, Will Hooley, Adam Hughes, Jeff Hull, Ryan Hunt, Carlin Isles, Patrick Johnston, Paul Keeler, Bryan Kelly, Alev Kelter, James Kennedy, George Killibrew, Kimball Kjar, Phaidra Knight, John Layfield, Steve Lewis, Peter Lucas, Dan Lyle, Michael Lynagh, Alex Magleby, Jason Maloni, Matt McCarthy, Richie McCaw, Cormac McCormack, Nigel Melville, Tendai Mtwawira, Brian Murphy, Chris Murphy, Peter Pasque, Jon Persch, Mike Petri, Rich Pohlidal, Stuart Proctor, Bryan Ray, Curtis Reed, Tony Ridnell, Chris Robshaw, Cristian Rodriguez, Owen Scannell, Rob Scott, Blaine Scully, Richard Sexton, Paul Sheehy, Will Snape-Rogers, Dallen Stanford, Aalina Tabani, Naya Tapper, Joe Taufete'e, Phil Terrigno, Mike Tolkin, Marty Veale, Lara Vivolo, Amanda Windsor White, Ross Young, Shane Young.

In journalism, any list of those who helped and shaped me is also bound to be incomplete. Here goes anyway.

At *Lex* magazine my first editor, Catrin Griffiths, thought my name rhymed with Llanelli, a citadel of Welsh rugby, and therefore gave me a try. So, I'm her fault, if still not Welsh. Mathew Lyons and Viv Timmins were Cat's deputies. David Cobb gave me a heap of instructive shit. At *Rugby News*, Graeme Gillespie gave me a chance when I needed one. Thanks also to John Edwards, Mark Hudson, Hugh Godwin, Tony Prince, and Russell Stander. Bank!

I made it to Fleet Street. At the *Independent on Sunday*, Neil Morton, Hugh Bateman, Gary Lemke, and Simon Redfern gave me a place on the desk. Also at the *Independent*: Marc Padgett, Mark Howe, Simon Jones, John Cobb, Andy Tong, Chris Corrigan, Saul Brookfield, Will Hawkes, Julian Cooper, Matt Gatward, Robin Scott-Elliott, Chris Maume, Stuart Price, Ben Walsh, Hildy Serle, Warren Howard, and more. I also joined the poor bloody infantry, a.k.a. the subs, at the *Guardian* and *Observer*. Among those I learned from: Chris Taylor, Russell Cunningham, Ian Malin, Steve Bradfield, Jeremy Alexander, Mike Baker, George Chesterton, Ed Gibbes, Matt Hancock, Andy Martin, Marcus Christenson, Claire Tolley, Philip Cornwall, Russell Thomas, Chris Cheers. At each paper, I edited rugby writers: Chris Hewett, Hugh Godwin (again), Tim Glover, Rob Kitson, Paul Rees, Mike Aylwin (whose book, *Unholy Union*, is a must if you want to understand world rugby) and Donald McRae. All shot the shit when it was quiet and worked like hell when it wasn't. All taught me to be a newspaperman.

At *Guardian US*, Janine Gibson and Stuart Millar took their own chance on me when I pitched up with a kid on the way, crap insurance, and not much else of a plan. They won a Pulitzer. I asked Steve Busfield to let me write about rugby. Tom Lutz, the next sports editor, gave the okay for the trip to West Point then deftly edited the story. There are too many others to thank. Among them: Tim Hill, Rusha Haljuci, Ashley Chervinski, Matthew Cantor, Mark Oliver, Paul Harris, Ankita Rao, Jo Walters, Ramon Antonio Vargas, Ed Pilkington, Dom Rushe, Oliver Milman, Adam Gabbatt, Bryan Armen Graham, Richard Luscombe, Amana Fontanella Khan, J. Oliver Conroy, Anthony DiPonio, Sidney Blumenthal, Robert Reich, Jessica Reed, Betsy Reed, Dana Canedy, Martin Hodgson, David Smith, Hugo Lowell, Chris McGreal, Julian Borger, Joan E Greve, and Lauren Gambino.

Among those who have left *Guardian US*, thanks to Tom McCarthy, Alan Yuhas, Amanda Holpuch, Enjoli Liston, David Taylor, Matt Seaton, Paul Laity, John Mulholland, Heather Long, Lee Glendinning, Matt Williams, Daniel Strauss, Megan Carpentier, Sabrina Siddiqui, Jon Swaine, Maraithe Thomas, Nicky Woolf, and Ben Jacobs. Among others in US media and publishing whose paths have crossed mine, Marty Baron, Molly Jong-Fast, Rick Wilson, Judith Gurewich, Clara Bingham, and Sebastian Junger would be rugby fans if only they knew. Mike Gartland of the *New York Daily News* has even been to a game. Tom Teodorczuk persists in believing soccer is superior. And yes, I wrote "soccer." It's an English word. Look it up.

Three *Guardian* names to repeat: Russell Cunningham, Chris Taylor, and Chris McGreal.

Russell and Chris Taylor are true friends as well as superb editors, which is probably why they agreed to read my manuscript and offer priceless advice. Chris did so despite loathing rugby with all his heart. Sorry, not sorry, old chap. Chris McGreal, meanwhile, is a fine reporter and author who read the book and made a great call on its structure.

Other readers and advisers: Steve Lewis (eggs and Bond); Lloyd Green ("Tinker to Evers to Chance"); Charles Kaiser (author, reviewer, friend); Rory Carroll (who generously discussed his time in Iraq and kidnap in Sadr City); Matthew Teague (the finest writer I've commissioned); Craig Mullaney (wise about Ranger school and Rhodes scholarships); Andrew Exum (wise about Ranger school and David Pocock); H. R. McMaster (so generous with his time and expertise, with his pen and with a beer or two at Old Gray and in the parking lot before the All Blacks game); Tom Ricks (whose books heavily informed the manuscript he generously read for errors); and Dan Lyle (the real Captain America, as any rugby fan knows). Any errors that remain are of course entirely my own.

Ted Widmer wrote a fine book about Abraham Lincoln (second row and captain in any Presidents XV), talked to me about it for the paper, and became a friend, believer, and adviser. He also turned out to know a president of a publishing house who played fullback for Harvard. To that fullback, Will Thorndike, a heartfelt thank you. To all at Godine, including David Allender and my editor Joshua Bodwell, with whom I bonded by Covid-enforced distance, chiefly over the Hardy Boys and Six Moon Hill, boundless thanks. To Dan Avant, for the superb copy edit, thank you, too. Sorry about the rampant Britishisms, from "arse" to "kit" and back again. To photographer Rick Starkman and designer Joe Montgomery, for the stunning cover, thank you. And to Dylan Gray, thank you for thinking of dog tags draped over a ball.

Given that playing second row for England was never really going to happen, true to my lefty roots, I only ever wanted to work for the *Guardian* or the BBC and somehow publish a book. Two out of three ain't bad.

Speaking of England, this book could not have been written (largely at 5:00 a.m. before taking the kids to school or logging on for a news shift) without the unrelenting example of the greatest player of all, "Iron" Mike Teague, rock of the back row for Gloucester, England, and the Lions. I've always wanted to write that. Other heroes I've always wanted to consecrate in print: Will Carling and his England squad, 1988–95, the 1997 British and Irish Lions, and two great men now lost: Doddie Weir, a Scottish giant gone too soon, and Cliff Morgan of Wales, the finest storyteller of all. While I'm here, thank you to Brian Eno, whose music scored each edit.

And so, at last, to West Point.

Mike Mahan, the man who *is* West Point rugby, may not have known what to make of me when I showed up in his office at Anderson Rugby Complex in 2015. Certainly, I didn't know what I was getting myself into. Mike was unfailingly generous with time, thoughts, and support. To be told (by Bryan Phillips) of Father Mahan's tears after the cadets finally won a national championship, in Houston in 2022, was to know what Army Rugby truly means.

Thank you to Matt Sherman, a successor to Father Mahan, who welcomed me and answered my questions while plotting that national title. A fraction of a chapter was rewritten in the team room before kickoff against Lindenwood one November evening. Thank you, Tom Hiebert, for your advice, help, and magnificent hospitality. Among the Old Gray: Charlie MacMaster, Steve Heidecker and Kathleen Byrne Heidecker, Lew Boore, Frank Kearney, Leo Brooks, Sean Mullin, Dave Biery, and Tony Ridnell. Thank you, too, to Ambassador Robert Kimmitt and to Chris Starling, a rare Marine in the army throng.

Thank you to those who played with or knew the class of 2002, among them Charlie Erwin, Al Bairley, Shannon Worthan, Brian

Anthony, Liam Marmion, Mike Ziegelhofer, Eric Stanbra, Trent Geisler, Wesley Pearce, Mike Izzo, and Brent Pafford. Among the younger brothers, Kevin Lynch was particularly generous with time, beers, car rides, and gripes about the FloRugby feed. Outside the rugby team, Eddie Johnson summoned painful memories to talk about Joe Emigh. Ken Wainwright, R. J. Johnson, and Jay Landgraf shared similar memories of Zac Miller. Nick Utzig and Brian and Terry Babcock-Lumish offered simple friendship and advice. From the faculty, thank you to Liz Samet, for her wise words about *Henry V*, and to Ty Seidule. From command, thank you to Daniel Christman, Leo Brooks, and Bill Lennox.

Thank you to those who served with the brothers of '02, who are named throughout the book. Nate Hadd, in particular, found numbers and pulled strings. I pulled them again, and members of Top Flite Security dredged up terrible memories. To Randall Mullally, Alejandro Michel, Zach Pamer, and Van Torres, thank you. Thank you, Caleb Hastings and Dawn Hurley.

David Finkel of the *Washington Post* talked about his own time at Rustamiyah and showed me the way forward. Brian Castner, who has written so vividly of his own time in Iraq, told me about IEDs and EFPs, and where to look for the SIGACT.

Thank you to the families of the brothers of '02. Ken and Helen Gurbisz were limitlessly kind and helpful, remembering terrible things. Kathleen Gurbisz Forte and Tori Chapel did the same. So did Rosalyn and Keith Miller, who welcomed the whole Pengelly family to western Pennsylvania. The girls will never forget the giraffes. Nate Miller spoke about his brother. George and Maryanne Emigh showed me where Joey grew up and remembered him and his mom, Joanne. Thank you to Jan and Clem Olearnick, to Diane Molstad and Zosha, and to Casey Olearnick too. Thank you to all the wives, teachers, friends, mayors, and others who spoke to the Brit with the pen. Thank you to Erin Blind, who looked after practically a full XV of rather "emotional" ex-players, and the Brit with a pen, one summer weekend in Cohasset.

Which brings me, finally, to the brothers of '02. Thank you, Matt Blind, the captain who still does so much to make the team work and did so much to make this book work too. Thanks for beers and oysters in Duxbury, for inviting me to Hingham and Cohasset, for organizing the reunion in summer '21 and the memorial in fall '22. In Cohasset, we recreated the senior photograph of twenty years before. Matt's porch stood in for Nininger Hall. Zac and Joe's places were empty. Dave Little, who didn't manage to show up for the original, stood in for Jim.

Thank you, Dave. Thank you, Jerrod Adams, Pete Chacon, Mo Greene, Jeremiah Hurley, Andrew Klutman, Brian McCoy, Bryan Phillips, Scott Radcliffe, and Nik Wybaczinsky.

Thank you, Zac Miller, Joe Emigh, Jim Gurbisz.

Thank you, Clint Olearnick. You spoke generously of your brothers and of Jim, the brother you lost, before your brothers lost you in turn.

A NOTE ABOUT THE AUTHOR

Martin Pengelly is an editor and reporter for *Guardian US* based in Washington, DC, where he lives with his wife and three daughters. Born in Leeds, England, he played rugby for Durham University and Rosslyn Park FC and worked for *Rugby News*, the *Guardian*, and the *Independent* before moving to the US in 2012. Since then, he has written about politics, books, and rugby in America. His work has also appeared in *Sports Illustrated* and the *New York Times*. *Brotherhood* is his first book.

A NOTE ON THE TYPE

Brotherhood has been set in Kepler. Named after the German Renaissance astronomer, Kepler is a contemporary typeface created by Adobe type designer Robert Slimbach and released in 1996. While Kepler is in the tradition of classic modern eighteenth-century typefaces, Slimbach's calligraphic detailing lends it warmth and energy. Walbaum has been used for display.

Design by Brooke Koven. Composition by Vicki Rowland.